UNTIMELY BOLLYWOOD

Amit S. Rai

UNTIMELY BOLLYWOOD

Globalization and India's New Media Assemblage

Duke University Press   Durham and London · 2009

Duke University Press gratefully
acknowledges the support of the
English Department at Florida State
University, which provided funds
toward the production of this book.

To

As'sia-Thara Rai,

Sarah Husain,

Leena Rai, Meera Rai,

and Shambhu K. Rai,

in appreciation and

gratitude for all you

have taught me

There are two ways of considering events,
one being to follow the course of the event,
gathering how it comes about historically,
how it's prepared and then decomposes in
history; while the other way is to go back
into the event, to take one's place in it as in a
becoming, to grow both young and old in it at
once, going through all its components and
singularities. Becoming isn't part of history;
history amounts [to] only the set of preconditions, however recent, that one leaves behind
in order to "become," that is, to create something new. This is precisely what Nietzsche
calls the Untimely.

GILLES DELEUZE, "Control and Becoming"

CONTENTS

Acknowledgments xi

Introduction: India and the New Nonlinear
Media Assemblage 1

PART 1 Cinema Becoming New Media

ONE "First Day, First Show": Bollywood Cinemagoing
and the New Sensorium 23

TWO Contagious Multiplicities and the Nonlinear Life
of the New Media 55

PART 2 Toward an Ontology of Media Durations

THREE "The Best Quality Cinema Viewing . . . Everywhere,
Everytime": On the Malltiplex Mutagen in India 133

FOUR "With You Every Moment in Time": On the
Emergent Ittafaq (Chance) Assemblage 179

Conclusion: Clinamedia 211

Notes 221

Bibliography 275

Index 291

ACKNOWLEDGMENTS

I have been writing and rewriting this book for about a decade, so acknowledging all those who have helped me to write it couldn't be anything other than untimely. Patricia Clough and Jasbir Puar have been my secret sharers in this adventure of political thought for many years: thanks for all the affects (no, really). My colleagues at the New School, Gary Lemons, Kian Tajbaksh, Ifeona Fulani, M. Jacqui Alexander, Greg Tewksbury, Steve Caton, and Jan Clausen, were constant inspirations and keen critics. My colleagues at Florida State University, Jerri McGregory, Chris Shinn, Virgil Suarez, and Delia Poey, have provided me with many different intellectual and emotional resources to negotiate my new institutional contexts and to reconceptualize this project. The support of Ralph Berry, Robin Goodman, Leigh Edwards, Barry Faulk, Bruce Boehrer, and Dan Vitkus has been a solid spur to action these past few years. At different points in my career I have been lucky to find students who have been infinitely patient and creatively engaged, including Diane Roi, Taimur Khan, Louisa Solomon, Emily Sogn, Krishna Mali, Iskandar Zulkarnain, Jonathan Dean, Krysten Davis, and Kathryn Wright. I thank Saleh and Ginger Assadi for accepting me into their family. Much of what I have been able to write here would not have been possible without their generosity and affection. Sudeep Shrivastava always gave me his untiring help through these many, many years. Dustin Anderson and Andrew McFeaters provided productive points of intersection and contrast (as well as sculpted tile and the philosophy of the Red Sox). To Tarun, Puppy, and Kenny I can only say that without your friendship and ironic guidance this work would not have come to fruition. To Sarah Fryett: thanks for the mutations!

The writing of this book was made possible by various grants and institutional support. The American Institute of Indian Studies Senior Research

Fellowship, the New School research support for archival work, Florida State's first-year professor grant and Committee on Faculty Research Support (COFRS) grant have enabled this work to proceed apace.

I would like to thank Ken Wissoker for his rigorous engagement with this project and for his encouragement, and I thank Courtney Berger for her meticulous and timely attention to the details of the manuscript. I would like to also thank the very helpful suggestions of the anonymous readers of the manuscript. All errors that remain are of course my own.

Chapter 1 appeared in a different form as "The Pleasure and Politics of Hindi Film Culture," in *Samar: South Asian Magazine for Action and Reflection*, no. 15 (summer/fall 2002): 44–49. A portion of chapter 2 appeared in a different form as "On Purple Pleasures: Digitally Assembling Bollywood," in *South Asian Technospaces*, edited by Radhika and Venkataramana Gajjala (New York: Peter Lang, 2008), 71–95.

India and the New Nonlinear Media Assemblage

In the DVD version of Farah Khan's intertextual masterpiece *Main Hoon Na*, the first chapter, a "secured" promotional video, presents the general business model used by the film's global distributors Eros Entertainment International (Kishore Lulla, chair and CEO). A deep, quasi-British-accented voiceover suffuses meaning through a rapid machine-gun movement between orchestral crescendos and pounding dance beats, digitally massaged star images, logos, and intertitles (as the viewer looks through a lens and takes aim). The comforting voice tells us of Eros's production of "spellbinding spectacles," "magnificence beyond belief" (a twirling Aishwarya Rai-Durga in *Devdas*), and "irresistible charm" (Sharukh as Devdas-babu). The voice continues:

> It's the magical trance of Bollywood. For the past twenty-five years one name has cast a spell across the globe. It's Eros Entertainment International. [Western urbanscapes, multicolored bowling balls, and the Statue of Liberty flow by in a quick montage.] As the largest Bollywood content provider . . . Eros will continue to bring you the best of Bollywood in times to come. At Eros it's a vision to create, enhance, and distribute content across technological platforms. As a pioneer in international home video markets, for Bollywood Eros provides a catalog of over two thousand film titles and song compilations on DVD, VCD, and VHS. Eros launched the world's first Bollywood pay-per-view service. [Kareena Kapoor in powder blue gyrates at the center of the crosshairs.] To repurpose its content for the broadband environment, Eros ventured into

video on demand. To delight TV viewers all over, Eros launched the hugely popular satellite channels B4U and B4U-Music. For millions of netizens across the world erosentertainment.com is the sought-after Bollywood website. For those flying high, Eros offers enthralling in-flight entertainment on all prestigious international airlines. The state-of-the-art Eros postproduction studio is breaking new ground in creative ideation and design. Now [pause in music, a slow reedy lilt builds as we follow Aishwarya's gaze to mark the pixels of a digital butterfly flitter across the screen and into the heavens] the extraordinary odyssey of Eros takes a big leap—film production and finance adds another splendid chapter in the dazzling saga of its pathbreaking success. Eros International is a fully integrated media company that's taking Bollywood places.[1]

In a review of the top Oscar contenders for 2006, Manohla Dargis laments the kind of shifts that Eros hails as their crowning achievements: "To judge by how executives at major studios often talk about their business, in their discussions about closing windows, new platforms and emergent technologies, the movies themselves barely count. What counts is when you can watch a film on your cellphone, not if there is something worth losing your eyesight over. In the age of the incredible shrinking movie, content equals quantity, not quality . . . A nation of iPod-people, each staring at his or her individually downloaded film on the delivery system of his or her choice, seems a poor substitute for the oceanic feeling that comes with watching a film with a crowd, finding communion in the dark."[2] For Dargis an era of cinema exhibition is coming to the end of its particular duration, and the shape of things felt in cinema is reforming. In the pages to come, this duration and its untold mutations will form the basis of what I wager is a stochastic or nonlinear experience of Bollywood. Something untimely unfolds through the changing conditions of media consumption in globalizing India today. Something untimely, as when one is witness to a patterned dissolution of moviegoing practices in the dynamic topology or emergent forms of the new media. And this, for critics such as Dargis, signals the end of a certain anonymous community of viewing, the quantification of cinema art, and the technological individuation of media consumption. In taking the cinephile's lament as seriously as Eros's global ambition, I argue for a media assemblage approach to the evolving problem of media and its habituations.

There is a set of terms that will come to resonate throughout this text, and I will introduce them in their place, but here I would like to map their "domain of validity" and the disciplinary fields with which they are correlated.[3] The overall aim of this book is to shift the analysis of audiovisual media from a representational frame where the image, discourse, narrative, signifier, and ideal are all in various ways master tropes that produce a linear causal relation to consciousness and identity. In observing media events whose effects are multiple, contradictory, implicative, and evolving, the necessity of making this shift came to me as an intuitive shock. When confronted with the protean embodiment of sensation through the time of these events, it seemed that all of my previous conceptual frames rendered the media event as the reproduction of the same or the similar. It was this shock that led me to a method of diagramming nonlinear processes of an assemblage that implicates bodies through their potential or capacity to mutate. By intervening in postcolonial media studies, film studies, new media studies, and eco-criticism, this study focuses on media as a contested production of sensation. In that regard, one dimension of this domain of validity is the cultural critique of identity (in terms of sexuality, gender, caste, class, religion, and transnationality) as an effect of discourse. For too long, representation has been thought in terms of an actualized product of given hierarchies of power. But what if representation is an event that performs anew with each repetition and with each new scene of circulation being an unpredictable but patterned trajectory of present conforming to past but open to future mutations?[4] If so then what needs prior elaboration is not the production of representation but the viability of its event: How does an audiovisual stream contagiously "catch on"? How does audiovisual technology circulate regimes of signs and sounds such that they seem to "catch on" to the very bodies of newly globalized consumers?

Pleasures circulate across populations and sensations proliferate paradoxes. The most banal media stream becomes a resource for a passionate attachment, and so Shahrukh "King" Khan reigns for over a decade as the premiere Bollywood attraction. Sensations resonate "at the point where body and population meet."[5] This is also precisely how Michel Foucault defined *sexuality*, and in pursuing this preindividual sense of sexuality as a question of the very movements of media events I argue for a notion of sexualization as a historical ecology of sensation. Sexuality emerges first as intuited sensation through the interactive capacities of the various elements of the assemblage, and then as codified contents, signs, or narratives. But the preindividual ecology of sensation is the very condition of the evolution of sexual identity itself, and that evolution is about the refunctioned *bios* in media technologies, the body in habituated populations, and the body mutating through these repetitive processes. Thus, I suggest that the key question of sexuality needs to be situated in a broader field of dynamic processes that take those very processes as objects to be tinkered with. (This notion of evolution as natural tinkering has been decisive in rethinking the various effects of bio/power, for instance through feedback loop relations.)

A closely related aspect of this domain of validity is the conceptualization of the body as an assembling whole that is open to change through its own indeterminations. The feminist and queer multiplication of the gendered, raced, and sexed body's resistant desires, pleasures, and intensities would mark this domain's disciplinary intervention. Drawing on anti-racist, post-colonial, and queer feminist theory, this argument highlights how the human body has evolved its capacities to change and be changed (affectivity) by developing specific kinds of connections between technology, energy, memory, neuronal activity, and the flesh. And these connections cannot be adequately grasped as the body adding to its powers through prosthetic coupling. This would be the body as an amalgam of prostheses on a unified body as in some forms of cyborg theory.

Instead, I focus on the body fluctuating across key thresholds, times, and technologies of digital control. This is the biopolitical domain of my study, and its disciplinary correlates are political philosophy and new media studies. Dargis suggests in the quote above that part of what is happening to film is its integration in portable computing interfaces that increasingly are shrinking in size and speeding up intensive consumption. But this gets at one of the important differences between Eros as business model and Dargis as film critic: the privileged position of film as master organizer of media effects. What happens to the consuming body when cinema is refunctioned, or repurposed in new media, as Eros hopes and Dargis despairs? One of the most important responses to this question of the body in media is Vivian Sobchack's film-based phenomenology, which reframes the question of the "cinesthetic" subject as follows: "What have we, as contemporary media theorists, to do with such tactile, kinetic, redolent, resonant, and sometimes even taste-full descriptions of the film experience?"[6] Sobchack shifts the terrain of film toward a broader mediascape and then moors that shift by privileging cinema as the origin of its governing sensations. I have two arguments against this approach. First, my focus on the body's affects modulated across these cultural and technological thresholds is committed to furthering ongoing explorations of the specific modes of address of Indian film genres as they articulate in *feedback loop relations* with active audiences and the global restructuring of the financial, labor, aesthetic, and creative infrastructures of a variety of transnational media.[7] The production of bodily affect is a continuous multiplicity, a multiplicity that is continuously varying with itself because of its intensive self-organizing activity and its open interfaces with outside forces, dynamics, and materialities. Also, given that the creation of surplus value within the affect economy fixates on the accumulation and revaluing of the affective capacities of life itself, this emergent affectivity implies that in the media assemblage there can be no privileging of cinema as original apparatus or industry. Second, the body under the conditions of the analog versus digital assemblage is a body that must be thought of as the site of creative indetermination *before* actual experience and *before* consciousness, at the level of what is called proprioception, which is the continuous monitoring of internal changes in the body by sensory nerve endings brought about by movement and muscular activity (i.e., the preindividual). As Susan Buck Morss, Mark Hansen, and Brian Massumi (in their different ways) have shown in their explorations of the nervous system, the affectivity of the body is a way of dynamically connecting with the world in all its profusion of sensation.[8] It follows then that the media phenomenon as a set of events assembled together through feedback loop relations is never fully experienced at the level of consciousness, representation, or identity. And so it is precisely the body as preindividual (that is, individual and populational at once), self-organizing (a mutating multiplicity far from equilibrium and intuitively open to its own becomings), and dynamic (simultaneously stochastic and patterned) that now comes to be situated at the center of a given media assemblage.

Finally, the domain of validity of this study is characterized by a thought of ontology as duration.[9] This suggests a shift away from thinking of media effects as products legible on a passive body and toward the intensive processes of consumption that give a media assemblage its particular durations. Duration here is understood in terms of both the nested temporalities that are lived through the assemblage, and the duration it has as an entity in its own right. Like a sugar cube on fire, when audio-visual media catch on there is a specific duration and intensity to its forms that comes from the "internal resonance" of its various capacities and its singular affordances vis-á-vis its ecology.[10] How do new forms of media come to dominance, and how can we best grasp their emergence in the preindividual, self-organizing, and dynamic bodies of its globalizing consumers? To account for this emergence we need a kind of analysis (the biogram, in Brian Massumi's terms) that unlocks the part of the media event that exceeds its actualization. As will become clear in subsequent chapters, the concept that to my mind enables such counteractualization is affect.

The terms that I will develop in my definition of media assemblages are drawn from a variety of sources in feminist and queer philosophy, the physical and biological sciences, and biopolitical cultural criticism. For instance, one way of modeling the assembling body-in-media is to trace out a continuous movement (or qualitative multiplicity) of audiovisual information across a population as a contagion. The notion of contagion seems particularly apt for my purposes since a diagram of contagious multiplicities distributed across technological platforms through dynamic thresholds is a way of keeping in mind a postcolonial feminist resonance of contagion as racial miscegenation and sexual degeneracy,[11] while also moving away from its analysis as metaphor (and resemblance) toward consideration of ontic durations of media pleasures that change in kind (i.e., qualitatively).[12] In such a view, the capitalist circulation of sound movements in the production of consumerist affect becomes an element in an overall resegmentation of audience populations, all with a view for new sites, strategies, and possibilities for value creation and accumulation. But media contagions are like parasites that draw energy and information into a dissipative cascade of events whose causes are multiple and whose effects are nonlinear.[13] The notion of contagion, thus, draws attention to processes that unfold through turbulent events that exceed their actualization.

Flashback

I began this book project twelve years ago through a consideration of how, in the context of Indian nationalism after independence, the iconography and discourse of Elvis Presley was deliriously re-created (as hybrid identity in representation) by the popular Hindi-Urdu film actor Shammi Kapoor. The connection, and its at least partial celebration, was of a piece with a politics of (reading) resistance rooted in discursive strategies, the performativity of gender, the political economy of the sign, and the disparate narratives of postcolonial subjectivation and desubjectivation as a shuttling of the gendered subaltern. Decisive here was the work of Gayatri Chakravorty Spivak. In some sense, the most challenging cultural studies work done in the fields of representational analysis in the 1990s was an ongoing conversation that began with the circulation of "Can the Subaltern Speak?" But perhaps we have yet to catch the full force of that brilliant question? Certainly in my own work this missed opportunity took the form of an analytical method that deployed film as the "metaphoric" ground from which political forms would be read.

For me a decisive shift has occurred in the thought of media over the years since 9/11. The memory of the suspended ashes of human flesh on the streets of Chinatown and Tribeca forcefully suggest that we return to the minoritized histories of globalizing and contested spaces through what Brian Massumi and Manuel Delanda call an "incorporeal materialism"; indeed, that event and the subsequent biopolitical settlement of the Bush administration caused me to reconceptualize a set of researches on communal riots and film exhibition practices that I had conducted for over a year in Bhopal, India (in 2000–2001, my first extended trip since 1991).[14] My immediate aim in my Bhopal research initiatives was to understand the life of Lily Talkies, a brilliant movie hall built in 1971. I fell in love with pictures at Lily. And for the first time I began attending to the body and its sensations (situating the problem of sexuality in an assemblage context) in the social processes of viewing film, just as a certain analysis of the biopolitical state of exception was making itself felt throughout academia. A changing domain of validity started to take shape, and I began asking how to live an untimely love, a kind of complicit extraction, of India's media assemblage as a diasporic Indian. What emerged was a cinephilia becoming tele-info-philia. But the love here also functions to open thought to the specific shock of bearing witness to the death of exactly that which you love: What does media pleasure have to do with the bare life of the state of exception? In what way are contemporary media assemblages and contemporary processes of biopolitical control creating new bodily modes of a potentializing power? These initial questions had to be themselves reformulated in light of the specificity of India's post-Hindutva globalizing economy, where forms of digital-binary control in fact function through caste, communal, privatizing, and patriarchal lines of becoming whose history cannot be enclosed by either the rupture or the unity of discipline and biopower.[15] This led me to pose how at the level of everyday experience new habituations regarding the future and its management were entering the nested spatiotemporal scales of my analysis: How had global risk management become folded into the media assemblage in India? Part of what is at stake in this study, then, is a reconsideration of the critical function of (Indian, Hindu, secular, Bollywood, diasporic) "culture" in postcolonial media assemblages. (In this regard the nation will be both key placeholder and site of displacement in elaborating the media assemblage of globalization; no national frame can exhaust the contagious dynamism of contemporary media.) In short, I began developing a methodological prism through which a diagram of the relationship between global risk, terrorism, homo sacer, and the audiovisual movements of contemporary media assemblages in India becomes both legible and virtual.

Most immediately, this effort brought me to the work of Madhav Prasad, Ravi Vasudevan, Geeta Kapur, Tejaswini Naranjana, Ashish Nandy, and Lalitha Gopalan. It is Gopalan's text *Cinema of Interruptions* that provided me with the initial coordinates for an exploration of the new media assemblage in India and its diasporas. There are moments in her study of action genres in Indian cinema where the thought of what I am calling media assemblages (contagious and continuous multiplicities, or ecologies of matter, media, and sensation) proliferates beyond the dialectic of interruption and continuity—that is, moments where a certain complicity is marked and made strange by its becoming something else. Gopalan's text pushes the terms of debate beyond their contemporary framings. She does this through the cinephile's odd and always risky combination of marking pleasure and launching critique—an interpretive pleasure in cinema that is profoundly ethical and itself interruptive. For instance, the beloved song-and-dance sequences, despite their profilmic integration into narratives (e.g., in the work of director Mani Ratnam), do not, in Gopalan's words, "totally escape their ability to circulate separately from his films to other economies of production and reception."[16] This line of flight traversing bodily and aural-imagistic economies limns the connectivities of what I will call India's media assemblage. My initial thought spurred by Gopalan's reading was that this separation is also a form of connectivity, continually unstable feedback loop relations across aleatory variables, stochastic channels of communication, technological-human substrates, and unpredictable but patterned trajectories. It is precisely this multiform connectivity of the circulation of film music that moves cinema from fetish object into the broader dynamics of the media assemblage. Indeed, this is an aspect of the production and consumption of the Hindi film music industry that from its inception in the 1930s has necessarily involved film music in volatile connectivities. Even though, as Alison Arnold argued in a still-relevant article on film music, song-and-dance sequences were more often integrated with narrative flow in the first phase of film music (roughly from 1931 to 1965), what needs to be posed, even more so today given the changes in sound recording and consumption (consider Ray Dolby in India, both his decisive trip to the country in 1963 and the emergence and proliferation of this technology of sensation along with portable stereos in the 1970s and 1980s), is the actual shift in affective flows, or intensive consumption from narrative to song-dance movement.[17]

Thus the differences across media—say from the cinema hall, to DVD, to cell phone ringtones, to JPEG/MPEG, to the Internet, not to mention from dialogue to song—could also be addressed as the qualitative, intensive shifts in the modulation of noise-desire-information-affect: namely, media synaesthesia.[18] Crucial here is that, like many digital technologies, the shift into digital modulation happens at a level below experience in the neural activity of the embodied mind;[19] one definition of MPEG (the acronym for Moving Pictures Expert Group), for instance, suggests that the MPEG algorithm achieves a higher rate of compression by storing only the changes, or intervals from one frame to another, instead of each entire frame. The video information is then encoded using a technique called DCT (Discrete Cosine Transform) that prepares the data for compression and reduction. According to one source, "MPEG uses a type of *lossy compression*, since some data is removed. But the diminishment of data is generally imperceptible to the human eye."[20] This example highlights how contemporary forms of digital control (encryption) are changing the nature of the body's functional connection to quickly reconfigured media technologies at a level *below*, or better, *before* perception (the media event), where the brain's activity of "neural filling-in" is retrained and reinvested. And it is precisely here, at the pre-individual level, that I situate the argument around sexuality in this book: ecologies of sensation modulate and potentialize the body's pleasures and distribute them as contagions across segmented populations not as master scripts that normalize but as self-organizing codes that modulate and tinker. To my mind, Gopalan's theory of Indian cinema as a constellation of interruptions enables this deterritorialization of film becoming media, where a dynamic threshold between text, media, sensation, and bodies becomes thinkable.

The force of this insight was brought home to me when I began research into the everyday travails and pleasures of a cinema owner in Bhopal and the diverse populations that flowed through his exhibition space. My friendship with the cinema owner, Varun Moolchandani, was enabled through a certain camaraderie that my cousin Sudeep Shrivastava, a professor of economics, and I shared with his graduate students. Varun was my cousin's star student. Brilliant, charismatic, and entrepreneurial, Varun is the scion of one of the most prominent business families in Bhopal. Although at one time the family members were staunch supporters of the centrist Congress Party, today the family leads the Hindu business community in supporting the Hindu chauvinist Bharatiya Janata Party. As refugees from Punjab after partition, Varun's family settled in Bhopal and started Raj Radios. In 1971, using profits from the very successful radio retail business, the family established Lily Talkies. Lily was once the pearl of movie exhibition in Bhopal. Located between the old Muslim city and the new Hindu-dominated urban sprawl communities, as if between two legacies of postcolonial modernity, and facing one of the beautiful lakes of the city, it attracted a strong "family-oriented" business and was considered among the best serviced and cleanest of the city's thirteen theaters. Throughout Lily's early years (1971–1982), its owners had the ear of Indira Gandhi when push came to shove—for instance, during protracted and (often bitter) labor disputes. Usually the owners got their way, but in the years to come the contestation between the layers of the Hindu-Sikh-elite management-owners and the Muslim-subaltern staff would come to affect the life of Lily Talkies with ever-renewed intensity.

From the mid-1990s, the traditional cinema exhibition business in the state was in rapid decline. Thus, after years of suffering severe losses, the family was forced to shut down Lily Talkies when, at the end of 2005, the police raided the theater for censorship infringement. By that time Varun had already launched another media retail venture—selling DJ equipment and producing training CDs—and he claimed to dominate 70 percent of the market share in the state. By 2005, business was growing rapidly. The career of this one Sindhi family, as their lives and work traverse the singular media assemblage of globalizing India by negotiating and creating within it, points to one of the central arguments of this book: namely, the question of what is at stake in the thought of a media assemblage—in the very "experience" of indetermination and of what it is to create something new today.

I pursue this question by considering different media events and their dynamic thresholds across affects and nested spatiotemporalities. I consider the possible biograms of "first day, first show events" in Bhopal (chapter 1). Following the insights of recent critics who have suggested that closer attention to exhibition is crucial for situating the precise nature of cinema's biopolitics, I look at one of the organizing events of Indian cinema—notably the practice of attending first day, first show events. In so doing I reconstruct an experience of going to an opening of *Mohabbatein* (dir. Aditya Chopra, 2000) at a single-screen talkie in Bhopal. In subsequent chapters I tie this experience to the qualitatively different experience of the media event in the multiplex. In looking at the kinds of continuities and displacements from the single screen to the multiplex, I mark how the moment of exhibition is still what cannot be brought within the algorithms governing digital encryp-

1. Lily Talkies theater, Jahangirabad, Bhopal, 2004. Photo by Amit S. Rai.

tion. Digital rights management technologies notwithstanding, the changing technologies and functions of the media piracy economies destabilize the production of value of any particular media assemblage. This far-from-equilibrium condition suggests that the media assemblage's social field is a site of indetermination because, at a basic level, it is the site of a struggle for securing image-sound contents and habituations.[21] But this indetermination is deepened as soon as we move into the realm of image-sound consumption where we confront an analog body open to its own outside forces of futurity, creating the new as well as circulating the pirated—that is, the oscillation between a flight out of time as naturalized habit (the shock) and a continuous multiplicity of movement. Bringing thought to these many infolding but never fully actualized becomings is one way of touching the Untimely.

Enter the DJ

The cosmopolitan DJ is the guru of the media assemblage. Her figure stands at the threshold of an emerging sensory-motor schema in contemporary popular Hindi-Urdu media. The DJ's navigable data, both digital and constantly reassembled along new lines of movement and always hybridizing styles, unfolds interactively with the collective movement of bodies, their flows and desires. It is a rhythmic synaesthesia. To think about this emergence—as digital technologies shift, converge, but also qualitatively differentiate embodied perception, dynamic interfaces, and divergent intervals—the evolving problematic returns again and again to affective control and becoming across media platforms.

Affective assemblages of bodies, populations, and media function through a kind of sticky symbiosis of what Baruch Spinoza called "relations of motion." In India, as also in Hong Kong (but for very different reasons), two figures of time—utopia and nostalgia—have assumed a new centrality in contemporary theorizations of media and politics in their postmodern mode.[22] This study, both informed by and departing from the terrain of those debates, privileges modalities of movement, and as such it follows from my central aims—from representation to diagram, cyborg body to assemblage, and from product to duration—that entail a focus on unpredictable but patterned trajectories within and of populations (becomings, or the untimely). In the pages that follow I give very different examples of such movements, some of which are folded into others and some are parasitic on another, but none of which resemble or analogize each other. Here, the styles and infrastructures of Hindi-Urdu cinema become newly global—its becoming as Bollywood. Thus, my first methodological move was to isolate and multiply the figures of time, or the sensorimotor circuits that could strategically be diagrammed in their moment of dominant and minority becomings. As such a certain topology of dynamic change, or what above I have called an ontology of duration, emerges across media technologies, audience populations, bodies, and spatiotemporalities.

In chapters 2 through 4, my argument is divided into four parts that are involved in each other and mutually constitutive of each other yet do not form a dialectical progression.[23] In the first part, I consider the potentializing excesses of film culture as sites for mapping this cinema's contagious multiplicities. My method is to look at the changing nature of cinema, notably its functional connectivities as well as its evolving capacities to affect and be affected through its proximate populations, its many bodies, microspaces, and speeds, technological promiscuities, consumerist habituations, genre segmentations, and proliferating interfaces. What emerges is a new diagram of the movements constituting the durations of Bollywood's media assemblage. The question that arises is what is the function of this potentializing *excess?* Or, what specific political charge should we "assign" to this excess given the informational nature of contemporary media assemblages?

There are variations in the use of this term in this text, but I see these variations forming a kind of regularity. On the one hand, my use of the term excess stands in contrast to those forms of cultural criticism that would locate political subjectivity at the chaotic center of excess and then fold that center into a narrative of resistance to (hetero)normativity. At the most basic level, the shift from representation to diagram necessitates a thought of media assemblages that exceeds the signifier and its attendant regimes of meaning or indeterminacy. This excess, however, is not a site of any straightforward (human) resistance, but rather is embedded in patterned (recurring) processes of nonlinear and co-dependent emergence. Thus, the question of excess can never be reduced to a possible identity position, but rather must be seen as potential dimensions of change within a media assemblage. The ontology of duration suggests that as media habituations evolve over time and across populations, mutations and variations (excess) spontaneously form their own trajectories (self-organization) that may become the starting point for a general phase transition (or global restructuring and refunctioning) of the media assemblage itself. This is the nonhuman, or preindividual, form of excess that I argue for in this book, and one that I return to in the conclusion.[24]

Initially, I trace a first movement from cinema cultures to media assemblages, where the dominance of the framings of image-sound, culture, and narrative of film criticism are put to flight along another trajectory involved in thinking and feeling the interpenetrating, co-implicated, and continuous multiplicities of the human-media interface (HMI). In the second part of the book, I consider the rise of the multiplex in India as an example of the overall transformation in the nature of film culture: the media assemblage of a globalizing Bollywood that I sketched in my first section finds specific interfaces and connectivities in newly multiplexed bodies. This emergence can be understood again in terms of the shifts in the management of cinema's risky excesses: audience-body, population-community, and theater-space have all been problematized in exhibition practices as sources or sites of contagion and possibly nonrecoupable, nonproductive expenditure. The multiplex in India seeks to resolve the problems associated with the single-screen theater in India by drawing on a technology that I am linking on the one hand to the non-resident Indian (NRI) and on the other to the history of loitering bodies that have evolved from north Indian bazaar culture. The second movement, then, is from populations segmented in the single screen to a transnational and multiplicitous regime of sensation. In the final chapter, I consider the regime of sensation (the sensory-motor schema) launched, habituated, and interrupted in the proliferation of insurancial and astrology technologies on Indian satellite TV. Here, I focus the diagram on elements of the media assemblage that take us from sexuality as identity to affect as bodily schema; I am specifically concerned with the image-sound connectivities of what I will call the ittafaq image (both chance and concordance in Urdu-Hindi and Arabic) as a continually deforming and reforming (topological) image center marking the emergence of risk technologies across contemporary media.[25] I focus on two contemporary social practices common to both South Asia and the diaspora: insurance and spiritual healing. I tie the transformations in narrative and characterization in Bollywood melodrama to shifts in concepts of temporality, sexuality, and risk in the wake of the "financialization of everyday life" in India: that is, a movement from discursive constructs to political ontologies of capitalist time.[26]

Interval

This study situates the media assemblage of globalizing Bollywood through specific case studies. It flows from a desire to shift focus from (sexual, religious, caste, gender, racial, and class) identity and its representations as a form of identity suture and begin the rather more dubious but nonetheless crucial diagram of representational and nonrepresentational conjunctures and functionalities. This diagram will chart the co-dependent emergence of perception-technologies, rhythms, intensities, spaces, bodies, and temporalities that constitute contemporary film and new media practice in India and the diaspora. Such a thought of cinema would keep open the tensions and contradictions of the effects and functionality of representation, but by deploying a pragmatic approach to language the sign becomes continuous with the material practices, or affections, of the body that an assemblage viably connects.[27]

I will explore this dual line of thought by considering different relations of motion among technologies of the body that I argue are transforming contemporary Bollywood within and through the very idioms of that cinema. The biopolitics of Bollywood's assemblage elicits correlated effects of power at the autonomic level of the preindividual,[28] in habits and collective enunciations that give a specific rhythm to its subjectivities and organizes its affects, fantasies, pleasures, and consumer pedagogies around a series of recurring processes peculiarly suited to the needs of a liberalizing postcolonial economy. At the same time, these processes are potentialized (excess as unpredictable but patterned trajectories) by the proliferation, or better, contagion of a diffuse counterfeit economy.

Throughout the mediascape of globalizing India we are becoming attuned to a moment of radical flux and profound retrenchments. We can discern the abstract potentialization of human technological matter and material capture as idealized abstraction, or put in another way, media synaesthesia as corporate logo. One consequence of this conjuncture is that all modes of potentializing *excess* in the body (affectivity) are always also open to various mechanisms of *branding affect* in the global economy. Thus the media assemblage of globalizing India finds new functionalities, dynamic thresholds, and articulations at a moment when we must see that recent economic and financial crises throughout the world have created disturbing and volatile social effects by correlating unemployment, massive displacements of populations, poverty, and social and political unrest. The recent ouster of the Hindu chauvinist government in India (fronted by the Bharatiya Janata Party [BJP]) by emergent and residual social forces—both from the Left and the Right, not to mention in the capitalist-oriented diaspora—shows that India has been profoundly affected by these global changes. Is the present moment, then, merely another case of what Antonio Gramsci once symptomatized as the specific liminality of the 1930s in fascist Europe? That, as Gramsci put it, the "old is dying and the new cannot be born: in this interregnum a great variety of morbid symptoms appear."[29] Morbid? Yes, if we realize with what affectivity—those multiple fluxes that vibrate, interrupt, and reassemble with qualitatively different intensities—this morbidity functioned under fascism, indeed at the level of affect such morbidity, even at its most murderous, was all life, nonnarrative vibrations moving through bodies and populations and moving them in unexpected ways. Yes as well, if we can think of the dis-*ease* of morbidity as contagion, as an unfolding process of constitutive openness, a sense of volatile bodies—the nexus of indetermination—framing perception before, and then beyond perception. A return to the event of framing, its virtuality, its constitutive outside (to think creatively with both Mark Hansen and Fredric Jameson—I will return to both thinkers in subsequent chapters),[30] this interregnum—this between-regimes—is the temporality we will attempt to address in a new thought of cinema's re-mediatization in the postcolonial context of Hindi-Urdu popular culture.

The nonlinear dynamism of the globalizing media assemblage of Bollywood yields multiple and paradoxical effects. This new sensorium for transnational media technologies and industries unfolds at many levels. A sensorium is a particular regime not only of pleasure but more generally constituted habituations of affect at the preindividual, subsensate level, keeping in mind that the preindividual is the mutational interface-limit between the subject and multiple populations.[31] It is a thought that must begin with the digital in order to constitute the specificity of what it is in the process of displacing. This is the basic premise of all the chapters that follow.

The diagram that emerges articulates a double movement of an untimely becoming. What are those untimely affects being created today through the multiple movements that constitute popular Hindi-Urdu media? The new-media critic Mark B. N. Hansen, whose work I engage with in more detail in subsequent chapters, draws on the philosopher Gilbert Simondon to define affectivity as a mode of bodily experience that forms durations of dynamic connectivity through unstable because stochastic feedback loops. Between the individual and the preindividual, the personal and the impersonal, thought is drawn to affectivity: "Whereas perception appeals to structures already constituted in the interior of the individuated being, 'affectivity indicates and comprises this relation between the individualized being and preindividual reality: it is thus to a certain extent heterogeneous in relation to individualized reality, and appears to bring it something from the exterior, indicating to the individualized being that it is not a complete and closed set [ensemble] of reality.' "[32] In keeping with the general avant-gardist spirit of Deleuzian art and media criticism, Hansen takes the notion of affectivity in the direction of a new experience of human becoming media. My argument in this book will be that this mode of bodily experience is also the primary mode of branding popular media under globalization the world over, and that it is unfolding in India in singular ways, as both potentialization and containment, control and becoming. How do we live this double movement otherwise? It is toward creative indetermination as an activation of the singular openness of the body that an untimely experience of embodied media draws us.

What is to become of Indian film criticism through such an engagement with the spatiotemporality of the body in the new media? As Søren Mørk Petersen has recently noted, framing the various forms of media in relation to their material practices is nothing new, although it is seldom done. For instance, scholars in television studies have studied the physical and aural effects of watching television instead of only focusing on the content broadcasted; cyberculture critics have shown how the physical setting of Internet cafés is a part of the construction of gender, and how the placement of computers in the home demonstrates their primary use and which members of the family are using them.[33] As Petersen argues, these analyses follow technologies becoming mundane and habitual and chart how new connectivities subtly alter the perception of our embodied timespaces. These processes inform all aspects of contemporary life across heterogeneous populations, and thus call for a multidisciplinary framework: in a phase transition, where the ontologies (durations) of consumption are serially tweaked producing quantum effects, a pragmatic combination of disciplinary formations helps to illuminate different facets of this new assemblage. In this study, then, media studies offers a body neurally implicated in audiovisual technologies of memory; postcolonial studies offers the critique of global capital as a violent and value-yielding machining of gendered, raced, and sexed population flows and the subjugation of historical contents and forms of sociality; feminist literary studies offers an attention to the resonances of narrative unfolding the expressions of a dissociated self, with an insistence on the material effects of language in and through the situated body; and political philosophy offers the strategies of correlating bodies and technologies as biopower. Foucault, in his 1978 lecture "Security, Territory, Population," defined this last concept as "the set of mechanisms through which the basic biological features of the human species became the object of a political strategy."[34] It is in fact biopower that brings together these disparate lines of enquiry by directing our attention to the aspects of preindividual forms of power, where sensation vibrates in the creative indeterminacy between habit and its repetition.

In this time of deterritorializing and reterritorializing media how is it that Hindi-Urdu cinema has come to assume the characteristics of a "national" cinema, and has done so for the first time? For unlike most national cinemas throughout the later half of the twentieth century, Hindi-Urdu commercial cinema was never a state-sponsored project. Tom O'Regan defines national cinemas as "simultaneously an aesthetic and production movement, a critical technology, a civic project of state, an industrial strategy and an international project formed in response to the dominant international cinemas (particularly but not exclusively Hollywood cinema)."[35] Now clearly popular, Hindi-Urdu cinema has been organized by a commercial ethic, one that, even when it was one with a nationalist or postcolonial civic project, maintained the necessity of the commercial character of Bombay filmmaking (these contradictions and legacies are still quite legible in censorship practices, as I show in chapter 3). On the one hand, as I shall argue, "Bollywood" (and I am fully aware of the gross inadequacies of this term) has never had a deeper global market penetration, and the impact of south Indian film populations, specifically south Indian directors, on Bombay cinema has enabled its entry into many new circuits. On the other hand, given the massive surge in Hollywood ticket sales spurred by the multiplex boom (2 billion rupees, in 2006), Bollywood is also confronting the gradual weakening of its own market dominance by becoming a "national" commercial cinema (even as non-Hindi–based cinemas in the south and in West Bengal continue, reinvent, and deepen their own regional dominance). These multiple becomings have their own speeds, and nothing but a teleology could yield predictions at a moment of such thoroughgoing restructurings.

I will, however, suggest certain tendencies in the social, bodily, technological, institutional, and commercial reorganization of Hindi-Urdu popular media, each of which has a duration that penetrates the others, thereby forming new "contact actions" and new relations of motion. For example, the contact action among digital technologies, new intellectual property laws (digital rights management), and encryption algorithms has yielded a new regime of capture and passage within the media assemblage, and the experience of media in India has been transformed by these elements of its ecology because they have expanded, accelerated, and controlled the capacities (affects) of production, circulation, and consumption.[36] Building on the notion of the "production of locality" in the apparatuses of globalization by Hardt and Negri, this articulation of contact actions by processes of assembling media ecologies is the site of a double movement of homogenization (overcoding of information and identities) and heterogenization (marketable difference but also unpredictable potentialization).[37] Within such a regime of overcoding and potentialization it is all the more necessary to follow closely the emergence of preindividual embodied perception and temporalities of consumption; these processes continue to deform and reform the topography of India's media assemblage. One important place to diagram this affective restructuring is in the creative engagement with processes of "branding" in piracy cultures. Taking this example as paradigmatic, the argument throughout this study is that an ecology of sensation specific to India's experience of globalization is restructuring and refunctioning the temporalities of Hindi-Urdu media experience. What is at stake is the specific conception and practice not only of the temporal processes of "sexual becoming,"[38] but more radically of habituated dispositions toward the very future itself: insurance and astrology meet Bollywood in a new ecology of sensation (cf. chapter 4). My research into exhibition practices and film population norms in a "nonmetro" north Indian city, Bhopal, and my interviews with South Asian Bollywood fans in the New York metropolitan area have focused on India's new media assemblage.[39] The analysis of such an assemblage calls for a method that focuses on the changing nature (or functionality) of specific kinds of connectivities (or intervals) between bodies—technological bodies, (non)human bodies, filmic bodies, and pulsive, proprioceptive bodies—toward a biogrammatics of media intervals.

A media interval is an emergent property of variously connected flows, human and nonhuman energy, capital, timespaces, and image-sound flows. In one of its capacities it functions as a gateway tracking the gradients of the very flows from which it emerges. Intervals thus organize these flows, and by assembling novel mechanisms and forms of connectivity and resonance they establish a phase separation from the flows through which they emerge. Intervals are the qualitative durations constituting the continuous multiplicity of a media assemblage, their mode of self-organization. Potential examples of such intervals are intermissions, shot length, exhibition schedules, rates of data transmission, attention spans, event anticipation, the public lifespan of a media stream ("catchy" media), and the evolution of a given media habituation. Obviously such a capacious notion of the interval can easily become so diffuse as to lose its analytic force, where any randomized gap in a flow becomes a decisive interval. It is important then to specify a set of concepts (drawn largely from biopower analyses) that can help us adjudicate the important interval from the unimportant one. First, media intervals are stochastic *and* patterned; as gradient-tracking gateways for a heterogeneous set of flows they organize statistically controlled populations of media culture that will always also swerve from their given trajectories (what I term in my conclusion clinamedia). Second, intervals render assemblages in perpetual nonequilibrium conditions, and yet they are more or less consistent over the lifespan of that singular assemblage. Third, and following from the second assumption, media assemblages are temporally bound structures through which definite sets and forms of information circulate, thereby producing variations that can form further novel assemblages (dissipative phase transitions). In these eddies of media various forms of energy and matter dissipate irreversibly through the interval gateway. Media assemblages are nonequilibrium dissipative structures,[40] with turbulent and mutating image-sound forms (infolding processes) and neuronal resonances that self-organize through the operations of the interval:[41] My contention, to be tested in the pages that follow, is that singular intervals reconfigure the fluctuations of media assemblages into contagious patterns of sensation, information, and resonance.

This book comes out of the belief that contemporary film and media studies must address the kind of contagion that audiovisual movement has become. Neither formalist analyses of film culture nor representational theories of subjectivation addresses the particular interval involved in the global becoming of control media: namely, the bodily dispensation of the digital. That untimely interval is in the production of affect, in the co-dependent emergence of human populations and media technologies. The interval happens in the very interaction of all the various elements of a media assemblage; those in-between processes through which constituting powers enable modes of negotiation and flight, processes that render relations of force at once most visible and least vulnerable. (That is also why different strategies of writing are called for to inhabit the same book.) It is in the interval, says Giorgio Agamben, where the question of the biopolitical subject itself can be posed. The interval is neither an absence or lack nor merely production; instead, it is a remainder. The interval subject can only be conceived "in terms of a process of subjectivation and desubjectivation— or rather as an interval or remainder between these processes."[42] It is here, in the emergent capacities of biological life, which is radically repurposed across the processes and technological substrates of media assemblages, that following Agamben, Deleuze, and Foucault we locate a certain ambiguity, a risk. This ambiguity is to diagram the event of media assemblages as an untimely becoming: to go, as Deleuze states, "back into the event, to take one's place in it as in a becoming, to grow both young and old in it at once, going through all its components and singularities. Becoming isn't part of history; history amounts [to] only the set of preconditions, however recent, that one leaves behind in order to 'become,' that is, to create something new."[43] To take a risk beyond calculation or the promise of security, to move thought along another trajectory traversing the political, biological life and remediated affects, is to give oneself to the promise of a future that remains untimely.

PART 1

CINEMA BECOMING NEW MEDIA

"First Day, First Show": Bollywood
Cinemagoing and the New Sensorium

"First day, first show." It's a common phrase throughout India, sure to
bring a smile to both speaker and interlocutor: a recognizable coding of one
of South Asian cinema's singular events. It conjures up images of Bollywood
faithfuls gathering, struggling, and scrambling to be one of the elect few to
say, coolly, "Dekhli [saw it]—first day, first show." In this quintessentially
Indian experience, one that is being re-created by new media practices and
global consumerist habituations, we can see how fans from economically
and socially diverse communities are renegotiating older structures of film
and media culture today. Over the past six years, I have had the privilege to
explore this film culture in various sites in India (Bhopal, Mumbai, Bangalore, Delhi), the United States (Times Square and Jackson Heights in New
York, and Artesia in California), and the United Kingdom (Birmingham,
Manchester, and London). The chapters that follow build on these site-
specific encounters, drawing most heavily from my extended research
into new media assemblages in Bhopal—the City of Lakes and the capital
of Madhya Pradesh. Bhopal is a city that was torn through by a rampaging
death-gas secreted by a Union Carbide plant in December 1984, which killed
thousands and thousands of mostly poor Muslim people within hours, and
which continues to claim the lives of fifteen people each month. It is also the
city of my birth and home to my father's extended upper-caste, middle-class
Hindu family. Historically it was a walled-in city ruled for over a century by
the Begums of Bhopal, the Muslim descendants of its founder the Afghan

Dost Mohammed Khan. Today, Bhopal is a segregated city: the old gated city, home to the now minority Muslim population, is overwhelmingly poor and overcrowded; the new Bhopal, Hindu dominated, is home to politicians, state legislators, landowners, businesspeople, and Dominos Pizza (and the Dalit workers who service them).[1]

Of the thirteen movie theaters in the city (all owned by Sikhs or Hindus), only three of them are in new Bhopal. The rest are all in the Muslim-majority areas of the erstwhile walled city. The difference is not only in location but can be seen in terms of numerous factors such as accessibility (quality of roads, density of traffic, availability of parking, etc.), regular programming clientele ("family" or soft porn genres, all-male clientele or gender mixed; single teenagers or families; poor, middle class, or rich; day or night crowds; Muslim or Hindu), services (box office, types of intermission snacks, ushers and "crowd control," cleanliness of toilets, lighting, drinking water), and theater "attractions" (Dolby sound, star and director visits, façade design, MTV-style digital advertisements and billboards, date of construction, style of architecture; condition of balcony, dress circle, stall seats; climate control via fans vs. water-cooled air, privatized dedicated power generators, etc.). This spectrum of differences indexes the emergence of a new kind of connectivity across the multiple dynamic thresholds of media technologies, cultural forms, subjectivities, neighborhoods, regions, nations, ideologies, and perception; it indexes as well the complex relationship between the new media and the changing strategies of India's globalizing elites.

Very simply, all these new connectivities imply a fundamental shift in the sensations of cinema. Certainly today cinematic practices, not just the cinematic image, are indissociable from the Internet, Dolby sound, or satellite TV as folds of each other. And certainly the form of bodily attention—exteroception, proprioception,[2] interoception; in short, affect—produced through the cinematic sound-image and its constitutive intervals (practices, institutions, sensori-motor circuits, and spatiotemporalities) has fundamentally changed in being folded into the new media. Thus, if a qualitatively different human-media interface is coming into dominance through these technologies and the active bodies of media consumers, then the thought of cinema itself must change. We chart these becomings through diagramming the body's sensations in and through the nonlinear dynamics of this new media assemblage.

But whose body? And which media technologies? In response, two initial "method" problems present themselves. First, does this suggest that all bodies, regardless of gender, religion, class, caste, race, sexuality, etc.

are equally implicated in this new dynamic threshold? Second, does this assume that satellite, Internet, and cable, etc. have transformed the totality of film-media culture in postcolonial India where access to and knowledge of such technologies are themselves technologies of social and economic exclusion and control?

To my mind these two questions should be reposed as: How can we think of the transformation in Bollywood cinema's ecology of sensation in the era of its new media assemblage as a qualitatively different kind of solicitation of the body's essential creativity, its openness as a center of indetermination—in short, its virtuality? Simultaneously, how can we think of the assemblage's specific form of power—as a violent machining, as the reproduction and containment, or reframing of deeply entrenched and repeatedly produced inequalities, clichés, and habituations across heterogeneous populations, a human multiplicity structured in dominance? Throughout this study I attempt to hold these lines of critique in productive tension: namely, Bollywood's global media assemblage as a historically specific unfolding of virtualization-containment, the unpredictable but patterned emergence of new media habituations. This approach follows through on Bernard Stiegler's startling suggestion that a "people"—ethnic, racial, national, regional, populational—is not defined by its past (memory, culture, traditions, "genius") but by its future; that is, by the line of mutation that orients it to a technologically constitutive outside, by its assembling along a machinic phylum. I will return to the question of the machinic phylum in the next chapter. Here I take up my initial point of departure and pursue some founding elements of this changing diagram of media, exhibition space, bodies, and power: Bollywood's biogram.[3]

Consider the site for this first day, first show: Jhumpa Talkies. Like thousands of other ardent fans I went to the first day, first show of *Mohabbatein* at Jhumpa, which is located in the Jahangirabad section of Bhopal—an overwhelmingly poor, and largely Muslim section of town. As such, I was warned repeatedly that there would be a mad rush for tickets and I was incurring needless danger by venturing into that part of town. Jahangirabad has a reputation: it is a highly policed subsection of the city, known as much for its narrow, potholed, underserviced streets and overcrowded slums as for the crime that, say the police, justifies their continual presence. In 1992, in the wake of the demolition of the Babri Masjid by Hindu nationalists, it was this neighborhood that was first engulfed by communal violence. The hostility subsequently spread throughout old Bhopal, where it was aided and abetted by the police and the army.[4] Eight months after the screening of *Mohabbatein* at Jhumpa, this same neighborhood movie hall would become the site of renewed communal violence as the blockbuster *Gadar* (dir. Sharma, 2001) sparked a national controversy by its chauvinist depiction of the partition of India and Pakistan.

But that was all yet to come, or it was already in the narrativized past.

It was the day after Diwali, and I made arrangements with my eighteen-year-old friend Abhishek (a lower-middle-class, upper-caste Hindu who never misses a first day, first show) to meet me at 10 AM. I got to Jhumpa before he did—but not nearly early enough, even though the show was supposed to be at 12:30. By 10 AM the line for the balcony seats, dress circle, and box seats was already beyond the outer gate. There were hundreds of people, mostly men, milling about the courtyard. Jhumpa is a single-screen theater, with seating for around twelve hundred. It is built in the molded concrete style of late 1970s and early 1980s movie halls in Bhopal—namely, a cross of classical art deco and administrative functionalism where shooting molded spires tiled with crumbling marble frame impassive grey blocks that are hidden behind faded white and red lime-paint. There are no fewer than three gates through which one must pass in order to get inside the theater: the outer gate leads into the hexagonal courtyard, whose centerpiece is the gnarled remains of an ancient tree; the heavily guarded theater gate leads into the inner courtyard lined with refreshment stands; and the final gate leads inside to the dress circle and stalls on the first floor, or up the staircase streaked in red *paan* juice to the balcony and box seats.[5]

The Connectivity of Art Deco

Here I will pause to consider the relations of motions established between a particular design style and exhibition timespace. Generally, the design of the art deco talkie in India is thus a series of enfolded half circles that funnel through strategic gates of passage and blockage, with the molded facades offering modernity, speed, and intensive image-sound. Art deco had a singular life in the Indian media assemblage; in spilling far beyond exhibition space it links experiences of consumption through a postcolonial temporality, and I will consider it a form of connectivity in this assemblage. No doubt, in its dominant spatial aesthetic, cinema in India has always been associated with a spatial and temporal disjuncture. Here the postcolonial temporalities of colonial materiality—European technology, African primitivist design, and a modernizing drive into the past and future at once—connect with the sensational intervals produced in the event of this material assemblage's functioning. It is not that the movement from village to city to diaspora and back is recapitulated or resembles the disjuncture of the stylized body within cinema and the disciplined body within exhibition space. Rather, we can speak of nested temporalities that have their own affordances in relation to various populations of material and phenomena. The movement invoked by the modernist ethos of the post-1950s talkie should be understood as a pedagogy of national belonging and a reductive coding (or subtractive image) of a potentializing excess of sensation.

Taken together this combination could be seen as an extension of what Gilles Deleuze calls cinema's sensory-motor schemata, but already this implies that we are no longer only considering what is specific to cinema but also what is specific about its becoming something else—a media assemblage. Consider the articulation (functional connectivity as dynamic feedback loop) of visual and musical style and exhibition space: India's art deco talkies deform into the globalized multiplex.[6] If we compare, for instance, the diverse visual and aural styles of Bimal Roy's *Devdas* (1955) and Sanjay Leela Bhansali's *Devdas* (2002) with the art deco talkies of the 1950s and the multiplex of today's globalizing India, we can discern how differently the media body can be articulated with cinematic space (I will return to these cinematic examples in the next chapter).

Art deco was a popular international trend that surfaced in Europe between 1910 and 1935. As a ubiquitous aesthetic style, art deco affected all aspects of world design including fashion, crafts, housewares, jewelry, statuary, architecture, and interior decoration.[7] Of heterogeneous origins with multiple branches, art deco was insistently modern, and as such it formed an assemblage with the machine age in its technologies, imagery, and graphics. As Lucy Fischer notes, not only did art deco adopt "a rhetoric of the mechanical," it also utilized new technologies of fabrication. In its commercial production, art deco employed synthetic materials like plastic (Bakelite, Lucite, Vitrolite) and metal (chrome, stainless steel, aluminum, and wrought iron). Stylistically, art deco was known for its streamlined, geometric, and symmetrical patterns—traits associated with Western industrialization. In keeping with art deco's stark high-tech facades, color was often reduced to the basics: black, white, and silver. Not unlike modernism itself, art deco was tied to the city and thus deemed the "skyscraper style." In its articulation of Western modernity, art deco also echoed various avant-garde movements. Through constructivism and futurism, technology became central to art deco's form; from cubism came a practice of pure form itself; and from German expressionism came distortion effects.[8]

2. Eros Talkies theater, Churchgate, Mumbai. Photo by Amit S. Rai.

3. The art deco design of the Goonj Bahadur theater, Jahangirabad, Bhopal, 2004. Photo by Amit S. Rai.

More significant in terms of its colonial and postcolonial deployment, art deco also assembled disjunctive temporal dispositions—enfolding its futurist tendencies into a pronounced fetishism for the "primeval." Like many styles of the era, it was influenced by what Euro-American elite culture understood as "traditional and even primal forms." Specifically, art deco evinced a fascination with the racialized and "primitive" other, as rendered through a litany of tropes. In Fischer's words: "From Egypt where King Tutankhamen's tomb had been discovered in 1922, Deco embraced Pharaonic imagery (from sphinx heads and scarabs to cats). From the broader Middle East, Deco recycled the Assyrian/Babylonian ziggurat structure—a pyramidal, terraced tower. So popular was this motif (as the base of furniture or objets d'art) that an entire strain of Deco came to be known as 'zigzag moderne.' From pre-Columbian Mexico, Deco drew upon the sunray image; and from Africa, it took the stylized mask as well as such materials as ivory and animal skins (zebra and tiger)."[9] Colonial flows of commodities, images, populations, and desire gave form to art deco by enfolding coded temporalities of exotic primitivism with the material duration of its substances, spaces, and media events. In these disjunctures a diagram of a postcolonial untimely emerges, with interruptions of linear progress embedded or nested in the intervals of its material and expressive form.

Art deco formed a machinic assemblage with Hollywood from its inception. Art deco greatly influenced set design through the work of a series of art directors associated with particular studios (e.g., Van Nest Polglase at RKO, Stephen Gooson at Fox, and Cedric Gibbons at MGM). As Fischer notes, art deco left its stamp not only on film costuming (especially that of women),[10] but even the physiognomy of actors was used to create art deco-inspired designs. Further, an aesthetic of art deco informed the graphic idiom of many movie posters of the era as well as the font and layout of studio logos (RKO and Twentieth Century-Fox, for example). Finally, art deco had a tremendous effect on the architectural design of American movie theaters, especially those elegant and luxurious spaces (such as Radio City Music Hall in New York) known as picture palaces. Donald Albrecht suggests that the ubiquity of the art deco mode on movie screens helped to popularize contemporary design in America: "The adoption of architectural modernism by the popular arts had [a] notable effect. . . . It successfully promoted the modern style to the general public, making it both more accessible and more palatable."[11]

In this light, look at art deco palaces like Eros, New Empire, or Regal Talkies in Mumbai (and recall that art deco was the style of choice for talkies throughout much of India well into the 1970s). On a more modest scale, consider the Eagle Theater in Jackson Heights, Queens (made famous perhaps most recently by Suketu Mehta in his memoir of a diasporic's life in *Maximum City*),[12] or the design of three film posters from Homi Wadia productions: *Lootaru Lalna* (dir. Homi Wadia, 1938), *The Return of Toofan Mail* (dir. Aspi, 1942), and *Magroor* (dir. R. D. Mathur, 1950).

In these theaters, the bodies invited to take their place in such monuments to urban modernity were epic, echoing, modernizing bodies—these image-sound-spaces give off desires of a directional, intentional movement and a buffered reverberation of sound. The lines of these beautiful structures give the impression of a rapid march, or better, a race into the future; as such, they play on and articulate the motion of the movement-image itself—of, say, the 1950s Hindi-Urdu social film, one of the most popular genres of this cinema, and one centered on the unfolding of a narrative space that was simultaneously linear and iconic. Keep in mind here Ravi Vasudevan's famous deployment of Geeta Kapur's notion of the iconic. He argued that the aesthetics of frontality and iconicity arises from mass visual culture, in instances ranging from the relationship between deity and devotee to the enactment of religious tableaux and their representation in popular artworks such as calendars and posters. When I refer to the iconic mode, I use the term not in its precise semiotic sense to identify a relation of resemblance, but rather as a category derived from Indian writing in art history that has been employed to identify a meaningful condensation of image. The term has been used to situate the articulation of the mythic within painting, theater, and cinema, and it could be conceived of as a cultural work that seeks to bind a multilayered dynamic into a unitary image. In Kapur's definition, the iconic is "an image into which symbolic meanings converge and in which moreover they achieve stasis."[13]

All three of the film posters mentioned above are deeply influenced by the framing devices of art deco,[14] and as such they attempt different multilayered bindings to yield the unitary image. In the first, the exotic deco-moderne costume of the action legend Fearless Nadia (Mary Evans Wadia) is supplemented with a montage of equestrian action shots, while the stitched double frame forms arrows of motion. In *The Return of Toofan Mail* the painted photographic heads of the lovers hover above the linear action of gun, train, and masked avenger. In the colorized *Magroor*, the bright strip of film and the scaled headshots mix frontality with the effect of contoured waves of color. Thus, in the art deco–cinema assemblage that produces bodily effects through both built space and image montage, the stasis of the iconic itself

4. Eagle Theater, Jackson Heights, Queens, 2006. Photo by Sarah N. Husain.

5. Poster advertisement for *Magroor* (dir. R. D. Mathur, 1950).

gives off the image and changing quality of movement. We might say that this is its immediacy and its intuited felt sensation, an almost hectic motion. On the one hand, and at the level of nationalist ideological coding, this intuition of movement is transfigured through the nationalist image of a postcolonial nation that had existed forever but was nonetheless rapidly developing through fixed five-year plans.[15] On the other hand, given its promiscuous anti-traditionalism, its hybrid genealogies, and its explicit ties to modern scripts of gender and sexuality, Indian art deco's iconic frontality is persistently in excess of nationalist pedagogies, which gave it its irresistible aura of transgression. And that is why space becomes intensive affect, an interval internal to the multiplicity of relations becomes operative throughout the assemblage. Moreover, if we consider Bollywood's art deco in terms of *aural* style—one that always doubles and departs from the iconic image—we can chart more broadly the heterogeneous effects at the level of the body of the kinds of nationalist primitivisms and pan-Asian hybridisms that marked the global musical repertoires of such brilliant music directors as S. D. Burman (with Dev Anand), Shankar Jaikishen (with Raj Kapoor), Naushad (with Dilip Kumar), and O. P. Nayar (with Guru Dutt). No rigorous consideration of art deco in 1950s Indian cinema can overlook the specificity of the song-and-dance track as it provided both the quintessential staging ground for art deco's aesthetic and also the potential for an entirely different kind of excess (the O. P. Nayar-Shammi Kapoor connection, with its creative mixtures of cabaret rumba rhythms, bhangra folk dances, and "light" pop music, would be exemplary in this regard).

Returning to my initial argument, we see that forms of connectivity—in this case between exhibition space, design style, and aural hybridity—enable specific relations of motion across a media assemblage. At the level of meaning and ideology, particular codings of iconicity take on affective actions as bodies moved through and are moved by the events (pathways-blockages, surface-screens: intervals) of a given assemblage. In these spaces where narratives unfold, media intervals distribute bodily intensity and qualitative duration, which feed back to modulate different elements of the assemblage and thus form gradients of various flows. Here distinctions between public and private space, modernity and the primitive, and stasis and flow enter into mobius-strip formations, inhere in each other as elements of each other, and produce zones of creative indetermination. The art deco talkie was one such zone, and in India the serial events associated with art deco yielded intensive populations of consumers who were habituated not through an image or story but through the patterns of pragmatic interactions within the assemblage. The swerve of such self-organizing patterns (the clinamen, or swerve, in media: clinamedia) is unpredictable, and it is in that irreducible chance of something going awry that we can say once again that such media events exceed their actualization.

Situating First Day, First Show

Let us pursue this patterning of interactions in the case of the first day, first show I attended. I found, to my surprise, that the experience of "first day, first show" can be a rather strenuous physical activity that demands different kinds of strategies for success. Success here is defined as occupying a ticketed seat with your acquaintances as the lights go out. This was something I learned when I tried to attend the first show of *Mohabbatein* (dir. Aditya Chopra, 2000). At the time (October 2000), there had been a series of films that had roared through Bhopal—*Dil Pe Mat Le Yaar, Shikari, Aaghaz, Dhai Akshar Prem Ke, Jis Desh Mein Ganga Rehta Hai*, etc.—all of which received little attention. Indeed, both *Aaghaz* and *Dil Pe Mat Le Yaar* ran for only about one week (although both would later have an indefinite lifespan on satellite and cable TV in north India and in the Hindi-Urdu–speaking diaspora). The critics all declared that the audiences (the "masses" and the "classes," the classic audience binary in Indian film journalism) simply were not interested in any of the stories and precious few of the songs. But with the coming of Diwali (the Hindu New Year, and usually the season for new big-budget film releases), things seemed to be different. A building curiosity about the new releases slowly crept through the city—the affective contagion of anticipation launched and spread by TV shows, film magazines like *Stardust* and *Filmfare*, radio shows, interviews, song prereleases, videos of the dance sequences, and rumors. And then the simultaneous release of *Mission Kashmir* (dir. Vidhu Vinod Chopra, 2000) starring Hrithik Roshan and Preity Zinta and the blockbuster *Mohabbatein* with Amitabh Bachchan, Shahrukh Khan, and Aishwarya Rai was like a filmgoer's fantasy come true.

Mohabbatein's story is familiar, but it has a particular globalized twist. As a "remake" (in the hybridizing vein of recent Bombay cinema oriented toward the non-resident Indian, or NRI) of *Dead Poet's Society* (dir. Peter Weir, 1989), *Mohabbatein*, a neologism meaning "many loves," tells the story of Gurukul College. The name references upper-caste Hindu institutions of Vedic learning, but in this cosmopolitan recasting the models are various elite north Indian boarding schools for boys such as the Doon School or Amitabh Bachchan's own alma mater Sherwood College in Nainital.[16] For the past twenty-five years, Gurukul's imperious principal, Narayan Shankar—played by the megastar of the millennium, Amitabh—has run the college on "Parampara, Anushasan, aur Pratishta" (or tradition, discipline, and honor). In other words, he runs the college on fear. The boys fear him and he thinks that their fear is a sign of their devotion. As the story unfolds, three young men enrolled at Gurukul fall in love with three young women, two of whom are from the neighborhood and one is enrolled in the all-women's college next door. They all know, however, that love is forbidden in Gurukul because years earlier a student had fallen in love with Narayan's daughter and, without even talking to the student, Narayan expelled him from the college. In desperation, Narayan's daughter Megha (Aishwarya Rai) committed suicide. Although the tragic event was long ago, the rumors linger and the girl's ghost continues to haunt. Meanwhile, a music instructor, Raj Aryan (Shahrukh Khan), is hired. The instructor insists that love is the inspiration for music, and he encourages the three students to reject Narayan's somber discipline and instead pursue their loves with abandon. After a series of catchy songs "picturized" in Switzerland, along with volatile dramatic scenes, we learn that Raj is none other than the luckless student whose love was sacrificed to Narayan's stubbornness. And so the scene is set for the epic generational struggle between fear and love, tradition and postcolonialism; and with a title like *Mohabbatein* you can guess who wins in the end.

It is a familiar narrative, with a familiar visual style. Yash Chopra (the producer and the director's father) is legendary not only for his evolving visual style but also for the "exotic" locales of his movies. By "exotic" I mean European: Chopra was recently given an honorary citizenship by the government of Switzerland in recognition of the profound contribution his films have made to Swiss tourism; indeed, a lake was renamed in his honor.[17] But Chopra also has diversified his exoticism of Europe—the actual setting for his idealized, Hinduized Gurukul is a palace near Wiltshire, England. Thus, part of what is being marketed as traditional Indian culture in Hindi films today is not simply a Sanskritized and chauvinistic brand of "national" memory, but one with global ambitions as well. Keep in mind that more and more of the profits from high-budget "A-grade" Hindi films come from "foreign exchange"—that is, collections from overseas territories, mostly in the United Kingdom and in North America. We can, then, appreciate this other simple fact: the Hindi film industry has actually profited from the considerable devaluation of the rupee over the past twenty years. The situation puts this film industry in a particularly curious position: it selectively sells a chauvinistic brand of national culture, thereby paying its debts to (Hindu) nationalism, while its financial and profit base is increasingly oriented toward the centers of capitalist accumulation in the West (this is a tendency of profit accumulation as much as ideological alignment, and given the devaluation of the dollar globally, there may soon be a reorientation toward the euro). Thus the nation is involved in a double movement that, on the one hand, in its name and through its discourses attempts to secure the image to a certain normalizing pedagogy (Narayan's "Parampara, Anushasan, aur Pratishta"), while on the other hand, floating or probabilistic logics of global risk assessment and the affective landscapes of an exoticized Europe deterritorialize cinema's infrastructures. Call this new connectivity the denationalizing finances of Bollywood's nationalist media assemblage.

These codings, contagions, narratives, and images give expressive force to the act of procuring a ticket for first day, first show. Generally, ticket checking happens only at the gate, but on a first day, first show for such blockbusters as *Mohabbatein* the groundskeepers, ticket collectors, and police work together to mobilize the three gates and the outer and inner courtyards as modes of differentiation, both population control and codification of desire. For us, standing in the back of an interminable queue and still in the outer courtyard, getting tickets seemed out of the question. I thus started looking around for other options. The nature of the gathering was a complex pattern of social relations and lines of force. Even the loiterers—those who weren't in line, and probably had no hope or even desire to see the show—were hanging out and watching the crowd while partaking of, commenting on, and contributing to the festival-like atmosphere and its specific spectacles. But the loiterers were almost entirely men, and this is an important aspect of how urban space and masculine performativity give to the event of media exhibition the suspense of an open threat.[18]

Loitering and the Swerves of Media

The loiterer at the scene of exhibition is male, urban, working class, and often from subaltern castes. This "subject" can easily become the agent of a romantic assimilation of loitering within an idealized discourse of cinema culture's resistance to bourgeois norms. But what if first and foremost loitering as a practice internal to the swerve of media is situated within varying sets of functionalities, sensations, gradients, norms, identities, capacities, and connectivities? This view would also include thinking historically of the evolution of the habituations of a media assemblage, the history of ecologies of sensation. I will return to the question of loitering in the next chapter, where I trace the emergence of the "malltiplex" in liberalizing India. Here I would like to anticipate that argument by noting that the malltiplex comes largely from the set of practices associated with the single-screen talkie, which in turn emerged from forms of consumption and circulation embedded in precolonial and colonial Indian bazaar culture. More specifically, habituations of media such as loitering have enfolded the bazaar into the bourgeois public sphere at the level of the autonomic body. But this is not without mutation: my contention is that the talkie and the malltiplex should be understood as different technologies of biopolitical control as well as embodiments for the creative indetermining of the very regimes that give them a relative stability. This is so because the assemblage of media that is the talkie or the malltiplex reorders time and sensation at the affective interface between bodies in population and technological evolution. In thinking through the diagram of this emergence, we are led to consider the ethnographic and historical work of Kajri Jain, Sandria Freitag, Woodman Taylor, Stephen Hughes, Rajat Kanta Ray, Christopher Pinney, and others who argue for a movement away from the static discourses of sovereign individualism to the embodied practices of value that circulate in the stratified but dynamic networks of Indian bazaar culture.[19] Most of these scholars have focused almost exclusively on the relationship between indigenous forms of vision and image circulation in colonial and postcolonial contexts by exploring the scopophilic mechanisms relating *drishti*, *nazar*, *bhakti*, and *darshan* (all different figurations of vision within Hindu and Muslim popular and sacred culture) to the materiality of the visual. In pursuing the implications for embodiment, I argue that the imagistic regimes of circulation that constitute the dynamism of the bazaar should be put into a broader media ecology or assemblage. One way of doing this is by following through on Kajri Jain's brilliant suggestion that the bazaar calendar image is not simply a text or sign to be read but rather a circulating or animated object that "as the common element between different constellations of value, draws them into a relationship where it becomes possible for value to switch tracks, to jump from one economy to another, drawing their subjects into each other's networks." She continues: "For the heterogeneous genealogies I have described do not inhabit different spaces, nor do they inhabit the same rectangular space of an image printed on cheap, flimsy paper. As modes of value they must form themselves as fleeting constellations between the image, other bodies or objects, and the quality, rhythm and intensity of time at a given moment. It is these heterogeneous qualities of time within postcolonial modernity that lie beyond what meets the ocularcentric eye."[20] Jain's

6. Sidewalk bazaar in Mumbai, 2004. Photo by Amit S. Rai.

7. Big Bazaar department store at the Phoenix Mills Mall, Lower Parel, Mumbai, 2004. Photo by Amit S. Rai.

work helps us, first, to question the privileging of vision in contemporary accounts of embodiment in popular culture in India; second, to situate the materiality of temporality in the rhythms of embodied practices; and finally, to explore the heterogeneous production of value across these relations of motion. In this chapter and the next, I take up Jain's challenge to South Asian media studies by focusing on the changing practices of loitering and "time pass" in the contemporary movement from the talkie to the malltiplex.

In its practices, popular Hindi-Urdu cinema has become a loitering technology. Loitering, in fact, is its mode of becoming, but this is what it has incorporated from the assemblages from which it has evolved. In bazaars or *mandis*, and then later at first day, first show screenings, or in the cinema lobby during intermission, loitering created self-organizing (patterned but unpredictable) traffic: jams, exchanges, interruptions, muscle contractions and extensions, density, gazes, clusters, and affective and population flows. Loitering is what popular media does in its nonlinear circulation. Through it and in it, the body waits for incoming and ongoing connections and modulated connectivities, the movements of which have defined class, caste, and gender power, or gradients of access across technological platforms and exhibition spaces in India. As we shall see, the occasion of first day, first show is an assemblage of bodies, some loitering and some "authorized," waiting for the inaugural unfolding of a media event. The authorized bodies either hold a ticket or go about acquiring one by standing in the queue or buying from scalpers. The loiterers are what give the first day, first show its *mela*-like (or festival) quality. Loiterers come mostly for the spectacle, and in standing, sitting, leaning, wandering—*fokat mein* (the colloquial Prakrit-derived phrase meaning having no exchange value)—without definite purpose or intention, they add density to the scene of exhibition. The first showings, indeed the first weekend, determine the future of any given film: a full house on the first weekend is the sign positive of a healthy return on investment, and the black marketeers whose money laundering schemes are the financial life of Bombay cinema breathe a sigh of relief.

This assemblage is today undergoing a qualitative change, a phase transition as indigenous financial infrastructures and aesthetic forms are transformed by transnational capital, Hollywood production companies, new insurance products, and the synergies of the new media. What are the coordinates of this changing media topology that derives new value as it were *fokat mein*? As a modality of nonlinear dynamics, loitering could be situated within a genealogy stretching back to the creation of an indigenous capitalist class in the colonial bazaar of the late nineteenth century and the

8. Imax Adlabs theater, Wadala, Mumbai. Photo by Amit S. Rai.

9. First day, first show for *Lakshya* (dir. Farhan Akhtar, 2004), Muskan Chhavi Grah. Photo by Amit S. Rai.

twentieth, or indeed back further to the precolonial bazaar, to the proliferation of bhakti cults, and also to the experience of bhava in rasa theory. The weekly bazaars, the seasonal melas, the marketing towns or mandis, and the holiday festivals that punctuated and gave rhythm to indigenous production between *rabi* and *kharif* (or spring and autumn) crops throughout the twentieth century were in fact media assemblages. As one colonial report on Chalisgaon taluka (in Maharasthra) in the 1890s put it: "The local bazaars . . . in the district are of very little importance as places for the disposal of any but small parcels of produce, the ryots [agricultural workers] resort to them as an outing, to hear the news, and to meet friends and acquaintances [more] than for serious business." Or consider another even more telling colonial account of Taloda's (Maharasthra) weekly bazaar in the late nineteenth century:

No more picturesque scene can be imagined than Taloda marketplace on Friday. On one side are piles of sugarcane, chillies and vegetables of different kinds, with heaps of wheat, gram, linseed and other grain. The main road is fringed with dealers on the smallest scale from copper moneychangers to venders of whiffs of tobacco, whose stock-in-trade can be reckoned in piece. In the main marketplace, under white canvas booths are cloths of all kinds and colours, brass and copper vessels, stone and glass beads, brass and tin bracelets, armlets, anklets and all the other rings with which the Bhil damsel adorns herself, kerosine, oil, and the hundred and one trifles into which the tinsmiths' ingenuity twists its tin cases, cheap cutlery, looking-glasses and Birmingham toys. The crowd is as varied as the wares. Guzars, Marathas, Gujarati Banias, Marwadis, Bhils of the plains, Powras from the Akrani with their quaintly bedecked womenfolk, and that village shy-lock, the Rohilla, besides coppersmiths, carpenters, potters and other artisans jostle one another, haggling and bargaining in their languages and as many patois, and raising a din and an atmosphere as difficult to describe as to forget. Considerable number of Powras attend the market, bringing grain and jungle produce such as charoli seed, mhowra flowers, honey, bees' wax, lac, gum and resin. As there is no cart trade from the Akrani, produce of all kinds has to be brought on bullock or by head loads.[21]

In other words, people came to the local bazaars to check the prices, to relax their minds and bodies, to feel new sensations in the circulation of goods and rumors, or to just be and become. Now each of these elements of this media assemblage—price, mental state, affect-sensation, being and becoming—is in fact translated by one word in Hindi: bhava. Indeed, bhava seems particularly relevant to understanding the stratified resonances of the loitering media assembled in the bazaar. As an experience of both value production and affective potentiality, bhava would be a kind of nonlinear movement from stimulus (*vibhava*), autonomous response (*anubhava*), and conscious reaction (*vyabhicari bhava*).[22] The broad semantic range of *bhava* in Hindi today helps us to configure loitering in its various aspects, or in other words as a mode of the nonlinear.

My argument here is that loitering is the general condition of affectivity—that is, of capturing value and producing sensation—of the media assembling body in the ecology of sensation that traverses the single-screen talkie to the contemporary malltiplex. This parceling of time, its divisibility and its continuous rhythms, acts on the body directly, producing both new habituations as well as potentially new assemblages. Loitering is the very condition of evolution in media assemblages. And the coils of control are in these relations of motion,[23] which is to say that the analysis of a media assemblage such as Bollywood can take no comfort in intellectual production as "resistance" retrieval.[24] The loitering mode is at once precolonial, colonized, and postcolonial, as affective dispositions with very different histories fold into, or nested within, each other in the event of media. This means that loitering media is not a gaze reducible to a subject position, but a mechanism of connectivity, memory, interruption, pause, lingering, stuttering; and also "time pass" (I return to this phrase in the next chapter).

Loitering is an aesthetic and a critique of bourgeois citizenship, even though the claim of belonging that may be legible in the practice cannot create an identity. Loitering always borders the misfit, a practice on the edges of propriety and property. This is why all loitering media traffics in the pirated. It is the loitering nature of Indian media that has enabled the gradual but thoroughgoing refunctioning of every element of the assemblage itself: the shrinking of the average shot duration in editing practices globally, the emergence of the halting, jerky camera style in new multiplex-oriented genres, the transformation of the *ittafaq* image (chance-harmony becoming fate-risk; see chapter 4), and the quotidianization of characterization in Bollywood acting are all elements that form new resonances in loitering media technologies but without resemblance or metaphoric condensation. To be more specific, each of these new aspects of Bombay cinema has emerged because there has been a change in the different durations of media; a shift in its speed, acceleration, flow, direction; a change in a given domain of validity. A modulation of duration: loitering. Each element of the assemblage has a duration all its own, an interruption specific to its looped feedback. Media ecologies evolve and at critical thresholds mutate when the feedbacks start resonating across the assemblage and new emergent properties take hold. But the aesthetic suggests another resonance, this time demographic, as hitherto excluded populations (lower caste, Muslim, queer, disabled, subaltern) find both a representative voice in the public sphere, being thus included in the liberal *econos* (household) of the nation (thus the grand narrative of the secular nation is duly extended), and at the same time potentialize the spaces of the public not merely by exposing its constituent contradictions but by opening those spaces to refunctioned connectivities and new temporalities, thereby affecting bodies irreducible to identity.[25]

Media Embodiment

At the scene of exhibition at Jhumpa Talkies on the first day, first show of *Mohabbatein* there was intense excitement in the air, as well as intense heat. (How is it possible to ignore the fluctuations of the autonomic body in such heat? What kind of media memory is activated at the body's "medium depth"—in its muscles, its sweat glands, its juices—through such stimulus?) The sun beat down upon us as if it were repeatedly slapping our faces (this phrase has a fantastic resonance in the Bhopali Hindi from which I have translated it—oh khan mamu, aisa lagriya hai jaise dhoop tujhe thappar mariya hai).[26] But everyone in the ticket line took the solar abuse almost agreeably—these were the hopefuls: ardent souls who come, without connections or advance bookings, seeking the pleasure of a first show; determined boys and men (and some girls and women) who will brave the late summer sun for hours if need be, all for that elusive ticket. These hopefuls had been waiting, first outside the gates and then in line, since the early morning. They had a little while longer to wait.

The ticket queues were long and sprawling, but they had a regularity to them as well. The women's line was much more orderly, and smaller. There were some women with children, all neatly lined up, but mostly they were women and girls. Altogether, the crowd was about 90 percent men and 10 percent women (another reason my friends warned me away from Jhumpa Talkies—again the gendered logic: where women can't go, it is unsafe for everyone). The courtyard at such events continues to be a masculinized space, crosshatched by different kinds of gendered gazes and bounded by a contingent kind of propriety. (I learned later that, as the crowd was dispersing from the first show, some men physically assaulted a young woman—

she cried out for help, and although eventually some police officers ushered her into a rickshaw, the potential threat actualized in assault.)

My experience of joining the men's queue for dress circle tickets strikes me now as itself something out of a Bollywood movie—an "NRI from New York City" (a stock character in Hindi-Urdu popular cinema since the early 1990s) trying to experience a "real" first day, first show "back home." But at the moment my eyes were set on the queue. The queue is where it all starts and ends: to become one with a tightly compacted, single file of lanky, sweat-drenched men, leaning on each other for support; and every now and then a massive surge, and a push-and-tug war would start and then die down. As my longing gaze wandered closer to the ticket counter the line seemed to proliferate into a kind of atomic cluster of moving limbs and hopeful faces. Every few minutes there was a slow, rising crescendo of shouts and hurrahs followed by a quickening kind of groan of anticipation when it seemed that the manager was actually going to give the signal to open the box office. But these events were just false alarms. Hundreds of hopefuls had crowded around those lucky ones who were first in line, hoping that their new best friend would buy them tickets (one particularly enterprising fellow had climbed over the railing and was trying to push his way to the very front; as a result he was quickly lightened of his shirt and actually lifted off his feet by the crowd and joyfully flung out of line). There was a heavy traffic in promised tickets, and I assume those who were first in line took a certain measure off the top for themselves. But regardless we were too late—the lucky ones had already promised people four tickets, five tickets, nine tickets. There was no point standing in line.

At the most general level, the movie ticket is the part-object, part-subject of the field of play of cinemagoing, cutting across all shows from first to last.[27] Not unlike, say, the ball in a soccer match, the movie ticket organizes human bodies in the fields of potential that constitute the exhibitionary sensorium of the talkie. Before we turn to the singularities of the ticket, let us clarify what we mean by the term exhibitionary sensorium. Stephen Hughes has suggested that a turn to the space-time performance of film exhibition is crucial to renew film criticism. He argues that we must attend to film exhibition as a performative social event with multiple histories. This implies that from the perspective of exhibition, films cannot be studied as "finished and timeless objects." Instead, "one must be attentive to how films are constantly rearticulated through the specific historical situations of public exhibition and reciprocally constructed through a complex social interchange with audiences. This decentres the abstract objectivist conception of film as codes, narratives and language, and reconceives films as constantly being reiterated, remade and contested as ongoing social events within each act of exhibition."[28] The event of cinema is more and less than film, it constitutes one of its intervals (though not always the most important). Sound-image streams, however, are only one dimension of change, one vector of a continuous multiplicity. The connectivities of this multiplicity are about qualitative change, as much as its infrastructure is enabled by interlocking systems of quantification: risk assessment, population control, capital investments, "content" security. I have already diagrammed some spatiotemporal aspects of this connectivity in my consideration of art deco and loitering in India. Let me pursue this diagram in the potentializing effects of the ticket. Film tickets are printed on the lightest recycled paper stock, and in a sweaty hand they are seemingly one step away from returning to pulp. No one pays much attention to the ticket, unless they don't have one, or can't get one. It is the unthought dynamic object catalyzing changing relations across the field of exhibition. Its exchange value rises or falls depending on the doubling, folding, and intensification of the media image: the bigger the "buzz" the harder and costlier it will be to get a ticket. This materiality always is in the process of melting into the infinity of circulation—its interface with money has been modulated by the Internet in specific ways: cash economy to credit card Internet "advance booking" purchases (albeit credit card purchases are still relatively uncommon in India). The ticket is a singular sign for at least four players in the field of exhibition. For a theater owner it is branded with the proper name of the event space ("Jhumpa Talkies presents . . ."), but in practice its selective release serves as a mechanism for maintaining gradients of access in an ever-expanding patronage circuit, while obfuscating its circulation is key to avoiding having to pay burdensome entertainment taxes. For the soon-to-be viewer, it is access-pass to image-sound consumption, as well as possible souvenir, proof positive of a past presence, both material and expressive.[29] For the ticket collector it is the most immediate mode of differentiating within this human multiplicity, while for the black market ticket seller the ticket functions as a variable rate of desire and as a mechanism of clientelism connecting him back to theater management. In that sense, owner, management, scalper, and viewer are all differential *objects of the ticket*. Like the game ball, the ticket must be considered in some way an autonomous actor because the effects of its displacement—its movement from ticket-counter clerk to hawker, viewer, ticket collector, tax collector—can be produced by no other element of exhibition practice, not even money: no ticket, no show, "sold out." The ticket's circulation—as sign, as exchange value, as memento, as pass, as desiring micromachine—returns each actor at each moment to a differential field of potential. I will return to this field of potential toward the end of this chapter.

A blockbuster first day, first show takes this part-object, part-subject and fundamentally intensifies it through a media doubling. The first day, first show ticket has already been doubled by itself: it is already an image of itself, precirculated through the successful media blitz of contemporary film advertising, and thus a kind of transduction from cinematic image to movie ticket. When a movie "catches on" prior to its release, tickets begin to sell long before its first show (generally through advance block bookings). The intensity that is mobilized at its circulation on that singular morning and then ratcheted up through its media doubling, has effects at the level of the viewer's body—standing in queues for hours, muscles tense from jostling through the crowd; calling in favors to the socially "higher ups"; the unbearable building of expectations; the essential (in)security of ticket possession. There are effects as well at the level of management—stricter enforcement of ticket collecting; closer integration of hawkers; reorganization of event space; active collaboration with local police.

What is the relation of these timespaces to the populations that are measured through them? If we take first day, first show as a critical interval in exhibition cycles, we can see that at a general level media intervals measure changing gradients in the self-organizing dynamics of a human multiplicity. Through their singular durations and tactility, their affordances and blockages, they correlate resonances across ecologies of sensation, captured and potentialized through unpredictable but patterned trajectories of felt flows. This is what I would call the sexualization of media populations. From the perspective of the managers of these timespaces, it is this potentializing of sensation felt between and through the flesh that needs coding, securing, quarantining, policing.

On this first day, first show for *Mohabbatein* the local police were indeed present in the form of two *havildars* (street cops) with *lathis* (bamboo sticks for crowd control). They had no qualms about using their lathis, and the crowd seemed to expect it. The regulars had gathered close to the entrance gate, which was plastered with digitally rendered posters of Hrithik Roshan/Coke and Shahrukh Khan/Pepsi. The regulars were those who had some kind of *jhugar* (connection for tickets) and exuded a kind of authority. The regulars also had a fixed agenda of fun. First, a few of them climbed atop the *Mohabbatein* hoarding and put a garland of flowers around the massive photo of Amitabh and Shahrukh (the media buzz had highlighted the fact that this would be the first time these two giants of Hindi-Urdu cinema would be seen on the same screen). Someone had brought up a small cutout of Aishwarya Rai (who everyone knew in advance was supposed to make a surprise guest appearance in the film), and they were trying to paste it on to the poster. Others were lighting fireworks by the gate—sudden deafening bursts of sound would occasionally tear through the air, leaving one temporarily unable to hear one's neighbor. And with each bomb, the crowd by the inner gate would scatter in a mad dash to get away from the explosion.

The police, as I have mentioned, had secured the premises. While I was taking a photo of a group of regulars who had climbed the hoarding, the havildar started to swear at them to get down or he'd do something unpleasant. But that's when the unpleasantries started. In an effort to get the crowd of loiterers away from the entrance gate, the havildars and the *chowkidars* (groundskeepers) staged what seemed to me to be crowd control spectacles, notably lathi charges aimed to clear loiterers away from the second gate. And then, of course, there was another mad rush, this time to save one's limbs from getting broken. (I had by this time given up on the ticket queue and had joined the general mass of people, mostly men, loitering about the courtyard.) At first, I must say that I had no idea what was going on—all I knew was that there was this push from behind me to move and I started running with the crowd. But it was like blowing on boiling milk—the crowd kept surging back and then forward again; first came the lathi charge, followed by the mad rush backward, and then the slow gathering of expectant hopefuls, confident regulars, and lucky ones would once more choke the gate. This ebb and flow defines an entire regime of passage that is now in the process of dissolution. It is useful to recall Brian Massumi here, who notes that what is pertinent about an event space is not its boundedness, or effects of closure, "but what elements it lets pass, according to what criteria, at what rate, and to what effect. These variables define a regime of passage."[30]

After a while the havildars left the lathi charges to the chowkidars, with one ingenious fellow using a whip made from a plastic belt. They performed their task of crowd control with commendable verve—rushing at the crowd, swinging their weapons of choice at the feet of the fleeing boys and men, swearing at them and putting on frightening faces, looking around making sure their audience got the full effect. Was the effort designed to cower the masses into discipline, or was it all for my camera? Everyone seemed to be striking poses and playing out scripts.

Contrary to my initial assumptions, the crowd had a discipline of its own. For the hopefuls who had been there since the morning, the four-hour mark since they'd been standing in line was approaching. They were close to the ticket counter, however, so they were sure they would get tickets. Thirsty, harassed, and sweating but expecting a great movie, they held fast to their place in the queue. And all around them, milling about, lighting firecrackers, and sizing up the women, the regulars were managing the space through their own rules, codes, and protocols. I continued to take photos, and a crowd soon gathered around. Quickly, the regulars swarmed, offering to strike appropriately *filmi* (film-like) poses—it was then it struck me that these people were the "subaltern" managers of this space—not the chowkidars, not the havildars, not the owners. These local kids—they must have been around the ages of fifteen to twenty-two—had a kind of privileged access because they were collectively the mediators between the white and the black ticket market. I knew that the nod and wink that my acquaintance Abhishek had just given one of them was the only way we were going to get in: we bartered the photos for tickets. A hundred rupees and a few pictures for two tickets that usually go for twenty rupees.

A taciturn older boy guided us outside the courtyard, and off in a side gully he sold us two tickets. Walking back in, we were greeted with the festivities still in full swing—fireworks, lathi charges, the tug of war in the ever-growing hopefuls line. After a little while Abhishek suggested that we gravitate toward the entrance door, and he encouraged me to use my English and my fake press status to get us in. I hesitated, and then tried the English bit, but to no avail. They were only letting women and children in—and those who had either made advanced bookings through the owner or bought their tickets on the Internet (an exhibition practice that had only just started in Bhopal and is still quite rare). The members of the latter group were conspicuous—mostly families clearly not from the area and from a socioeconomic class entirely different from that of the locals. After they carefully wound their way through the crowd as if maneuvering around a contagion, they approached the entrance gate and walked right in. As the "advanced-booking crowd" they may or may not have a ticket, but they do have some connection to the owner or other talkie official—or their access is created through the use of new technologies. The hopefuls generally don't have such connections, or such computer literacy/access and money. What they do have is the desire to see their favorite hero and heroine on the first day, first show screening; to be a part of the pleasure of dancing in the aisles when an-already popular tune comes blaring out of the speakers; to be able to say, later, "Yes, I saw it. It was just okay. . . ." But desire doesn't open doors, at least not for long. After standing in line for four hours, to the dismay of the hopefuls they saw the ticket counter open for all of ten minutes, when at most a hundred tickets were sold. The rest had mysteriously already found their way into the hands of the regulars—who were dealing them at their own discretion, with their own rules, and certainly at the agreed-upon rates (they will split their earnings with the ticket counter clerk, or perhaps the talkie manager who has supplied them).

So Abhishek and I waited by the side of the entrance gate with the others who had bought tickets on the black market. Squeezed up against the wall, we hoped that the chowkidar's irritated gaze—or the strips of his lathi—would not fall on us. We were lucky, although worried: looking at our tickets, we noticed that they had no seat assignments or dates. I can't say with any certainty what happened next. What I saw was the door open a crack, and then from behind me a massive, surging pressure rushed me forward. My glasses nearly fell off, a sweaty hand was pressed against my shoulder, and the next thing I knew I was caught up in a mad dash to get in with the rest of the crowd. And the chowkidar was trying desperately to stop the rush and close the door; even as I was pushing through, my bag got caught in the lock. Ripping it away, I squirmed my way in. Running, I stumbled, as did a number of people, but there was no possibility of stopping—if I fell there was no doubt that people would run right over me to get a seat. It was then that I realized that this collective panic was partly due to the fact that there were no seat assignments on dress circle tickets.

I didn't fall. I kept pace with the rest, hanging on to Abhishek as we made our way to two empty seats in a moderately good location. Settled in, we waited for the movie to start. The mad mela of the courtyard had turned into the relieved celebration of the movie hall. Everyone sitting around me was involved in this self-congratulation, a kind of momentary solidarity created through the exquisite agony of getting a seat at this first day, first show. Shouting, running, dancing in the aisles, and laughing, the male members of the audience in the dress circle (at 90 percent, the majority) were reeling in the *nasha* (intoxication) of a first day, first show success, while the women mostly sat apart, smiling but quiet and watchful. The house, needless to say, was full. And the lathi-wielding chowkidar was also in full swing, so to speak—apparently some people without tickets had slipped into the hall, so he beat them back out.

After a few scenes of this *tamasha* (spectacle, show, attraction), the actual tamasha started—*Mohabbatein*'s opening shots were greeted with an ear-splitting shriek of joy. As the lights went out at Jhumpa Talkies, I settled into my seat with a kind of giddiness.

This feeling of giddiness can be a critical starting point in resituating Hindi-Urdu film culture beyond the seemingly fixed narrativity of its structured experiences, and within what I am calling Bollywood's globalizing media assemblage, its historically specific ecology of sensation. It is an intuition about the changing nature of socially differentiated bodily experience in this assemblage. In turn, this bodily intuition can help us interrogate the management of the talkie's social space, its stratified histories, the at times antagonistic audience cultures, and the forms of power that cut through, divide, and tie together all of these disparate elements: the field of potential of movie exhibition. It is first day, first show as *event*, as that which *exceeds* its actualization as productive overflow, as the topology of value-added virtualization. For structure, as Massumi warns, is the place where "nothing ever happens, that explanatory heaven in which all eventual permutations are prefigured in a self-consistent set of invariant generative rules"—in other words, the supposed "structuration" of culture. Time is reversible in a static structure at equilibrium boredom. But nothing is prefigured in the nonlinear event of media. "It is the collapse of structured distinction into intensity, of rules into paradox."[31] The event is the suspension of the prefigured, and the emergence of the new—which can also be a corporate strategy: at no other point in the history of capital have the processes of commodification been so thoroughly saturated by both potentializing and containing forces.[32] As I noted above, the suspenseful buzz on that hot day for such a mediocre movie as *Mohabbatein* was created by the new corporate media strategies of slowly intensifying advertising blitzes through convergent media, and then ramified by an assortment of cross-merchandising schemes that have transformed the experience of the A-grade film: cell phone jingles, Internet interviews on RealPlayer or YouTube, movie-poster wallpaper for your PC, music trailers on TV and CD, cross-merchandising with fast-moving consumer goods such as chips and sodas (items also consumed during the still-requisite intermission), hoardings, posters, interviews, etc. (The massive proliferation of Internet cafés throughout India suggests that the kinds of collective access to these public spheres are their own regimes of passage.) Suspense is central to this approach, and it is maintained through very different strategies. For instance, until the very eve of *Mohabbatein*'s release, the trailers for it were carefully edited so as not to disclose Aishwarya Rai's surprise guest appearance. And yet, it was an open secret. Such a multiply mediated event, with its carefully orchestrated modulation of affects, images, and intensities, challenges us to understand contemporary film culture as a complex, even paradoxical negotiation of history, pleasure, and commodity circulation—as a sometimes raucous, comedic, but always also differential bodily experience of social and affective power. As we have seen, these sites, especially when overloaded with the event of first day, first show, continue to be spaces that from the standpoint of the administrators of law and order must be policed. There are many modes of such policing, and gender and sexual stratification (e.g., loitering) is perhaps the most obvious and most subtle. This mode interfaces with the digital as contemporary film culture brings copyrighted "content" into circuits of motion with socially, sexually, and economically diverse elements of the population yielding a dangerous admixture in need of control and security.

Here we can begin to diagram the dimensions of change in media contagions. As I noted in the introduction and will argue in the pages that follow, contagion is not only a metaphor for Indian film culture. If one characteristic of nonlinear dynamics is to facilitate self-organizing movements that find resonances between correlated elements,[33] then entrained resonances of practice, intensity, habit, and intuition move an incorporeal contagion across metastable bodies. And these movements are codified in practices of postcolonial social hygiene. It is in this intuited sense of the media event where we locate the organization of sexuality as ecologies of sensation. Here, in the co-dependent emergence of nonhuman technologies (Bollywood becoming "digital content" and the globalized art deco talkie becoming corporate malltiplex) with the body's affect, a media ecology evolves by circulating eddies dissipating carbon- and silicon-based matter and energy and spawning mutations. These nonlinear dynamics are the recurring patterns of overlapping populations, rhythmic temporalities, and stratified spaces.

First day, first show: in Bhopal, people will vie for this title. It names the originary moment of a film fully emerging into the mediasphere of Indian cities. And yet films no longer (if they ever did) can be said to have a pure originary moment—no discrete release into viewing pleasure, so to speak—given a context so thoroughly saturated with image interfaces of cinema advertising. Is this supersaturation of the multimediated cinematic image another example of what one *New York Times* critic called Bollywood's "purple pleasures of the moment"?[34] Or are there other sensations to be had in a different thought of this cinema's new media changing durations and connectivities, its virtual durations and globalized codifications?

Two aspects of the story I have told of first day, first show must be highlighted as essential modes of connectivity in Bollywood's media assemblage. First, as Brian Massumi suggests, social or cultural coding and state-administrative codification are forms of "event self-referentiality" that fold the event back onto itself, toward its repetition: "The folding back, the self-referencing, is what converts the event into an event-space." The physicality of the event space (house or stadium or Talkie) is doubled by a dynamic abstraction proper to it. This is what allows event spaces to proliferate. Houses proliferate into suburbs, stadiums into leagues, and talkies into exhibition circuits. When codified, the event space becomes reproducible: "Its reproduction provides an inductive ground for the serial emergence of subsequent events. These are deemed to be the 'same' by virtue of occurring in what has become a recognizable space. A type of space. . . . Recognition makes an event typical. That is to say, boring."[35] What we find in the specific case of north Indian cinema exhibition, and as I will argue at length in subsequent chapters, is that the event space of the traditional single-screen talkie or the globalized malltiplex is, first, a "type" of inductive exhibition space that generalizes the nonspace of viewing policed and authorized by state administration. Second, the exhibition space has been and continues to be a culturally coded space of danger and pleasure, which lends force to the rumors circulated about Jhumpa Talkies, for instance. Third, and paradoxically, these event spaces are singular commodified triggers for nontransmittable events where different strategies of branding proliferate through, for example, Dolby digital technologies, retailing, "boutiquing," or unique locale. This implies that a culturally marketable singularization is constitutive of the codification of a movie hall—it must both double the event space in a kind of discursive and material regularity (its contained recognizability as cinema space) and, on another level, proliferate a discursive and material differentiation (its viral marketing or serial branding, in other words). As I will argue in subsequent chapters, the regularity and differentiation of contemporary media technologies converge on the terrain of digital security. In the corporate strategy of today's globalizing malltiplexes, typification and branding (the paradoxical reproduction of singularities) go hand in hand; in India this dual strategy has a genealogy in film exhibition tied to the spatial distribution of the modern urban single-screen talkie from the 1950s on.

Second, media transmission involves the dimension of "event-transitivity"; that is, a change in quality, *a process of pure differentiation and interrelation in excess of the reproduction of singularities.* In other words, how do media contagions proliferate? The transitivity of the event is proliferating, suggests Massumi. But this proliferation crosses a "qualitative threshold." When the event passes from the stadium to the home, or from cable TV to the talkie, carried through televisual sound-images or by loitering subjects jacking-in through their cell phones, it changes in nature: "Whereas self-referentiality has to do with reproduction, event-transitivity has to do with differentiation." As the event transits through media it transforms, returning to its becoming as pure immanence. This is why media intervals—their transformational transit across technological platforms and conditions of reception—are the modal life of media assemblages. We become loitering in clinamedia. "The interval of transmission is thus very different from the interruption of regulation. In the media interval, the event is a material but incorporeal immanence (an electron flow) moving through a dedicated technological milieu."[36]

What happens when the interval event *comes after* its interval of (TV, radio, Internet) transmission, as in the case of *Mohabbatein*'s postmedia blitz first day, first show? This is not a simple reversal but rather a different kind of proliferating transitivity. We have a contact action of affect generated between open bodies, screen images, ticket objects, precirculated commodities, and event space that achieves a certain duration of connectivity, a catalysis of the event's ecology of sensation in the collective performance of first day, first show.[37] First day, first show is a trigger for accreting potential—its seething indetermination—accompanying a film's media blitz: that is, it has caught on. This catching, however, is not simply the capture of a film's media potentiality but also its unleashing.

The mode of power specific to the media assemblage has been characterized by Massumi as "the transitivity of intervals." As the new technologically assisted channeling of event transitivity proliferates beyond film, necessitating a thought of media assemblages, we diagram an emergent mode of power different "than either the regulating codifications of the Static or the regularizing codings of the 'social' or 'cultural,' at whose self-referential thresholds it is continually knocking." The transitive mode of power is what connects coding to coding, codification to codification, and each to its own repetitions "in an ebb and flow of potentialization-containment. The network distributes. Interlinks. Relates. The network is the relationality of that which it distributes. It is the being of collective becoming." The media assemblage is what results from the self-organizing, nonlinear interactions of each of its constitutive elements.[38] The transitive mode of power—a pure immanence of transition—from one coding to another, from one event space to another, calls us to attend to those incorporeal materialities that constitute the field of potential of such events as first day, first show. It allows a new thought of the interval, not as the interruption of an assumed continuity at the level of narrative but as a bodily affective mode of power that in itself proliferates the contagions of the media event. Again, it is here in the proliferating contagions of the unpredictable but patterned trajectories of an entire ecology of sensation that we will situate the changing nature of a preindividual sexuality. By returning the question of sexuality to the sensations of the media event we chart the co-evolution of a sensorium in the intervals between the stratified body of its consumers and the repetitions it sets in motion.

Throughout this book I will explore the transitivity of power, the continuous multiplicity of becoming-time, the proliferating connectivities of various media, and the body as nexus of indetermination, through an extended argument about machinic affect (to borrow from John Johnston)[39] in the context of India's globalizing media assemblage. For instance, there is a curious temporality embedded in this phrase "first day, first show."[40] The phrase not only marks a precise present but one with multiple durations and intensities (and thus other pasts and potential futures), which we can only perceive through images, or what Henri Bergson once called subtractions from these durations and intensities (thereby deducing perception from matter). In other words, we only perceive that which in a sense puts us in motion, has effectivity, or interests us both out of the infinite flux of affect images that constitutes the world, and the multiplicity that constitutes both affect and image; in this sense, thought and perception are always after the event that exceeds its actualization: "A creature's perception is exactly proportioned to its action upon the thing."[41] We can only experience durations and intensities at the level of humanized affect or emotions, because the temporality specific to nonhuman affect is in excess of the body and quicker than consciousness or language (this is also why in certain ways language will always fail us in such biogramming). That potentializing excess is the virtuality that constitutes it—its "spirituality" as well as its material functionality and empirical actuality. The time of first day, first show as spectacle must be addressed as a mediatization of narrativeness—suspense, openness, contingent time—and in that very contingency opens thought to the specificity and virtuality of affect.

Massumi suggests that the effective dimension of the interrelating of elements, of "their belonging to each other," is the event-dimension of a field of potential. If we think of the contagious intensities of a movie hall on first day, first show contingently moving through material bodies themselves mobilized by the ticket's part-object, part-subject we can begin to discern the field of potential as an effect of the "contingent intermixing of elements, but it is logically and ontologically distinct from them." In itself the movie ticket is composed not of parts or terms in relation, but of modulations, "local modifications of potential that globally reconfigure (affects)." The field of potential is exterior to the elements of a first day, first show, "but it is not inside something other than the potential it is. It is immanent. It is the immanence *of* the substantial elements of the mix to their own continual modulation. The field of immanence is not the elements in mixture. It is their becoming. In becoming is belonging."[42]

What is the becoming that belongs to Indian media today? My argument here and throughout this study is that first day, first show references an entire sensorium that is in the process of becoming something else, the constitution of a new dominant media assemblage. Through such film becoming media events as first day, first show, we can begin to grasp how in all major cities in India film populations are specific political forces with their own nonlinear histories. This force has not been organized through parties but rather through informal groups, or somewhat more structured societies or clubs (although in specific film populations of the South—most spectacularly in Tamil films—actors and actresses have spawned political parties, even full-fledged political dynasties).[43] In these diverse spaces, these eddies within eddies, the general viewer, the avid fan, and the committed cultural "worker" come together to create and participate in film populations and to share in the unpredictable experience of the visual, gastric, tactile, and aural pleasure of Hindi-Urdu film. Samosas and Lata Mangeshkar, Aishwarya and paan, and Pepsi and power outages are all part of this bodily experience. It is in the historically contingent experience of pleasure, and more radically in the autonomic nature (will-independent functioning, as in the nervous system) of film's habituations (or affectivity) that identities of caste, gender, religion, and class are made and contested, where social space is redrawn and sometimes blurred. An autonomic sexuality potentializes the media assemblage. This is not the same as asking is there a natural sexuality, since all autonomic living systems have a nonlinear history. Instead, it is to pose a question regarding the co-evolution of sexuality within capitalist apparatuses of image-sound-sense. It is here that affects are linked to or diverted from consumerist disciplines, and where the overlapping complexities, the contagious multiplicities of media assemblages, social power, and visual and aural pleasure can be felt literally on and through the active body loitering in clinamedia.

TWO

Contagious Multiplicities and
the Nonlinear Life of the New Media

At key moments throughout the past century, British colonial and Indian
nationalist claims to cinema and its varied media technologies aimed to educate the nation's sensation. But as I demonstrated in chapter 1, the assemblage self-organizes its unpredictable and patterned trajectories through
forms of popular unruliness (loitering and first day, first show activities)
and a well-known but obscure black market economy. These two key elements of Indian cinema's phase space are vectors with their own frequencies
forming a field of emergence and practice. The constant struggle between
these elements gave cinema a resonant intensity produced in the repetition
of processes correlated across media platforms. In the discourses of postcolonial administration, cinema was figured in two contradictory ways. As
part of the general denigration of popular subaltern culture, cinema was
positioned as a mass delirium that was more of a distraction than anything
else. Certainly there were loud paeans to *Mother India* (dir. Mehboob Khan,
1957) and nationalist celebrations of Raj Kapoor and Nargis in Russia.[1] But
cinematic pleasure never escaped the charge of being essentially in excess of
national development, even when, as in the two examples just cited, cinema
could function as an ideological supplement to the postcolonial apparatus
of development. Cinema, then, was a kind of contagious practice that the
censor board chief, excise commissioner, and state's chief medical officer
could quarantine among them. Nonetheless, as in the nationalist films of
Manoj Kumar (*Purab aur Paschim* [1970], *Roti, Kapada Aur Makaan* [1974],

Kranti [1981]), cinema could also be one of the key cultural sites for the staging of nationalist integration.[2] In any case, however, cinema proliferated as through affective contagion, the shock of sensation catching on and becoming population-wide habit. More than a metaphor for the cinema, contagion is the modality of historically stratified media assemblages. This colonial and postcolonial assemblage for the administration of Indian film culture would include the historical shift in the dominant cinema space design from European art deco moderne to postindustrial multiplex. This shift in exhibition design was part of the overall refunctioning of theater, radio, and TV with cinema's audiovisual commodities; with the advent of downloadable pirated torrents (peer-to-peer distributed audiovisual content in a variety of formats) cinema folds into computer interfaces. Exhibition strategies have also differentiated with the globalization of film finance, as the circuits of black market profiteering have been newly integrated with so-called transparent business models and transnational financial circuits. The economic and political contexts of media ecologies chart the body's potential in relation to patterns of religious and social segregation of lived space throughout India, while changes in censorship legislation and practice (from "censorship" to "certification") recode the state's claims on sensations produced in these ecologies.[3]

My itinerary in this chapter proceeds through contagion, with one thought affecting another and then another until a kind of critical "mutagen" is created. I begin with the deterritorialization of sensation, audiences, and genre in contemporary Bollywood narrative in the context of a "potentializing" reading of two versions of the cinematic classic *Devdas*. In subsequent sections, I draw this thought forward toward a definition of the media assemblage in its mode of connectivity: contagious multiplicity. My aim here, as in the next chapter, is to write a nonlinear history of media assemblages as an evolution of sensation. Not unlike a history of military technologies written by and about robots,[4] the tale of sensation assembling with biomedia would not be the progressive narrative of humanizing emotion, but rather a set of diagrams of preindividual affect potentialized through the resonances and networked interactions (feedback loops) between qualitative duration, image-sound, capitalist timespace, and media technologies. Specific frequencies correspond to each of these movements, and at threshold moments these frequencies form resonances across the media assemblage,[5] thus triggering new organizational structures and new potential energies in the interaction of the frequencies.

On the "Purple Pleasures of Bollywood"

Perhaps since its inception, cinema in India has drawn its commercial force from the image of film culture as contagion—as an exuberant devotion infecting bodies by virtue of their promiscuous mixing. But contagion, again, is not only an image but also the key mode of assembling this open whole. This implies something crucial for Hindi-Urdu film criticism. If each connection of body, technology, image-sound, and space of consumption is a timed portal (interval) for fluctuating flows we must conceive of media itself as a potentially infinite topological movement with historically specific dimensions of change. This potentiality has often been relegated in Indian film criticism to a "remote possibility" in a field that, while torn by political struggle, has been equilibrated through a structural dialectic.[6] For instance, consider two important castings of the "assemblage" of popular commercial film: Madhava Prasad's exploration of Bombay cinema's mode of "heterogeneous manufacture" (Marx), and Priya Jha's more recent recasting of the interruption of "gender difference" into the formulaic narrative of genre films. As Prasad notes: "If we consider the Hindi film is conceived . . . as an assemblage of pre-fabricated parts, we get a more accurate sense of the place of various elements, like the story, the dance, the song, the comedy scene, the fight, etc. in the film text as a whole. . . . What makes this method of functioning unsuitable for Hollywood is the fact that a material substratum—the story—is the point of departure of the production process and its transformation into a narrative film is the final goal of that process."[7] Note that in Prasad's "mode of production" analysis film production is prosthetic, and cinema's assemblage is an always already preconstituted addition of already assembled parts, where one part (song) is sutured to another (dance) by a cohering thread (story). This assemblage is a "quantitative multiplicity" that is discontinuous and spatializing: 1 plus 1 plus 1. I will return to these properties of multiplicity below, but for the moment what I would like to highlight is that as one of the dominant forms of institutional analysis of Hindi-Urdu popular cinema, modes of production analyses such as that by Prasad have the overall effect of presenting a cinema of static reproduction: reproduction of ideologies, narratives, social structures, identities, infrastructures, and even prefabricated heterogeneity: a "preestablished realm of possibility," more of the same.[8] In partial contrast, Jha's work, which is meticulously attentive to gender and difference, focuses on the interruptive qualifications of cinema's performativity. Jha writes that, in the quote cited above, Prasad gestures toward the recognition of the filmic system itself as the creator of cultural meaning espoused through the contents of the filmic space. The whole film cannot be understood without all the elements that Prasad catalogs . . . Because of a liberal "borrowing" from Hollywood, Bollywood films often reflect the growing need of India to convey its entry into metropolitan modernity after colonialism. The Bollywood apparatus, as a highly charged institutional tool, joins past and future at threshold moments. In this sense, the interruption of the formula with genre draws attention to the artificiality and construction of history while allowing "difference" to be part of the formulaic narrative. This is where I think songs do a particular kind of historical work that cannot be translated purely as "musical" across national borders.[9]

What is most striking, indeed compelling, about Jha's recasting of Prasad is her insistence that the apparatus undergoes a kind of potentialization at threshold moments: difference interrupts the static reproduction of genre conventions. But in signal ways this zone of potential is reduced to the possible-actual circuit of gender hierarchies, performative subversions of national territorializations, and melodramatic codes. That is, the eruption of difference at threshold moments is already figured as that which is exhausted by the possibilities of a particular configuration of actuals. Thus, "the recuperation of the melodramatic mode as 'feminine,' the alternative triangle of the diegesis, the song space, and the spectator are always shifting and adapting themselves to the dictates of the spectacular vernacular of the cinema. In this sense, the erasure of women from the song space rather than the exclusion of women from the national imaginary instead reinscribes them even in their physical absence."[10] Despite their differences in style and framework, what both Jha and Prasad effect is a discursive closure of the zone of potential of Bollywood's media assemblage, and they foreclose a thought of the virtuality enabling its mode of interrelations: its becoming in belonging. What is it that virtualizes a media assemblage? Thus far I have used words such as "co-dependent emergence" and "co-implication" to describe the mode of interrelation of the constituent parts of an assemblage, but I now must specify what this entails both analytically and politically.

This line of thought, far from being a depoliticization of film criticism, obliges us to consider the ethical stakes in the body's potentialization through specific media assemblages—that is, the body's changing capacities to affect and to be affected. The autonomic processes of perception within a media assemblage are organized by the habits of bodily attention, and they are potentialized in their very repetition (the swerve of a clinamedia). Since that repetition happens under conditions that are in varying degrees far from equilibrium, habituated media practices are open to swerving from their course just slightly and thereby find new resonances (media contagions), or more radically they jump from a basin of attraction into another less defined and emergent singularity (a phase transition).[11] Now my argument is that media contagions are operating a general phase transition in moviegoing practice today in India; an overall reorganization of media practices has brought different forms of thought (computer engineering, visual, aural, and interior design, architecture, viral marketing and advertising, and neoliberal urban planning) to a common threshold of apprehending sensations specific to a given human multiplicity (the new niche audiences). Throughout this study I query the ethics of Bollywood's media assemblage. The potential of the diagram also changes when different perceptual capacities are tapped, modulated, refunctioned, or dampened by a configuration of the assemblage. A new connectivity is emerging through media habituations, and the body feels different because it is beginning to belong to new collectives and new populations. In a way that has absolutely nothing to do with performative sexual identity, this volatile situation is precisely a question of sexuality if we understand this term as a diagrammatic logic of the assembling of ecologies of sensation. This is what I mean specifically by co-implication, and it is my belief that such assemblages call us to another form of sexual politics, one that can effectively intervene in the interactions between bodies-populations, image-sound streams, and media technologies as a continuous unfolding of unpredictable but patterned trajectories. Clearly then the issue here is not merely a reduction of cinema's effects to representational or cultural codings of gender or sexuality but rather an opportunity to think about the radically new (the forms of media durations, or intervals lived at the autonomic) still gripped by or in conformation to the residual.[12] For instance, how have the capacities of consuming populations evolved through the specific changing connectivities of protocapitalist bazaar culture, popular theater, radio, and cinema from the mid-nineteenth century onward, and then in specific filmic genres through social films of the 1950s to the 1970s emergence of homosocial melodrama and then to 1990s diasporic, neonationalist, and digital deterritorializations, and the constitutive destabilizations and blurrings of these genres and forms of consumption? What becomings belong to the specific interval of interactions of the shift from black-and-white 1950s montage to the new algorithms and postproduction color adjustments of the digital?

To consider these questions, I return to cinema. As noted above, in the past decade and a half the neat genre distinctions that divided Bombay cinema into art films and commercial films (at least relatively) have broken down. In the heyday of art films (roughly from the late 1960s to the early 1990s), social topics ranging from colonialism, feudalism, gender inequality, westernization, and the tyranny of elite traditions formed the narrative whole in a cinema whose visual style was relentlessly realist and explicitly noncommercial. Movies such as Shyam Benegal's *Ankur* (1974) and *Bhumika* (1976), Basu Chatterjee's *Swami* (1977), Girish Karnad's *Godhuli* (1977), Ketan Mehta's *Holi* (1984) and *Mirch Masala* (1985), Mahesh Bhatt's *Arth* (1982), Govind Nihilani's *Aakrosh* (1980) and *Ardh Satya* (1983), Sudhir Mishra's *Dharavi* (1992), and Vijaya Mehta's *Pestonji* (1988) were self-consciously part of the "parallel" genre of art cinema, one that was founded in a clearly legible political and social commitment, an auteur-signature, and a state-sponsored aesthetic—the long take, realist montage, onsite sound recording, and on-location shooting. In the postparallel cinema of the late 1990s, best represented by the work of Shyam Benegal (*Zubeida* [2001], *Hari Bhari* [2000]), Ram Gopal Varma (*Satya* [1998], *Jungle* [2000]), Mahesh Manjrekar (*Vastaav* [1999], *Astitva* [2000]), Kalpana Lazmi (*Rudaali* [1993], *Daman* [2001]), Sudhir Mishra (*Hazaaron Khwaishein Aisi* [2003]), Mani Ratnam (*Dil Se* [1998], *Bombay* [1995]), and Vidhu Vinod Chopra (*Parinda* [1989], *Mission Kashmir* [2001]), the few Bollywood music sequences are folded into social critical narratives, most often in an extension, commentary, or deepening of the narrative itself. Combined with a narrative-governed montage logic, a realist camera eye, and big-name Bollywood stars this cinema signals the end of clear-cut genre distinctions in Indian cinema. Bollywood cinema today has broken with its own law of genre.

One can lament this break as an erosion of the "artistic" in the face of the massification of all South Asian culture through globalization; however, a better posing of the problem is also possible. If genre distinctions are breaking down between the stark social realism of art cinema and the pure fantasy of the commercial film (and this genre binary was never as rigorous a distinction as it might appear in hindsight), we can begin to distinguish different combinations of form, emergent modes of address, and the production of qualitatively novel affects that are all entailed in this shift. In one sense, commercial cinema—in its narratives, its visual style, and even its choreography—has incorporated aspects of the former parallel cinema, which has opened the possibility for new audience segmentations. More, this folding of the two genres has multiplied the functionality of the commodity form of

Bollywood cinema; its mode of address, always in itself heterogeneous, has become a way of correlating and modulating constantly changing branded styles with consuming populations. What styles of visuality and aurality have functionally assembled in commercial cinema, as a result making it more or less commercial? What relationships circulate and connectivities function among fantasy-travel, narrative-interruption, and exhibition space in the new postparallel cinema? What is the work of music, specifically the detachable song-dance in this new cinema?

The dominant framing of these questions in mainstream Western film criticism has come to affirm the essential nature of Bollywood as a nonnarrative, sensation-based entertainment: a cinema for saps and sensualists. This repeats and displaces a colonial trope (the animalized pagans reveling in the riotous night of unreason, from James Mill to Thomas Babington Macaulay to Winston Churchill and beyond).[13] And yet my argument in the text that follows will also suggest that popular Hindi-Urdu cinema is both nonnarrative and traversed by an abstract machine for the commercial harnessing of affect. I will argue that the human-technological assemblage of contemporary media is transforming the sensations of cinema toward new media horizons and new consumer habituations that fragment, interrupt, and jam the sensory-motor schema enabling narrative. This intensifies the human-media interface as a site for indetermination (potentialization), and simultaneously deploys this indetermination as value-added immersion in such technologies as Dolby sound (8.1 channels) and the multiplex-commodity-sensorium.

Take, for example, a "near" hit in recent Hindi-Urdu cinema, one that translated Quentin Tarantino's *Reservoir Dogs* into a Bombay idiom: *Kaante* (dir. Sanjay Gupta, 2002) is the all-male multistar film that brought together on the same screen Amitabh Bachchan, Mahesh Manjreker, Sanjay Dutt, Lucky Ali, Kumar Guarav, and Sunil Shetty. It was shot entirely in Hollywood, with "largely American" technicians, as Dave Kehr writing in the *New York Times* notes.[14] Given the American production background, what makes the film Bollywood? According to Kehr, Bollywood embodies a "tradition of excessive generosity," in which "too much of just about everything" finds its way into the film. Although he admits that there are a couple of "snazzily edited music videos," he adds that such scenes "make you realize that Bollywood is essentially a nonnarrative art form, in which coherent storytelling plays a distinctly secondary role to the purple pleasures of the moment."[15]

Narrative (or coherent storytelling) in this view is seen as marginal and secondary to Bollywood; it celebrates the "colorful" pleasures, which, through the form's fleeting nature, perhaps provides its critic's favorite adjective for popular Hindi-Urdu cinema: ephemeral. Bollywood is the realm of the ephemeral pleasures (alternately known as "cheap pleasures"). Even more "sympathetic" Western critics are invested in the discourse of the essential otherness of Bollywood as a kind of excessive pleasure. For instance, David Chute in an article in Film Comment writes: "Bollywood cinema's peak achievements, like those of Hong Kong, devote immense amounts of creative energy, ingenuity, and highly evolved craftsmanship to the life-affirming task of delivering intense pleasure to the largest possible audience. But while Hong Kong cinema works by radical compression, Bollywood operates by expanding in all directions."[16] Of course, there is also an important strand of cultural criticism from South Asia and its diasporas (for instance, the work of Ayesha Jalal and Vijay Mishra) that argues precisely about and sometimes for the nonnarrative nature of Bollywood.[17]

In what follows, I argue that one issue for which Bollywood cinema draws criticism is toward an interrogation of the very potentiality embedded in narrative itself; that this popular media presents us with a way of accessing a level of reality that is virtual and material, and always in the process of multiple becomings. But does that mean that Bollywood cinema is nonnarrative? I will attempt to answer this question through a consideration of Ravi Vasudevan's justly famous reading of the deification of heterosexual masculinity in Bimal Roy's 1955 version of Devdas.

Although Bimal Roy's Devdas is not the most successful version of the story, in many ways it set the standard not only for the cinematic adaptations of Sarat Chandra Chattopadhyay's novel (there have been eight film versions of the novel) but also for subsequent filmic representations of heterosexual companionate love itself. It is often said that Dilip Kumar's performance as Devdas is the epitome of emotive acting.[18] The story revolves around the doomed love between Parvati (Suchitra Sen) and Devdas (who are socially mismatched through caste and class inequality), and Devdas's unconscious rejection of the loving devotion of the prostitute-dancer Chandramukhi (Vyjayantimala). Many viewers have told me that when Devdas was released in 1955, both the new and the old conversations about the effectivity of the tragic lover, the social constructions of the family and lineage, as well as the issue of women's subordination under Hindu patriarchy all became part of the cultural discourse of the film. We can discern aspects of this in the pre-release publicity for Roy's version; in Filmfare's full-color "Star Profile" of Suchitra Sen (she played Devdas's true love, Paro) for the August 5, 1955, issue, we learn that there is a great deal of buzz around Suchitra ("whose real name is Rama Sen") because *Devdas* is her first Hindi film (she was already "Bengal's reigning box-office queen"). Moreover, atypical for Bombay actresses, she is married and the mother of a four-year-old daughter: "In 1947 she married the man with whom, she says, 'I had been in love for as long as I can remember.'" Suchitra is a thorough professional: "An artiste who takes her work seriously, Suchitra is an early riser and, at the studios, is ready in her make-up well before the others." And she does her own hairstyling. The caption reads: "Suchitra has rich, long tresses, and takes great pains over her coiffure. She combs and twines her hair herself."[19] The piece also notes that she drove a "brand new Buick convertible" from Bombay to Calcutta. Coupled with the bright red lipstick in the color photos, these extra-diegetic elements of the star aura both compete with the character Paro, and complete the narrative (unlike Paro, Suchitra marries her long-time love).

In viewing Roy's *Devdas* today, and thus after Sanjay Leela Bhansali's elaborate and luxurious translation from 2003 (at over $13 million, Bhansali's version was at that time the most expensive film ever made in India), we can see why Bhansali dedicated his version to Roy: Roy's *Devdas* is a singular example of 1950s-era Bombay filmmaking. In that sense Roy's *Devdas* comes to us from what many call the golden age of Hindi-Urdu cinema. For some critics, 1950s cinema was "a transitional period between the popular culture and mixed social audience of the 1930s and 1940s and the mass audience emerging from the 1960s."[20] However, Ravi Vasudevan, in his justly famous essay "Addressing the Spectator of a 'Third World' National Cinema," takes issue with such a periodization. He suggests that 1950s cinema in its deployment of "a rhetoric of traditional morality and identity" to bind its imagining of social transformation already prefigures some of the dominant methods of the subsequent periods of Hindi cinema.[21] More specifically, Vasudevan analyzes how hierarchies of patriarchal power develop around the image of a character. "This character image becomes the authoritative focal point of a scene, occupying a certain privileged position which structures space as a force field of power." As I noted in the last chapter, in understanding the sacralization of this image, Vasudevan deploys Geeta Kapur's notion of the iconic, where the iconic is "an image into which symbolic meanings converge and in which moreover they achieve stasis." In Vasudevan's redeployment of the iconic, the term is used "to situate the articulation of the mythic within painting, theater and cinema, and could be conceived of as cultural work which seeks to bind a multi-layered dynamic into a unitary image."[22]

The crucial point here, as with all effects of closure in film, is that the unitary iconic is *one* effect of the process of decoupage and montage in cinema and not their natural outcome.[23]

I would like to pursue this point by looking again at the segment that Vasudevan argues stages the deification of masculine authority. In Roy's version of *Devdas*, the first glimpse we get of the adult Devdas is apparently from Paro's perspective: it seems that she is looking at his shoe-clad feet first, with eyes downcast and her head down, in the proper pose of the devoted bhakti wife awaiting the coming of her Krishna lover. For Vasudevan this moment is iconic insofar as the male desire of the camera is established through a process of deification: Devdas's feet activate a chain of signs tying him to Krishna, and her to Radha. The film thus utilizes, on Vasudevan's words, "continuity conventions to the highly 'traditional' end of deifying the male as object of desire."[24] First, for Vasudevan, the ideological effect of male deification is produced through a process of continuity editing. Second, the sequence in question narrates Paro's point of view. And third, the agency of masculine deification is the filmic image. As Vasudevan continues: "In anticipation of Devdas's arrival, Parvati hurriedly starts lighting a *diya*, a devotional lamp, and the melody of a kirtan, a traditional devotional song expressing Radha's longing for Krishna, is played." We hear the sound of Devdas's footfall on the stairs—if the filmic image deifies the masculine, it is the ear of Parvati that opens another kind of agency. Supplemented and split by the soundtrack, Parvati's anxiety to light the lamp before Devdas enters her room is caught by a suspenseful intercutting between her hurriedly lighting a match and shots of the empty doorway. "The doorframe in this sequence suggests the shrine in which the divine idol is housed. Devdas's entry is shown in a highly deifying way: first his feet are shown in the doorway, followed by a cut to the lighted lamp. Finally his face is revealed. There follows a cut to Parvati, suggesting that this is the order through which she has seen Devdas's arrival. As she looks at him, in a classical point-of-view arrangement, conch shells, traditional accompaniment to the act of worship, are sounded. The future husband as deity, object of the worshipful gaze, is established by the narration's deployment of Parvati's point of view." Thus, Vasudevan insists that we must "acknowledge the framework of masculine authority within which female desire is finally held."[25] What concerns me in Vasudevan's reading is the excision of zones of potentialities inhabiting this "hold" on Paro's subjectivity, as well as the closed determination of narrative structure by the imperatives of a certain patriarchy. By considering Paro's agency as a complex articulation of desire, narration, and a field of potentiality we can also begin to address the overdeterminations that both structure and deterritorialize "the framework of masculine authority."

In breaking down this segment into its constituent frames (something that DVD technology itself facilitates through "frame stepping"),[26] it becomes clear that the camera's first cut after Paro lights the diya is an eye-level shot of an empty doorway. But rather than simply a question of what is the actual sequence of editing, this becoming-image allows us to return to the plane of incipiencies and deformations. Is this empty doorway the male under erasure? The shrine of the male idol? If so, an obscure, empty doorway is a potential space as well, the spatiotemporality of a certain interval that comes between cause and effect and retrospectively blurs both. It is a potentializing opening: time, space, movement, echo, threshold, passageway, void, emergence, and means of communication. As a cut between cause and effect, it is the very site and means of becoming.[27] In that sense the empty doorway establishes the prior level of communicability, the immanence that "precedes the *what* of thinking, saying, feeling."[28] If we can think of this suspenseful doorway as a channel of potential, then the elements of Vasudevan's masculine iconic are organized around and through this virtual passage, this interval of becoming. We should remember that for Gilles Deleuze the virtual intercedes and suffuses the real as that which is expected, anticipated, predicated, or even imagined of the real. It is the originary evanescence, the incipient, intensive process without the emergence of which nothing in reality would be actualized—"the virtual is the very proceeding of the actual."[29] If the shoe-clad feet of Paro's master are iconic, then no less so is the empty space of the threshold. And the one is a becoming that emerges from that other, virtual timespace of the interval.

Moreover, if we maintain with Vasudevan that the camera movement narrates Parvati's perspective, then it in fact narrates a much more complex (nonlinear) subjectivity than simply the victim of a male fantasy. What is the force of becoming that resonates in this scene? Vasudevan misses the full force of the first shot after the iconic feet of Devdas: two unevenly positioned flames—the devotional diya and the dying match that lit it. It is only then that Devdas emerges from the shadows; it is only then that we see Paro not with downcast eyes but with the direct gaze of an adoring lover. Something other than subjectivity is being signed with these cuts, and with the panning of the camera that precedes it. Indeed, as Paro looks out toward the virtual space of the empty doorway we can grasp that moment as the repeated assertion of an unequally positioned but no less intense desire with Devdas: becoming flame. Later in the movie she will be made to suffer for it by his hand, as he scars the pure moonlight face of his beloved. But I suggest that we forget Parvati's indomitable agency only at our peril: another portal-passage always haunts, indeed enables, the masculine iconic.

It is by keeping this potential in play that the question of whether Bombay cinema is a nonnarrative form can best be posed. What this segment does is open up narrative time to the nonlinear presentness of the moment. It is through this multiplicious presentness that anything like suspense is possible in the first place. Gary Saul Morson in his theses on narrativeness provocatively asserts that all narratives do not have narrativeness, and that the necessary condition for any degree of narrativeness is the aleatory unfolding, patterned but unpredictable, of different processes. "The sense of process, the activity of tracing possible futures from a given past, is essential to narrativeness."[30] Note that here too the temptation would be to reduce this zone of potentiality, which is the very unfolding of the real, to already predetermined "possibles." Rather, since this process must be articulated through a series of presents ("the present moment must matter," asserts Morson), it cannot be a totalized derivative of earlier events or dictated by later events, that is, by the structure of the whole—the process is present in that it follows a temporality that remains open to outside forces of futurity, as well as a patterning conforming to the past. "And what gives a moment presentness? In a phrase, open time. For a present moment to matter, to have real weight, more than one thing must be possible at the next moment. We may define open time as the excess of possibilities over actualities. For a determinist, one and only one thing can happen at any given moment, what did not happen could not have happened. In open time, at least one thing that did not happen could have." Again, we must refuse the reduction of the open time of narrativeness to already given possibles; indeed, narrativeness is constituted by process, by presentness, by events that exceed their actualization, by contingency, messiness and unpredictability: suspense.[31] So although Morson, like Jha, reduces the question of fields of potentiality enabling narrative to the possible-actual circuit by mooring open time in narrative to merely a question of what is possible, we should reframe narrative as an agonistic process of potentializing, contagious, and mutating effects given the closure of representation.

It is in this sense of narrativeness that Hindi-Urdu cinema at its most challenging can help us to rethink the very nature of what constitutes narrative itself. The empty doorway, the virtual space of the interval, not only frames the iconicity of Devdas but also launches that other line of flight that describes Paro's desire. This desire, indomitable and yet overcoded, proceeds from the sensation of anticipation, from the event of potentiality, which implicates the viewer through the intervals of shot/reverse shot. As a nonactualized event of an indeterminate sexuality, it is a present moment because more than one thing could and does happen through its narrative processes: that is, also its suspense and lingering indeterminacy. In subsequent chapters I will develop the force of this suspension as an interval between causes and their actualizations. The concordance of heterosexual romance (the Devdas-Paro circuit) is preceded by the contingencies of a stochastic communication portal: the doorway as Ittafaq-image (both harmony and chance in Hindustani; a coincidence that I will return to in chapter 4). The moment is a nonactualized event in that lines of force converge in its unfolding without ceasing to resonate beyond the frame of its timespace. It is this proliferating resonance, the unpredictable but patterned populations and trajectories through audiovisual media, that "causes" sensation at a level prior to consciousness, or preindividually. To anticipate my argument, the Ittafaq-image is a nonlinear ecology of sensation; it is sexuality's mechanism of capture and coding as well as line of flight in this media assemblage. For now let us note that the framework of masculine authority and women's agency staged through this segment of *Devdas* is an effect of a process that allows us to consider other potentialities that not only haunt but also are the intensive processes of the iconic narrative of male sacralization.[32]

This potential otherness constitutive of the image-sound regime diagrammed above is both captured as algorithm and lit as a becoming-flame in one segment of Bhansali's *Devdas*. The segment is from the song "Silsila yeh chahat ka" ("An Affair of Desire") and is an obvious quotation of precisely the scene that Vasudevan focuses on in Roy's version. It is staged in part as a devotional prayer to the goddess Durga (an incarnation of Devi or Parvati); in the last shot of the segment she is shown, wearing a red sari, in the traditional frontal pose before a lion, her ten arms wielding various weapons ready to wipe out all the evils of the world. The lyrics, however, tell of an affair whose flame has never been extinguished, and that is the visual conceit of the song. A whirling Parvati (Aishwayra Rai), dressed as Durga, defies the mockery of her girlfriends as she precariously cradles a diya in the palm of her hand, keeping the flame burning brightly through rain, wind, and dazzling pirouettes ("Silsila yeh chaahat ka na maine bujhne diya / Piya, yeh diya na bujha hai, na bujhega / Meri chaahat ka diya"; "I did not let this affair of desire grow cold / My love, this flame has not died, nor will it / My desire's flame"). Bhansali deploys an active camera, with numerous pans and angles, continuous 360-degree shots, and rhythmic movement from one color-space to another for the sake of a different deification. The perfusion of color from lyric sequence to musical refrain is dominated by the red of Durga's sari and the vermillion that explodes in bursts of reddish haze. . In the initial sequence this montage-sound-color strategy builds with the expectant tempo of the lilting song (sung by Shreya Ghosal), carefully cropping Parvati's face from visibility (the faces of gods and goddesses in Hindu temples are often hidden before devotion begins; the *darshan*-circuit, the gazing on and the gaze of the goddess, is only activated through devotion).

And then—a sudden illumination courtesy of digital animation. Parvati (Ghosal-Ashwarya) starts to sing ("Silsila yeh chaahat ka na maine bujhne diya") as a flash of lightning illuminates her face. Lowering her arm, the flame "catches the mirror" on her bindi and, digitally enhanced, it momentarily flickers in a moment of nonmotivated cinematic excess, to recall Kristin Thompson's famous essay.[33] The potentializing face is an interval of manipulable pixels, which suggests that potential is only given as such through specific media intervals and their protocols. These pixels are massaged in a variety of ways through algorithms common in commercial digital filters: the face today is an open doorway that confronts the viewer as a graphical user interface. Together with the signature color saturations and active camera that characterize Bhansali's style, the digitized face engulfs the viewer in a careful orchestration of movement, sound, color—Parvati's rhythm into flame.[34]

This is a qualitatively new sensory-motor schema that implicates the body of the viewer through a particular synaesthesia of sound, light, texture-color, duration, and movement. Bhansali's visual quotation is in fact a refunctioning of the entire assemblage that enabled Roy's "deification of masculine authority" by staging cinema as an event of a new deification and new relations of power, thus establishing the ecology of a new media assemblage. These assemblages are not comparable in the sense that the (post)modern is the maximalization of the dream of the other, always figured as resemblance, analogy, identity, and/or contradiction.[35] The embodiment of the senses and

----

(opposite)

10. The direct gaze of Paro (Suchitra Sen) in *Devdas* (dir. B. Roy, 1955).

11. Paro (Aishwarya Rai) protecting her diya in *Devdas* (dir. Sanjay Leela Bhansali, 2002).

12. Digital compositing: Paro becoming diya becoming bindhi in *Devdas* (dir. Sanjay Leela Bhansali, 2002).

the affective multiplicities (sensation ecologies) are qualitatively, intensively different in both. The nature of this difference is what is at stake here. There is no doubt that gender hierarchies are crystallized through both scenes, but their intensive processes and the specific way in which they implicate the desiring machines they assemble are singular events irreducible to the capture of heterosexual demand. The media assemblage returns thought to the singularity of sensation's emergence, its nonlinear dynamics in excess of the crystallization of desire. The excesses of Bollywood are not the purple pleasures of a cinema expanding in all directions, but rather the excess of events opening narrative to the intensive processes constituting it.

Globalization and the Media Assemblage in India

What is at stake both for Bollywood (defined as Urdu-Hindi popular culture) and for its analysis is an engagement with the sensations of a globalizing media assemblage. Evolving technologies and shifting diagrams of power implicate embodied sensations through repetitive practices, the assemblage gives rhythm to and partly actualizes virtual becomings. It is the material, expressive, and virtual unfolding of sensation that we are naming sexuality, where the individual and population meet in stochastic but patterned trajectories, practices, and pleasures. This assemblage has enfolded the totality of cinema, not because cinema is dead but because it is an essentially open totality, a constantly shape shifting, vigorously reorganizing body-machine becoming newly global and differently informational. Such an analysis would inhabit cinema in the middle and in the interstices of its multiple movements, a criticism that both diagrams and moves through and with a specific media assemblage.

What is a media assemblage?[36] Jay David Bolter and Richard Grusin in their persuasive genealogy of new media argue that in the West today the mediasphere is necessarily constellated, remediated, and multiply overlapping. "Our culture conceives of each medium or constellation of media as it responds to, redeploys, competes with, and reforms other media. In the first instance, we may think of something like a historical progression, of newer media remediating older ones and in particular of digital media remediating their predecessors. But ours is a genealogy of affiliations, not a linear history, and in this genealogy, older media can also remediate newer ones." In noting how television can and does refashion itself to form connectivities to the World Wide Web, and film can and does incorporate and attempt to contain computer graphics within its own linear form, they suggest that "no medium, it seems, can now function independently and establish its own separate and purified space of cultural meaning."[37]

This is a good place to begin a definition of Hindi-Urdu cinema's new media assemblage. Crucial to an understanding of the publicness of cinema and its biopolitical topography is the notion of media connectivities—for instance, information circulating between platforms such as the Internet, cellular phones, and satellite TV, or generative sensations between bodies and a graphical user interface. These connectivities shall be diagrammed as dynamic technologies of becoming, with their own thresholds, habituations, and vectors of evolution. Some, but not all, dynamics that happen in and through these interfaces are self-organizing and proceed through neural contagion at a preindividual strata. Contemporary marketing strategies operating through the connectivities of the assemblage invest (in) these neural contagions as value-added services, but the contagion of a media assemblage is stochastic and durational and always exceeds its capture (without necessarily constituting an identity or political resistance). Image-sound practices correlate in an assemblage, yet their trajectories are never given since these connectivities are positive feedback loops of capital, affect, pleasure, and time. While these feedback loops generate novel information as consumer profiles that are then used to modulate advertising streams, the circulation of information also produces noise that overflows those streams (entropy). There is always potentiality in noise to develop into a novel line of flight and to generate a new self-organizing assemblage by dissipating entropic information, energy, and matter to form a new phase space and new sets of media intervals.[38]

In India today, and indeed Bollywood globally, we see eddies within eddies of new functional connections forming. Cinemagoers are continuously implicated in new digital media through these connectivities and these (de)territorializing interfaces. Through such a method we can diagram the capture and codification of sensation as affective regularities or the evolving habituations of a media culture. This implies that sensation, in the co-dependent emergence of the individual and population (the preindividual), is the volatile "place" where contemporary capitalist media segments local audiences (for instance, through exhibition events). The media assemblage draws its specific analytic and political force from a framework that allows us to pose in the same breath (as breath is both a medium of language and a possible mode of contamination) how new regimes of risk management and population security establish temporary and partial relations of motion with the desiring machines of Hindi-Urdu cinema.[39] Media assemblages, functioning in the intervals between the subject and multiplicious populations, are preindividual, affective technologies for mutating heterogeneses.[40]

And they are also sticky. As we shall see, media assemblages activate and draw out the virtual openness of particular bodies-populations to refunction, correlate, and revalue images, sensations, technologies, capital, and pleasures by forging new lines of connectivity, asymptotic gravitational forces that aggregate materialities, force, and energy in open but resonant configurations (unpredictable but patterned trajectories and populations). Three modes of assembling bodies in media are to refunction, correlate, and revalue. The outlines of this emergence can be seen in the following excerpt from my Bhopal field notes.

August 29, 2000

Another *mehfil* (social gathering). With Manoj (son of a construction tycoon) and Raj (son of the owner-manager of Deepa Talkies, located in an upscale business district in New Bhopal). My cousin, an economist, is their drinking buddy (and former professor), and he put the event together for me, thankfully.

So the night began with Manoj coming to pick us up, and there was Raj too in the car (a newish sporty Zen—a/c, CD player, the "works"). They were playing Indian techno music. Raj began to interview *me* immediately. So you are doing a project on film or what is it? Who funded you? How much money did you get? etc., etc.

So then we went to this bar, where we sat outside and the conversation started after a few drinks. It was whiskey (Royal Challenge) for the regulars, and some beer for me.

According to Raj the cinema industry is on the decline in Madhya Pradesh and throughout India. Video and cable are the cause. But lifestyles are also changing, he believes. "Five years ago when we used to watch TV with our parents, we used to leave the room in embarrassment when a condom ad came on—now it's like, who cares." It is an indication of the explosion of media. Images and commodities are the stuff of everyday life so much so that every little thing seems different.

Where in all this are Indian values? Or is this even a relevant question to this class of people?

They were both giving me a sense of how much things have changed. New finances are everywhere. Banks are willing to fund just about anyone, they were saying. Where are the banks getting all this money? Multinational corpo-rations have flooded the country with cash. And the interest rate here, at least for mortgages, is like 13 percent or more. . . .

Jamuna (a theater in Muslim-dominated old Bhopal) and a couple of other talkies can install digital sound because they don't pay taxes (at least one of the theaters is a money-laundering machine for the former Congress Party chief minister of the state; not surprisingly it is one of the two talkies in Bhopal with digital sound). They can afford it. Raj said—almost as if he were boasting—that there is a lot of money in the theater business if you knew how to make it. Money like you wouldn't believe, he said.

So it was an evening of contrasts, if not contradictions. By far the larg-est part of the evening was spent with Manoj and Raj complaining about the government corruption that is eating into not only their profits but their self-esteem. This in a state that is still nearly 65 percent rural, and one that in January 2001 launched a much-touted experiment in direct-village democracy *gram swaraj*—village self-rule.[41] Despite this political veneer of a new anti-corruption ethos, for large parts of state governance an entrenched clientelist culture of governmentality continues to fight the proponents of globalized "transparency." Such as these two twenty-something businessmen; they style themselves as "forward-looking" young entrepreneurial men (who have inher-ited a lot of money). But people who also have a different kind of business ethos too—I mean it seems that they are mostly fed up with the way things have gone in this country. They want liberalization, even demand it as their right as so-called global citizens, repudiating their parents' clientelist ethos and the pastoral state they venerated. But they know too that all that they have their parents have built in some measure because of this *vyavastha*, system.

Manish was saying how much the government people bother him, how much they expect of him, how often they come to him for free tickets. The taxes are extreme, that's why the business isn't so profitable he was saying. There is not one AC movie hall in all of Madhya Pradesh [in 2000]. And Manoj explained how the government will not allow buildings larger than three stories to be built. Except PVR [a popular and successful multiplex chain throughout India]. When he threw that in the faces of those government agents, they said produce the plans for PVR and then we'll see if you can build a theater like that. It turns out the plans for PVR have disappeared. They seem not to exist. It is almost as if in some places in India a whole new set of rules are being implemented and enforced. This is also the unevenness of globalization—the necessary uneven-ness as national territoriality is punctured by zones of exception.

Manoj said, "My dad used to say not too long ago that whenever you pass a car on the road make sure you wave because most probably *jaan-pehchaan reha gaa* [it will be someone you know]. Today, forget it. Every *banda* [joe-shmo] has a car." Raj was also adamant that the expectations of the audiences have changed, new kinds of titillations have become necessary with the media explosion.

Globalization in India, at the level of the everyday, even for non-elite subjects in Bhopal (but quantitatively and qualitatively differently), is proceeding through the unprecedented proliferation and amplification of these temporary and partial relations of motion; what determines their duration, of course, is how effectively, or, better, profitably does each specific media assemblage combine the forces of standardization and differentiation necessitated by a transnational capitalist economy. No doubt, globalization as it has entered into everyday language is a notoriously difficult term to analyze, like postmodernism or curry.[42] I use the term to name that historical conjuncture of productive, security, bodily, and cultural forces that have come to characterize a very uneven dominance over the course of twenty years of deregulation, privatization, flexible production, cold war dissolution, structural adjustment, and telecommunication convergences: India's integration into new circuits of global capital. This period has been termed by some the epoch of the "de-territorialisation of capitalist rationality."[43] In other words, the organization of legitimate violence as a function of state sovereignty has in some profound ways been adapted by transnational capital, which has in turn empowered local nonstate groupings of a kind of "scattered hegemony" in many postcolonial nations (especially volatile under conditions of U.S. occupation coupled with civil war, as in Afghanistan and Iraq).[44] The global imperatives of this new capitalist rationality are that trade will flow uninterrupted and the market will determine exchange rates and capital convertibility. As Don Kalb argues, "Liberals and neo-liberals joined their forces in the aftermath of the fall of the Berlin Wall in an effort to shape George Bush senior's 'New World Order.' This was a genuine globalizing alliance, reflecting the belief that liberal capitalism was now 'the only game in town.'" The premises of this alliance were: (1) if commodities are freely exchanged between people and places, (2) actors everywhere will discover their self-interests as producers and consumers and will let these interests prevail over collective passions and hot politics; (3) they will then form into modern "independent" and productive "middle classes," (4) who will demand civil rights and vote against inefficiencies and insider interests,

(5) which will foster trade, prosperity, freedom and growth, and will further deepen global interdependence among mankind.[45]

This conjuncture between neoliberal political economy and American-led empire produced a decisive shift in all the political, economic, and cultural apparatuses developed by and for transnational capitalist accumulation throughout the 1990s. More than one critic has characterized this entire epoch as one of implosion.[46] Indeed, the dizzying rate of capital flight from the erstwhile "Third World" to the (dominant and emerging) core countries is immediately tied to the transformation of the social organization of industrial production (e.g., flexible or "lean" production, subcontracting, new consumerist disciplines linked to global media, etc.) and an infusion of information-driven technologies at every stage of the industrial process, from design to marketing.[47] These epoch-making processes are fused in an ethic that seeks to integrate cultural, work, and technological factors within a specifically transnational structure. Moreover, as Ankie Hoogvelt suggests, a new political economy of "relationship enterprising" or "economic networking" (which makes it possible for firms to relocate an ever-widening range of operations and functions to wherever cost-competitive labor, assets, and infrastructure are available) has developed in which national laws play an increasingly marginal role. "As these cross border alliances develop their own rules of engagement, so, step by step, a global governance structure, whether entirely voluntary or assisted by inter-nation government agreements may emerge."[48] Today, transnational capital, the International Monetary Fund, and the World Bank are the harbingers and purveyors of a new kind of governing apparatus, in which Western multiculturalism seems to be an integral part.[49]

What is crucial in all this in the context of a fast-changing postcolonial nation like India is the nature and extent of the technological, labor, and aesthetic transformations in production and everyday life. Some have suggested that the microelectronic and telecommunications "revolution" of the past thirty years has resulted in an overall but uneven fall in communication and transaction costs with far-reaching consequences. Brishti Guha, writing in the *Economic and Political Weekly*, has specified at least six consequences of this so-called revolution. First, there is an increased mobility of vast volumes of capital "in a near-frictionless financial market." Second, different kinds of services no longer have to be consumed at the point and the moment of production: due to integrated forms of database management they can be traded across not only spatial but also temporal barriers (they can be electronically stored or archived on the Internet). This expansion of technological platforms signals a shift in regimes of cultural production (that is, the production of culture for economic exchange) that describe a move from a regime of cultural production ordered by authorship, originality, and signature to one ordered by the brand, branding, and simulation; indeed, all forms of production today must be analyzed as part of the wide-ranging process of the patenting of matter previously coded as natural and/or social—a process of "type or kind becoming brand."[50] This expansion of the modalities and timespaces of biomedia and biocapital consumption has given rise to definitions of economic value based on processes of reception, or what Walter Benjamin termed exhibition value. As Lisa Adkins notes, "Ownership of that labour is made less in terms of claims concerning the creativity and uniqueness (that is the capacities and abilities) of the cultural producer (the individual) and more in terms of process of reception, that is, in terms of the commercial effects of cultural goods vis-á-vis the intended audience."[51]

The third consequence is that the globalization of markets and supply sources associated with the fall in search and transaction costs has reduced or at least limited the economic importance both of specific large markets (as greater numbers of producers can now access a global market) and of capital-rich regions (which earlier were the main focus of growth but are now no longer so due to capital mobility). Global markets and supply sources also imply an intensification of competition, which has triggered "winner-takes-all" effects on income distribution. Globalization has forced adaptations in technology with firms switching from large fixed investments to computer-controlled "flexible specialization." The attempt to evolve through new networked connectivities so as to be able to respond rapidly to changes in global market conditions has led to changes in the structures of firms, such as a flattening of the hierarchical pyramid and a redistribution of power, responsibility, and initiative. Adkins notes that substantive studies of the new economy attest to this more open character of economic action. Such accounts stress the retreat of socio-structural formations that previously framed possibilities for action (for instance, those of occupation and organization); an intensification of self-regulation and self-reflexivity; how working practices are increasingly networking practices; the proliferating significance of intermediaries; and how workers tend not to share narratives or life histories and how continuous effort and emphasis are placed on working at making and remaking networks and relationships—"people do not 'have' relationships, instead there is a focus on doing relationships and on relationship management."[52] As Adkins goes on to argue, all of these shifts lead to a kind of "overflowing" of all economic contracts; "It is precisely this overflowing which makes the *contract productive*. . . . In short, the very elements that stabilize a contract are sources of overflow (since frames are never entirely closed off or sealed), and it is this overflowing that produces *productivity*." Overflowing may thus be thought as "the production of production" since economic action is not framed or constituted by (relatively) closed or fixed sources but is found in open, moving, heterogeneous networks.[53]

Fourth, the smaller role of fixed asset investments coupled with lower fixed costs in research and advertising has reduced the importance of economies of scale, thereby increasing the scope for variety in product differentiation. The standardized mass market has given way to "niche markets" and "narrowcasting" for differentiated products and media. Fifth, the tradability of services across space, the declining attraction of large markets and capital-rich regions, and the diminished importance of scale economies all combine to give countries of the global south an "advantage" as producers and exporters of labor-intensive services and manufactures (and also as consumers of services not available locally). No doubt, this so-called advantage reinscribes an older colonial and racial international division of labor, and, given the intensified mobility of capital, has weakened the bargaining power of organized labor globally. Sixth, the large corporation that integrated all of its operations has given way to the small, in many cases "virtual," firm that outsources most if not all of its operations. This is partly because with increased competition among suppliers the firm's vulnerability to opportunistic extortion by any particular supplier falls, and so does the incentive for vertical integration—a tendency that seems to exist side by side with that of flexible, flattened, and networked production within multinational corporations. Both tendencies are due to the opportunities created by new communication technology that has increased the span of coordination and control and just-in-time technology-driven production, and which consequently has reduced inventory requirements; "These enable the firm to function as a virtual presence coordinating a global network of producers and marketing outlets, and achieving flexibility by avoiding fixed commitments."[54]

Fundamental to these overall shifts is a reinvestment by capital in circuits of affect. Patricia Clough has shown that in this global situation the connection of affect and capital is not merely a matter of a service economy's increasing demand for affective labor or media's modulation of the circuit from affect to emotion. Rather, "pre-individual affective capacities have been made central to the passage from formal subsumption to the real subsumption of 'life itself' into capital, as the accumulation of capital has shifted to the domain of affect."[55] In other words, the overflow of productivity taps into the potential of emergent capacities of both biological and nonbiological life. This subsumption of life itself within a posthumanist capitalism is what Eugene Thacker calls biomedia, in which biological components and processes are rendered as information and recontextualized for purposes that may be either biological or nonbiological (or computational).[56] Capitalist biomedia expands affective labor and qualitatively shifts media modulation of the body's connectivities to the media assemblage. Capital accumulation in the domain of affect assembles energy resources, including the human body and "life itself," through their informational substrate, "such that equivalencies might be found to value one form of life against another, one vital capacity against another." With information as the unit, capital accumulation in the domain of affect is an accumulation and an investment in information as the dynamic immanent to matter, its capacity for self-organization, emergent mutation, and creation.[57]

Another way of thinking about this revaluation of potential within capital today is through Gilles Deleuze and Félix Guattari's notion of the "machinic phylum," through which self-organizing processes in both organic and nonorganic "life" produce order out of chaos.[58] The initial point of reference for this concept is Gilbert Simondon's earlier work on morphogenesis and the evolution of the technical object in a "phylogenetic series," which, as a defined stage of evolution, contains within it "structures and schemes that represent the principle of an evolution of forms. The technical being evolves by convergence and adaptation to itself; it becomes unified interiorly according to a principle of internal resonance."[59] As Manuel Delanda notes, these processes reach a critical point (a dynamic threshold for phase transitions) at which correlated elements begin to "cooperate" (or resonate, in keeping with the language of nonlinear dynamics that I have been using) to form a higher-level entity. As he further states:

> To provide a clearer idea of what these processes of spontaneous "cooperative behavior" are, consider a few examples: the individual spin of atoms in a metal "cooperate" to make the metal magnetic; the individual molecules in a chemical reaction "cooperate" to create the perfectly rhythmic patterns of a chemical clock; the cells making up an amoeba colony "cooperate" under certain conditions to assemble an organism with differentiated organs; and the different termites in a colony "co-

operate" to build a nest. On the face of it, there would be no reason to assume that processes as different as these could be related at a deeper level. But recent advances in experimental mathematics have shown that the onset of all these processes may be described by essentially the same mathematical model. . . . Behind self-organization there is a "machinic phylum."[60]

Delanda goes on to show that tracking the nonhuman life of the phylum involves discovering the "emergent properties" of different assemblages; these are properties that arise from the actual interaction of the various elements of the assemblage but are not present in any of the elements taken alone.[61] Connecting this with what Adkins shows is the overflow necessary to production today suggests that the emergent property (capacities, affordances, affects) of the globalized assemblage of new media and bodies is the property to produce overflow itself, as the potentiality of all forms of excess becomes a mode of self-organizing the assemblage itself. There are dangers here, though: I am not arguing that there is anything "natural" to the social inequalities generated by the globalization of communication technologies; neither am I suggesting—á la the Extropy group—that free market capitalism articulates the principle of spontaneous self-organizing.[62] I am arguing, however, that nonhuman forces of self-organization such as the variable flows of media technologies combine through secured and pirated flows with human and nonhuman energies, expressions, and matter to form new assemblages of media-population-body-value. In other words, the media assemblage organizes and connects the capacities of local ecologies. It amplifies the far-from-equilibrium dynamics inherent in this process, catalyzing phase transitions and a new stabilization of an always-precarious order.[63] It is this assemblage of resonant processes with its own emergent properties (affects) that we have been calling an ecology of sensation, where preindividual sensation is potentialized and captured in the theater of the machinic phylum. To clarify the diagram of the machinic phylum in the media assemblage of globalization let us return to our discussion of the various elements that have been decisive in the present conjuncture in India.

There is, for instance, the question of how and where we situate the nation-state today. Certainly, such global shifts in speed, computer-network interfacing, affect-accumulation economies, and flexible production are undeniable. But here we must be wary of totalizing proclamations that take David Harvey's argument around the timespace compression of capital (i.e., as technological advances are exploited by capitalist rationality, the time it takes people, services, commodities, information, and capital to go from one space to another is radically shortened) or Paul Virilio's elaboration of the increasing material sensations and technologies of speed in postmodernity as signaling the end of territoriality or the nation-state.[64] Thus, in contrast to Hoogvelt and others who have too hastily declared the death of the nation-state, critics such as Don Kalb and Ellen Meiksins Wood have recently noted that throughout the world territory and space have become more important as master signifiers, or that they order words of patterned bundles of social relationships and institutions.[65] The nation still sticks (around). Indeed, globalization is an epochal imposition of markets by centralized transnational institutions dominated by the core (and emerging) capitalist economies. In respect to actual trade in goods, the global economy is actually much less internationalized than the Britain-based world economy of the late nineteenth century.[66] The intensification of social struggle around space (residual and emergent ethnicities, diasporic nostalgia, global environmentalism, informal-sector street vendors, etc.) and the spatialization of time (the congealing of culture, commodities, subjectivities, and populations through technologies such as culturally specific insurance marketing or narratives of development, underdevelopment, and overdevelopment) can be seen as a complex interaction: as both implosion and rearticulation. Moreover, as the world becomes informatized across all sectors of production and consumption, a legal (both national and transnational) framework for informatization is taking shape under the aegis of the World Trade Organization (WTO) and with active inputs from multilateral agencies such as the International Telecommunication Union (ITU). As Pradip Thomas notes in the case of the global south, "the developing world is far less enthusiastic, even apprehensive about these developments, given their levels of competitive disadvantage vis-a-vis the developed world, in the emerging information-based industries but also in traditional sectors." The specter of a "privatized knowledge regime" enforced through standardized intellectual property law will radically constrain room to maneuver for the nations of the global south: "Today the WTO functions as the 'Lord of the Market' with extensively invested powers related to devising, interpreting, policing and maintaining the parameters of global trade."[67]

Thus we situate the very different but increasingly resonant trajectories of capitalist restructuring globally as capital is newly potentialized on the plane of the machinic phylum but with unpredictable effects. One of these unpredictable effects is the complex relation between the microstates of local or regional economies and the macrostates of globalization. As numerous authors have suggested, the "real" economy may well be regionalizing rather than globalizing, giving rise to three regional clusters of national economies: the Triad of the European Union (EU), the United States via NAFTA, and East-South Asia.[68] These political economists have shown that roughly two-thirds of all transactions remained within these regional clusters. Such internal transactions were "embedded" in a texture of local institutions in labor markets, housing, education, law, networks of trust and familiarity, and so on, with all of them ultimately anchored in a more or less "public institutional heritage" organized by states. And so real economic growth, as distinct from the nominal growth in the virtual economy of stock markets, does not first of all depend on the freeing of flows in global space but rather on the maintenance of production cultures on the ground. "Such production cultures came in various genres, among others East Asian development states, European continental welfare states, and Anglo-Saxon liberal and stock-market-based regimes. It made no sense to impose one version as the only rational one."[69] Similarly the work of "historical institutionalists" such as Alice Amsden, Linda Weiss, and Robert Wade on East Asian states underlines "the centrality of state action in preparing economies for successful export performance. East Asia, thus, squarely denied the path to export earnings recommended by the globalists. Not shock-therapeutic opening, but patient and carefully managed integration was the lesson."[70]

In India this narrative of globalization is familiar, but in its material proliferation in everyday life it also has taken singular forms. At the general level of economic and public policy India's liberalization path is something of a cross between the East Asian experience of "carefully managed integration" and the IMF's forced shock treatment administered throughout Latin America.[71] Because of a complex internal and international historical conjuncture (the 1987 stock market collapse, the first Gulf War, a sudden rise in oil prices, a fall in remittances from the Middle East, the gradual break-up of Nehruvian-Congress hegemony, new populist rural and subaltern class formations, the rise of Hindu nationalism, and capital flight), by the end of the 1980s India's elites were confronted with a decisive political-economic crisis. (The machinic phylum was on the move, a moment when the material flows of capital, information, and energy were beginning to resonate in an entirely new way, a system beginning to establish new gradients of flux and creating a clear-cut phase separation between one hegemony and another.) By the beginning of the 1990s imports exceeded exports, which led to a balance of payments deficit totaling $6.8 billion.[72] India was thus forced to borrow more and more money, with external borrowing rising from $18 billion in 1980 to $56 billion in 1989. This massive increase in the fiscal debt fueled inflation and pushed up prices; this was accompanied by a devaluation of the rupee, skyrocketing public debt, and a growing inability to generate the revenue necessary to meet the debt.

In 1991 the Indian government sought to resolve the fiscal crisis, but of course it had little autonomy to do so. By June its foreign exchange reserves were down to two weeks of normal imports, and it was forced to negotiate loans from the World Bank and the IMF and in so doing to undertake the loan in accordance with certain "conditionalities" relating to the movement of capital and the role of the state. Under the broad heading of free market "structural adjustments," the Indian government was obliged to devalue the rupee by 19 percent; bring inflation under control through draconian budgetary measures; reform the financial sector; eliminate protection for most industries; privatize significant sections of the public sector; remove import licensing controls for a large range of capital goods and raw materials; lower all import duties; "rationalize" indirect and direct taxes; and introduce pro-capital labor laws.[73]

India's external debt grew from $63 billion in 1991 to over $100 billion in 2000. And although the budget deficit has been reduced, if not actually wiped out, it has been at the cost of social welfare and education.[74] Ironically, individual nation-states across the developing world, under pressure from the new regime of structural adjustment, have been unable to use capital expenditure to create the infrastructure necessary for productive foreign investment. Simultaneously, there has been an enormous growth in the finance sector, which has been fueled by speculative capital, thus adding to inflationary pressures brought about by the devaluation of the rupee.[75] Under the so-called discipline of market forces, the rupee has spiraled downward with rising prices: by June 1995 the price of grain was already 60 percent higher than it was when India initiated its economic policies in 1991, so that, even though the government had in storage over thirty million tons of grain, the poor could no longer afford it.[76] From 2000 to 2005 the transnationalizing Indian economy all but reversed many of these macroeconomic indicators,[77] without however reversing the process of proletarianization, exploitation, or immiseration: the killing blight of "India Shining" (the much-derided election slogan of the Hindu chauvinist party BJP, voted out of office in the 2004 elections). The massive influx of displaced agricultural workers into the unorganized sector and the increasing insecurity of organized labor throughout India give some sense of the changing Indian labor market in the era of globalization.[78] And while in sheer numbers India's "poverty headcount" declined markedly throughout the 1990s, certain regions such as southern Orissa or the *adivasi* (indigenous) reserves of Madhya Pradesh have seen an intensification of poverty and a concomitant contraction of political power for the majority in those areas.[79] These are zones of exception that are internal to the logic of globalization in India.[80]

What we mark then is the profoundly uneven character of liberalization (as state policy) and globalization (as transnational cultural and economic process) across India and indeed across urban and rural space.[81] This unevenness indexes both the heterogeneous nature of capitalist restructuring and the stratified histories of local political economies in the process of negotiating regional, state, national, and transnational fluxes. Kaushik Sunder Rajan, in his *Biocapital: The Constitution of Postgenomic Life*, has carefully traced the ways that contemporary biopower is constituting surplus populations as "experimental subjects" in the wake of the massive displacements of Mumbai's deindustrialization. These same experimental populations provide the genetic data for the development of various pharmaceutical therapies for the sovereign consumers of the West.[82] But as his work shows so well, this suggests that there is a fracturing of the national terrain itself in the constituting and redeployment of such postgenomic life. Arjun Appardurai situates the fractured heterogeneities of globalization in this way: "Cities like Bombay—now Mumbai—have no clear place in the stories told so far that link late capitalism, globalization, post-Fordism, and the growing dematerialization of capital." Their history is characterized by "disjunct, yet adjacent," histories and temporalities. In such cities, Fordist manufacture, craft and artisanal production, service economies involving law, leisure, finance, biotechnology, and banking, and virtual economies involving global finance capital and local stock markets live in an uneasy mix. Here are the loci of a predatory global capital, placing Mumbai with Bangkok, Hong Kong, São Paulo, Los Angeles, Mexico City, London, and Singapore. Here are the social black holes mired in the effort to embrace and seduce global capital in their own particular ways, "which are tied to varied histories (colonial and otherwise), varied political cultures of citizenship and rule, and varied ecologies of production and finance." Such particularities appear as the cracked and refracted fool's gold of globalization.[83]

Much like the social situation in Argentina and Turkey in the 1990s, India's economic crisis unearthed the legitimacy and governing crisis of the postcolonial state whose clientelist and corruption-producing mode of social regulation had marked politics since the 1960s.[84] Thus India's integration into this proliferating system of global expropriation has produced new apparatuses of security that are negotiated in singular ways. The globalized malltiplex in all of its infolded affectivity and proliferating commodity fetishism is also an apparatus of security; its aspects include the production and continuous regulation of populations, their market images (audience segmentation such as masses vs. classes gives way to gradients of desiring populations, the niche audience), and the brand images and sensations they potentialize and consume. An exploration of the possible connections and ambivalences between the media assemblage and the new security apparatus of globalization must begin with a diagram of the becoming-information technology of India's economy, that phase transition in the assemblage where the circulation of information and its different structures and platforms forms new resonances with the neural life of sensation (the preindividual) on the plane of the machinic phylum, yielding new habits, affective dispositions, and security risks. In other words, if thought of as a biogram that shows the globalizing relations of motion in Bollywood's media assemblage, we can follow the infolding of media into the security regime of India's newly informatized economy. But what is singular to the Indian experience? I will argue that we consider this articulation of media and security not as a cultural extension of Western-dominated globalization but as localized and global ecologies of affective capital, where catalytic actions of global lines of flight produce singularities that are integrable across the assemblage: in Bhopal one can buy the best fake Nike shoes in India because the regional economy has for decades been a vibrant nexus for the grey market and the black market in a variety of consumer goods. Simultaneously, new econo-technological rationalities have spurred transformations in media production; film finance is enabled by the so-called frictionless transparency of computerization, for instance. New econo-technologies of subjectivation render everyday financialization through pedagogical strategies and temporal dispositions embedded in, for instance, insurance and astrology. All of this has been folded into the assemblage as well. These mutual and uneven foldings limn the dynamic thresholds between laboring-desiring bodies, affective flows, normalized populations, reterritorializing states, and capital flashing forth in unexpected ways, always open both to virtualization as well as branding.

Enter the new media. In the early 1990s, technological changes swept through Indian cities. In May 1991, only a few months after the Gulf War, the STAR TV network (Satellite Television for the Asian Region, owned by Rupert Murdoch) brought international programming to India. The STAR network was a slick media outlet for advertisers, and it was seen by the upper classes as an immediate "improvement" over the bulky, state-run broadcasting system. Globalized media giants such as CNN, HBO, and MTV soon followed, and they brought international news, films, and music as well as lifestyles rooted in the appeal of privatized consumption.[85] Introduced in 1959, television in India was seen as a means for disseminating state policies and public information—in other words, public service broadcasting. The main aim of the national broadcasters—All India Radio (AIR) and the national television network Doordarshan (DD)—was to educate, inform, and create a feeling of national identity-integration and help maintain national unity.[86]

By 1998, nearly seventy cable and satellite channels were operating in India, including major transnational players such as STAR, BBC, Discovery, MTV, Sony, CNN, Disney, and CNBC, as well as scores of Indian companies. Recent forecasts have suggested that by 2015 India is set to emerge as Asia's leading revenue-generating market for pay TV, with the multichannel video industry (cable, DTH, and IPTV) turnover growing from $3.6 billion in 2005 to $7.2 billion by 2010 and $10.5 billion by 2015.[87] Now, in order to maintain ratings and advertising revenue, the transnationals have had to "Indianize"—that is, adapt their programming strategies to suit the Indian context.[88] The social impact of an onslaught of Western-produced audiovisual satellite feeds in the early 1990s spurred Hindu chauvinist pandering to an endangered "Bharat Mata" (Mother India) as well as catalyzed an unprecedented explosion after 1995 of aggressively "Indianized" new media entertainment, visual art, and pop music centered on indigenous consumption and youth culture.[89] The Hindu-ized nation and its MTV deterritorialization are in fact verso and recto of the same dynamic. As Vamsee Juluri has noted, the postliberalization era in India has been marked not only by the rise of a qualified form of youth culture in the context of music television broadcasters such as MTV and Channel [V] but also by a broader shift in television content that could be characterized as a move from "worshiping senility" to "worshiping juvenility." The emergence of the teenaged media consumer in India is fraught with cultural tensions inflected along lines of generation, gender, class, religion, nationality, and globality. It represents a particular historical assemblage of technology, economy, and culture in which a new charge of foreign and domestic investment in youth markets seeks to secure a youth identity premised on the equation of consumption with the national interest and the global imperative. In other words, being young is not only a metaphor for the message of commercial television but also a particular dynamic connectivity to media technologies in India, articulating with emerging notions, practices, protocols, and intensities of being one's self, in Juluri's words, "as a youth, a student, a friend, a son or daughter, a fan of music and popular culture, and as an Indian in a visibly global context."[90] Jaluri goes on to argue that, considering the marketing strategies of globalized media, a fundamental difference between the experience of youth in contemporary Asia and that of different generations of youth who have grown up in a media-saturated environment in the West since the 1950s is that although the latter have successively "rebelled out" from their parents' generation, the former are in the process of "rebelling in" to the middle class. In India, marketing executives have also understood the generational experience of nationalism and globalization along similar lines: "Young, middle-class Indians, it is believed, are ready to become aggressive consumers—and consumers of national identity—because their parents' generation had finally tired of nation-building Nehruvian ideals of austere consumption and was vicariously consuming through its children."[91]

What does it mean to be an aggressive Indian consumer in today's globalized new media ecology? I conclude this section by affirming the fact that television as we knew it died on October 18, 2004. That's what Mark Pesce, one of the early developers of Virtual Reality and the co-inventor of Virtual Reality Modeling Language (VRML), tells us, and I think he's got that much right. In "Piracy Is Good? New Models for the Distribution of Television Programming," Pesce argues that BitTorrent technology is the "killer app" (i.e., the decisive application) for broadband technology, the application that gives new functionality and intensity to the technology itself.[92] This is another example of the machinic phylum harmonizing resonances between technology, pleasure, and practice, thereby reorganizing the media assemblage along new intensities and new gradients of information and capital flow, and moving it toward a phase transition. Let me elaborate briefly on Pesce's argument and draw out the implications for Indian new media practices with a different example.

For Pesce, BitTorrent has changed the way television content is consumed today, marking the advent of "hyperdistribution." Audiences are more and more technically savvy, and less and less inclined to pay for content that's downloadable for free. Widespread piracy has short-circuited the chain that tied producers to broadcasters and advertisers, as BitTorrent consumption has "disintermediated" the distribution channels, potentially connecting producers directly to audiences. Noting that, per capita, Australians are the most profligate downloaders of television programming in the world, Pesce shows that today's "digital ephemera" media has subjected media oligopolies (such as the one in Australia) to "digital arbitrage," which can hollow out empires in an afternoon. In this context, according to Pesce's quasi-apocalyptic, quasi-utopian musings, the hollowed out networks will return to their origins in live, real-time broadcasting. Thus, hyperdistribution will reorganize the consumption of digitized content, "harnessing piracy for profit," as Pesce blithely puts it. Basically, Pesce's idea is to harness the viral power of the "bug," the smallish, semi-transparent station ID that has become the constant onscreen companion to all television broadcasts. By tying up directly with major advertisers in a given region, whose bugs will flit across the mise-en-scène of hyperdistributed content globally, producers can both harness piracy and establish a continuous symbiosis with branded advertisers.[93] This continuous symbiosis means that the thirty- or fifteen-second advertisement interval has reached its own duration: the future belongs to uninterrupted branding of digital content that integrates the marketing interval into the attention of consumers contagiously. Thus, the interval of viewing is expanded by excising the advert while simultaneously contracting the interval of attention by quantifying the multiplied microspaces of the screen. This paradoxical expansion and contraction of attention is the biopolitical nature of contagion in the viral media assemblage. But media contagions swerve imperceptibly from their trajectories: clinamedia (the clinamen in media—I speculate on the future of this concept in the conclusion to this volume). Their populations fluctuate stochastically among an ensemble of microstates; while all of these microstates are not equally probable, they are equally consistent with one and the same macrostate.[94] Thus, the BitTorrent phase transition into hyperdistribution is marked by gradients of audience attention and gradients of marketing tolerance. In India video pirates and cable providers have for at least a decade covered nearly a third of the screen with continuous advertising content, and there was never anything transparent about it—it was simply a solid band of nonstop color adverts. This was tolerated in India, primarily because the distributors had monopolized the stream, but it has also produced an entrained audience that expects to have to piece together just what is happening in a given program above the advert band. But this is not the case with people who use BitTorrent globally, and this is the crucial shift in the new ecology. As an Internet respondent to Pesce notes about the new business plan: "The model [Pesce] suggests to 'save' television is the very model that's driving me 'away' from television. And it could be that others who already use 'torrents' to acquire programming do so to escape the bugs. Add the bugs to torrents and you may very well kill the reason behind piracy . . . but at the same time, kill the viewer's interest in watching a given program in any distribution. He suggests that 'word of mouth' advertising between friends would spread the popularity of a program. But frankly, if a friend recommended a program to me that was full of 'bugs,' I'd probably reconsider that friendship."[95]

Broadband technologies are developing according to the functional specificities of Indian media ecologies, but they have not achieved that decisive saturation in which BitTorrent protocols could change the very nature of distribution and consumption. (Although in a 2007 YouTube interview, the NRI Ashwin Navin, president and cofounder of BitTorrent, expressed the company's desire to expand numerous operations in India.)[96] This is not the case with cell phones, and the technological "leapfrogging" that expanded 3G bandwidth promises (up to two megabytes per second in fixed applications) has produced a flurry of speculation on the forms of "value added" applications and services (VAS) that may soon be available to the average Indian subscriber.[97] What is at stake here is the very nature of value itself in this new media: How is value potential actualized? In India cellular phones had a staggeringly quick penetration and now are indispensable in contemporary life, traversing (unequally) the urban-rural divide. In fact, India has the world's fastest-growing wireless market, and as of November 2006 the total number of cell phone users stood at 143 million.[98] But as a recent report by the Internet and Mobile Association of India notes, voice remains the most common function for cell phones in India, and most users opt for low-end cheap phones with limited capabilities for high-definition content, thus making VAS at times prohibitively expensive for the majority of people. Mobile value-added services are not part of the "basic voice offer" and subscribers use these services separately, which turns the cell phone itself into a divisible node of heterogeneous practices and functions. However, the development of VAS will depend in part on the expansion of the wireless infrastructure throughout India, which will make location-based, language-specific VAS a viable option for application developers, service operators, and average subscribers.[99] Now these services are tools for product differentiation, allowing mobile operators to develop other streams of revenue: "The nature of value added services changes over time. A VAS may become commoditized and becomes so commonplace and widely used that it no longer provides meaningful differentiation on a relative basis."[100] Thus, the future of mobile VAS will be based on developing "alternative revenue streams as voice has become commoditized and has ceased to be a tool for differentiation . . . Operators are facing cutthroat competition and with the call rates in India being one of the cheapest in the world, the margins are very low."[101]

It could be said then that there is an industrial brand coding of VAS. By brand coding I mean a discourse on and mechanism of capturing and quantifying the intensive, qualitative processes constituting this new media assemblage (processes that cannot themselves be divided without changing in kind). Central to this brand coding is the rhetoric of "commoditization" and "differentiation." Obviously the function of these concepts in the business models of brand coding is always already a form of deterritorializing emergence, and it is not at all far-fetched to suggest that the preemption of emergence in the war on terrorism that Cooper details becomes a kind of mad vector of quantified heterogeneity in corporate new media. So the business model is to situate value production in the processes of emergence—emergent practices, technologies, protocols, and identities (VAS as "self-expression"). But in the interaction of these elements of the assemblage—in the resultant distribution of their vectors of change—emergent properties take form in the assemblage itself. And this process is not quantifiable because these emergent properties are tied to changing capacities in the stochastic events of the media assemblage. Consider in this regard one of the predictions of the Internet and Mobile Association of India (IAMAI) report: by 2010 there will be a displacement of the dominance of Bollywood entertainment in mobile VAS in favor of infotainment (information useful to the subscriber concerning movie tickets, news, bank accounts, etc.) and m-commerce (transactional services such as buying tickets or placing orders).[102] This view completely misses the particular affective relations and the kind of folding and ratcheting of intensity specific to the media assemblage itself. The affective charge of Bollywood content, like movie-based games, branded wallpaper, or ring tones and callback tones,[103] at the level of perception, through the perceptual apparatus of the user is out of proportion to its consciously perceived and practical value because it is assembled with an entire ecology of media events and sets of practices of "self-expression."[104] This is even more apparent in the case of television. As the report notes, "television is another culturally entrenched constant in the life of the average Indian. Typically TV viewing has been a passive affair, however following the global trend TV channels have been focused on making programming interactive. Thus programs, especially music [and] contest shows have started giving the option to their viewers to participate through SMS [short text message]. A popular show like *Kaun Banega Crorepati* (KBC) generated 58 million SMS over a 3 month period."[105]

These intensive vectors are channeled through a number, the protocol of the "short code." For instance, a satellite TV corporate buys their own short code (e.g., 8888, 3456 etc.), they then sell to a third-party client access to the code, assigning a keyword and a specific duration. These clients have a tie-up with multiple operators to ensure that customers of all the operators send an SMS to the same number. So if TV programmers want to get participants for a show, they advertise "Type 'x' on your mobile phones and send to 3456." The server at destination 3456 identifies the message with the keyword "x" and routes it to the owner of that short code.[106] What are the emergent properties of the assemblage of the short code? The short code multiplies revenue streams, and given its wide range of applications it is serially deployed; its cognitive associations circulate through specific mediatized marketing strategies, but its functionality is dissociated from these discourses as any given code enfolds numerous protocol-specific keywords. The short code, in other words, allows for a widening flux of intervals in a media stream. It is, on the one hand, a way of stretching the duration of a film or TV show beyond its exhibition by penetrating the microtemporalities of everyday consumption. The keyword code is with you wherever and whenever your cell phone is on and the feedback loop follows you continuously, thus increasing the probabilities of its vibrating contagion. On the other hand, the code concentrates these media streams into their most contagious denominator, their brand image: the catchy tune reduced to simple tones, a narrative imaged as digital wallpaper, or a star-centered interactive game. In short, multiple mechanisms temporally modulate events and allow for their stochastic proliferation. Thus, the very concept and experience of value in VAS is potentialized—patterned and unpredictable—as an emergent property of assembling intensive vectors. (One could go further—and in subsequent research the aim will be to do just that—by specifying the connection of cell phone value-added to the *fokat mein* bhava of loitering that have evolved from bazaar economies.)

In sum, I have stressed the catalytic folding of global economic changes in India's media assemblage. New capacities for media are emergent and they are harmonizing across heterogeneous populations on the plane of the machinic phylum. There is nothing innocuous about these resonances, they are volatile and variable precisely because wars of gradients of energy and matter—meshed fields of intensive, intersubjective, and governmental forces—constitute their emergence. In the intervals between there is nothing but differential forces. I have argued that the media assemblage is the premier theater of postbiological life, the timespace of irreversible processes of energy expenditure, material recombination, and techno-genesis unfolding stochastically in new dissipative systems that render order at the edge of chaos. The shift to the accumulation of affect in different forms of biomedia, where the body's neural pathways as well as its genetic information are deployed as the material substrate for various kinds of algorithm-based procedures, is predicated on the openness of economic networks, where openness or overflow is the central mechanism of value production itself, the stochastic production of productivity. These changes, in turn, have given rise to an audience-based consumer economy replete with its own protocols, pedagogies, and potentialities. Through all of these changes, however, I have also sought to show that the quotidian life of biomedia is a central concern to crisis-driven national initiatives in media policy and social reproduction in India. In what follows I will draw these elements of my argument forward into a consideration of different aural-imagistic regimes and infolding timespaces in the emerging media assemblage of India.

Pirating Dolby: Digital Sound and the Sensations of Cinema

Consider, in light of these global transformations, the image and technology of Dolby digital sound. In the Western metropole, the digital strategy of Dolby sound refunctions the film experience as a more intense configuration of sound-image-sensation-space (sound, as Deleuze points out, acquires the status of image with the advent of the electronic and digital regimes).[107] According to the Dolby website: "This premiere surround sound format delivers realistic digital audio via 5.1 discrete channels. The three front channels (Left/Center/Right) deliver crisp, clean dialogue and accurate placement of on-screen sounds, while twin surround channels (Left Surround/Right Surround) wrap around the audience and immerse them in the action. The LFE (Low-Frequency Effects) channel delivers real impact for explosions and other effects that can, literally, be felt as well as heard."[108] Dolby technology projects modulated sound at once stabilizing the media image (the function of digital sound is not, therefore, a departure from reality but rather its fundamental intensification)[109] and creating value through the circulation of its brand logo. More to the point, Dolby sound produces affects that synaesthetically correlate sound waves with nonaudio visual forces: "literally . . . felt as well as heard." This is what might be called affective synaesthesia—not the desire-effect of the lack of the mother's voice (as Michel Chion would have it),[110] but the virtual and actual proliferation of a preindividual and continuous multiplicity of sound waves felt as much as heard.

Although, on the one hand, such a technology must function unobtrusively (not calling attention to the apparatus itself), on the other hand this aural and affective rendering of cinematic space explicitly remarks on its branded specificity (singularly important in India, as we shall see). But beyond its integrated presence and branding, it literally extends the sense of sound to the sensation of touch through vibrations. In the market of American consumer "high fidelity" this means that, according to Lloyd W. Phillips, "you can add a transducer (a device that converts an electrical signal into mechanical motion) that will extend your audio coverage far below the response of the best subwoofer available. This goes below the range of hearing, and enters a new realm: sensation (vibration)."[111] And the latest extension of this vibratory sensation—Sonic Whole Overhead System (swos)—is a sonic compression from above as Dolby's Digital Surround EX places its eighth channel on the ceiling of theaters. (Although this overhead channel was successfully tested in Tempe, Arizona, during a screening of the action film *We Were Soldiers*, it seems to be particularly ill suited to the exhibition conditions in India, given that overhead fans are needed in almost all theaters.)[112] A new unique selling point (USP) is that as Dolby sound kinesthetically saturates the space of the theater, as sound becomes moving sensation, it also doubles back on itself and becomes a detachable, value-generating image.

But is this an "extension" of the body, as I seem to imply above, or is it a fundamental refunctioning of the "brain-body achievement" of affect? Mark B. N. Hansen, in his finely textured study *New Philosophy for New Media*, argues that the digital image effects a profound displacement of the human role in perception. In contrast to earlier visual technologies such as the cinema, which functioned by extending the physiological capacities of the body, "contemporary vision machines bypass our physiology (and its constitutive limits) entirely."[113] Hansen goes on to provide provocative readings of new media art by subtly tracing modifications at the level of embodied behavior that are triggered by the new body-computer interface, and in turn trigger new, different connotational consequences: "All of these aesthetic experimentations with the digitization of photography exemplify the Bergsonist vocation of new media art: in various ways, they all channel perception through the computer, not as a technical extension beyond the body-brain, but as an embodied prosthesis, a catalyst for bodily self transformation."[114] We will have occasion to return to—and problematize—the body's prosthesis, but for now I would like to emphasize what I take to be the originality of Hansen's thesis. Hansen notes that the digital image—and he focuses almost entirely on the digital image, excluding the affectivity specific to digital sound—entails that we rethink the very basis of perception, that the new media in fact implies a body reconfigured by "broadening . . . its function as center of indetermination."[115] This should be the starting point, I argue, for a consideration of the digitization of contemporary media assemblages: the reconfiguring and refunctioning of an essentially volatile body-brain achievement of sensation as *launching differential nonhuman becomings across heterogeneously produced audiences*, as different forms of image-sound technologies converge and blur. I will return to this argument below, but it is necessary to flag it here.

Let us return to the adventure of sound in contemporary exhibition practices. Already Dolby has been encompassed and thus superseded by Lucasfilm's THX technology (originally the name of a sci-fi film George Lucas directed in 1971: THX 1138).[116] Consider the branding and marketing of "THX—The Science of Sensation." As the advertising copy for THX technologies informs us: "As consumers seek entertainment experiences with greater sensation and sensory immersion, using precision science to invent new technologies has become paramount. THX Ltd. is continually enhancing these consumer experiences by enabling the creation, delivery, and presentation of digital content through more efficient, more powerful, and more enjoyable methods. With structured certification programs and innovative technology development, THX is embedding the science of sensation in diverse entertainment venues and influential products. Today, the world's premier commercial cinemas, post-production studios and home entertainment products incorporate THX technologies and have achieved the coveted THX Certification."[117] A THX Certified Cinema offers "movie-goers the ultimate cinematic experience." Why? Because every THX Certified Cinema is designed and tested to ensure that it meets "all standards for sound and picture excellence in categories" such as background noise—"controlled noise from HVAC units, projectors, exhaust fans [and] transformers; room acoustics—crisp accurate cinema sound through controlled reverberation and sound isolation; image quality—high resolution, clear images with standardized screen illumination and minimized distortion; projection—audience viewing angles, image cropping, and projector placement that result in the best possible picture presentation; sound system—only THX approved equipment and alignment for optimal sound reproduction."[118] Thus THX is, first, a technology for the radical spatialization of the body's senses, its quantification as gradient of affect; second, an intensification of the real (I return to this below), as directly produced bodily sensations precede and enable narrative immersion; third, a scientifically precise standardization (structured certification) and a value-adding differentiation (one of an elite class);

and fourth, a competitive advantage (both in the sense that it puts space to its most efficient usage vis-á-vis the demands of blockbuster cinema and stadium seating; and that it responds to the demands of more discerning, elite patrons). Indeed, THX maximizes the body's capacities for immersion; as Tim Schafbuch, director of sales, puts it, THX provides some key "value points": uniform "natural" sound balance reaching every ear in the auditorium evenly; improved dialogue; decreased bass distortion and higher frequency range. "So, audiences experience higher frequency sound the highest and lower the lowest."[119]

There are currently three THX certified multiplexes in India—INOX (Pune), Jaipur Multiplex Entertainment (Mumbai), and Star City (Mumbai)—and more are on the way.[120] In Pune (a major college town and the site of the National Film Archives), INOX Leisure Ltd. (a subsidiary of Gujarat Flurochemicals) has followed the "developer model" of multiplex construction, thus creating a movie experience that is closely tied to "lifestyle brands—Barista, McDonald's, and Pantaloon—to offer a mix of movies, food and shopping." According to Shishir Baijal, CEO of INOX, "Inox is a fundamental shift in the way consumers watch movies. Here a movie will start every 30 minutes and ten titles can be showcased in a day."[121] You can text message a booking on your cell phone for any of the movies playing at INOX. The connectivity of this assemblage is emerging: INOX Leisure is technology in motion; its objects, spaces, and screens retail the image of exotic transnational travel; its technologies are centered on intensifying all sensations—tactile, visual, aural, and oral—as they are mobilized through a kind of cross-platform synaesthesia of commodity fetishism; its design and economic rationale is oriented toward families as (intra- and inter-)divisible market segments, different populations; its imaginary is culturally split between cosmopolitan India and PG-13 Hollywood; its bottom line is integrated with global corporate capital; and its regulatory regimes dovetail with American population security. Pantaloon Group (a national retailer that has just tied up with INOX)[122] and its privileged customers just migrated with a green card: "Through its chain of Pantaloon stores, the Company has brought to the Indian masses an ambiance conductive for shopping, and offers customer tremendous convenience to shop. In addition, the superstores also offer a varied range of brands which encompass every aspect of modern dressing in India. . . . As Pantaloon moves into the era of Multibrand and Multi-product retailing, it is time for its privilege program to mature. In our constant effort to offer our customers the best service, we are migrating to a new privilege card—the GREEN CARD."[123]

13. Is it a mall or multiplex? The Malltiplex, IMAX Adlabs, Wadala, Mumbai. Photo by Amit S. Rai.

We should note that, as with the IMAX theaters in India, the THX theaters originally screened fewer Bollywood or Indian regional films; rather, their marketing edge came through a close association with Hollywood block-busters. (This is now changing as niche and boutique theaters, and their new market segmentations, are integrated into retail development projects in the outskirts of major cities.) But outside the "metros" exhibition practices shift dramatically, and other dynamics come into play. Indeed, throughout many north Indian cities and towns it is the pirated image of Dolby or DTS (Digital Theater Systems) that circulates and creates value, rather than the technology itself, which would entail as well an entirely different human-technological interface in the production of sensation. Although only two talkies in Bhopal (out of twelve)[124] have actual Dolby or DTS sound technol-ogy, many others insist they do and they prominently advertise these tech-nologies as their own competitive advantage. There is a historical irony here. Ray Dolby, in remembering his first conceptualization of a commercially vi-able noise reduction system, recalls that "it was in India, while I was doing some calculations on the distortions to be expected from one of the older noise reduction systems, that I suddenly realized that everybody else had been working at this problem from the wrong end."[125] Right or wrong, the imme-diate benefit of the Dolby logo in India today is slightly higher ticket prices at such talkies, which allows these theaters to attract a more affluent clien-tele. The futures of these kinds of digital-aural technologies (that in some sense they represent the necessary future of cinemagoing—crucial to their cultural capital) circulate in postcolonial India as always potentially counter-feit. And that is also their affective pull—a counterfeit mode of futurity.

The proliferation of the piracy infrastructure of old and new media in In-dia has been specifically addressed by the new global regime of commerce. Briefly, under pressure from GATT, the multinational lending agencies and trading partners in the West, the Indian government amended its copyright and intellectual property laws as a guarantee of its intent to liberalize and as a condition for favorable trade partnerships. This led to changes in copy-right law enshrined in the Copyright Act of 1995. This act provides extensive protection both for traditional content as well as for computer-generated content. Enforcement agencies have been set up and the National Associa-tion of Software and Service Companies (NASSCOM), the Business Software Alliance, and government agencies have begun extensive combing opera-tions to curb software piracy. The new copyright law also protects content transmitted by satellite and cable, rental rights of videocassettes, and ex-tends extremely heavy penalties for infringements. One of India's largest private security outfits, Tops Copyright and Intellectual Property Rights Enforcement (Topscaipre) was established on July 2, 1998.[126] It deals with cable piracy and other forms of "cultural" piracy. While the protection of Hollywood films is a priority concern, the severe recession in the Hindi-Urdu film industry in the late 1990s, allegedly also caused by cable piracy, has led to copyright protection becoming a priority throughout the Indian film industry. However, with more than sixty thousand cable operators, only a third of which are registered, the possibility of copyright law enforcement seems elusive.[127]

Notwithstanding the piracy of logos and software, clearly something is happening in the experience of machinic sound in India. For instance, the wave-field of sound achieved by a thousand-plus seat theater like Bhopal's Lily Talkies was accomplished by putting multiple hundred-watt speakers directly behind the screen. The orientation of sound signaled the economic, affective, and symbolic breakdown in the segmentation of sensation: an intense vibratory blare for the lower-priced stalls and floor seats (for working-class individuals), a more encompassing echo for the middle-class families in the balcony. Sound and space worked together to produce a continuous social segmentation within and between audiences. This experience of sound complemented the overwhelming public use of audio (and later audiovisual) media outside of movie halls throughout India at least since independence. Consider in this regard an anecdote that a sixty-something college professor recounted for me of her first temptations by the contagions of film music and sound: "We are talking about around the late 1940s. I was not allowed to sing in the house, by orders of my very strict, serious father (who himself had his acting ambitions thwarted by his older brothers). I never went to the movies, or almost never." So I asked her was it possible when you were young to have a hit soundtrack and the film be a flop? "Yes," she said, "because you have Radio Ceylon. We listened to the radio every chance we got. As soon as my father would go off to court (he was a lawyer), I would turn the radio on. And I loved to sing Bengali songs. I learned them because my father didn't know Bengali. Then one day the owner of the building, he was of a very romantic nature, the owner said to my father, your daughter has such a lovely voice, I want to adopt her. Maybe he had heard me when I was in a friend's circle? I was such a fool back then that I thought he would adopt me. I kept trying to impress them in the hopes that they would take me away. My father kept laughing him off, but would treat him with respect. We lived near a theater back then, and when the show would get out, they would blare music from the theaters. We loved loudspeakers back then. Now, I curse them because they are so loud, they ruin the very holy days they are supposed to help us celebrate, but back then I loved them. Those songs, they flew through the air with such fullness. We all waited for that moment."[128]

The curse is as important as the gendered memory. As a flashpoint for communal tensions, the loudspeaker attached to almost all Hindu temples as well as masjids in Bhopal must be understood in its specific history to social sound in India. This is at least part of my respondent's curse, and I return to it toward the end of the next chapter. I read this as a testimony to sound's public vocation, as well as to the particular sonic quality of such open-air transmissions in colonial and postcolonial India. It is that public quality of sound that is being refunctioned in today's media assemblage, as embodied sound finds new resonances on the plane of the machinic phylum. Writing from another context, Peter Kvetko has noted that with the veritable explosion of Indian pop music (Indipop) in the globalizing 1990s, one of the clearest distinguishing features of the production of this music form has been the lack of the heavy reverberation that characterized much of film music throughout the 1980s and 1990s. According to Kvetko, "Indipop producers prefer a clear tone that will sound good on headphones, personal stereos, and in other modes of *individual* consumption." This is in clear opposition to the echoing sounds sought by film music producers, who attempt to create a sonic space compatible with "the modes of *public* consumption associated with films—such as movie theaters, rickshaws and taxis, and open-air bazaars where film music is blasted from loudspeakers." In another shift of production aesthetics, Indipop producers turn down the treble and boost the bass in their mixes. Although Kvetko at times stereotypes "Bollywood music" with its "high screeching strings and stratospheric women's voices," his broader point seems sound, so to speak. He argues that the older assemblage of sound was more useful in outdoor, crowded spaces and open-air rickshaws. Today's sound seeks the privatized event of consumption: "The bass sound and deeper, softer voices of Indipop music come through better on personal stereos, and inside air-conditioned cars with the windows rolled up." Thus, he points out the topological relationship between physical space and sonic space, each folding into the other. Indipop music finds for commercial sound a new dimension of change and proliferation in the more atomized physical world inhabited by middle-class urban Indians.[129]

But from another perspective—that of a thought of cinema as functional part of a broader new media assemblage—film music is becoming Indipop, and Indipop has folded back into contemporary 1960s and 1970s Bollywood remixes as well—the differences have to do with the kind of dynamic thresholds that define the media assemblage between exhibition space, digital audiovisual technologies, and consumer habituations of private versus public sound. Sound is central to the multiplicity of such an assemblage; it is one of its catalysts, one might say, because sound "is something that is essentially relative—silence for example can only be perceived in relation to something—and dependent upon time. We cannot isolate and break up sound into individual components as we can with film."[130] Relative and temporal, *contagious multiplicities in relations of analog motion moving bodies that are far from equilibrium through algorithmic modulations of subsensate proprioception.*[131] Attending to sound as affect, in short, we access a dynamic threshold where a new regime of consumption is reorganizing the body's entire sensorium, not just the level of meaning, discourse, representation, and the imaginary. For instance, Leela Fernandes has argued that "the specific material conditions of globalization in India, manifested in policies of economic liberalization, have produced a national political culture which increasingly centers on a culture of consumption. Images of the consumption of newly available commodities serve as signifiers that assimilate globalization to the Indian nation-state."[132] In contrast to this in some ways dominant strand of media and cultural studies whose focus on the imaginary circulation of consumable signifiers of the global has limited its effectivity, I suggest we attend to the multiplicities of sensation in the process of their reterritorialization; relative and temporally bound, such multiplicities incorporate image-sound regimes as a dynamic strata of doubling and divergence in an overall production of sensation—but never without paradox and a certain enabling, creative indetermination. As I will argue in the next chapter, the technologies of the media assemblage—the creation of a particular synaesthesia or "occult sympathies" between, say, the body's changing sensations and rhythmic aural space—are central to the globalizing pedagogies of contemporary multiplex space or the contested regularities of population segmentation (balcony, stalls, front benchers, upper caste, lower caste, outcaste, Muslim, Hindu, youth, student, adult male, mother and child).[133] More, the emergence of DJ culture in Bhopal over the past five years suggests that such relations of motion expand the potentialities or lines of the media assemblage itself: from cinema sound systems attracting audiences with a new image, if not experience of sound (in the late 1980s and early 1990s in Bhopal) to compact DJ speakers and mixing equipment used in party and wedding events that further segment and refunction populations already moving through differential flows of this assemblage.

Contagious Multiplicities: Another Name for Media Assemblages

We can trace with some rigor the circulation of image, sound, and affect through Internet websites and TV trailers in new strategies of integrated marketing, thus tying together the libidinal and consumer economies of the café-bedroom-livingroom-theater with pirated video compact disks (VCDs), radio, print publications, etc. For instance, there are obscure but definite connections between digitally produced film hoardings and handpainted ones. The latter have had an enormous resurgence in Bhopal and its surrounding locations since 2000—they are made in nearby Indore, a major commercial and entertainment center in Madhya Pradesh. The bazaar for film memorabilia (for instance, in a place like Chor Bazaar in Mumbai) has a feedback loop relationship to other elements of the media assemblage: as if by digitizing the force of the handpainted creations (themselves a tracing-diagramming of photographic stills),[134] contemporary music video shows and channels (Channel V, MTV India, B4U music, for instance) and satellite film-based channels (Sony Entertainment, B4U, Zee, etc.) maintain a constant demand for an absolutely contemporary nostalgia through the very animation open to the digital.[135]

As I have already suggested, to begin an effective biogram of this assemblage we should grasp it through the modality of a multiplicious contagion.[136] Two provocative feminist rereadings of the nature of this Deleuzian modality have recently appeared. Diane Currier draws on Elizabeth Grosz and Gilles Deleuze to bring a critique of identity to bear on our thinking of bodies, media, and assemblages. Currier notes that for Deleuze and Guattari assemblages are "functional conglomerations of elements" but, importantly, the component elements are not taken to be unified, stable, or self-identical entities or objects—that is, "they are not grounded on a prior unity." Particles, intensities, forces, and flows of components meet with and link with the forces and flows of the other components: "The resultant distribution of these meetings constitutes the assemblage." Currier argues that this formulation obviously presents a challenge to "a straightforward prosthetic account of the meeting of bodies and technologies, where a preexistent unified body and technology meet."[137] Of course the very meeting of these particles, intensities, and forces occurs in the context of other meetings, other multiplicities, and other articulations—in other words, through always unequal relations, unfolding morphogenesis, and histories of power. But assemblages are not "in" history, rather they are its enabling condition as its virtual substrate. For instance, Félix Guattari notes that the term

14. Handpainted film hoarding for *Main Hoon Na* (dir. F. Khan, 2004), Bhopal. Photo by Amit S. Rai.

15. Digital poster for India's first "lesbian" film, *Girlfriend* (dir. K. Razdan, 2004). Photo by Amit S. Rai.

16. Retailer of Indian film memorabilia, Mutton Street, Chor Bazaar, Mumbai. Photo by Amit S. Rai.

17. Aamir Khan for Coke. Photo by Amit S. Rai.

assemblage does not imply any notion of "bond, passage, or anastomosis between its components."[138] It is an assemblage of fields of potentiality in dynamic processes, of virtual as much as actualized elements, "without any notion of generic or species' relation."[139] For her part, Currier ties this question of virtual articulation to a critique of the prosthetic notion of the cyborg, urging a shift toward thinking of Deleuze's notion of "continuous multiplicities" that differ in kind rather than quantity. As Deleuze states in his famous study of Henri Bergson (Bergson himself was drawing on the physicist and mathematician, G. B. R. Riemann): "[There are] two types of multiplicity. One is represented by space (or rather, if all the nuances are taken into account, by the impure combination of homogeneous time): It is a multiplicity of exteriority, of simultaneity, of juxtaposition, of order, of quantitative differentiation, of differences in degree; it is a numerical multiplicity, *discontinuous and actual*. The other type of multiplicity appears in pure duration: It is an internal multiplicity of succession, of fusion, of organization, of heterogeneity, of qualitative discrimination, or of *difference in kind*; it is a *virtual and continuous* multiplicity that cannot be reduced to numbers."[140] Extending this thought in a feminist critique of cyborg theory (specifically Donna Haraway),[141] Currier argues that to think assemblages as "interpenetrating multiplicities" offers a radically different formulation to that of the prosthetic in two ways: first, the mode of connectivity is no longer that of one object meeting another but rather of linkage, exchange, and dynamic phase transitions; and second, the components of any connectivity are multiplicities themselves, rather than unified objects.[142] Further, as Guattari noted, machinic assemblages are "autopoietic machines" that undertake an incessant process of replacing or refunctioning their components as they must continually compensate for the external perturbations to which they are exposed (or what Brian Massumi calls "outside forces of futurity").[143]

Quantitative multiplicities have dominated the thought of media assemblages. For example, Jay Bolter and Richard Grusin, in their pathbreaking work *Remediation*, in the process of describing the movement of attention in the graphical computer interface from one window or website to another, write:

> The new material usually appears in the original window and erases the previous text or graphic, although the action of clicking may instead create a separate frame within the same window or a new window laid over the first. The new page wins our attention through the erasure (interpenetration), tiling (juxtaposition), or overlapping (multiplication) of the

previous page. And beyond the Web, replacement is the operative strategy of the whole windowed style. In using the standard computer desktop, we pull down menus, click on icons . . . all of which are devices for replacing the current visual space with another. Replacement is at its most radical when the new space is of different medium—for example, when the user clicks on an underlined phrase on a web page and a graphic appears. Hypermedia CD-ROMs and windowed applications replace one medium with another all the time, confronting the user with the problem of multiple representations and challenging her to consider why one medium might offer a more appropriate representation than another.[144]

Bolter and Grusin attempt to push beyond the limit of representation-as-media and suggest a body that "both remediates and is remediated."[145] Yet, as Eugene Thacker notes in *Biomedia*, for Bolter and Grusin the body and technology are ontologically distinct entities. Indeed, as long as we think of media as preeminently a kind of discontinuous visual-textual medium of representation that implicates the body from outside, bodily remediation returns us to the prosthetic framing of this interface. But as soon as interpenetration, juxtaposition, and multiplication become part of one immanent and continuously changing sensation—that is of a body-technology assemblage of audiovisual-tactile proprioception—another thought of multiplicity (and the mediated body) becomes necessary.

Unlike multiplicities characterized by difference in degree, which are discontinuous and homogeneous in that they are comprised of discrete units and can be accounted for with a single measure (thus the individual elements can always be identified and understood as self-identical within an always prior unity), multiplicities that differ in kind are of an entirely different order: heterogeneous and continuous. Departing from the framework of quantifiable identity that defines multiplicities of the "One and the Multiple," multiplicities characterized by differences in kind are always in a perpetual mode of differing in themselves, forming assemblages that increase the dimensions of change of the multiplicity itself.[146] Differing in kind describes a movement whereby any change is not one of quantity, but of quality, a change in nature, capacity, potentiality. Multiplicities composed of heterogeneous elements are continuous to the extent that through positive feedback the interacting elements differ in themselves rather than being different from each other, are traversed by a continual movement, or dynamical process of differing. As opposed to discrete multiplicities, such continuous multiplicities are "intensive magnitudes whose nature changes each time they are divided."[147]

One mode of differing for such continuous multiplicities is contagion. Luciana Parisi in her incisive critique of phallocentric filiation in Darwinism offers a view of information trading across phyla through modes of contagion. Urging a radical "reconstruction of the notion of sex, which, far from determining an essence, entails nonlinear transmission of virtual potentials, operating by means of contagion rather than filiation," Parisi shows how the prolonged symbiotic, parasitic associations that precede the appearance of a new organism (a process termed endosymbiosis) challenge the "model of evolution based on linear transmission and demonstrates that each animal cell is the unexpected result of long symbiotic contagions between bacteria."[148] Such contagions and parasitisms are "ecologies of information trading suggesting that a body, far from being completed, is suspended in a field of virtual partialities." Thus, a body, or assemblage, is always "open to its potential contagions arising from the indeterminate transfer between molecular bodies."[149]

Mark Hansen, in pursuing the radical implications of this virtual (non)human body for media studies, makes a strong case for what he terms the "Bergsonist vocation" of new media (art). Through a vigorous and original critique of Deleuze's ontology of cinema, Hansen recasts the fundamental insight of Henri Bergson—that affectivity grounds perception through embodied framing. First, Hansen builds on such thinkers as Crary, Mitchell, Massumi, Simondon, Manovich, Levy, and Virilio,[150] whose work has enabled a new thought of digitality. He shows how the embodied human observer with her or his habituated repertoire of techniques for decoding sensations is displaced by a new abstract regime of computer code where "machinic processes of pattern recognition and statistical sampling" set standards of vision. Computer technology allows a satellite, MRI scanner, or tunneling microscope to capture and process an image then send it to another computer where the image is analyzed and interpreted in terms of other algorithms and data-processing techniques—thus, "vision becomes machinic; and in the process human observers are placed on the same place as machines of vision."[151] More specifically, Hansen builds on Bergson's understanding of the embodied basis of perception (from Bergson's project in *Matter and Memory* to overcome the symmetrical errors of idealism and realism by deducing perception from matter). According to Bergson, the world is composed of an aggregate of images, and perception demarcates the selection of a subset of this aggregate by a "center of indetermination."[152] Bergson reconfigures perception as "a *dimunition or subtraction* from the universe of images: what distinguishes my perception of a material object from that object as it is in itself is not something internal to my brain or something added by me (as it is for idealist positions), but the fact that I can perceive it only isolating certain of its aspects, leaving the rest aside."[153] Exploring the body as a center of indetermination necessitates a thinking of the virtualities of the body, its openness and its constitutive (form-giving or potentializing) excess; the creative body directly through its sensorimotor nexus opens itself to its own indetermination.[154] As Brian Massumi notes, sensory stimulation is folded into the body, except that there is no inside for it to be in, "because the body is radically open, absorbing impulses quicker than they can be perceived, and because the entire vibratory event is unconscious, out of mind."[155] Hansen calls this "affectivity": "The capacity of the body to experience itself as 'more than itself' and thus to deploy its sensorimotor power to create the unpredictable, the experimental, the new." In turn, Hansen reverses what he insists is Deleuze's trajectory in his studies of cinema: from the frame (back) to the body. The frame in any form—the photograph, the cinematic image, the video signal, and so on—cannot be accorded any qualitative autonomy. Its form (in a concrete media event) reflects the demands of a historically contingent negotiation between technical capacities and an ongoing "evolution" of embodied (human) perception.[156] "The bottom line is that we are able to perceive images only because we sense ourselves as form. Perception . . . depends on affectivity,"[157] which is itself preperceptual and autonomic. Thus Hansen launches his compelling exploration of the framing function of the human body as center of indetermination.

For our purposes, Hansen's analysis of "the contagious dynamics of affectivity" is most relevant to a rigorous diagramming of the techno-human promiscuities of India's new media assemblage. Hansen suggests that supplementary sensorimotor connections capitalize on "the contagious dynamics of affectivity in order to attune the body to a stimulus that is novel—and . . . that is so precisely because of its radical heterogeneity to already developed human perceptual capacities. Affectivity steps in precisely where no perceptual contact can be made."[158] This process of affective attunement virtualizes the body by continuously carrying out a "fundamental reindividuation" of the body, which expands the body's capacity to mediate between its own on-going individuation and the individuation of the world itself. For Hansen, affectivity is "the privileged modality for confronting technologies that are fundamentally heterogeneous to our already constituted embodiment, our contracted habits and rhythms."[159]

Does the framing body itself have a frame?[160] Hansen argues that the flexibility constitutive of the digital image "operates a modification of the time-image, a new mode of framing of the actualizing of the virtual: specifically, it resituates the source of the virtual from the interstices between (series of) images to interstices *within* the image itself." Moreover, for Hansen framing is the activity through which consciousness actualizes the transpatial domain constitutive of human (organic) life.[161] But as I have been arguing in these pages, this transpatial domain is in fact itself constituted by technological-human durations of media, and intensive dissipative processes scale these bodily durations as eddies within eddies. Thus, the virtuality of the body must be situated within the evolution of what Hansen, following Simondon, calls the ongoing technogenesis of the human, which would problematize any hypostatization of a given frame of consciousness as resistant excess. What is (non)human about this virtual, excessive body? How can we continue the project of provincializing Hollywood as well as Euro-American technological framings of the body through a contestation with and of Hansen's thought of affectivity as a confrontation with the new?[162]

What is at stake, again, is nothing less than the production of fundamentally, qualitatively new (non)human bodies in the context of changing media assemblages across historical, technological, cultural, discursive, and political contexts. What Hansen never discusses, but which functions as the "given" in his theorization of the framing body, is precisely the "frame" of the body—the location- and duration-specific affectivity of historically varied centers of indetermination, topological image centers in the process of becoming history's untimely body. Despite suggestions to the contrary, he writes as if the body's affects are a transhistorical reserve of indetermination, affectivity as ideal (bodily) form. This is the force of his paradoxical suggestion that the virtual is actualized in the (non)experience of affectivity in the new media. But if we begin with the rather more obscure (yet distinct) premise that the virtual is never actualized, and that intensities (which Hansen isolates as digital affectivity directing technogenesis toward the revitalization of the human) are already partially actualized possibilities, whose field of emergence must be thought as the *unmediated* processes of assembling the contagions of image-sound, the synaesthesia of affect, and variable populations along "ridges" of critical points in their resonating self-differentiating, the media assemblage becomes less a story about us and more of questions pragmatically posed. These questions, as problems that unfold, would take as their conceptual frame a field of potential where past and future meet in pure tendencies, and which in itself is never actualized. For instance, given that all of Hansen's "concrete" examples are staged as decontextualized—*deframed*—confrontations with Euro-American avant-garde new media installations, the question of which human virtuality, which technological frame—not to mention which form of political economic infrastructure—must be privileged to produce this new human is never rigorously questioned.[163] In the next section, I will return to thinking of the specificities of the body's "registration of the in-betweenness of the incorporeal event,"[164] the specific presensate "mesoperception" that the multiplex boom in India is in the process of restructuring.

Continuous multiplicities open to their own specific potential contagions bring forth new spatiotemporalities, rhythms, tempos, and intensive pulsations: precisely what is happening *between* the terms and technologies of Bollywood, Indipop, and Dolby/DTS. Breaking with the measurable linearity of homogeneous time, contagious multiplicities or multiplicitous contagions return us to the untimeliness of chance, to the thought of an always-open risk. (The thought of this risk is internal to the biopolitics of insurance; it is a guarantee against possible [not potential] futures—hence the insistence that media assemblages are folded into security functions across the abstract machines of societies turning more and more toward control and management. I will return to this notion in the last chapter.)

My argument here is that Bollywood, indeed any globalizing media, is an assemblage of interpenetrating multiplicities that establish partial and temporary relations of motion, sticky synergies, or pulsations with and through populations, bodies, image-sound regimes, technologies, timespaces, affects, and potentializing capitalist practices. How can we characterize the nature of Bollywood's media assemblage in the present moment? We could begin by noting how the speed of Bollywood seems to be increasing and its effects intensifying, and that this is the case for two interrelated reasons. First, because the media lines of dissemination are proliferating, Bollywood, and its connected media cultures, can be found all over the world, from Kenya to Iran to Trinidad to Kansas. Hyperdistribution has been the modality of Bollywood at least since the advent of VHS technologies, which suggests that this proliferation is in fact an intensification and refunctioning of an earlier mechanism of Hindi-Urdu film and video distribution: videocassette piracy and its informal circulation was oriented toward the Arab Gulf-states from the 1980s on. But as Wendy Chun has noted, the vector of speed cannot fully specify the multiplicity of intensity in biomedia capture—all of these lines and forces proliferate and are stored in the memory machines as the instantaneously available "enduring ephemera" of desire.[165]

Each site is a potential singularity. While Shahrukh Khan in Port of Spain, Trinidad, is not the same affect-image for the diasporic community in Toronto, Canada, a regularity of sensation traverses the sites. Assembling with stochastic populations of media events, cultural practices, and human multiplicities, an image stream forms a singularity over time, not because it is opposed to other sites of media consumption but because it is "broken or fractured according to the different trajectories of the forces that constitute it."[166] Its resilience depends on the distributive force of resonances between its elements. These event-sites have variable connections to the globalizing circuits of exchange, consumption, and viewing that define contemporary Bombay cinema's regimes of bodily pleasure.

We should note that Indian production houses were only recently granted "industry status" by the government, thereby opening up new avenues of legitimate, or "nonblack," financial underwriting—only for a small but growing minority of top production houses. And even when we acknowledge the creativity of active audiences in the moment of the body's implication in these assemblages, we must understand the overwhelming numerical strength of Hollywood. Considering that as far back as 1992 the United States was yearly exporting around US$3.7 billion worth of media products (as opposed to the European Union's US$300 million), this dominance has only increased in the subsequent decade. Hollywood's presence in India is strong and getting stronger. With a potential audience of fifty million, Hollywood is committed to competing for a market share in India, with a goal of at least 10 percent of the market in the coming years. The Hollywood majors of course welcomed India's decision in 1995 to liberalize the import of foreign films and to raise the quota from one hundred films to two hundred. The government has also agreed to the private negotiation of film imports, which until 1992 had to be channeled through the National Film Development Corporation. The dubbing of Hollywood films into Hindi and south Indian languages has generally been a great success and has focused Hollywood's interest in multiplex exhibition. As Thomas notes, "While *Jurassic Park* cost US$30,000 to dub, it grossed US$6 million in India. Furthermore, marketing 'synergy' for each new release with multinational corporations like Pepsi and Kellogg's has inaugurated an era of intense competition for audiences. Hollywood is also looking towards building multiplexes in India. Time-Warner has explored the idea in Bombay but has met resistance from domestic theater owners."[167]

But Hollywood is looking for synergy in Bombay—not in the vein of cultural imperator but more along the lines of parasitic catalyzer.[168] Thus, Hollywood-dominated economic models for a globalizing media assemblage are spurring the proliferation and profusion of Bollywood's own media lines: Twentieth Century-Fox recently produced *Ek Haseena Thi* (2004) starring Saif Ali Khan and Urmila Matondkar and directed by the new prince of Bollywood, Ram Gopal Varma. Varma terms his strategy as that of pursuing the best of the West: "There's going to be a massive change. A lot of old filmmakers are going to go out of business. Anyone who looks at a film as a formula of one song, two comedy scenes and three action scenes, who doesn't look at the totality of the film, is lost now. Anyone who follows the old prudish traditions, of showing a bush's shaking leaves when they mean people are f—ing behind a tree, is gone. And anyone who doesn't follow the West is gone. For many people in the business, their pride won't let them. But following the West is not surrendering. Following the West, the best of the West, is following originality. Western innovation is superior, and I think we're just beginning to understand that. With my films, I'm targeting the urban multiplexes, the sophisticated media-savvy young crowd. Frankly, I couldn't give a f—for the villages."[169] While it certainly could be argued that Gopal's position is one of the autonomy of Indianness (content) and cosmopolitanism (aesthetic form), unfortunately, rural and poor peoples across India do have to "give a f—" since Gopal's new cinema is helping to define the very consumerist regime that has once again relegated rural life to some kind of vestige of an arrested development.[170] Indeed, the cross-merchandizing pleasures on sale at the new Bollywood multiplexes (both in India and in the diaspora) are mapping ever more territories of bodies and population for ever more speedy dissemination, but through very specific community and subjective controls and modulations.

Bollywood accelerates also as the types of media lines multiply: digital, satellite, wireless, print, Internet, radio, optical cables, DSL, and telephone wires. We should note further that these accelerations in media speeds and these ephemeral, searchable, instantaneous data streams are discernible at the level of diegesis and cinematography: narratives are speeding up, the average shot duration is shorter,[171] long- to medium-range shots enable quicker and more economical editing, the number of songs is reduced, and there is a shift from mass lighting to spot lighting, new pop-formatted music videos, etc. But just as crucially, and contradictorily, the digital sensorium is discernible in the profusion of genres, subgenres (*Dil Chahta Hai* with *Jogger's Park* and with *Mango Souffle*), minimarkets (Chor Bazaar [Mumbai] or Hamidia Road [Bhopal], as black or grey markets for Bollywood memorabilia and media technologies), and through the thinking and extension of surfaces of creative friction in acting, directing, cinematography, choreography, musical direction, lyric and dialogue writing, and the integration of different technologies associated with each of these elements of production. All of these forces establishing relations of motion and difference between and within themselves generate new forces of pulsation. Hence the change in the very nature of Bollywood: multiple becomings, many controls.

Contagious Multiplicities II: The Subjects of Media Assemblages

Here is the thought of the becoming-media of cinema. The habituated modulations of the proprioceptive body—processes catalyzing the contagiousness of multiplicities—trace the diagonal flow of desire that traverses the assemblage, constantly moving from one outlet to another, adapting Walter Benjamin's take on Nietzsche's eternal return: the becoming-media of cinema "is an attempt to reconcile the mutually contradictory tendencies of desire: that of repetition and that of eternity."[172] At one point in my research I interviewed a serious Shahrukh Khan fan; we both agreed that Khan probably is the original "King of Bollywood." The fan had come to New York City as a college graduate in her twenties—a transplant from the small immigrant Hindu community in Minnesota. She remarked that New York provided the fan with so many more "outlets" to connect to Bollywood. For this fan, the Internet was a mode of connecting to the oceans of information on Hindi film, to fanzines, and finally to the affecting body of Shahrukh:

Q: How have you found the experience of Bollywood on the Web?
A: I think it's great. There's just a lot out there, you know. There's almost too much out there, to a point where do you want to read about the stars, do you want to read about their love life . . . I feel you can just read everything now. Um, you can have chat room discussions if you want, though I've never done that. But it's like a whole new level that they've taken it to. Bollywood's definitely . . . it's kinda become like a lifestyle rather than a trend. Like, people are doing everything [through it]. You know, I subscribe to *Stardust*.
Q: You do?
A: (Laughs.) Actually I don't subscribe to it but, because I've been called such a FOB [fresh off the boat], it was my birthday present from a friend of mine.
Q: Ah, but you kept it?
A: But I kept it.
Q: And you read it?

18. DVD cover (UK release) for *Main Hoon Na* (dir. Farah Khan, 2004).

A: Um, the whole subscription . . . So I get it every month now. . . . I mean, you can see all the pictures and the, you know, the photo shoots and whatnot. But I was recently an extra in the *Kal Ho Na Ho* movie . . . Karan Johar's movie with Shahrukh Khan, I did three scenes with them . . . mind you, I don't think a lot of people would because they pay you nothing for an all-day thing in which all you do is, like, sit around and wait. You know, I don't know if you've ever done that thing, but you seriously just wait, and I was . . . just there because the whole, like, aura of being around Shahrukh Khan was so amazing. He is one of the most intense people I've ever been around. Seeing him is definitely an experience. Like, you can see him on film, but to see him act in real life is definitely something.

Q: He's a great actor.

A: He is. He's a great actor and has his expression, and not only just his face but his whole body expression. He's really intense. You know and even just watching him, he makes you just feel what he's feeling. There's a scene where he's sad about it and he's just crying and you want to go up to him and tell him that it's gonna be okay 'cause he just looks so sad.[173]

We could consider these moments—Internet, *Stardust*, movie set, Shahrukh, and affection—not as sequential stages, or lines of a narrative, but as implicated in one another, infolding continuously, and taken to a new level of intensity, and in moments we glimpse the outlines of a phase transition to come. The meeting, for instance, of Internet-friendly digital cinematography (which would include within its own assemblage both technology and brand logo of T-1 lines, Lucasfilm THX, and miniDV) and Bollywood melodrama has produced many skins, many relations of motion, many affects. Its diagram will be a sensorimotor schema. In one way or another it signals the death of Bollywood—which is not to say the end of Bollywood: both Benjamin and Derrida remind us that what is dead wields a very specific force: the force of becoming.[174] The futures of Bollywood are being born within the different fetishisms specific to this cinema—that is, its own fetishes (in no particular and nonexhaustive order: light-skinned virgins, Switzerland, muscular *jawans* [male youths, soldiers], colonial nature, the workerless City, cosmopolitan consumer, and the global Logo) and the fetish that it is turned into in the West (middle-class European Americans were dancing "authentic" bhangra in the aisles during the screening of *Lagaan* [dir. Ashutosh Gowariker, 2001] at the artsy FilmForum in Manhattan)—the proliferation of these fetish surfaces—the skins of an assemblage—guarantee a mutational future, monstrous or not.

A sensorimotor diagram differs from itself, continuously. In this passage from an interview with the queer diasporic grandson of a prominent Delhi talkie owner, a diagram emerges of a system of transformations:[175]

Q: What drew you to Bollywood at that age?

A: "Um, I think it was, you know, the sheer thrill of it all. I mean it was thrill, it was glamour, it was beauty, it was fighting, it was conquering, it was, you know, reinforcing the family spirit, it was, uh, it was a common language between everybody, between my cousins in India and my family in America and my friends in America. It was something for us to talk about. Now most of the kids I grew up with didn't really watch Indian movies, and didn't go to India, yeah a lot of Indians kids didn't—and, later on started to, but they were kind of like, they were struggling with identity in a different situation, and I'll explain later why for me it was more of an Indian thing. And so, later, see I think later on they kind of realized the importance of being Indian. I always felt really mature that way, I really understand the value of being Indian. My parents were like, I mean I started Indian classical music, my parents were really surprised, they were like, "We never played Indian music at home, but you both, kind of, took an affinity to it." We loved it. And I think that's because my parents loved the Indian culture so much that we, in many ways, wanted to please them. So then I went to undergrad and I stayed away from the Indian community a little bit, kind of was trying to foster my own, and then eventually, um, my last two years got involved with the Indian association, and it was a celebration . . . it was the fifty years of Indian cinema. So I did a documentary on, I did a mock Indian movie, fifteen minutes on campus . . . we had so many songs and there was a struggle and, you know, we wrapped it all up on campus . . . And Bollywood has a sheer kind of . . . theater quality to it and whatever, you know, right. So, and I choreographed dances and was designing clothing at that time for the show and stuff. And then the second year we did a movie called *What Would Happen if Fifty Million Indians Took over America*, and that was a study of television. If you're watching television, and there were fifty . . . million Indians in America, the person's changing the channels, what's going on television? So we did Okra and we did Singhfeld. We did, um, *Flintstones* in Hindi, and . . . we addressed issues of parents being like, "Well where was your daughter last weekend?" "Oh, she was studying." And then we'd play a tape of her drinking in a bar and then, parents would be like, "Oh, that's not my daughter. Uh, that's somebody else's daughter," that, you know, we believe in denial. It's the best way, as long as we pretend our children aren't doing it, it's not happening. So, kind of, really . . ."

The acute hilarity of this diagram bustles with many lives. A common language? A cultural code, an identity, a (theatrical) performance, an exclusionary discourse, and an enabling strategy: all of these lines of force suppose a material substrate. What is that substrate? A changing combination of media—writing, TV, film, theater, video, dance, fashion modulating a kinesthetic body. Such a capacious, contagious ecology yields specific sensorimotor schemas that open the self to the thrill of Bollywood as diasporic Indianness, but only to jam its schemata, jam the combined narrative clichés of Bollywood Indianness and American sitcom. But the jam turns into cliché: parental denial.

The proliferation of this cosmopolitan commodity, the globalized Hindi film, has also multiplied the production of these skins, surfaces, plug-ins, hat ke-folds,[176] and amplitudes from Jackson Heights (Queens, New York) to Jahangirabad, Bhopal. The media of the multitude-become-celebrity unfolds its synaesthesia across South Asian life, implicating it in the morphogensis of the newly biotechnologized life of contemporary biomedia.[177] (The question arises, to what political end? What are the politics of a contagious multiplicity? Parisi and others suggest that what is at stake is the thought of a feminist sexual agency—a nonhuman, open, mobile, multirhythmic becoming. I agree with this characterization, but the forces of globalized homogeneity-standardization and the proliferation of (transnational) difference compel another thought as well: privatization and subnationalisms are both "contagious multiplicities"—beyond their spatializing quantifications of human multiplicities, they also generate and function through affectivity, rhythmic durations, and qualitative differences. In that sense we can see that what is contagious about Bollywood can also be habituated in practice and for increasingly greater profit. Here is the short annoying answer: Bollywood's media assemblage does not have an essential politics, but it is always and everywhere political.)

Consider for instance the multiplicities (and their overlapping politics) in the narrative quoted below. A middle-class Hindu woman in her thirties recalls her "first" time going to Lily Talkies with a group of her friends—it was in the mid-1980s. The story is remarkable for its different articulations of urban danger, spatial segregation, communal tensions, and collective viewing practices. It is important to note that Lily was shut down by the city authorities early in 2005 for screening pornography; the operation had been loosing 200,000 rupees for the past two years. Also, long before the idea of the multiplex became all the rage (seemingly everywhere but in Bhopal!), Lily Talkies was in fact a hierarchical duplex—the original twelve-hundred seater Lily built in the early 1970s was for first-run family films, and a smaller one-thousand seater, attached like a protruding appendage, called Goonj Bahadur was built in 1978 and screened second runs, B-grade films, and reruns.

> As a young woman growing up in Bhopal back in the eighties, to my mind and my crowd, Lily was much more [than a movie theater].[178] It was one of the most sought-after fun destinations. One was not allowed to go to Lily often. It was after all situated too close for comfort to the main city, where things were quite "sensitive," and young women had no business being in such places. But Lily being Lily, was the irrevocable queen of cinemas. It was to Bhopal's cine scenario what the Gateway of India is to Mumbai. Movies were the first to come here. The only air-cooled "talkies" of Bhopal at that time, Lily was the place to go. I remember the time when Lily lured me and my group of friends, when we were about sixteen. We were in school and not allowed to go for movies on our own. But the idea was tossed around and a successful strategy devised to win over parents, which included home visits by group members. So there we were. A brightly dressed group of eight smart girls celebrating the end of exams, and attracting in the process hundreds of amused looks. It's not easy to forget one's first movie seen with friends. The Lily complex at that time had two halls, both promoted by the same owner. One, Lily and the other, Goonj Bahadur. Now this name was enough for us girls to go on a giggling spree. The show timings were so adjusted that one could catch the other hall's show in case it was "house full" at Lily. Unfortunately, this was the case that day. We ended up watching Love 86 [dir. Esmayeel Shroff, 1986] at Goonj. I remember clearly how, seated on the Rexene chair with coir beginning to peep out at the sides, I had fallen in love with Govinda that day![179] As we were returning a little disappointed because we could not watch a movie at Lily, we struck a deal. None of us were to divulge it to anyone, especially the other girls in the class that we had

seen the movie not in Lily, but in Goonj. So that was our story when we returned to school after holidays, faking triumph.

At the level of personal narrative, the story is familiar: the excitement of a first nonsupervised outing to a popular movie theater with girlfriends. A gendered experience, no doubt, and yet sexuality as an emergent property of the intercalated sensations of a media ecology functions at a level before experience, in the (non)experience of an event exceeding its actualization, where excitement always verges on paradox. The lure of Lily as a center of multiple attractions: its communal danger and its image-sound-aural pleasures. Govinda in his presuperstar rising. The bonds of secrecy uniting the friends. The disappointment of a full-house show. The awe and love of the filmic image merging with the discomfort of a worn-out balcony seat. The one surface bleeding into another across an indeterminate interface has a modulation, a quality all its own, which exceeds its perception, or narrativization. In some profound way, this experience of cinema, while already an assemblage, is still dominated by the filmic as a kind of node of organization; its connectivities are distributed across typified social space (the dangerous talkie), seasonal fluxes (the end of school term), familial-social layerings and negotiations, the fundamentally collective experience of cinema consumption. What we find in the transformations from this experience to today's "whole new level" of the media assemblage (see above) is a qualitative shift of modulations specific to a media assemblage and a certain delimitation of the individualized interface of consumption—TV-computer-body. Without nostalgia, without lament, we must also see that the displacement of Bollywood's assemblage has necessitated the production of a profoundly different set of presensate habituations catalyzable by today's mediasphere. From talkie to malltiplex the experience of "dwelling" in the *chchavi-grah* (the Sanskritized name for a "house of images"), leaving material traces as a practice of image consumption (recall the overlapping red streaks of paan-juice spit lining the stairs of a typical talkie, or the coir poking out of the seat as traces of past bodies) has become at once dematerialized in the cybermodulation of consumption and reembodied in the singular intensity of the transdurational rhythms of the media assemblage (digital sound and image work directly on the body as receptor; the screening time of a film is multiply folded by its durations as TV trailer and cell phone jingle and product placement and so on). This is not a movement from simplicity to complexity but rather from discipline to the modulation of qualitative differences; neither is it a narrative of a lost past into an ever-renewed present, but a pastness continuing to shape the singular quality of the emergence of the media assemblage.

Excessive Bits of Sensation: Pornography and Censorship in India

Here I begin again from the discourse, as discourse, of a certain excess in Hindi films. Historically there has always been a specific moral charge to the functional relationship between representatives of state and exhibitionary power (constables, tax collectors, gatekeepers, managers, and producers of desiring social flows, or film culture), on the one hand, and the contagions of the film industry on the other hand; a complex interplay of administrative strategies and counterstrategies, pedagogies and transgressions, institutions and singular tangents mark this history.[180] Yet, as only one example, we could analyze the entire development of the state-funded National Film Development Corporation (NFDC) as a kind of national pedagogy to produce examples of productive expenditure in Indian film culture. As the corporation's official website tells us:

> NFDC: Where Ideas Grow . . . National Film Development Corporation of India is the central agency established to encourage the good cinema movement in the country. The primary goal of the NFDC is to plan, promote and organize an integrated and efficient development of the Indian film industry and foster excellence in cinema. Over the years NFDC has provided a wide range of services essential to the growth of Indian cinema. The NFDC (and its predecessor the Film Finance Corporation) has so far funded/produced over 300 films. These films, in various Indian languages, have been widely acclaimed and have won many national and international awards.[181]

All of the elements are here for a certain calculation of productive expenditure: good cinema will plan, promote, and organize an integrated and developed Indian film industry to win national and international awards. The model is arboreal or pastoral, either way the unpredictable becomings of cinema and its contagious excesses authorize this discourse on national film development (as if it were a squandering of national resources), and enable its pedagogies of production, its specific "education of desire" (as Ann Stoler suggests about race and sexuality in a class-divided colony).[182] This pedagogical vocation of Indian cinema was codified around 1928 with the publication of the *Report of the Indian Cinematograph Committee (1927–28)* (which has been well analyzed by Priya Jaikumar): "The pictures produced by these [indigenous] companies are mythological or religious, historical, and social dramas . . . These mythological films are less affected by provincial differences than the social dramas; they have an especial appeal for the uneducated people, and, if they are of good quality, they appeal to the deep-rooted religious instincts of all classes . . . In the social dramas there is frequently a tendency not only to borrow plots and incidents from Western novels, but also to imitate the Western films both in action and treatment. This kind of mimicry is not pleasing or successful. Though much can be learned from the Western films this sort of crude imitation is to be avoided. Indian pictures should be faithful to Indian life and should preserve its essential character."[183]

If this is one dominant conceptual and institutional coding of the role and development of film and its cultures in India, then in this framework popular Bombay cinema is never dissociated from "that glorious operation . . . useless consumption";[184] in other words, moviegoing as sheer "time pass" (I return to this singular spatiotemporality below). One indication of the resilience of this view is the curious but no doubt quite profitable entertainment tax that is levied on all film rentals, a chief cause cited by exhibitors that I have spoken with of rampant tax evasion and dwindling profits. Again in keeping with this productivist framework, only "meaningful" films—often, "women-centered," "social issue" films such as *Astitva* (dir. Mahesh Manjrekar, 2000), *Daman* (dir. Kalpana Lazmi, 2001), or neonationalist films such as *Lakshya* (dir. Farhan Akhtar, 2004)—are bestowed with the coveted prize of "tax free" screenings. The rest are always brushing up against the utterly meaningless, the useless, or the morally depraved, but whose sumptuary excess is effective in both bringing in a steady tax collection and defining a kind of permissible transgression of certain representational and bodily norms.

In what way do these norms constitute a discursive and bodily regularity across a population? One site for the interrogation of this question is the "voluntary cuts" website of the Central Board of Film Certification (CBFC) for a "C" grade, "A" (adult) rated, semiporn domestic production. The codes of editing and framing, of the montage of the ubiquitous rape scene in this well-established genre of films, are overdetermined in light of India's history of censorship legislation. The constitution of a review panel for films shows some of the assumptions regarding sexuality and cultural norms: the balance of national and regional representation; and the relation of power between men and women. First, the film, various documents, the censor fee, and the cess (processing) fee must be submitted to the regional officer where the film has been produced. Next, the regional officer will form "an Examining Committee to view the film." This committee, "in the case of a short film, will consist of an officer of the CBFC and one member of the advisory panel either of whom shall be a woman, and in the case of a long film/feature film, one officer of the CBFC and four members of the advisory panel of whom two persons shall be women." After previewing, an advisory report indicating the category of certificate recommended and deletions and/or modifications is submitted to the chair of the CBFC; there is also a specified appeal procedure.[185] The objectives of film certification are to ensure that, first, "the medium of film remains responsible and sensitive to the values and standards of society"; but, second, artistic expression and creative freedom must not be "unduly curbed"; third, the certification process itself must remain "responsible to social changes"; but certification must also ensure, fourth, that the "medium of film provides clean and healthy entertainment"; and, finally, as far as possible, certification determines if "the film is of aesthetic value and cinematically of a good standard."[186] Thus, the biopolitical reach of "certification" as a procedure of the state mutates beyond the content of film narrative. Every Examining Committee is guided by the "detailed guidelines for certification" published by the CBFC. These criteria are worth quoting in full:

(i)   anti-social activities such as violence are not glorified or justified;

(ii)   the modus operandi of criminals, other visuals or words likely to incite the commission of any offence are not depicted;

(iii)   scenes

        A showing involvement of children in violence as victims or perpetrators or as forced witnesses to violence, or showing children as being subjected to any form of child abuse;

        B showing abuse or ridicule of physically and mentally handicapped persons; and

        C showing cruelty to, or abuse of animals, are not presented needlessly;

(iv)   pointless or avoidable scenes of violence, cruelty and horror, scenes of violence primarily intended to provide entertainment and such scenes as may have the effect of de-sensitising or dehumanising people are not shown;

(v)   scenes which have the effect of justifying or glorifying drinking are not shown;

(vi)   scenes tending to encourage, justify or glamorise drug addiction are not shown;

(vi-a) scenes tending to encourage, justify or glamorise consumption of tobacco or smoking are not shown;

(vii)   human sensibilities are not offended by vulgarity, obscenity or depravity;

(viii) such dual meaning words as obviously cater to baser instincts are not allowed;

(ix)   scenes degrading or denigrating women in any manner are not presented;

(x)   scenes involving sexual violence against women like attempt to rape, rape or any form of molestation or scenes of a similar nature are avoided, and if any such incidence is germane to the theme, they shall be reduced to the minimum and no details are shown;

(xi)   scenes showing sexual perversions shall be avoided and if such matters are germane to the theme they shall be reduced to the minimum and no details are shown;

(xii)   visuals or words contemptuous of racial, religious or other groups are not presented;

(xiii) visuals or words which promote communal, obscurantist, anti-scientific and anti-national attitude are not presented;

(xiv) the sovereignty and integrity of India is not called in question;

(xv)   the security of the State is not jeopardized or endangered;

(xvi) friendly relations with foreign States are not strained;

(xvii) public order is not endangered;

(xviii) visuals or words involving defamation of an individual or a body of individuals, or contempt of court are not presented. EXPLANA-TION: Scenes that tend to create scorn, disgrace or disregard of rules or undermine the dignity of court will come under the term "Contempt of Court"; and

(xix) national symbols and emblems are not shown except in accordance with the provisions of the Emblems and Names (Prevention of Improper Use) Act, 1950 (12 of 1950).[187]

Let me take two examples from the "voluntary cuts" website of the film Certification Board for the "A" rated film *Pagal Jawani* (2000, dir. unknown; dubbed in Hindi from the original Tamil). These cuts were as follows: "Deleted the dialogue 'Hindi film me bhi dhekneko nahi miltha'" (In Hindi films also you don't get to see [sex]); "Deleted the visual of hugging the girl from behind, first by man servant and then by brother-in-law"; "Deleted the visual of breast cleavage of Devi"; "Deleted the visual of swinging the breast during skipping"; "Deleted the visual of lady in bikini in the beach"; "Reduced the visual of blood smear on the lady's face. (Retained suggestively)."[188] Similarly, the voluntary cuts for the "A" rated Hindi film *Hello Girls* (dir. Ravi Kumar, 2001) consisted of the following: "Delete the visuals of man kissing woman especially on chest and close visuals of bare legs"; "Delete the entire sequence of the two girls in tub"; "Delete the visuals of Ajay lying and kissing Neha in song and dance sequence" (twice); "Delete the visuals of Neha undressing blouse in song/dance sequence"; "Delete visuals of policeman undressing girl"; "Delete visuals of man and woman scratching themselves against each other especially the close visuals of embracing each other"; "Delete the word 'Haramzada'" [bastard, scoundrel]; "Delete the words 'tang uta le' [lift your leg] said by Babulal"; "Delete the words 'Jalianwala baug.'"[189]

These cuts, voluntary or otherwise, present a certain ideal regularity in film production and certification (censorship). It is a regularity because the types of cuts listed repeat themselves again and again and are supposedly enforced across genres, but they are ideal because in practice they are applied differentially and selectively. The expletive *haramzada*, to take only one example, is not uncommon in top-tier Hindi films and rarely is it the object of censure. Such an ideal regularity in film certification suggests the most basic and very old figure of the proper viewer—the mass viewer. Impressionable and essentially carnal, the explicitly masculine viewer is projected by a pastoral power that redirects his gaze toward a multicultural, antisexist nation. The visual cuts and dialogue cuts function at different levels, implicitly acknowledging an effective rupture between them. More, often the cut of offensive dialogue is mimed by a voiceless mouth and thus it is clear what was said.

A particular cinematic dispensation for an emerging postcolonial nation cohering a human multiplicity is legible in the guidelines and subsequent censorship practices; the entire procedure of censorship and certification dates its own regime of legitimation from the early 1950s, but its many genealogies tie it as much to the protracted overthrow of Mughal rule by the British East India Company and the contingent functions of an interventionist, pastoral state as they do to the new scientism of twentieth-century biopolitical racism.[190] Indeed, taking a page from Foucault's important series of lectures, through film certification postcolonial Indian society will, from its own ecology of sensation, have been defended.[191] Both the *right* of enunciation (as artistic creation or the production of intervals as cuts) and the production of strategic caesuras in a human multiplicity (state racism) are vectors of the technology of film certification. The delimitation of antisocial, criminal, pedophilic, misogynist, addictive, misanthropic, communal, obscurantist, and antiscientific taboos (referencing, at times, statistical subpopulations) bespeaks the implicit norm: the properly nationalist human order. More, an assumption of the particular effectivity of representation is crucial; not only are the visual and the spoken equated in their direct action upon the sensibilities of viewers (thereby delimiting the domain of validity and effectivity: discrete visuals and collections of words, or "bits"), but "dual meaning words as obviously cater to baser instincts" are expressly prohibited (modulating the sensations in language and in the field of vision). As all nationalist pedagogies of collective expression, what is most threatening is not the indeterminacy of meaning and nonmeaning (obscurantism, double-entendre, etc.), but the very contagious perversity of audiovisual communication: the *body's* implication in collective expression. How can such contagion be stopped? The failure at the heart of all nationalist censorship programs is that film and in fact all audiovisual media proliferate through the contagion of affect, at a presensate level, before meaning, and to the side of language or the visually codeable, fringing it as its emergent potentiality.

Is it possible to legislate for affect? No. But as we have seen it is possible to generate value from its capture and production. Censorship and certification is central to the creation of value within the assemblage of capital, image industry, branding, and state, thereby intensifying the affectivity of this media. Its effect is to channel value by acting as a modulating regime of passage. This is what is missed by critics who insist that either censorship doesn't exist or that the CBFC has been bought out by the ruling bloc for its own ends. For such critics, the industrial status of cinema, and by extension of all media entertainment, renders passive viewers not only anti-art, but in fact anti-human. One seasoned political critic writing in the pages of *Economic and Political Weekly* recently suggested that "films today . . . testify to the fact that this censorship does not exist in reality. Violence is glamourised, degrading and humiliating images of women reinforcing traditional stereotypes are an integral part of today's cinema. Whether it is out of respect for the freedom of expression or a general disinterest, we the public are passive spectators. . . . The State Censorship Policy declares that it is this mesmerising quality of cinema that makes it different from other forms of art requiring greater attention. What makes it far more important for us is the magnitude of capital investment that entertainment like cinema needs. The political economy of cinema is significant as the control of the film industry is in the hands of those who consider it purely as business not in the hands of the minority those who consider it an art."[192] The old oppositions don't concern me here, not because they have been transcended but because they are in the process of reorganization: such classic oppositions as art versus commercial cinema, where art is an island of humane resistance in a sea of prurient sensation, have been rearticulated not just by films as different from each other as *Masala* (dir. Srinivas Krishnan, 1991), *Daman* (dir. Kalpana Lajmi, 2001), *Menaxi* (dir. M. F. Huasin, 2004), *Kya Kehna* (dir. Kundan Shah, 2000), *Mrityudand* (dir. Prakash Jha, 1997), *Main Madhuri Dixit Banna Chathi Hoon!* (dir. Chandan Arora, 2003), *Veer-Zara* (dir. Yash Chopra, 2004), *Zubeida* (dir. Shyam Benegal, 2001), and *Black* (dir. Sanjay Leela Bhansali, 2005), but by the fact that such functional hybridity is also a mobile form of capture specific to globalization.[193] More, the passive spectator has nowhere been more thoroughly discredited as a static template for reception than in studies of the specific modes of engagement of Indian cinema audiences.[194] But, returning to my argument around media ecologies of sensation we must also see that the effects of Bollywood refinancing have numerous planes of operation that are themselves reorganizing. Indeed, the effects of financing changes at the level of narrative, visual style, and ideology must be connected back to the level of bodily affect. But such criticism is incapable of seeing the qualitative change implied in that connection. Instead as Volga, the critic for *Economic and Political Weekly*, has it: "We witness daily what the real estate mafia has done to cinema. A capital investment, which will tolerate only those artists who can fulfill its purpose. It controls the freedom of expression of both audience and writers." But this argument draws closest to the national pedagogies of the Certification Board when it shows the body implicated in this machine of desire: "Recently a group of friends went to view a film together primarily to protest. I see all films—commercial, art or alternative. I attend all the international film festivals in the country. So I have the capacity to tolerate the worst films. My companions were people who chose to view only good films. We were all physically ill after seeing the film. Not a simple headache. We suffered from nausea, vomiting and fever. In the class in which we were sitting there were about 10 people. The cheaper seats were all sold out and packed with working class youth and lumpen elements. It took them around 40 minutes to fully grasp and respond to the horror of that film. Once they had done so they responded and fully enjoyed the film for the rest of the 80 minutes. The violence of that stimulus and response needs to be understood. Youth who have no good schools to provide an education, whose schools have no blackboards or teachers. Youth who have no jobs or have jobs with no security. All they have is air-conditioned theatres with digital sound systems that systematically destroy their aesthetic sense and any shred of human values left."[195] At first it is unclear whether the lumpen elements are themselves triggers for the critic's nausea, but then the humanist sympathy kicks in. Digital sound and temperature control seduce misguided, jobless youth whose habituations are turned away from human aesthetics. To what? To the sensational contagion of cinema's media assemblage.

As one journalist wisely summarized, the problem of censorship and certification is "a complex one." Geeta Seshu marks the issue of soft- or hardcore porn as a defining element in the process of certification. Such films, DVDs, VCDs, cassettes, and print materials are smuggled into the country in clear violation of the laws governing possession and distribution of what is termed "obscene" material. Section 292 of the Indian Penal Code terms as "obscene" anything that is "lascivious or prurient," aimed purely at the sensations and liable to disturb "moral sentiments." The Rajiv Gandhi government passed the Indecent Representation of Women Act of 1989 to cover visual material, an effort that was "widely seen as an attempt to establish its reputation as a pro-women government." The Cinematography Act of 1952, designed to ensure that "healthy entertainment" is provided for citizens, has various guidelines governing the depiction of sexuality. In 1975–1976, the G. D. Khosla committee report recommended that "kissing and nudity be shown on Indian screens provided these are shown aesthetically." Such legislation has been very difficult to enforce given the vague and uncertain definition of prurience or indecency.[196]

Without doubt, in the discourse of certification many of the categories of nationalist film pedagogy—from humane aesthetics to healthy entertainment—were transposed in the early years of independence from the colonial apparatus. As Priya Jaikumar notes in her analysis of the *Report of the Indian Cinematograph Committee (1927–1928)*, "Film historians and scholars refer to the ICC interviews primarily as a product of Britain's racial anxieties over the impact of Hollywood films in India." These scholars, she observes, note that the ICC's stated mission was responsive to an increasingly vocal concern in Britain about the kinds of American films screened in India. "Undeniably, the ICC's self-proclaimed focus was on 'the question of as to whether the censorship was lax and particularly whether a certain class of [American] films were being exhibited which were harmful to the prestige of the white people.'"[197]

In contrast to these critics, Jaikumar urges that we not treat the policy process as "reactive to social context" but rather as an intrinsic part of it; she thus considers "regulatory discourses to be open to the kinds of analysis that postcolonial cultural critics have brought to bear on cinematic narratives and images." She turns her attention to a historical moment when the coherence of imperial ideology ruptured along the lines of a fractured (rather than a unified and dominant) imperial state. Considering that the ICC interviews were a preliminary step toward a consideration of regulatory change, and the British government ignored the ICC report resulting from the interviews, Jaikumar argues that it is precisely the interview's function as a failed preamble that makes it an ideal locus for studying how and why imperial ideology collapsed, adapted, and re-presented itself in different forms when under attack.[198] Her work shows that in this dynamic and volatile context, the danger of cinema was located quite explicitly in its solicitation of the body's sensations. Jaikumar quotes one committee member's opinion thus: "Based on witness responses, Mr. Hamill (member of the Indian Cinematograph Committee) pointed out that the 'danger [of immorality] will remain no matter who produces the film. Whether it is a British or an American company that produces, they will have to cater for people who want sensation.'" But the contagion of sensation mixes with the necessity of colonial racial segregation (the contemporary critic's "lumpen elements" finds one genealogy here): "Rustomji Dorabji (proprietor of Wellington, West End, and Venus Cinemas) screened Western films in his theaters. According to him, after he screened an Indian film titled Lanka Dahan in his theater, he had to disinfect it to convince his regular [mostly White or upper-class Indian] audiences of its cleanliness, confirming his belief that 'The modes of life of different people are different. The type of people who like Indian pictures—their way of living is quite different and generally they are people who chew betel leaves and they make things very dirty.'"[199]

Cut to 2002. The then newly appointed chair of the CBFC—the well-known film director Vijay Anand announced that the Kerala regional board of certification had proposed screening pornographic films in select theaters in an attempt to "save" mainstream cinema in the state.[200] Politicians, media, and consumer groups erupted in protest; even before Anand could put the suggestion before a core committee he resigned in disgust at the (then Hindu nationalist) central government's directive not to discuss any such proposals. The new incumbent to the post of chair, Arvind Trivedi (a television actor and former Hindu nationalist BJP member of parliament), declared: "I am completely against the proposal. It is against our culture and does not reflect nicely on our society." Trivedi was against not merely porn but any depiction of sexuality, yet he endorsed kissing between mother and child and between siblings.[201]

Yet what such heavily mediatized debates obscure is the actual functioning of pornography in Indian cinemas. As Geeta Seshu observes, "In some places, more commonly in small cinema houses in satellite towns across the country, theatre owners interpolate 'sexually explicit' scenes into films certified for public viewing. In Sangli (Maharashtra), for instance, a theatre showing the English film, 'An Officer and a Gentleman,' suddenly began screening sex scenes. Journalist Vasant Bhosale said, 'The actors were obviously foreign and so was the locale. They had no connection with the story and the sequence went on for 15 to 20 minutes. We were startled, but others in the audience hardly reacted. Obviously, this was a common occurrence.'"[202] These "bits," as they are called in the exhibition industry, are interpolated at different times during a screening. At one screening I went to in Mumbai they interrupted the intermission trailers; at another screening, about forty minutes into the first reel a screech and a flash signaled the hard-core porn interpolation.[203] Police constables are often present in the movie hall as these bits are screened, and I have sat in the balcony with fully uniformed officers through an entire screening of such films. The point here is that the very bits of obscene visuals and words separated out to yield "clean and healthy entertainment" through the codes and processes of certification come back in the form of interpolated Western-produced porn bits, thus further dividing an always already interrupted film. This machine of division, and the desire is in the division, is what enables film—not just such films, but film *as such*—to open itself to new connections and new becomings, and assemble with other kinds of media. In a small north Indian city like Bhopal these cinematic bits of Western porn have found a new home on cable TV. As noted in an excerpt from my field notes: "October 2000: MEGA—Movies Easy Get Anytime. Basically, after 11 PM it was until recently a porn channel—full nudity (with a grey patch around the genitals, as if deflecting the finality of the gaze, 'Hindi porn mein bhi dhekneko nahi miltha'). The significance of this is that about one month ago the BJP government proclaimed that all cable operators would be responsible for all obscene material on their channels. The cable operators went on strike. After a protracted battle lasting weeks, they finally won certain concessions from the state government. Approximately one week after their victory, MEGA started broadcasting in Bhopal.

For the past couple of days though it has been a blank. Tonight I saw some new programming on it—they were showing *Star Wars*."

Bits of sensation: I am suggesting that the pornographic bits of C-grade cinema and late-night cable channels—not at the level of content but in their temporality, form, production, and effect, that is, at the level of media ontologies—have connected diverse media under the changing economic scenario of domestic Hindi-Urdu film production. As Vivian Sobchak argues for the digital: "Digital electronic technology atomizes and abstractly schematizes the analogic quality of the photographic and cinematic into discrete pixels and bits of information that are then transmitted serially, each bit discontinuous, discontiguous, and absolute—each bit 'being-in-itself' even as it is part of a system."[204] Working through this thought, consider the multiplication of genres in relationship to the production of bits of sensation across media. As the well-known cinema industry critic Taran Adarsh writes, "In the recent past, there emerged two categories of film producers. One, those who produced lavish, big-budget ventures and the other, who were content producing films with new faces, completing the shooting within fifteen days. Most of them were, of course, soft porn films, catering [to] a niche audience."[205] This soft-porn production process has been adapted to create niche genres in Bollywood's globalizing moment. In Bhopal (and this is true of every town or city in India) the talkies are themselves segmented—split between two or three big-budget film venues and those venues that exclusively screen low-budget, soft-porn, *dakait* (bandit) flicks (often starring Dharmender) like *Ganga ki Saugandh* (not the 1978 version starring Amitabh Bachchan-Rekha; the C-grade version starring an aging Dharmender was playing at Lakshmi Talkies on February 28, 2001). But Adarsh argues that films like *Kasoor* (dir. Vikram Bhatt, 2001) signal a change in the industry: Mukesh Bhatt (the producer of *Kasoor*) started *Raaz*, with two well-known models, before starting on an expensive Anil Kapoor production; Subhash Ghai completed the low-budget *Rahul* in three months, while the big-budget *Yadein* was being edited. This reorganization of production schedules has continued and deepened, as if these fluctuations of duration were indices of an industry undergoing a phase transition. (We could simply call this globalization in *India*, as long as we think of the immanence of processes drawing together the many singularities of the urban and rural timespaces stretching from Lahore to Dhaka, from Colombo to Srinagar— the British administrative territory.) These movies are completed in about three months, within a specified budget and sold for about 3.5–4 million rupees (between US$80,000 to US$90,000) per major territory, and the producers make a "decent profit" at the end of the day. But crucially, as Adarsh also notes, these films must be aggressively marketed in all forms of media to achieve total saturation. As he states: "Let me cite the example of Kasoor which was marketed excellently before its release. Slick promos and an aggressive promotional campaign helped the film fetch a fantastic opening at several places." The modest hit Kasoor was made for about 40 million rupees ($919,000) while a major flop like Raju Chacha was made for 300 million rupees ($6,900,000).

Along with an aggressive blitz across media, but especially through song-dance bits (rarely full sequences, often edited to follow a narrative montage) on music-trailer shows on cable and satellite TV, the development of the mall-multiplex nexus in the major metros is another decisive feature of this new niche genre strategy. Writing in India Today, Anupama Chopra calls these new genre productions "the little big films."[206] Faced with a shortage of stars and chronic box office failure (with figures regularly exceeding two hundred releases for one blockbuster), Bollywood seems to be discovering a "new formula." The new formula seems to speak directly to what I mean by a commercial entertainment industry undergoing a phase transition— central to that becoming would be the articulation of a new winning formula, except that the industry has exploded the very function of a formula: "Films with little face-value that are high on concepts, low on budgets and are completed in a given time frame." Chopra points out that these are not artsy films but mainstream features, "complete with songs and aggressive promotional strategies." (The trend was perhaps started with the popularity of Satya [1998], directed by Ram Gopal Varma.) "Stars, super-exclusive and superbusy, are forcing makers to look at other alternatives. At any given time, at least 50 reputed banners are chasing 10 heroes. But the money and the effort don't guarantee a hit."[207] The key to the success of these new films, according to Chropa, will be expert promotion and distribution strategies. The example of Kasoor's 94 percent of tickets sold during the opening in Mumbai,[208] with its "high adrenaline television commercials" set the standard. The other tie-up is that the new malltiplexes will also help the small film (if not the poor viewer). As the director Raman Kumar states, "We can't make more than 30 big budget movies a year, and we need at least 130 to sustain our theatres. This is the only alternative."[209]

Who is the target audience for these films? In the case of Kasoor (a remarkably faithful remake of The Jagged Edge) the audience was largely made up of young urbanites. Generally, one can see that the traditional domestic market strategy is being supplemented by the constitution of the NRI audience as another crucial element in this developing media assemblage. Thus there are at least three cinema audience tiers now fully in place: the big-budget class-mass flick, the low-budget urban commercial film, and then the dakait or soft porn films for the rural and small town centers. I will return to the role of the NRI as well as the malltiplex in the following chapter.

To conclude: from its earliest days this media of useless consumption has put into play national or imperial pedagogies with exuberant sexualities "deflected from genital finality," as Bataille once put it.[210] Exuberant and excessive bodies perform in the space of the talkie in its policing, in its relation to urban spaces, and in the diegetic worlds that it projects for its always stratified audiences. (As I noted above, the examples of Bollywood's "active" audiences are many, and the literature here is growing.)[211] The analysis of the policing of cinema's excesses in India has often focused on the banning of kissing in the late 1960s in a moral paroxysm following Indira Gandhi's "roti, kapada, makan" (food, clothing, housing) style of nationalism. But filmgoing strategies were never brought to heel through these pedagogies. In one hilarious cartoon from the September 26, 1969, issue of Filmfare the cartoonist parodies both a national morality obsessed with the purity of representation and the violent sexism of male-dominated Hindi cinema. But finally it is the space of the theater, as the lights go down, that is a potential site of unpredictability, danger, and contagion. The last cell of the cartoon reads: "So let them ban the kiss on the Indian screen by all means . . . But let us movie-goers carry on the tradition of our ancestors . . . unhampered." Let me say that nothing of what I have argued necessarily implies that these exuberant sexualities are resistant in and of themselves but rather simply that they are to be objects of multiple and contradictory forms of control, discipline, and pleasure giving off their own potentializing excesses, which in turn authorize new strategies of policing and new pedagogies of productive expenditure. But this potentializing excess is also a contagion, and its multiplicities are unpredictable but patterned. Who knows what they will become, or what we are becoming through them? Rather, the question is how do they work, and how might their diagram facilitate a critical immersion into other never-to-be-actualized potentialities? In the next chapter I aim to elaborate this concept of the contagious multiplicities of Bollywood by looking at the divergent convergence of media and consumerist pedagogies in the space and time of the malltiplex.

PART 2

TOWARD AN ONTOLOGY OF MEDIA DURATIONS

THREE

"The Best Quality Cinema Viewing . . .
Everywhere, Everytime": On the Malltiplex
Mutagen in India

In Corey Doctorow's "0wnz0red" (pronounced "zone-zord") the character
Liam, a computer programmer-hacker from Silicon Valley, becomes a Hol-
lywood-military experiment.[1] Liam's body, which is infected with the AIDS
virus, is retooled: military personnel implant a biomedia interface between
his autonomic processes and a microcontroller. A suitable contagion is
needed first and foremost. Mutagen is an AIDS-specific "bug" that prepares
Liam's brainstem to emit and receive weak electromagnetic fields that can
be manipulated with an external microcontroller ("this latter has a serial
connector that connects to a PC that instructs it in respect of the governance
of most bodily functions"). Liam's body thus becomes a "platform" where
coders run a series of applications that modify his cells to become "virus-
hardened." The aim of the experiment is to create "zombie soldiers." But
Liam hacks into his own source code and edits a variable in the configuration file to "respawn" the process. "Where before he had been running at a
pace that would reverse the course of the HIV in his body in a space of three
weeks, now he was set to be done in three hours."[2] Along the way, Liam escapes from the Feds, goes underground, and remasters his own source code
for the "works" (metabolic controllers, increased dendrite density, muscle
builders, at-will pain dampeners, immunity to everything); he then reverse-
engineers the interface bug to become a "safe virus" that sexually transmits
"wellness," and he infects his best friend and lover, Murray, a "leet haxor"
(highly skilled hacker) like him, with the "Cure." For his part, Murray takes

the mutagen in stride, and together they plan a new startup: "We go into business in some former-Soviet Stan in Asia or some African kleptocracy. We infect the locals with the Cure, then the interface, and then we sell 'em the software. It's *viral marketing*, gettit?"[3] So, given that in Asia and Africa being a hacker is an "honorable trade," how do Liam and Murray plan to make trillions selling the software for the Cure? They deploy it on—you guessed it—Hollywood-developed, double-copyright-encrypted hardware. It is called Honorable.

I begin this chapter on Indian malltiplexes with Honorable hardware and its mutagen becoming to highlight the strategic, functional connectivity developing between autonomic capitalism—*viral, virtual marketing and everyday financialization*—and India's postcolonial media assemblage, where Honorable is not honored. If proprioceptive (preindividual, affective) technologies are the stuff of science fiction, then the contemporary media assemblage draws us to a future that more and more tightly loops through our vanishing present. The future, in fact, is a mutagen.

Consider how one Indian filmmaker and cinephile, Ravi Deshpande, describes the urban cinemagoing experience in the wake of new technologies associated with the malltiplex: "Look at the way you go to the movies in any of the metros today—You've logged in & checked the reviews, you've zapped into the slickly made promos, which in turn, have been made out of slickly shot songs somewhere out there—on the prairies, the mountains, the clean & nice streets—but almost always 'phoren' [foreign], & at other times with lavish sets, costumes & at very ethnic-Indian locales; you have heard the new music that is familiarly a rehash from a groove sampled from a CD—again from 'phoren'; you've found time, you've called amidst stressed city travel & connected cellularly to other stressed but 'wanting-to-check-out-the-film' friends, you have found the money for that Dolby/DTS experience with non carbon arc 'xenon lamp' projection, you have left the sweat-n-smell land & entered the cool-n-clean theater. The lights dim & you settle to view a crisp positive on the new 'Vision' (Kodak stock-stunning skin tones & cinematography)."[4] These are the elements of a continuous multiplicity—cell phone exchange, new multiplex-oriented genres,[5] Internet research, and the digitized cool of the multiplex are synaesthetically co-implicated in the modular body of today's media assemblage—these are the media intervals that are intercalated in the enfolded sensorium of this ecology. The new Bollywood-media interface has changed the very nature of cinemagoing, but it has also defined particular trajectories for the commercialization of the human-computer interface in India. The multiplex is central to this transformation.

This situation diagrams an emergence: a news report from April 30, 2004, on cinemagoing in India announced that Bollywood revenues would more than double by 2008, to $2.3 billion, which would then be supported by "a boom in multiplex building and the deployment of digital cinema to speed distribution."[6] According to *Cinema Systems* magazine, by the end of 2006 there were 145 multiplexes with more than 550 screens, which is still relatively small compared to the approximately 12,900 single-screen theaters throughout India (although some claim this figure is closer to 7,000).[7] But the multiplex boom is still booming, in part because the state, in an effort to encourage the restructuring of film exhibition under India Incorporated,[8] has declared an unprecedented tax holiday for multiplexes for what seems like an indefinite period. Another reason is that the multiplex has been folded into specific strategies of global retailing, given that the vast majority of multiplexes—around 75 percent—are located in or adjacent to those highly secured, private playgrounds of public consumerism, India's new transnational malls. This co-evolution has been facilitated by the assemblage of media platforms aimed to increase revenues by seamlessly multiplying interactive interfaces in the act of consumption. The recent development of movie-based value-added services in cell phone technologies is one example of such an assemblage; another example is the tie between INOX, a pan-Indian multiplex operator, and the retailer Pantaloon Group, which will ensure preferential access to all real estate development by Pantaloon. But as we have seen, new digital technologies do not merely speed up distribution, since the interface between broadband and BitTorrent (or some other peer-to-peer protocol) will most likely transform the entire field of distribution itself; so these revenue forecasts remain in the realm of "science fiction." From first day, first show frenzies at single-screen talkies to the new multiplex boom, the globalizing media assemblage of contemporary Bollywood is emerging through its new connectivities: digital images, spaces, sounds; cross-merchandized consumption; population resegmentation; immersive experiences focused on the autonomous life of the sensations. Honorable and pirated, this is cinema's sensorium multiplexed.

My title for this chapter comes from the brand tag for PVR, Ltd., "a pioneer and a trailblazer in Multiplex development in India" (the largest multiplex in India is owned by PVR).[9] My thesis throughout is that the malltiplex is a diagram of a power that acts by multiplying the body's connectivities (its ecology of sensation) through specific channels of controlled consumption (digital security). Currently there are eight major multiplex companies in India: PVR, E-City, Inox Leisure, DT, Cineline, Adlabs, Wave, and Shringar.

Contemporary Bollywood news shows are claiming that the rich have returned to the movie halls because of the multiplex.[10] The malltiplex offers glamour, clean toilets, a variety of viewing choices, and different kinds of family entertainment. To encourage this numerically massive market audience, many states have waived for multiplex owners the entertainment taxes for a given period of years (and have reduced taxes for a period after that time).[11] In the short term, this allows the owners to charge high ticket prices, which translates into bigger profits for distributors as well as a narrower, more docile audience segment. This shows as well the close collaboration between new exhibition strategies, the new media, and state economic policies; the new media timespace, deterritorialized in its self-image, diverges and converges with the liberalizing (and also protectionist) Indian state.

In coming years much more will be written on the social and economic history of the birth of the malltiplex in India; this chapter is a contribution to that conversation. I begin with the affections of the multiplexed body. My method in this analysis of converging media and postliberalization capitalist technologies correlates different kinds of connectivities emerging between the community, media technologies, the remediated body, and capitalist timespace in India. What is at stake, again, is how the question of sexuality is posed during a phase transition in its ecology of sensation.[12] My argument is that proprioceptive technologies such as the malltiplex are targeting the affections of the body in an unprecedented way. This is unprecedented precisely because the overflow so central to capitalist accumulation in the realm of affect is a way of harmonizing resonances in the body at the paradoxical limit (or incipience) of emotion, where hate is love if only because the matrix of sensation pushes the body to action, yielding new habituations of attention, new durations of media intervals, and new pre-individual sexualities. It is here, and only here, in the durations of media intervals, that an assemblage analysis of sexuality can diagram an ontology of becoming. This line of thought pushes us to ask how is the spacetime of the body reconfigured in the new multiplexes? Which gendered, aged, communalized, classed, and caste bodies activate what rhythms of pleasure and desire in the social act of viewing, in the struggle over the gaps of interruption of transmission and intermission? In drawing out the implications of an analysis of sexuality as an ecology of sensation multiplexed, I explore the set of phenomena that point toward an emergent diagram of the body in the shifting domain of affect.

A certain image of multiplicity, the social demand for a new kind of security, and minority becomings of sensation draw the multiplexed body toward specific consumerist habituations. The malltiplex mobilizes the affections of the body, which are linked to a zone of potential—the immediately virtual body, where experience is presensate proprioception, and thus cannot strictly be experienced or perceived. As Brian Massumi warns, this requires a reworking of how we think about the body: "Something that happens too quickly to have happened, actually, is virtual. The body is as immediately virtual as it is actual. The virtual, the pressing crowd of incipiencies and tendencies is a realm of potential. In potential is where futurity combines, unmediated, with pastness, where outsides are infolded and sadness is happy (happy because the press to action and expression is life). The virtual is a lived paradox where what are normally opposites coexist, coalesce, and connect; where what cannot be experienced cannot but be felt—albeit reduced and contained."[13] The solicitation, reduction, and then containment of affect are the bodily effects of the contemporary multiplex biogram. What happens in the interval, in the serial movements,[14] if the pure transitivity of its spatializing and rhythmic operations is unstable and riddled with the aleatory? For instance, the population flow from box office through ticket collection gate to concessions stand to auditorium seat and to restroom and then back is designed to control (but never quite can) the possibility of individuals or small groups sneaking off into another auditorium, then back into the restroom, and then off again into a different auditorium, and so on. (In the United States I have heard people recount gleeful stories of passing whole summer days going from show to show in air conditioned multiplex bliss.) On the one hand, we can see that such possibilities are already a kind of capture of the zone of potentiality suggested by Massumi; such sabotage is internal to the multiplex diagram and its probability has already been factored into the calculations of risk that constitute its design for utility maximization and "relative" accumulation.[15] On the other hand, I argue that in India it is in the feedback-driven thresholds that are forming between multiplex technologies and mediatized bodies, indeterminately folding into each other (rather than forming a static prosthetic relation), where something more obscure but profoundly effective is emerging.

In the media assemblage, sensory-motor habituations infold and unfold in the production of sensations. These processes have distinct and obscure relations to an always contagious outside (futurity); the schemata are systems of transformations that follow an analog logic, branching off from an algorithm-determined digital: a qualitative topology in partial conformation to what the past is for it. Massumi glosses topology as the "science of self-varying deformation." A topological figure is defined as the continuous transformation of one geometrical figure into another—a purely qualitative science. It is not empirical, in the sense of progressing from description to prediction: "It has no predictive value." Incapable of directly referencing anything other than its own variations, it is more analogical than descriptive. Without model or referent there is only infolding and unfolding, or self-referential transformation: "The analog is process, self-referenced to its own variations." It resembles nothing outside itself, and its diagramming begins with a rupture from the regime of representation. A "topological image center" makes the virtual appear, in felt thought or intuition, an ontology of the apparitional as much as the empirical. Sensation always emerges as a transformative feeling of the outside, "a feeling of thought, matter becoming in an analog mode; analog in the sense of a continuously variable impulse or momentum that can cross from one qualitatively different medium into another. Like electricity into sound waves."[16] Or like reproducible digital light processing images into an excessive haptic vision: the image breaks with the ontological grounding of representation in the Signifier, returning the topological image to the synaesthetic body.[17] It is in this sense of incipient movement where a series of singularities establish volatile channels of information flow that function as dynamic thresholds opening the assemblage to outside forces of futurity that we should pursue a diagrammatic analysis of aural-imagistic regimes.

Further, the image-sound-sensation field is a "pure" field of synaesthetic vision, sound, touch, and taste, which means it is a virtual field of resonant emergent properties. The interconnected units of vision as a separable sense themselves arise from this level of emergent perfusion. That is, even if they are always already there, when they will have been there visually, it is "on the more encompassing condition of intersense fusion." Distinct and obscure, always the almost-something of prior levels of an indeterminate synaesthesia, the visual is never sufficient in producing vision. If the other senses have abstract surfaces of skin and muscles (proprioceptors), the nose (olfactory receptors), the tongue, and the ears combine with the limit-field of vision to form the open containment field of experience. "The virtual self-standing of vision actually takes place in a crowded bubble."[18]

A sensory-motor schema, in other words, virtually diagrams the body-technology assemblage as an event of nonactualized and actualized futures. It is a virtual diagram because the level at which the schema operates is a continuous multiplicity of deformations, lines of flight, deterritorializations, potential and actual functionalities, and modulated intensities, pure resonances spontaneously self-organizing, without mediation. It is the unformed substance—the material substrate—from which discourse, representation, ideology (cliché), and regimes of truth take their form and specific force. This is not because the sensory-motor schema is the truth of representation, but just its enabling condition, its condition of effective force. Deleuze was fond of quoting Sartre, who said that "every image is surrounded by an atmosphere of world."[19] This atmosphere of the image (I have been calling it an assemblage; Gilbert Simondon called it an "associated milieu")[20] is the sensory-motor field, its plane of functionality. It is not what the schema is, then, but what it does. And part of what any image-sound-sensation regime does is open the body to the virtual incipiencies of events yet to come, of futures that will exceed their actualization in events that proliferate through contagion and sheer potential.

Consider the qualitative passage through image-regimes from flat-screen computer-controlled interface in the lobby (where viewer is also user),[21] to immersive, full-wall projection screen, to looped video display over a urinal or inside of a stall door, to three-dimensional promotional plastic soda cup "toppers";[22] or the tunneling of sound from diffuse chatter resonating from wall to ceiling to floor to ear in the lobby, to the science of individually "feeling sound" in the digitized experience of THX in the auditorium. Unlike the experience of the ticket as virtual object on a first day, first show, the field of virtuality in the multiplex has been generalized as the solicitation of affect, which occurs at every moment drawing the body in multiple and yet continuously modulated directions, thereby producing a regularity of sensation that is formalized through mathematization into algorithms, probabilized by calculating populations of events for a given set of recurring risks, and technologized in the assembling of the differentiated body through specific navigable data interfaces.

My argument here is that contemporary corporate malltiplex design globally considered aims to bring together more and more finely calibrated regimes of sensations, thus producing an ecology that dissociates pleasure from any specific expression of sexual identity and implicates it in a virtual-actual circuit of preindividual sensation. In other words, modular technologies of sound, sight, taste, and tactility engender a bodily experience of synaesthetic sensation, or sensation implicated within each other, with ever renewed intensity: the total dream of cinema is "virtualized" in the media assemblage.[23] In the malltiplex singularity, we confront the continuous quantification of the image through various forms of digitizing image technologies and their ever more sensational projection; the illusion of infinite if banal freedom in the "choice" of movies, locales, show times, food, drink, types of seats, video games, etc.; and the "full" immersion of the body in image-commodity consumption through the simulation of reality as its intensification.[24] Potential thus moves into possibility: corporate malltiplexing.

But if we take affect as the virtual point of view we follow effects that are synaesthetic, where the senses participate in the durations of each other. The "measure of a living thing's potential interactions is its ability to transform the effects of one sensory mode into those of another." Massumi diagrams affects as virtual synaesthetic perspectives anchored in or functionally limited by the actually existing, particular things that embody them. And the autonomy of affect is its participation in the virtual. "Its autonomy is its openness." Massumi argues that affect is autonomous to the degree to which it escapes confinement in the particular body whose vitality or potential for interaction it is. This escape would be a line of patterned but unpredictable differentiation across a channel of communication—a form of stochastic connectivity, in other words. "Formed, qualified, situated perceptions and cognitions fulfilling functions of actual connection or blockage are the capture and closure of affect. Emotion is the most intense (most contracted) expression of that capture—and of the fact that something has always and again escaped."[25] This escape is the participation of the singular experience of affect in the virtual and not the resistance of a sexual identity to heteronormativity (although it may involve such resistance on another level of experience). Rather, it is the constitutive openness of the body in the process of implication or co-emergence in media assemblages: interpenetrating continuous networks of sensation, matter, image-sound technologies, and codified, codifying control space. Here we follow a thought of the multiplex as duration, space, and discourse. So beware: synergy is not synaesthesia, nor is virtual escape revolutionary resistance, or subversive excess: it is the continuation of the event beyond its actualization. At the unstable and unpredictable interface of dynamic connectivities, bodies-technologies yield a remainder of indetermination, as an imperceptible echo infolding multiple futures.

The Malltiplex in a Transnational Frame

Other national examples can be useful in understanding the Indian singularity. In China and Hong Kong, the malltiplex boom has been in full swing for at least a decade, and it displays some global regularities. As Stephen Teo writes in "Postmodernism and the End of Hong Kong Cinema": "One concrete example of 'postmodern' restructuring in the 1990s is the virtual disappearance of the old picture palaces in the territory to make way for multiplexes and mini-theaters. In their own way, the rise of the new multiplexes shows Hong Kong succumbing to the pressure of Western-style 'uniformity.' But . . . postmodernism in Hong Kong cinema shows quite another proposition: Hong Kong society reacting against cultural uniformity."[26] As Teo goes on to argue, this uniformity together with its reaction is postmodernism. Multicultural uniformity can be thought of as one of the global regularities that the malltiplex heralds.

Specifically, first, malltiplexing cinema culture necessitates a corporate strategy of transnational copartnering. In 2004 the IMAX Corporation announced the official opening of the first commercially operated IMAX theater in the People's Republic of China. The IMAX theater at Peace Cinema, operated by Shanghai Evershining IMAX Theatre Co. Ltd. and Shanghai United Cinema Line Co. Ltd. (one of China's largest commercial exhibitors), will be the first in the region to show Hollywood event films that have been digitally remastered into IMAX's 15/70 format using the company's proprietary IMAX DMR technology.[27] The use of specifically proprietary technology folds the logo DMR back into the experience of the technology itself (as we saw in the case of Dolby in India); this folding, in turn, doubles another—the national company is reterritorialized by multinational "pacting." For instance, when Warner Bros. pacted with Shanghai United Circuit to build and operate two more multiplexes in Shanghai, it also partnered with the distributor Shanghai Paradise and the Hong Kong–based Broadband Investment; Warner announced intentions to take majority stakes in the theaters when the Chinese government, acknowledging that the industry needs an international financial base, signaled that it would raise the 49 percent cap on foreign investment.[28] (Another similar example is the partnership between Christie and major Korean exhibitors such as CJ Gold Village Co. Ltd., Lotte Cinema, and Eugenetek Corp., and Mexican exhibitors like Cinemex.)[29]

In India the malltiplex boom is fueling contemporary film production and helping to segment the possible audiences in terms of class, caste, gender, and religion. Without question, one of the key sources of capital for this massive expansion comes from North America, and more specifically Hollywood. Indeed, the malltiplex has been explicitly marketed for Hollywood productions. "Plexes" in Mumbai, Delhi, Gujarat, Bangalore, Chennai, Pune, Kanpur, and, recently, Kolkata—a total of thirty in all—drove up 2004 earnings for Hollywood by as much as 75 percent to $20 million. Bollywood movies have soared at the box office by as much as 60 percent to $250 million. India's first multiplex chain, PVR, which is owned by the Delhi-based Bijli

Group, is adding two luxury auditoriums to its five-screen multiplex PVR Gurgaon, located in New Delhi, in order to draw the "kinds of urban, sophisticated viewers increasingly targeted by plexes."[30]

The first wave of multiplex construction swept through the major metros in the late 1990s, accompanied by a boom in mall construction: the mall and the multiplex, the twin arcades of postmodernity, thus emerge from one technology. The malltiplex adapted and transformed older new media assemblages throughout India—an example of which is the local bazaar (haat), typically near a major bus stop, which had different shops selling cassette technology.[31] This older media assemblage, which dominated the national and regional media markets from the late 1970s well into the 1990s, relied on patterns of distribution and consumption centered on Hindi-Urdu (or regional) film. The relative flexibility of cassette technologies—cheaper, more durable, and more portable than vinyl, with low power requirements and more easy to produce and, in turn, to dub—encouraged a very high proportion of pirated music cassettes circulating through these circuits.[32] As we shall see, both this flexibility and its attendant piracy are targets of the new media security regimes of mall and multiplex.

Indeed, the rise of the malltiplex, with its inexhaustible ambitions for a commodified sensorium, spilling far beyond the acquisitive gaze of film, is perhaps a turning point in the organization of cinema's sumptuary practices. Bodily and monetary expenditure as absolute loss, as useless consumption has now consciously been integrated into pedagogies of capitalist consumerism across a variety of integrated media in India and globally.[33] Aparna Sharma has noted that although the Indian malltiplex is patterned along the malltiplex model developed in the West, it sports all the features of an upscale playground. The retail boom unleashed by the economic liberalization policy sustains the malltiplex, and it is thus aligned with and extends the transformation of India's urban milieus within the framework of globalized consumerism. The malltiplex's steady proliferation in the metropolis and simultaneous penetration into some smaller cities and towns testifies to its close association with a globalized modernity, which coincides with the rise of disposable incomes in the hands of the urban Indian family.[34]

One could argue that this practice has adapted and narrowed an older habituation common to north Indian film culture—namely, the ubiquitous practice of "repeat viewings." Going to see a favorite film ten times or more was not only common but a key marker of authentic fandom for the filmgoers I spoke with in Bhopal. The convergence of the malltiplex with image-branding strategies and with satellite and digital cable technologies has irrevocably altered this habituation. What happens to the sensation of experiencing an image-sound stream when the elaborate and elongated prerelease media campaign that today accompanies major productions modulates the duration of the stream itself by folding in websites, cell phone jingles, product tie-ins, radio promos, TV shows, fanzines, posters, and hoardings (on buses, trains, taxis, etc.)? Is this merely a technological extension of the old dream of film executives to saturate audiences with differently paced and placed film images? Certainly in this case technology has extended the reach of film advertising, but the act of deploying micronarratives, plastic "collectibles," songs, and visual, aural, and aesthetic styles in integrated platforms, I argue, implies a qualitatively (not only quantitatively) different experience of the image-sound stream itself. The stream becomes brand. The effects of this branded saturation can be felt spatially: the city becomes a palimpsest for the film's signature visual—usually a man and woman in some form of rhythmic embrace, with a specifically stylized title and subtitle—on massive digitally produced hoardings; on flyers pasted on any remotely flat surface; on bus, taxi, rickshaw, and train advertisements painted on bridge walls and along train routes. And from rickshaw speakers, CD/tape shops, and car speakers the latest "hit" soundtrack floats through the air.

As I've already suggested, this transformation has a specific temporal dimension as well: what, for instance, does the popular Indian phrase "time pass" actually name historically in relation to the social practice of cinema in India?[35] This is where an assemblage analysis of Bollywood media should begin: in practices of time, in the specific durations of a multiplicity. And this is also where politics begins: by changing the media's ontology of duration we extract experiences of the untimely in Bollywood today. The singularity here, the durations of the media event, is a fuzzy set of correlated practices that function as a sensory-motor circuit of media consumption, a strategic halting, stuttering, a pausing over and in sensation.[36] There is no anticipation in time pass, it happens all at once and not at all—when time passes loitering in the mixed streams of contemporary media one finds oneself in the middle of events that exceed their actualization, waiting, wondering, the banal mixing with the monstrous. This excess, which is not representational but mutational and virtual is the basis of an embodied politics of dominant Hindi-Urdu cinema. There is nothing but pure untimeliness in the gaps of time pass.

One of the implications of time pass, the popular image or, better, sensory-motor circuit of moviegoing, is, I think, a habituated form of affective open time[37]—time's divergence from itself in the act of cinemagoing, as when time bifurcates, halts, or "dies" as one's body is implicated in a media stream. Such regulated but volatile durations of media experience were central to this film culture, and are now in the process of becoming something else. Thus open time is also in the sense that in consuming or "partaking" of extra-diegetic star auras, the renewed past of cinema unfolding activated the memories of viewers who in turn rendered that memory audible in anticipated but involuntary shouts of acknowledgment for heroes, heroines, songs, scenes, or intertextual allusions. Time pauses as an immediate memory contracts the image-sound in the timespace of the media event, viral memory as a kind of interactive repetition of indices or attention-attractors distributed throughout the media ecology, and finding resonances in the feedback of active audiences. The time of cinema opens as well in anonymous hoots of displeasure for power outages, audiovisual failures, broken fans, bad dialogue, or zealous ushers and ticket checkers (an active antagonism between the managers and workers of exhibition spaces and working-class and youth audiences). More, the notion of time pass has often been integrated into the idea of its pleasurable return—that is, in the future of repeat viewings, cinemagoing as pastime and as a way of killing time is not its dissolution but rather the rendering of time into a repeatable packet of memory. Here in the open time of filmi time pass, the fragmented present of cinemagoing (so well analyzed by Lalitha Gopalan in *Cinema of Interruptions*) seems infinitely divisible, reopened as it were, in the form of talk back, sing alongs, crying, bathroom breaks, diegetic gaps, waiting in line, forced scene or song replays,[38] and of course the ubiquitous intermission. These differently experienced aspects of cinema culture's temporalities break apart the discrete packet of time that defines the pedagogies of film culture in the West (although one could show that elements of fragmentation and interruption also structure cinematic temporalities in the West).[39] Time pass films, despite their generally acknowledged formulaic mediocrity, were social events that integrated the specific theater into the body's social passage; in that sense the singularity of the event was indissociable from the specificity of a theater's space. (I return to Bollywood's time pass below.)

It is this sensation of killing time, its passing as a space-specific form of unproductive expenditure that is being fundamentally refigured both through the technologies of discrete pleasures in the malltiplex (most noticeably with the deletion of the much-loved intermission, at least in certain diasporic settings such as Loews Cineplex in Times Square, New York) and the forms of bodily and communal security emerging through discursive practices of the non-resident Indian (NRI).[40] The malltiplex has mapped its own relation to temporality and filmic duration through a new economy of cross-genre integration, genre and audience segmentation, and multiplication of rentable exhibition space. Aparna Sharma points out that the multiplex has not followed the conventional 12–3–6–9 time schedule prevalent in most single-screen cinemas. The multiplex created opportunities to schedule and program films on different screens, thus allowing for films of varying lengths to be screened. This encouraged the production of shorter, more Western-oriented films, with few or no songs.[41]

Manipulable schedules presuppose films of different length that can be slotted into specific time spots: thus dominant cinema's "formula" is heterogenized *as the new itself*. Such changes imply that the very durations of film at the level of production—length, but even average shot duration—are shifting to meet this new media assemblage context. In what follows I will diagram the relations of motion in this new connectivity, and then I will turn to the multiplex and its attendant habituations. First, we must grasp how the nature of Bombay cinema facilitated an integral connection to TV: due to its fragmentary narrative and musical form a new functional connectivity was enabled with the consumer cultures of malltiplex-satellite and cable TV throughout India. And yet we must resist the assumption that the experience of image-sound regimes in these different media remains static across technologies. John Sinclair and Mark Harrison argue that "the staple popular genre on television is the Indian film, with its characteristic music and dance."

> As well, some of the most popular panel and game shows are based on film music, notably Sa Re Ga Ma and Antakshari . . . This has meant that the proliferation of channels has also been a stimulus for the Indian film industry, and not only Bollywood, the Mumbai-based Hindi industry, but also those in some regional languages, especially Tamil. To that extent, film retains its preeminence as the powerhouse of mass-mediated popular culture both in India and for Indians abroad . . . Indeed, a recent report suggests that due to the profusion of Indian films and film music programs on television, cinema attendance within India is dwindling. Nevertheless, film remains profitable, thanks to the sale of television rights in India and the international cinema and music rights, especially for diasporic Indians in the United Kingdom and the United States.[42]

I have argued in this study that the nature of Bombay cinema—its qualitative durations, its functional connectivities—changes in the context of the new media assemblage, and the assemblage changes from itself as well, as a continuous, self-differing multiplicity. This qualitative change is missed when we assume that Bollywood on cable or satellite TV, and film music traveling, for instance, across national borders through the Internet doesn't do something fundamental to the experience of cinema. No doubt it maintains a certain regularity, a certain consistency, but does that mean we must assume that regularity and consistency is homogeneity, the banal repetition of the same? Indeed, this bias against the qualitative changes of the media assemblage of contemporary commercial cinema comes from a basic misunderstanding of the nature of the aural-imagistic regime of Hindi-Urdu cinema itself. Indeed, much of what Dick Hebdige argued for the "pop video" in the 1980s could be said to characterize not only the song-dance segments of Bombay cinema but the very cinema itself. Hebdige argued that Britain, as the home of the pop video, developed the potentiality of the pop video into a protean (ideal) commodity. Drawing on his argument, we can see the filmi song-dance sequence as neither "pure entertainment" nor "straightforward promotion," rather it is a commodity in itself (i.e., it is sold in shops, consumed on TV, radio, cell phones, and Internet); it is designed to sell another commodity (the movie, the singer or band, the music director-choreographer, the clothes style, the image, the attitudes it forms an assemblage with); to "tell," often through nonlinear narrational devices, an image or a story—the image and narrative of the movie, the brand of an actor, a production house, a singer, or group. From a viral marketing strategy, the symbiosis of song-dance and cinema stream turns in such a way that the image and the sound, the song and the movie, "chase after each other (i.e. sell each other) in a double helix which seems to promise cash for all concerned."[43] Many of the conditionalities that Hebdige argues for the emergence of pop videos were central to Bombay cinema from at least the late 1960s onward; certainly the current connection between the branding of a star's image-aura, the proliferation of new fashion industries, the continuing popularity of satellite TV trailer shows, the malltiplex boom, and changes in the production, finance, and codes of cinema show that these connectivities have reached a critical ridge inaugurating a general phase transition in the affect-based aesthetic of Hindi-Urdu cinema itself. Recall Gopalan's suggestion that these potentialities open "the film text to other economies of production and reception."[44] Indeed, this globalizing media assemblage has radicalized the "undecideability" of Bombay cinema. In the context of dwindling profits from single-screen theaters, and the synergy of image-sound and consumerist regimes established between Internet, TV, music channels, fashion designer boutiques, CDs, and cinema, the malltiplex developed its own unique selling point (USP).[45] It is here that we must probe for the emergence of the biogram of the new media assemblage: a virtual synaesthetic capacity in excess of the multiplex's bodily regime of consumption.

The Co-emergence of Perception and Media

The synergistic consumerism established by the malltiplex has been crucial to the history of cinema in America, but it must be situated as part of the more general restructuring of Hollywood since 1975. As is well known, Hollywood's initial response to globalization took the form of specific mergers throughout the 1980s that were characterized by vertical integration (starting with Columbia Pictures in 1986, the major film companies bought or acquired stakes in important theater chains around the country), the desire to control the production of programming, the distribution of programming (starting with Rupert Murdoch's acquisition of Twentieth Century-Fox in 1985, the majors began a new era of horizontal integration by controlling media distribution) and the exhibition of programming. As one industry watcher put it in the early 1990s, the rationale for merging was a "faith in synergy, a belief that one plus one could equal three."[46] A second kind of response to globalization was to establish an international base of motion picture financing. For instance, to reduce its debt load Time Warner restructured its film and cable business and created Time Warner Entertainment as a joint venture with two of Japan's leading companies, the electronics manufacturer Toshiba and the trading giant C. Itoh. The deal netted Time Warner $1 billion and was "unprecedented."[47]

The multiplex has come to be possibly the single most important development in film exhibition history, one that was both enabled by and in turn catalyzed the franchise-based blockbuster mode of filmmaking from the mid-1970s on. Kevin Corbett notes that in the 1920s the motion picture theater established an expanding connectivity with mass marketing and economies of scale, and the movie palace embodied that connection: in its art deco lines of forward progress and of flow and speed. In the 1960s and 1970s, that connectivity was refunctioned through the multiscreen theaters built along with or near suburban shopping malls, the first malltiplexes. "This transition," writes Corbett, "represents the last major technological transformation in theatrical movie-watching in the twentieth century, but it also reveals the film industry's continued pattern of pursuing its audience/market." As was the case with the drive-in, part of that pursuit was geographical: when the audience moved to the suburbs, so did movie theaters. Another factor was the movie theater industry's collaboration and new symbiosis with "the broader retail sales industry just as that industry's primary technology—the shopping mall—was greatly expanding." From 1950 to 1980 over 22,000 malls were built in the United States, and while the number of indoor movie theaters had remained remarkably constant from 1965 to 1974 at just over 10,000, after 1975 multiplexes increasingly began appearing inside these new malls, with a profound incorporation of 22,750 theaters by 1990.[48] "The result was that the movie theater as technology achieved the ultimate physical and symbolic connection to the most obvious form of conspicuous consumption: shopping."[49]

As Fredric Jameson argues, these new public spaces were in fact extensions of the privatizing drive of late capitalism. Unlike the modernist project, these public ventures "underscore the exclusion of private life," necessarily reincorporating the paradoxes of private property after the end of civil society ("by way of the more classic antinomy of a public space that is privately owned").[50] Indeed, the assemblage constituted by the mall and the multiplex offers within its new type of closure a simulation of all the "chaotic libidinal freedom" of the now dangerous outside world. In the passage from the amusement park to the mall, private police and concealed cameras sanitize the unruliness of the older collective experience and make it accessible to aesthetic and postmodern reception.[51] Although Jameson assimilates this experience to the depoliticization of an earlier modernism in the postmodern "ludic," what my own analysis of the media assemblage of globalizing Bollywood shows is that the closure of signification (ideology) is both undone and newly territorialized by the affective contagions of the body and its new habituations (far from the waning of affect, the mode of mutation and control of this consumerist technology is affect itself).[52]

From the inception of the multiplex boom, proprioceptive technologies aimed at producing bodily affect directly, and quite apart from narrative, sign, or montage, were central to its form of media consumption. Consider, for instance, the effect of the introduction of xenon lamps into film exhibition, which in 1954 replaced the older carbon short-arc lighting and "created a revolutionary change in the cinema industry." As one Osram (a brand of xenon lamps) executive explained, carbon-arc lamps used disposable electrodes that literally made an "arc of light," which was then projected onto a screen by a reflector. The system was inefficient and labor intensive. By contrast, xenon lamps provided a consistent, reliable light source and reduced labor costs. Before the introduction of xenon lamps, there had to be a projectionist in every booth for every movie. At every reel change, the carbon rods had to be trimmed or replaced, and the carbon-arc regularly burned or damaged film. By contrast, the xenon lamps offered theater owners immediate cost efficiencies because of their extended service life (two thousand hours or more) and low maintenance. The intense white light produced by the xenon lamps allowed manufacturers to optimize optical components such as coated reflectors and projection lenses into their systems, thus providing brighter, sharper images on the screen. Over time, the efficiency of the modern xenon lamp, coupled with advances in film-handling systems, helped usher in today's generation of multiplex movie theaters, where a single operator can oversee the projection systems in multiple auditoriums simultaneously. The same movie theater that had a balcony could be partitioned into four theaters all showing different movies simultaneously, thereby attracting four times the audience while only one projectionist was needed to run the shows. Then, as Hilary Chalmers puts it, they "build a cinema with six auditoriums in a shopping mall, and before you know it, we're all going to 20-plexes and 24-plexes. The growth in business was exponential."[53] Here we see exhibition practices, distribution, and eventually production reorganized through the reduction of residual inefficiencies and the emergence of new synergies, as self-organizing dynamics in technology and design intersect in the machinic phylum. As Simondon notes, "There are two kinds of improvements, then: those which modify the division of functions, increasing in an essential manner the synergy of functioning, and those which without modifying the division in question diminish the harmful effects of residual oppositions."[54]

Xenon lamps are in the process of being replaced by Digital Light Processing (DLP)—yet another unique selling point "revolution." The DLP technology is a "revolutionary" display that uses an optical semiconductor to manipulate light digitally. It is a highly reliable, all-digital display chip that delivers the best (commercially available) picture across a broad range of products, including large-screen digital TVs and projectors for business, home, professional venues, and digital cinema. The DLP chip is used in small projectors (under two pounds) as well as movie screens up to seventy-five feet. "The result is maximum fidelity: a picture whose clarity, brilliance and color must be seen to be believed."[55] (The fantasy of fidelity—the intensification of the real—that seems to be the order word of the digital is repeated here as well, but it combines with the notion that this new digital image is the truth of the artist's intention.)[56] How does digital light processing work? Developed in 1987 by Texas Instrument's Larry Hornbeck, the

DLP chip houses a digital "micromirror" device made up of a rectangular array of around two million hinge-mounted microscopic mirrors, each of which measures less than one-fifth the width of a human hair. Coordinated with a digital video or graphic signal, a light source, and a projection lens, micromirror device can reflect an all-digital image onto a screen or other surface. The three-chip system found in DLP Cinema projection systems is capable of producing no fewer than thirty-five trillion colors. The on and off states of each micromirror are coordinated with the three basic building blocks of color—red, green, and blue. For example, a mirror responsible for projecting a purple pixel will only reflect red and blue light to the projection surface; our eyes then blend these rapidly alternating flashes to see the intended hue in a projected image.[57]

Strictly speaking there is no purple but the alternating flashes are too fast to be perceived, thus pushing vision to its proprioceptive incipiencies that rely on "neural filling-in." As Francisco Varela, Evan Thompson, and Eleanor Rosch argue in their classic study of emergent capacities (affects) in the "embodied mind," since the visual system is never simply presented with pregiven objects, a patchwork of visual modalities (form, surface properties, and three-dimensional space and movement) correlate to form vision. This suggests that these modalities themselves are emergent properties of concurrent subnetworks that work together to produce a relatively coherent visual precept. Vision is an achievement of correlated embodied perceptual capacities.[58] It is this achievement that contemporary DLP technologies turn into an "adventure of vision" where the object is not visible as such but functions at the level of the emergent properties of the vision assemblage itself. What, more specifically, has happened to the body's sensation of vision in these successive "revolutions"? According to Caramagna, "xenon lamps were immediately more uniform and stable than the carbon-arc systems." They achieve full brilliance almost immediately, with a light that most closely matches the sun, and have a color temperature ideally suited to the accurate rendering of color film.[59] In the case of DLP you get "the best image quality available"; that is, clarity, with thousands of mirrors spaced less than one micron apart, resulting in a very high "fill factor." By minimizing the gaps between pixels in a projected image, DLP creates "a seamless digital picture that's sharp at any size." Brightness is more consistent given that it is mirror based and thus uses light more efficiently—"a whopping 15,000 lumens," with a superfine gradation of thirty-five trillion colors. Thus both xenon and digital projection are marketed (the discursive doubling) as the body experiencing a thoroughly naturalized image: a light closest to the sun (xenon bulbs), a more faithful rendering of the original (the mirror), the most accurate rendering of color (xenon), and nonpixilated seamless digital image (DLP). And yet at the level of the body's assemblage with projection lighting, at the level of its proprioceptive effects, both of these technologies function by addressing the ontologies of vision, its emergence in processes of embodiment. The access to nature here is inconceivable without the prior assemblage of body and spatiotemporal technologies of light, sound, and image, which as Lev Manovich notes, has a genealogy extending well back into the eighteenth century: the popular spectacles and entertainments such as magic lantern shows, phantasmagoria, eidophusikon, panorama, diorama, zoopraxiscope shows, etc. In the West, this history seems to culminate in the telos of the "seamless" digital object. "Digital compositing exemplifies a more general operation of computer culture," writes Manovich, one that is focused on "assembling together a number of elements to create a single seamless object."[60]

But the circumvention of the seam/pixel by the proprioceptive rendering of the image is not the focus of its incorporation into exhibition practices in India; indeed, that is almost a side issue in its discursive doubling in this postcolonial context. The DLP technology entered India in May 2005 with, appropriately enough, the global release of *Star Wars: The Revenge of the Sith*. Sathyam Cinemas, an upscale five-screen multiplex in Chennai, installed the technology specifically for the projection of the third of the *Star Wars* prequels. The cinema is equipped with two digital projection systems—one from the Belgium-based Barco and the other from the Canada-based Christie. Both use DLP; the feature film is prepared and encoded on GDC (geodetic datum code) format supplied by a Singapore-based company fronting Hong Kong capital.[61] The digital contents are then downloaded onto the GDC server. The DLP projector, connected to the server, will project the image on the theater's 65.5-feet-wide screen.[62] Its benefits seen from the point of view of an Indian exhibitor are indicative of the relation between a proprioceptive technology-body assemblage of media consumption like DLP and its social deployment in a postcolonial context. The key concerns here are, first, securing digital film property from the erosion of repeat screenings and the rigors of the Indian summers and monsoons; second, combating rampant piracy; and, third, maintaining the social and class segmentation of the population that has been the hallmark of the multiplex strategy in India: "Apart from the non-diminishing quality of each digital print, one of the greatest benefits of digital cinema is that it is encrypted right up to the projection, and there are inbuilt anti-piracy tools . . . [Sathyam Theatre manager] Mr. Reddy said that for the first few weeks, the price of tickets for the RDX showings would be increased by Rs. 20 for the I and II class, and by Rs. 30 for the balcony."[63] As Ganesh S., the business development manager for Texas Instruments in Bangalore, puts it, "CineLink [the proprietary security software developed for DLP] ensures that movies and other content are kept secure. An encrypted link is provided between server and projector to ensure safe delivery. Recently, a watermarking technique has also been developed that allows in-theater pirating to be traced back to the theater and showing time."[64] Here the very history of the multiplex in the West as a mass consumption strategy is inverted; it is as if the Indian malltiplex has materialized by privatizing the classic dichotomy of audience segmentation in single-screen Talkies—namely, the masses vs. the classes: "You have found the money for that Dolby/DTS experience with non carbon arc 'xenon lamp' projection, you have left the sweat-n-smell land & entered the cool-n-clean theater."

Let us return to the dreams of Honorable in "0wnz0red."

Ring Zero, the first registers in the processor, was where your computer checked to figure out how to start itself up. Compromise Ring Zero and you can make the computer do anything—load an alternate operating system, turn the whole box into a brain-in-a-jar, executing in an unknown environment. Ring Minus One, well, that was like God-code, space on another, virtual processor that was unalterable, owned by some remote party, by LoCal and its entertainment giants. Software was released without any copy-prevention tech because everyone knew that copy-prevention tech *didn't work*. Nevertheless, Hollywood was always chewing the scenery and hollering, they just didn't believe that the hairfaces and ponytails didn't have some seekrit tech that would keep their movies safe from copying until the heat death of the universe or the expiry of copyright, whichever came last.[65]

Such dreams of securing the digital through God-like encryption is really not the stuff of science fiction; it is the security protocol surrounding the base-code of more and more digital media. In Doctorow's tale, Liam and Murray discuss a new "entertainment chip" that replaces God with "crypto":

"Who's God, then?"

"Crypto . . . Really good, standards-defined crypto. Public cipher-systems whose details are published and understood. AES, RSA good crypto.[66] There's a signing key for each chip fab—ours is in some secret biometrics-and-machineguns bunker under some desert. That key is used to sign *another* key that's embedded in a tamper-resistant chip—" Liam snorted again. "No, really. Not tamper-proof, obviously, but tamper-resistant—you'd need a tunneling microscope or a vat of Freon to extract the keys for the chip. And every chip has its own keys, so you'd need to do this for every chip which doesn't, you know, scale. So there's this chip full of secrets, they call the Fritz chip, for Fritz Hollings, the Senator from Disney, the guy who's trying to ban computers so Hollywood won't go broke. The Fritz chip wakes up when you switch on the machine, and it uses its secret key to sign the operating system—well, the boot-loader and operating system and the drivers and stuff—so now you've got a bunch of cryptographic signatures that reflect the software and hardware configuration of your box. When you want to download Police Academy *n*, your computer sends all these keys to Hollywood central, *attesting* to the operating environment of your computer. Hollywood decides on the fly if it wants to trust that config, and if it does, it encrypts the movie, using the keys you've sent. That means that you can only unscramble the movie when you're running that Fritz chip, on that CPU, with that version of the OS and that video driver and so on . . . So basically, whatever Hollywood says, goes. You can't fake an interface, you can't make any uses that they don't authorize. You know that these guys sued to make the VCR illegal, right? You can't wrap up an old app in a compatibility layer and make it work with a new app. You say Microsoft loves this? No fucking wonder, dude—they can write software that won't run on a computer running Oracle software. It's your basic Bond-villain . . ." "—world-domination horshit. Yeah, I know."[67]

Despite the fact that everyone knows encryption does not work absolutely ("Not tamper-proof, obviously, but tamper-resistant"), Hollywood keeps dreaming of that algorithm that will keep "their movies safe from copying until the heat death of the universe or the expiry of copyright, whichever came last." For these "leet haxors" there is always a way to break the code, and that is to find the string that unwinds the code. And then sell it to Africa or Asia, where copyright is radically deterritorialized.

With the advent of digital cinema in India, cracking the code in the media server is not the central point of its "public corruption" (i.e., piracy). Rather, the moment of exhibition—that is, the moment of its conversion from digital light to analog processes in the act of consumption, the affective mobilization of its audiovisual signal in the body—is the moment of its radical vulnerability as well. One doesn't hack the system when one can just copy the projected content and reproduce it cheaply; the analog pirates sneak in fairly simple digital cameras and simply tape the projection on mini-DV and then encode it to VCD format. This is acknowledged by contemporary exhibitors of digital cinema in India (and many other exhibition contexts across Asia), even as they keep looking for that "seekrit tech" that would guarantee that their content is safe until heat death. "The current security mechanism ensures protection to content only at three stages of [the] 4 stage process: production, transmission and in-booth operation (to a limited extent). But the fourth stage, i.e. the on-screen exhibition is still vulnerable to sophisticated means of piracy. Fingerprinting and watermarking methods could be evolved to prevent or trace the source of camcording. However, the model hasn't yet been developed. The other aspects of [the] security mechanism that need to be addressed are rights management with digital keys, link between projector and the server, encryption of movie and distribution vehicle."[68] So the media assemblage is leaky, and this is the case for essential reasons: such continuous multiplicities are open to the indetermination of the analog at every moment, in every node of their interface with the body.

Contemporary Tendencies of the Malltiplex in India

These highly publicized proprietary and proprioceptive technologies are supplemented by other computer-based design innovations in the contemporary multiplex, innovations whose effects are at times more subtle because they have no preestablished exclusive logo to identify them (less discursive noise). Generally, we could say that they work (i.e., generate surplus value and are perceived as value added) by a kind of contagious multiplying of the sensations in the malltiplex. As Bolter and Grusin note, when we look at what happens on the screen (in a darkened theater), we can see how film "refashions the definitions of immediacy that were offered by stage drama, photography, and painting." More, when the film ends, the lights come on, and we stroll back into the lobby of a mall theater, we recognize that the "process of remediation is not over." We are confronted with all sorts of images (posters, computer games, videoscreens), as well as social and economic artifacts (the choice of films offered and the pricing strategy for tickets and refreshments). This assemblage, in its unfolding, constitutes the medium of film in the United States today, and it is now a global standard.[69] It is in this continuously self-differing experience of mediatized sensation that I would situate the qualitative multiplicity of the malltiplex's media assemblage.

We can map some general directions in the development of multiplex design in the West, and indeed globally. Current malltiplex design consists of the tight articulation of specific consumer effects for a "total entertainment experience." First, as we have seen, the multiplex more and more is anchored in a mixed-use development linking image consumption to retail shops and restaurants; these are some of its key modalities of multiplying the sensations of consumption in the experience of cinemagoing: cost effectiveness, reduction or elimination of labor-based turbulence, and technical functionality.[70] Second, the population is differentiated into specific age groups: youth audiences require music, video, games (the "x-boxers"); mature audiences want martinis, espresso, etc. as they arrive early and leave later, thus providing more consumption opportunities for additional amenities and services. Third, modernizing multiplexes are bringing in the latest technologies as smooth surface interfaces, and they are accessorizing passageways and screening rooms: wall-mounted aisle lighting, motion-sensor toilet-flush valves, faucets and hand dryers, vinyl composition flooring in auditoriums, hard flooring in lobbies and promenades, custom lighting, plasters, more-durable surface treatments, decorative lightweight ceiling treatments, way-finding signage, larger restroom stalls, more lavatories, extra fixtures in the women's room, family restrooms, party-room promotions for working parents, etc.[71] But these are all standardizations— today's multiplexes also deploy specific differentiation (branding) strategies. This entails the use and development of a specific design feature such as a tapas bar tucked away in a dimly lit corner of the reception area, or a full-function bakery, or the latest video games in a futuristic "play station." These strategies of branding focus, then, on the "lobby experience." The lobby is the nexus of desire and population flow that has come to be the central moment-space from the point of view of the exhibitor. Consumers are offered more and more finely modulated information on movies, food, services, entertainment, and other enticements; better and more services centered on maximizing convenience govern the logic here (self-ticketing machines, user-friendly websites facilitate Internet purchases, cash ATMs in the lobby, etc.). The lobby is also the prime theater of operations for concessions companies that promise to deliver, according to one website, "innovative in-theater marketing and concessions solutions to theaters worldwide. With 100% of our focus on the international cinema industry (we currently sell in over 40 countries), we leverage our worldwide manufacturers to bring you high visibility promotions in the product style, size and language that is best for your market. Our strong studio relationships allow us to bring the most creative in-theater solutions—'movie graphic' concessions, collectible premiums, sweepstakes and corporate partners . . . a new world of promotional ideas."[72]

The fall in flat-screen monitor prices (providing both labor-maintenance and cost benefits) has facilitated the transformation of the older theater information into a fast-paced collage of advertising, promotions, trailers, television, video games, and Internet. This is supplemented by floor- and wall-covering products, namely laminates and metals that have been designed to match new patterns, materials, colors, and color combinations to produce that "theatrical feeling and then take it up a notch."[73] In terms of projection and sound, the projection booths in the latest multiplexes have the physical capacity for both a digital projector and a 35mm one (consequently power and exhaust requirements are also increasing). Consumers expecting to "feel the sound" necessitate new strategies focused on quantity, placement, quality, and physical size of speakers; auditorium sidewall design and sound isolation details follow the standards set by the newest sound engineering technologies such as Lucasfilms THX. Screens are also, generally speaking, getting larger in multiplexes in the United States, often filling up the entire front wall (given the more tight constraints on space in the Indian malltiplex, screen size will more than likely decrease in the coming years); the strategy here is balancing the cost of additional building height and excavations with the latest technologies of sightlines, view angles, projection angles, and disabled-seating positions. In the contemporary multiplex, "all the material becomes expressive. It is the affect that is metallic, crystalline, stony, and so on; and the sensation is not colored but, as Cezanne said, coloring."[74]

What then is different about the malltiplex in globalizing India, or more precisely how does the multiplicity of media difference unfold given the singularities of local, national, regional, subcontinental, cosmopolitan hybridities? Clearly, there are different economic, technological, and cultural requirements that India's media assemblage makes functional in the malltiplex. The traditional single-screen talkie was a different kind of assemblage. As rentable space it was a machine for money laundering under the radar of state tax systems (hence all the elaborate schemes that developed to circumvent the tax officers, from double tickets to nonreporting to outright bribery); rarely was it directly vertically integrated into the production model of the major film studios. As physical space it functioned by differentiating itself from the given neighborhood in which it was built (in terms of architectural art deco design and its infrastructure—exclusive power generators, gated parking lot, building access roads), and over time it redefined that very neighborhood economically and culturally as it became the central landmark for the area. Also, as commercialized physical space it claimed proprietary relations over any merchandising on or around its premises, granting concessions-merchants contracts that extended its network of clients into the surrounding neighborhoods. This last point gets at the specific cultural specificity of the exhibition industry in north India that I have alluded to in previous chapters. A form of patrilineal kinship-based ownership and clientalist networking structured in a clear communal (caste- and religion-based) labor hierarchy defined the cultural-economic system of the single-screen talkie. Lower-caste, adolescent, nonunionized but organized maintenance workers, living within walking distance of the talkie, gradually asserting their precarious rights in the face of an intransigent and lower-middle-class male manager, while upper-caste, upper-class family-owners step in to mediate, as if benevolent but stern trustees of the communal good. At the level of the body, the talkie was both a total immersive space (centered on the film) and one of radical discontinuity and interruptions. On the one hand, going to a particular talkie was about entering the viewing space and not leaving it until intermission or the end of the show—in other words, it was a space apart, discrete, contained, with its outer and inner gates (almost always some variation on a kind of reticulated metal barrier) serving as passageways into a more and more enclosed space of exhibition: exhibition tactics. On the other hand, some combination of power outages, intermissions, singalongs and shout backs, technological anomalies, delayed reel delivery (due to double booking of the same movie reel, often in cross-town theaters), as well as other collective interventions (students demanding song replays, communal tensions, labor strikes, etc.) punctuated most screenings: everyday viewing tactics. This recalcitrant experience of cinema was always also an acknowledgment of the workings of the body's autonomic nervous processes—breathing, sweating, muscle contraction.[75]

Every manager, owner, or worker I have talked with for the past four years has told me again and again that the once dominant experience of cinema is fast disappearing. In an interview with V. S. Singh and Varun Moolchandani, the Sikh manager and the Hindu second-generation owner of Lily Talkies in Bhopal, Varun declared to me, "In the early 1980s, in family meetings, my father would say that now we've built a movie hall, the next three generations won't have to work. Today, people in this business cannot even imagine such a time coming back." In the same conversation, the middle-class manager told me in a subdued tone, bragging but careful not to be heard by the owner (who was on his cell phone), "Once even the gatekeepers of a cinema hall were local celebrities, people bribing them to get into shows. And the manager was above the most powerful people in the whole city, women would throw themselves at me, and in the evening men would come to shower me in gifts and drown me in the best liquors. That's because when something had to get done everyone turned to the manager. But who can even recall those times now? The whole business has fallen off, and the glamour has gone. You know even managers can afford new Marutis or Zen cars nowadays. But the owners cannot keep up their status if they run the theater honestly. Managers can outdo the owners now in their lifestyles. There is no way the owners can maintain themselves in the cinema business."[76]

The Value Chains of Exhibition

The entire film industry in India is being restructured: affectively, financially, technologically, socially. Consider Metalight Productions Pvt. Ltd. Formed by its parent company Production Facilities, a Singapore-based Indian television production company, Metalight is a "Strategic Motion Picture Venture" focused on the "complete value chain," that is slated eventually to produce twelve films per year (so far it has released three, *Dil Vil Pyaar Vyaar* [2002], *Satta* [2003], and *Teen Deewarein* [2003]). The company aims to distribute these films in major territories across the country and overseas, and to exhibit them in India through a network of theaters that will be managed under a distinct brand name.[77] The malltiplex is central to this "complete value chain" strategy.

By the end of 2004, the city of Gurgaon, just outside of Delhi, had around 15 malls while the national total was 245. Most of these malls were built between 2002 and 2004, and the plan is to have 400 malls in place by 2008.[78] According to the International Council of Shopping Centres–India there is already about 60 million square feet of mall space across India. The National Capital Region (NCR)—Delhi, Gurgaon and Noida—will account for 40 percent of the total. Indian and transnational retailers like Reliance and Wal-Mart are banking on a boom in consumer spending as well as a reorganization of it ("farm to fork logistics chain").[79] Two of the connectivities of this mall-based consumer revolution are modes of each other—in doing the one, you are necessarily engaged in the other. These malls attempt

19. Inside the Big Bazaar department store, Phoenix Mills Mall, Lower Parel, Mumbai. Photo by Amit S. Rai.

to provide "a world-class shopping experience." These are, in other words, human-commodity-image flows with a euro-based exchange rate. "As the economy upped northwards and conspicuous consumption became a habit, department stores, shopping complexes and malls made their entry."[80] Middle-class habituations connect buying in the space of the malltiplex to movement and modernity through technologies of the global (credit cards, privatized devoted energy generators, cell and land phone lines, wireless and fiber optics, English-speaking salespeople, regularized quality control, standardization—in short, "India shining").[81]

As a recent report on shopping at the new specialty multiplexes in India noted:

> The jewelry shops at the souk include Kerala's Alukkas, Mumbai's SR Ornaments, Kolkata's B. C. Sen Jewelers as well as what the owners, Ae-rens, call India's largest brand store—Avenue Montaigne, which retails branded jewelry, watches and lifestyle items. Top Indian jewelry designers like Rosily Paul, Ruhee Nanda and Sabina Batra have outlets at the complex. A food court, children's play area, beauty salon, ATMs and a security system are the other attractions. The building is physically-challenged

friendly and has conference rooms and business centres. "Since it is near the international airport, it will attract NRIs from around the world," says G. S. Pillai, president of the souk. More souks are being planned, notably in Mumbai, Ahmedabad and Kochi.[82]

Malls bring together, while simultaneously winnowing out, disparate parts of the nation through a single commercial and discursive space, and they provide a plane or stage of contact with the global Indian. Malls allow for the convergence of competitive and profit-driven commerce with the ideological narrative of national unity. Further, in contrast to the loitering media of bazaar culture, malls simultaneously galvanize and control the chance of the accidental. "A mall is a planned aggregation of shops," remarked Suresh Shingaravelu, CEO of Bangalore's Forum Mall, in an interview in *The Week*.[83] "In a shopping centre, success is an accident, while in a mall, [it is] a planned effort. Positioning is everything." But does positioning remove the accident? In the consumer statistics cited by the CEO we have a calculus correlating population flows with consumer desire, merchandise positioned in an object-based visual space, formulas for the maximization of the quantity, speed, and profits of "foot falls"; the strategy is to keep the viewers attention as they move from parcel of space to parcel of space. "Shopping is about placing temptation in your path," says this CEO. Food outlets at the Forum Mall are on the upper floor because "the moment you put popcorn in a shopper's hands, he turns into a window shopper," says Shingaravelu. The swerve from one form of consuming to another is based on the continuous implication of one sense in another, as they flow into each other; the act of keeping alive the possibility of a fixation, an object-choice, also keeps alive the potentiality of the swerve, an irreducible stochasticity in patterned fluxes. One pleasure must be tied to the exchange value of another, in an infinite chain: cinema, desire, movement, eating, family,[84] shopping. The only exit for moviegoers who visit the PVR multiplex at the Forum Mall is through the shopping area.[85]

We should recall here Susan Buck-Morss's elaboration of some Benjaminian motifs in the emerging consumer cultures spawned from the Arcades. She notes that in the *Passagen Werk*, Benjamin documents the contamination of public space by phantasmagoric forms. In the Paris shopping arcades, where the rows of shop windows created a "phantasmagoria of commodities" on display, panoramas and dioramas engulfed the viewer in a simulated total environment in miniature. The world's fairs expanded this phantasmagoric principle to areas the size of small cities. These nineteenth-century forms, she argues, are the precursors of today's shopping malls, theme parks, and video arcades, as well as the totally controlled environments of airplanes (where one sits plugged into sight and sound and food service), the phenomenon of the "tourist bubble" (where the traveler's "experiences" are all monitored and controlled in advance), the individualized, constantly modulated audiosensory environment of an iPod, the visual phantasmagoria of advertising, and the tactile sensorium of a gymnasium full of Nautilus equipment.[86]

In India today, as in the West, the overlapping and constantly shifting imperatives of achieving relative accumulation (beating the profit curves) determine the multiplex phantasmagoric as spatial and temporal strategy—a thought as of the moment. Aparna Sharma writes that the multiplex intervention, "as of the moment, can be termed as appropriating varying audience segments to stabilize and secure its own position, establish its distinction and engage the audiences in a varying film viewing exercise." She notes that the multiplex strategy of exhibition in India has emerged as a mix of seemingly contradictory strains. Taking cues from each other, chasing each other, multiplexes and malls throughout India are making for variables that don't just originate in, or correspond with, the existing consumer needs of their audiences, but also have identified, created, and accommodated overlapping tastes and preferences by readying access to fare, which may previously have been considered as lacking the numerical encouragement vital for profitability.[87] In other words, in India the malltiplex is part and parcel of a broader form of population segmentation that itself draws technologies from global consumerism as well as diverse kinds of risk management and security apparatuses, each element reciprocally catalyzed on the machinic phylum. This shift suggests a radically new market segmentation within an already stratified social field: stalls and balcony (masses and classes in the same viewing space) have been reterritorialized into single-screen C-graders versus cosmopolitan malltiplexers.[88]

But the value chain doesn't stop there. Consider the new PVR "Paradigm" multiplex of eleven screens at the Forum Mall in Bangalore, which was, until recently, India's largest theater. Partnering with the Australian-based multiplex designers Village Roadshow and the Bangalore developers Prestige, PVR created "a colourful, bright and people-oriented space celebrating the experience of watching movies."[89] In this multiplex, the orientation toward people means strategic population segmentation around differentiated luxury: Paradigm has seven regular stadium seating screens, two Cinema Europa screens, and two Gold Class Lounge screens. *Theatre Magic*, overwhelmed by the Gold Class Lounge, gushed, "Simply put, its luxury objectified—a red lounge saturated with red beckons the patrons into its warm embrace. The branding itself suggests a setting for the best. . . . The exquisite food offering and service at table are all integral to the customer experience. Lights imported from Spain and custom design artwork as light boxes with black and white faces of movie legends impart the ambience with a moodsetting for the ensuing unparalleled experience. The two auditoriums, each with 32 fully reclinable seats in pairs with centre tables is simply the final statement in movie viewing."[90] Here PVR is banking on one of the tested theorems of global multiplexing: build it and they will come. As Matthew Heyman, the American creator of the biggest theater chain in Mexico (he is now helping to start one in Pakistan), notes: "There has yet to be a failure in consumer demand around the world once new cinema infrastructure has been developed."[91]

Value and Affect in the Indian Malltiplex

The media assemblage internal and transversal to the malltiplex modulates blocs of sensation in the serial expansion of value chains. What happens to the open, assembling body as it moves through and is moved by these spaces of desire, these blocs of sensation? In reorganizing what Benjamin suggested were the three "original satanic promises" of modernity—the triple illusions of freedom, independence, and infinity[92]—the malltiplex translates this coiled promise into a modulated multiplication of the body's senses. In that sense illusion becomes felt sensation: isn't the malltiplex in its material organization, in its discursive foldings, in its bodily effects, a project to sell the potentiality of the body, its indetermination as a feedback loop of freedom? Deleuze and Guattari contend that affect goes beyond affections. "The affect is not the passage from one lived state to another but man's nonhuman becoming. . . . This something can be specified only as sensation. It is a zone of indetermination, of indiscernibility, as if things, beasts, and persons . . . endlessly reach that point that immediately precedes their natural differentiation. This is what is called an *affect*."[93] Looping back to that point before human differentiation is also the dream of total cinema, a dream that the new media assemblage of the contemporary multiplex turns into an algorithm or, better, a database of hyperlinked algorithms. The digitization of cinema culture—from server to screen, from purchasing tickets to Internet research on movies and their simultaneously released video games and action figures, from the incorporation of lens-based analog footage (once the defining technique of cinema) into a broader process of digital compositing and 3-D animation to the spatialization of montage in the image-information-interface—takes the form of a quantitative multiplicity of sensation: discontinuous and numerical, sensations just keep adding up, one shock at a time. This is *not* what is called an affect, and yet it is parasitic on the *qualitative* multiplicity of affect.

The key to situating the social and bodily effects of the malltiplex in globalizing Indian film culture is to keep in mind the changing relationship between two assembling multiplicities: the affections of the body catalyzed by new simultaneous connectivities among populations, flesh, technology, and image-sound. As I have been arguing, here in the new media sensorium a continuous, qualitative multiplicity unfolds on the self-organizing plane of the machinic phylum, whose nature keeps differing from itself, and so shifts, retrains, dissolves, or fuses each of its functionalities. In this multiplication of possible sensations produced through new globalizing habituations the contemporary malltiplex draws the media assemblage toward a specific stabilization of media durations.

This tendency consists of a majoritarian projection of a consumable and multiple present: malltiplexed. What they sell is the spatialized concentration of difference: many screens, many genres, many ages, many functions, many flows. Standardized heterogeneity (Fredric Jameson), or individualized customization (Lev Manovich)—either way it is the commodification of media durations.[94] Manovich writes of the temporality specific to the interactive computer object: websites, virtual worlds, computer games, and many other types of hypermedia applications are characterized by a peculiar temporal dynamic—constant, repetitive oscillation between an illusion and its suspense: "These new media objects are reminding us of their artificiality, incompleteness, and constructedness. They present us with a perfect illusion only next to reveal its underlying machinery."[95] The temporality of cinema viewing in the contemporary malltiplex is launched by the initial caesura historically common to all forms of cinema exhibition for the past four decades or so: the two and a half hours (closer to three and a half in Hindi-Urdu popular cinema, although this is shrinking) of image-sound consumption is like a gap, or cut in time, both illusionistic and suspended. One's relative immobility in the act of viewing coincides with a conscious withdrawal from the world's rhythms: as I noted above, in India going to the movies is commonly referred to as "time pass"—a phrase that throughout north India (and also in many urban centers of south India) is applied to all forms of absolutely unproductive expenditure, from pursuing a lukewarm love interest for sheer amusement to doggedly going to watch a guaranteed flop.

Time pass derives from the middle-English word "pasetyme," which the OED describes as "a diversion or recreation which serves to pass the time agreeably; an activity done for pleasure rather than work; a hobby; a sport, a game. Also: a practice commonly indulged in." Time pass is about pleasure in killing time, a practiced art that consists in feeling time's passing so as not to feel its accretion. This desire transforms the malltiplex into a space with no outside, like the Benjaminian dream: "Arcades are houses or passages having no outside—like the dream."[96] Benjamin's method and project in his study of the Paris arcades is peculiarly suited to understanding the hybrid temporalities of the contemporary malltiplex in India, and I will suggest some relevant connections here. In commenting on "the panorama of gaiety and tears passing before us like the dust of the rails before the windows of the coach" (Benjamin Gastineau, *La Vie en chemin de fer* [1861]), Benjamin wrote, "Rather than pass the time, one must invite it in. To pass the time (to kill time, to expel it): the gambler. Time spills from his every pore.—To store time as a battery stores energy: the flâneur. Finally, the third type: he who waits. He takes in the time and renders it up in altered form—that of expectation."[97] To kill, expel, store, spill, and render time: divergent pasts and futurities folded into the act of cinemagoing. They name different strategies of cinemagoing in India, aggregated in the phrase "time pass."

To kill, expel, store, spill, and render time are also different aspects of the rhythms of film culture's media *duration*: time pass is an emergent quality of sensation in the interactions of Indian cinema's media assemblage, and it is that experience of duration-pleasure that is being transformed today through new media intervals. And it is here, in the immanent duration of the media event, where sexuality becomes preindividual and potential. Recall Deleuze's thoughts on a cube of sugar: "It also has a duration, a rhythm of duration, a way of being in time that is at least partially revealed in the process of its dissolving, and that shows how this sugar differs in kind not only from other things, but first and foremost from itself." This alteration— which is one with the functional nature, or what Deleuze calls the "essence" of a thing—is what we grasp when we conceive of it in terms of duration. "It signifies that my own duration, such as I live it in the impatience of waiting, for example, serves to reveal other durations that beat to other rhythms, that differ in kind from mine. Duration is always the location and the environment of differences in kind; it is even their totality and multiplicity."[98] Notice that for Deleuze an essence here is not a substance or presence as such, but the differing in kind of a thing *from itself*: a changeful duration in an associated milieu. My argument here is that to kill, expel, store, spill, and render time is the general condition of affectivity of the media assembling body in the contemporary malltiplex. This parceling of time, its divisibility, its continuous rhythms act on the body directly producing both new habituations as well as potentially new assemblages. The potential malltiplexing of the body-technology assemblage is also a marketing gimmick. Brian Massumi suggests that potential is singular: a multiple infolding and unfolding into each other of "divergent futurities, only the *divergence* of which is reproducible." The particular nature of each divergent conjunction in the series is what is problematic. "Multiple in- and unfolding: singularity is multiplex." The multiplex divergence of the singular, writes Massumi, is not to be confused with the "disjunctive simplicity" at the basis of a "system of possibility." The multiplex mutually includes. Possibility develops disjunctively, one might even say quantitatively, toward the extension of a next actual step. "Multiplex potential envelops, around an intensely suspended (virtual) center."[99] The disjunctive simplicity at the basis of an audiovisual system of digitized possibility is how the machinic evolution of contemporary malltiplexing captures the singular affectivity of the body and renders time through a specific organization of interruptive, quantified *bits of pleasure*. Malltiplexes aim to divide film's interruption in time through a highly selective but also partly arbitrary refunctioning of the body-image-duration-space-pleasure-commodity topology. This entails the commodification or value-generating capture of potential connections that the body can make in the present moment: through food-thirst-hunger, through a certain appetite for star aura, or by attending to and consuming visual and aural affects less and less centered on the auditorium itself, that is, attention as continuous distraction. Always, the multiplexed body is drawn into a presentist temporality of total immersion that functions through an always changing and seemingly expanding combination of sensation: but never to the point of excess (no fainting, heart attacks, or extreme-sports-like viscerality, hopefully). That is its passive danger. The active danger would be something like Tyler Durden's method of movie projection: interpolate Indian-style bits (thirty seconds of hardcore or softcore pornography) in the middle of projecting a G-rated Pixar-Disney-DreamWorks film: edit your own fucking *Incredibles*. That would be an active danger, but again not necessarily resistant—and who is to say, after all, that inter-bit porn and digital Disney are not phenomenologically continuous? Simply, this malltiplexed presentism both solicits and controls potentializing excess.

How? The malltiplex launches becomings through a desire to perform subjectivity at the intersection of a network of gazes and a modular unfolding of cinema space. But like killing time, the viewing subject performs the script of an anonymous patron, a valid ticket holder, within a controlled timespace of loitering. Ushers, ticket-counter clerk, security personnel, manager, maintenance personnel, concession-stand attendant, cashier, closed-circuit TV—all these gazes crosshatch each modular and continuous space. In the malltiplex the concession stand and the "box" office have two related functions: present discrete, smooth-surfaced cells of consumption—the ticket counter identifies and validates your presence through exchange (and usually this moment of exchange involves the collection of data through credit or debit cards),[100] and moves you along to the gate where the ticket collector revalidates your presence, and then directs you toward your theater number ("theatre number 12, straight down, to your right"). That movement is interrupted by the unmistakable spectacle of the concessions stand, where uniformed attendants scramble to fill impatient orders before the end of the trailers: popcorn, chaat, nachos and cheese, coffee, chai, soda, samosa,[101] Twizzlers, ice cream—everything to make you more thirsty: "It's a fact—The more Ricos Products your customers enjoy, the more Soft Drinks they want to buy . . . And that's a Winning Combination You Can Bank On!!"[102] Space, desire, spectacle, and value generating exchange fold into each other through a constant pedagogy of movement, consumption, surveillance, break, and flow, all with varying intensities. The multiply connected body provides and activates the occasion of the event-space through its surface, its flesh, its indeterminate neural pathways, its brain—the target and instrument for affect. This activation does not happen each time, and indeed after each time, after each further turn of the habituated screw, the intensive pulsations (the feedback loops of affect) attenuate, and the sensorium that once seemed both so hidden and spectacularized in the multiplex becomes banal: mere time pass.

Thus in India the multiplexed body is born at the intersection between a segmented population and a reterritorializing nation-state—the biopolitical question for entertainment policy, theater design, and market analysis is how to proliferate globalized consumerism among the rich while securing the spaces of consumerism from the impoverished multitude outside (and using the labor of the socially excluded to secure and maintain this space). Indeed, the fact that productive expenditure is still the dominant mode through which cinema's cultures are managed in urban spaces in north India is no longer the question—rather, the problematic has shifted.

Where are the movements, the differences taking effect? One difference is that before liberalization, cinema's music-image-sound regime (the image and musical style of cinema) was seen as both possible enemy (hence, for example, ban rock 'n' roll, but enable the popular actor Shammi Kapoor to achieve stardom as Elvis's postcolonial double) and model citizen of the nation—its prodigal son, so to speak (Raj Kapoor and Nargis in Russia); today, into the open arms of a shining Mother India dominant Hindi-Urdu cinema has returned bearing the mask of the NRI.[103] As I have suggested above, in the past decade in India the proliferation of global consumerist sumptuary practices, tied to transnational travel and capital accumulation, has been enabled by and has in turn spurred the convergence of film and new media and marketing in India. As I have tried to show in this chapter, this new assemblage brings together film exhibition with transnational cross-marketing strategies.[104]

Which brings us back to our original question: Where does the notion of virtuality fit in this Indian experience of the malltiplex? Massumi calls that substanceless and durationless moment the "pure event." The time of the event, he suggests, does not belong per se to the body in movement-vision or even to the body without an image. "They incur it. It occurs to them. As time-form it belongs to the virtual, defined as that which is maximally abstract yet real, whose reality is that of potential—pure relationality, the interval of change, the in-itself of transformation." In such a temporality, time does not pass, it only comes to pass. It cannot be suspended because, unlike empirical time, it does not flow. "The event is superempirical; it is the crystallization, out the far side of quasi-corporeality, of already actualized spatial perspectives and emplacements into a time-form from which the passing present is excluded and which, for that very reason, is as future as it is past, looping directly from one to the other."[105] It is as if, given the arrow of time that is becoming, in the event time kills itself. In terms of time pass, if, as I have been suggesting, the virtual has been discursively doubled and thus captured in the simulation-sensorium of the global malltiplex, then what escapes this capture—is it the excess of the body's affectivity, as Mark Hansen would have it? Moreover, if the virtual emerges into potentiality by affect returning the body to a realm of incipiencies, then what happens to those nonactualized, nonterritorialized proliferations, the contagions of the multiplexing body?

In the context of an argument about affectivity in avant-garde new media art that assembles cinema and video, Hansen points to that viewer who takes in this intensely oversaturated temporal object. For Hansen the event unfolds through the guiding mechanism of cinematic temporality—the perceptual coincidence between the flux of a film and that of consciousness—and opens through "a kind of affective contagion." In this contagious media, consciousness, confronted with what it cannot properly perceive and yet what constitutes the very condition out of which the perceivable emerges, "undergoes a profound self-affection." In this body-digital assemblage, affectivity is the capacity for the body to be radically creative, "to be the agent of a framing of digital information that generates images independently of all preexistent technical frames."[106]

What if the malltiplex—as an oversaturated temporal practice, one that is based on the perceptual coincidence of cinematic temporality as one distinct element of its spatio-temporal assemblage, but also one that through proprioceptive technologies aimed at the preindividual level of the body multiplies sensation through a kind of affective contagion: *malltiplex mutagen, viral marketing*—what if this technology of commercial media by combining the qualitative and quantitative multiplicities of the body both elicits the radical creativity that Hansen champions (what, in following both Bataille and Massumi, I have called a kind of potentializing excess) and catalyzes it as surplus value, as accumulation in the realm of affect? Simply put, the malltiplex captures and integrates the proprioceptive body (which it can never totalize or calculate) into various kinds of quantifying mechanisms: counting bodies, probability algorithms, tickets sold, concessions sold, bigger screens and better technology attracting more viewers, more design innovations (all of which have their own constantly changing curves of relative accumulation). While each of these levels—digitally stratified and analogically folded into each other—proliferate and infect each other, it is the work of the multiplex to extract from them both a relative security and the (relative) maximum of profit.

Toward a History of Media Ecologies

To summarize, I am arguing that in considering the exhibition practices coming into dominance today in India we shift our focus from sexuality and its representations as a form of identity and begin the rather more dubious but nonetheless crucial analysis of the confluence of technologies, affects, rhythms, intensities, spaces, bodies, becomings, and temporalities in India's contemporary media assemblage. Here, in diagramming an ontology of media durations we feel a sexuality becoming multiplicious incipience in an ecology of sensation poised on the critical ridge of an indeterminate phase transition. The biopolitics of Bollywood's assemblage elicits effects of power at the level of the subindividual, in habits and enunciations that give a specific rhythm to its subjectivities, a modulated intensity to the connections interfacing with its flesh. What we have seen is that, on the one hand, the media assemblage territorializes the body in the diasporic-national family through a future-oriented nostalgia, a presently lost but always open possibility of return and reintegration. This movement can be mapped in the aural and image-sound regimes of films such as *Kabhi Kushi Kabhi Ghum* (dir. Karan Johar, 2001),[107] or in satellite TV ads for international calling cards, chapatti flour, or personal insurance (see chapter 4), or in what David Bordwell has called the "intensified continuity" of contemporary film practice (from shorter average shot durations to unstable, short-range, single-character shots): "Intensified continuity represents a significant shift within the history of movie making." This style aims to generate a keen moment-by-moment anticipation. Techniques that directors in the 1940s reserved for moments of "shock and suspense" are the new norm for film sequences today. Closeups and singles render each shot utterly legible. Rapid editing obliges the viewer to assemble discrete pieces of information at a commanding pace—look away and you might miss a key point. In the alternating close views, in the racking focus and the edgily drifting camera, the viewer "is promised something significant, or at least new, at each instant." Synergized with the satellite television form, the style tries to suture the viewer to the screen through what we can now see is a kind of neural "filling-in," adapting a strategy from the digital mode of perception of new media: "Here is another reason to call it intensified continuity: even ordinary scenes are heightened to compel attention and sharpen emotional resonance."[108] But in this very movement in postcolonial India, by opening bodies to new transnational forms of connectivity something else is also discernible—a kind of contagion of the body that has, for instance, interfaced film culture to the communalization of everyday urban life and the transnational rhythms of dance hall, reggae, calypso, Ibiza, dub, hip hop, and techno in a new filmi DJ culture with its specific economies. This is precisely what is happening in Bhopal today. Of course, as Manovich reminds us, there is signal importance in this new transnational cultural figure digitally modulating already existing sound frequencies to create mixed aural spaces:

> The DJ . . . creates music in real-time by mixing existing music tracks and . . . is dependent on various electronic hardware devices. In the 1990s, the DJ acquired new cultural prestige, becoming a required

presence at art openings and book release parties, in hip restaurants and hotels, in the pages of *Art Forum* and *Wired*. The rise of this figure can be directly correlated to the rise of computer culture. The DJ best demonstrates its new logic: selection and combination of preexistent elements. The DJ also demonstrates the true potential of this logic to create new artistic forms. Finally, the example of the DJ also makes it clear that selection is not an end in and of itself. The essence of the DJ's art is the ability to mix selected elements in rich and sophisticated ways. In contrast to the "cut and paste" metaphor of modern GUI [graphical user interface] that suggests that selected elements can be simply, almost mechanically, combined, the practice of live electronic music demonstrates that true art lies in the "mix."[109]

I end this chapter by considering the proliferation of DJ culture in Bhopal on one such night in summer 2004. This cultural proliferation articulates elements of the Hindi-Urdu popular media assemblage along new vectors. Although the music is assembled with film-based media, in a typical DJ repertoire in Bhopal it is incredibly eclectic and shows as much the influence of the hip hop transnation as A. R. Rahman on youth dance culture. My guide that evening was Varun Moolchandani, the son of one of the brothers who own Lily Talkies, and himself once an active force in the day-to-day functioning of the theater. He had big plans for Lily, he told me once—he dreams of making it again a center of media life in Bhopal by updating its technologies, services, and design and refunctioning its relationship to its smaller cousin, Goonj Talkies. But the intransigence of his uncle (the other active owner of the theater), the politics of labor and management, as well as the Byzantine zoning and construction laws aimed to maximize bribes and to minimize any actual material change greatly disappointed him and wore him down. This conversation was over five years ago, and since then Varun developed an entirely different entrepreneurial venture that is to be all his own: the retailing and servicing of DJ party equipments, including everything from the mixing board and speakers, to strobes, fog machines, drum machines, to producing training CDs. Through an aggressive marketing strategy he had cornered 70 percent of the market in the state of Madhya Pradesh (or so he claimed). His business style both continues and breaks with the traditions of his father's generation. Much like his father who mastered the engineering of radio transmitters in the 1950s before going into the family business, Varun bases his business on an almost artisan-like expertise of the science of rhythm creation and projection. Breaking with another tradition, Varun is friends with many of his customers and would not hesitate to dine with them or be seen publicly with them (although rarely would such public outings include his wife or children). Most of his clients are of course of his class—the majority of the more than fifty DJs in Bhopal are middle to upper-middle class. But Varun thinks of this as business networking, which is a direct critique of the style of business embodied by the distant and distracted masculinity of the shopkeepers of his father generation (indeed, his business style would be to associate freely across caste, class, gender, and religion to produce the critical overflow that contemporary economic networks use to extract value).

Varun's sudden turn to selling DJ equipment came as something of a surprise to me when I met him again after three years. His state-of-the-art office—a narrow but elegant room of carved-wood paneling lined with DJ equipment, interfaces, computers, and musical instruments and located just off of Bhopal's central commercial strip, Hamidia Road in the old gated city—is across the street from the original radio store founded by his Sindhi refugee grandfather in 1949. As I sat down in front of his desk, I was expecting his eyes to glaze over as I tried to interest him in my film book project (I had been pestering him for information for years), but the conversation took another turn. When I mentioned DJ Rekha's crazy bhangra parties in New York City he immediately suggested that we do a trial of some new gear he'd just got in from Mumbai. At the slightest encouragement from me, he scrambled together his staff (who were all clearly of a different community and class background). As if following a set protocol, they drew the shutters, plugged in every component, and Varun started blasting a techno beat while manipulating lights, the fog machine, the drum machine, and lasers—smiling tautly but concentrating, it seemed, on the totality of effects. After the demonstration, he told me that he learned everything he knows about acoustics from the speaker system at Lily Talkies. It would be more accurate to say that his interest in the social power of effective acoustic projection began from the cinema space. He studied carefully the creation of echoes, decibel range, power generation, and placement and design of speakers in single-screen cinemas, and he kept up with the latest research on exhibition sound through both the Internet and his many contacts in the field of sound engineering (e.g., developing a personal relationship with India's premiere speaker manufacturing family, the Ahujas). Further, he completed a six-month training course on new media in Mumbai. He brought all of this knowledge together with his undergraduate degree in marketing, and with capital borrowed from his family he opened the first DJ equipment retail business in the state. Between 2002 and 2004 sales grew 100 percent (in contrast, Lily Talkies has been losing about 200,000 rupees a year). Businesses like Varun's—quasi-traditional, quasi-modern, old capital with a new entrepreneurial style, technologically avant-garde and yet rooted in communal rituals—are the future of new media in Bhopal.

Later that week, on a particularly auspicious day in the Hindu calendar, Varun took me to the hills of the old city, where converted palaces of the Muslim Begums of Bhopal (the pre-independence rulers of the state) are rented out for mostly Hindu wedding receptions. The Januma Hotel sits on top of one of the highest points in the city; below in the flat maidans laid out toward the big lake the middle and lower-middle classes were having their own receptions (the average cost of an upper-class DJ *barat* [the bridegroom procession to the bride's house or reception hall] and reception was soon to approach 600,000 rupees). On the hill the upper-caste, upper-class wedding party was gearing up for the ritualized arrival of the bridegroom. Varun took me around and introduced me to the DJ and his producer who were just setting up for the barat that would arrive shortly. College graduates in their early twenties, they were an odd mixture of totally cynical and genuinely excited. Clearly, they loved the DJ experience even though they complained bitterly about arrogant rich male patrons demanding really bad music and generally not letting them get their groove on, so to speak. The setup struck me as something out of the Brooklyn West Indian Day Parade (where dancehall and calypso bands would ride down Eastern Parkway in DJ trucks). Here, the DJ is boxed in the back of a flatbed truck, with a laptop or small desktop computer plugged into a mixer, two turntables (usually CD players), and various other components; facing out the back are stacks of speakers framed by a fog machine and rows of strobe lights. Two lower-caste workers manage a portable power generator perched atop a handcart. The members of the barat, who will surround the veiled bridegroom riding astride a white horse, arrive in waves and assemble about fifty yards from the bride's family waiting on the steps of the open portico of the hotel. By then the DJ is ensconced in the back of the truck, completely hidden by the truck's side walls and the stack of speakers in the back. Suddenly, the first driving beats burst through the night, lights flash, and the DJ's assistant strategically modulates the other effects (fog machine, strobe, etc.). The barat party (mostly men) gathers behind the slowly moving truck and start dancing madly to songs like the Baha Men's "Who Let the Dogs Out?" or the controversial "sex kitten" showcase song "Kaanta Lagaa" (a remix of a "sober" Lata Mangeshkar–sung film tune).[110] These are crescendo songs saved for the last surge before the bridegroom dismounts from his horse; leading up to that climax is a mix of film songs and contemporary Western club "classics." The strobe lights are synchronized to the music (the over-wrought generator shadowed by the two haggard-looking, dark-skinned workers guarantees a variable flow of juice); but the CD is skipping and the sweaty, drunk men look aggrieved through their forced smiles.

The infolding of singular temporalities multiplies the affects of the DJ-barat scene. That function of multiplying (intensifying, rhythming, fold-ing, and modulating) is performed by concatenating different temporalities through different technologies: the DJ truck opens the path for the bride-groom riding his horse, and yet the master modulator, the DJ himself, is out of sight. Then the truck veers off, finally reversing back and engulfing from behind both the groom's procession and the bemused bride's party (whose men have now joined the dancing in a restrained, off-beat manner). In that movement of clearing and infolding, we have the materialization of an aural space that is itself a kind of affective doubling. The pattern of movement has been established for perhaps hundreds of years in north Indian Hindu wed-dings, but it is the DJ's modulation of mixed beats through the computer-generated playlist that connects the space to a projection of a typical scene from an average night in clubland. Here, memory and the flux of bodies are the preexisting *analog* flows that the digital DJ must rework and remediate to produce a complete immersion in the movement of the moment.

Later Varun takes me to the plains below the hills to check out another DJ setup at a middle-class reception, and on the way we encounter another barat slowly creeping to one of the reception halls. The contrast with the one at Januma couldn't be more striking. A live band (with male singer sitting in an open jeep, singing into a scratchy microphone) blares out Hindi film songs, as the bridegroom procession marches guardedly beside the groom and horse, halting and jamming traffic. Varun gleefully points out to me that even though there is no DJ there, it is still his speakers that are ampli-fying the band. The political economy of this entire situation is crucial to its proliferation. Live bands doing mostly film-based music for middle- and working-class barats; DJ trucks for the clubhappy, privatizing rich; aural space projected by 100-watt speakers in a Hindu ritual (the labor for which is provided by poor lower-caste boys, girls, and elderly workers) and moving through a mostly Muslim part of town, thereby communally reterritorial-izing urban space through that very projection. This is the scene in a city that has witnessed communal tensions turn to riots numerous times over the past decade and a half since the demolition of the Babri Masjid by Hindu

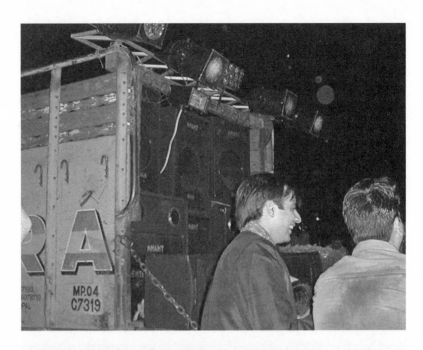

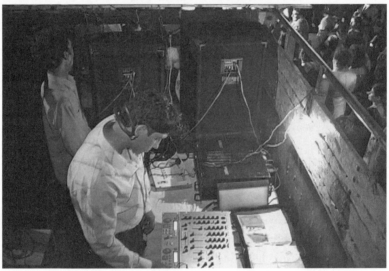

20. A DJ truck with speakers on the bed, followed by barat party members, Bhopal. Photo by Amit S. Rai.

21. Interior setup in a DJ truck, Bhopal. Photo by Amit S. Rai.

22. A barat with a live band, Bhopal. Photo by Amit S. Rai.

chauvinists, and where the speaker-based amplification of religious hymns from Hindu temples and masjids has been a serious point of contention between the two communities.

Finally, then, how can we situate this new technology emerging throughout India? Bolter and Grusin argue that in the West "new digital media oscillate between immediacy and hypermediacy, between transparency and opacity. This oscillation is the key to understanding how a medium refashions its predecessors and other contemporary media. Although each medium promises to reform its predecessors by offering a more immediate or authentic experience, the promise of reform inevitably leads us to become aware of the new medium as a medium. Thus, immediacy leads to hypermediacy."[111] As we have seen in the past two chapters, the new media explosion in India, either in its pirated circulation as logo (Dolby Digital in talkies in Bhopal) or in its proprietary release as the absolutely new and totally secure (Digital Light Processing), certainly traffics in immediacy, as a category that is both epistemological (unmediated transparency of an object) and psychological-affective (the feeling that the medium has disappeared).[112] I would suggest, however, that immediacy has never been the dominant cultural framework for audiovisual media in India. The latest technology does not take the form of the elemental (the "flame" of the lightbulb, as in Benjamin's example), but of a constantly shifting assemblage of materiality, memory, flesh, and sensation.

In this sense, the advent of the digital must be situated in a broader gene-alogy of the incorporation of oral and vernacular media into print technocul-ture in South Asia. Anindita Ghosh has recently suggested that the colonial historiography of print (and media) technology in India needs to become critical of the "technologically-armed elites modernizing backward rural population" scripts. Her study suggests that the borders between orality and print, marked by collisions and negotiations, resulted in a productive and volatile mix in the world of Indian commercial vernacular publishing, as-sembled through indigenous exchange in bazaar-centered economies. The spread of literacy and the availability of cheap print technology contributed to the growth of enormous popular markets for "ephemeral genres" that encapsulated the desires of a reading public still geared to preprint tastes. Elaborate efforts by the educated Indian elite to "improve" literary standards and sanitize tastes remained unrealized in the face of this "unbridled and ca-cophonous print revolution."[113] She concludes that the imperatives of a mar-ket economy and the flexibilities of its consumption patterns—developing functional assemblages of speech, song, image, poetry, prose, and thauma-turgy, and bringing together preprint, vernacular, and collective practices of spiritual "exercises" dating back, in one form or another, as early as perhaps the seventeenth century—combined to thwart the ready assimilation of the printed book and modernity in colonial India. "Far from displacing earlier traditions, and freezing writing habits into standardized norms and predict-able genres," writes Ghosh, "print actually equipped them with more endur-ing and resilient technologies." Ironically, then, the new print technology, instead of fixing formats, genres, and languages, offered opportunities for the interplay of many forms. "Most noticeably, print sustained earlier read-ing and writing traditions."[114]

There are specific topological changes in India's media assemblage from the rise of print technoculture to the proliferation of audiovisual technolo-gies in the twentieth and twenty-first centuries. First, from its inception in the late eighteenth century and the early nineteenth, the elite discourse (mostly colonial missionary, and, later, urban upper-caste literati) govern-ing the dispensation of print sought to curb the contagious excesses of vernacular traditions proliferating along specific gradients of circulation and consumption in the colonial bazaar. In that sense, the biopolitical ped-agogies of a media assemblage—aimed at public hygiene, human security, cultivating savings and productive expenditure—are tactics of de-vernacularizing and de-loitering media practices. But media contagions are always forms of vernacularization, gaps of time pass, spontaneously generating swerving vectors, bodily and discursively. Initially this pedagogy took the form of creating a new literary prose language and literature, in order to distinguish it from earlier traditions, allegedly polluted by rusticity, loose colloquial forms, and an abundant sexuality. This "civilizing drive" reordered ideas of the "obscene" (vernacular) and the "genteel" (modern) in the emerging print culture through the application of new standards. The civilizing of vernacular language established supposedly clear hierarchies between written and spoken language and imported a predominantly Sanskritized vocabulary. Of course, this was a marked departure from the folk language of medieval Bengal, which had been a layered hybrid shared by Hindus and Muslims alike. It employed both colloquial and Perso-Arabic words and borrowed idioms freely from local myths, beliefs, and the practices of both communities. The reformist literati hoped the printed book would modernize and purify the language.[115] These modernizing dreams were largely set aside during the first commercialization of printing in the middle of the nineteenth century. Although the preprint book trade had been carried on by scholars and scribes, as initiative and enterprise passed to more profit-oriented hands, cheap and popular print genres swept the market.[116] Further, the collective consumption of narratives, images, and songs and poetry was a defining feature of this media assemblage, and its genealogies have been traced back well before the advent of print. *Kathakata* is one example of such collective enunciations. Kathakatas, or collective narrative sessions, where religious works based on Hindu religious epics and mythology were read aloud by professional Brahmin narrators, or *kathaks*, were in great demand during the late nineteenth century and survived well into the print age. The texts were Brahmanical in spirit and content, and usually rendered in an ornate style of composition, with "resounding alliteration and elaborate metaphor." The reading event was divided into two sessions—morning and afternoon. In the morning the reader merely read from old tattered volumes, and sometimes more primitive wooden tablets, while in the afternoon what had been read earlier was explained in the vernacular. The kathak retold the existing story while interspersing the narrative with suitable songs, poems, popular tales, and moral lessons, thereby heightening the experience of listeners.[117] If these kathakata events were a focal point of community living, they were also a site of social contestation, technological assemblage, and the body's potentializing. The moral authority accorded to the narrator and the deep faith of the attending audience certainly gave him an extremely involved role, but one that was enabled by an always already active audience. As Ghosh notes, the audience evidently gave their full and implicit belief to the tales related, "for, as a contemporary observed, 'frequently the whole crowd makes some sudden impulsive gesture, illustrative of the progress of the story.'" Although many among the subaltern castes were literate, they would often join the illiterate groups at these sessions. Young and old, men and women, would flock daily to such gatherings, which sometimes continued for months on end. There was an undeniable participatory nature to these kathakata sessions: "Everyone had a share: the patrons, the performer, and the listeners were all expected to play their respective parts. This was undoubtedly an extraordinary celebration of shared emotions and listening experiences, cementing the community and encouraging piety, virtue, and conformity." If, as Ghosh further argues,[118] these popular performance traditions continued to thrive and almost invariably escaped fixation by writing, then what was at stake in their performance for the constitution and regularity of social power was the possibility of their affective contagion leading precisely to impiety (heterodoxa), depravity (bodily potential), and nonconformity (creative indetermination). This "escape," thus, is not a dialectical contradiction but rather an infolding and unfolding zone of indetermination internal to the social-technological field of a media assemblage, one whose effects exceed always its actualization, but in ways that are always immanent to the abstract dynamisms (field of potentiality) of a given assemblage. As we have seen, popular image-sound regimes continue to proliferate through and infect the sensation machines of media. In so doing they always overflow their fixation by the digital and in that overflow produce new sources of value.

FOUR

"With You Every Moment in Time":

On the Emergent *Ittafaq* (Chance) Assemblage

As I suggested in chapter 3, the new hero of Hindi-Urdu cinema is the cosmopolitan DJ. In keeping with global cultural and economic trends, DJ culture has exploded in India in the past ten years. The DJ has become a ubiquitous figure creating intensive aural timespaces everywhere including music videos, films, art exhibition openings, and wedding receptions. How do we think about this emergence? The DJ, spinning a careful mix of old filmi favorites and club anthems, creates interfaces and intervals in the movement of bodies, the projection of aural space, and the proliferation of digital media. These are new ad-hoc media publics, marked by the politics of negotiation, and yet their effects at the level of the body remain obscure because what is partially at stake in their thought is the return of the body to a level of experience before experience (phenomenology cannot address this contagious stratum in its specificity without reducing it to forms of consciousness). As others before me have suggested, this level of experience before experience is called the virtual, or affect.

"Ajeeb ittafaq hai" (It's a strange coincidence): we should consider this line so common in commercial Hindi-Urdu films as a limit experience in contemporary media. It signals a threshold into a qualitatively different kind of modernity in India. The term *ittafaq* is derived from an Arabic compound whose semantic range includes accordance, harmony, accident, conspiracy, agreement, concord, chance, event, and opportunity.

Ajeeb ittafaq hai is what, in the film *C.I.D.* (1956), Inspector Shekhar (Dev Anand) says to Waheeda Rehman when, after he is wounded by her thug accomplices, he awkwardly stumbles onto her house. And so the stage is set for Waheeda's famous performance of iconic facial gestures in the song "Kahin Pe Nigahein Kahin Pe Nishana" as she tries to seduce the villain and allow the hero to escape.

Ittafaq is one of the two words that General Bakshi offers to Major Ram Prasad Sharma to explain how his daughter (in desperate need of military protection) and Sharma's long-lost brother have ended up in the same elite college in a remote northern hillstation in *Main Hoon Na.*

The other word is *kismat* (fate, destiny). There, too, it sets the stage for the digitally composited transition to the paradigmatic college song of the era, "Chale Jaise Hawayein" (Let's Go Like the Wind), with its long shots, fast editing, moving cameras, digital effects, and explosive dance beats.

I am suggesting that accordance, accident, agreement, concord, chance, event, and opportunity—that is, ittafaq—have been and continue to be the order words governing the intimate passage from narrative anticipation to song-dance movement and back. Think of the field of emergence for the ittafaq image: What does such an image do to articulated sets of relations, singularities, events? The ittafaq image relates specific vectors or basins of attraction that energize the suspenseful transition of the body from chance dialogue to anticipated song. From at least the 1950s on, this passage has been seen as the advent and necessary mastery of chance. Indeed, as Peter Brooks pointed out long ago, part of what melodrama does as a technology of subjection is tame chance through the narrativization of coincidence.[1] Both Ravi Vasudevan and Esha Niyogi note that this is one of the legacies of the translation of the cultural form into popular cinema in India.[2]

I believe that a decisive aspect of what we are witnessing today is the rapid dissolution of the empire of signs, gestures, habituations, spatiotemporalities, and generic codes that governed this passage into and mastery of chance: the ittafaq image's new dispensation. The ittafaq image names a passage from a romantic dialectic of accident-concord to the proliferation and capture of chance as nonactualized event, or as a value-producing pure potentiality to affect and be affected. In short, a new quotidian practice of the ittafaq image is coming into being in the contagious becomings of a body that, on the one hand, orients practice toward a noncalculable, always emerging, and even noninsurable future, and, on the other, a body overcoded through the probabilistic apparatus of population statistics. I argue that a number of correlated developments have led to a qualitatively new ittafaq image in contemporary Hindi-Urdu cinema and in the social practices assembled with media multiplicity. Of signal importance has been

23. Ittafaq harmony: the handshake in *Main Hoon Na* (dir. Farah Khan, 2004).

24. Ittafaq sound: digitally composited photo in *Main Hoon Na* (dir. Farah Khan, 2004).

25. Ittafaq dance: "Chale Jaise Hawaien" performed by Amrita Rao in *Main Hoon Na* (dir. Farah Khan, 2004).

the explosion of DJ culture and the specific rhythms and intensities of the audiovisual database as an embodied cultural form in India. The very practice of sampling and harmonizing chance resonances across audio tracks in DJ practice gives ittafaq a new contagious capacity by linking chance to an ontology of media intervals: patterned but unpredictable. More, the displacement of the bazaar talkie by the malltiplex is also correlated with this emergence of new population segmentations, risk experiences, and chance subjects, given that the malltiplex is the new arcade where the chance encounter harmonizes with populations of encounters unfolding their own regularity and their own singular creativity (loitering media, clinamedia). Finally, the emergence of the jump cut[3]—understood as a cut in time *and* space[4]—in the visual style of certain commercial film genres has refunctioned narrative in terms of what Gary Saul Morson has called the open time of narrativeness. These vectors of change assemble in the medium of the digital, their interactions are synchronized but swerving toward a new experience of ittafaq. It is here in this emergent timespace, where the regime of human security transforms and orders disparate practices of work, pleasure, and life, that the potentializing of kismat and ittafaq becomes a matter of sexuality understood as an ecology of sensation. All this suggests that at the level of sensorimotor schema (the diagram of connectivity to historically specific ecologies of sensation) a dissociated body accelerating with the dynamic functionality of a globalizing media assemblage has transformed the mode of address of frontal iconicity that so long has been characteristic of commercial Indian cinema.

Assemblage, Control, Media

As Gilles Deleuze writes in his examination of Discipline and Punish, Foucault describes the West as moving away from disciplinary societies where individuals are confined in hospitals, prisons, schools, factories, and barracks toward "control societies that no longer operate by confining people but through continuous control and instant communication."[5] Patricia Clough has rigorously drawn out the political implications of this shift toward biopower: "Control does not operate within the enclosed institutions of civil society. Indeed, control is a response to the crises of these institutions, which have become turbulent and let to function as far-from-equilibrium systems of information." Clough points to that deployment of biopower through control which is much more dispersed than disciplining. The target of control is not a subjectivity expressing internalized social norms; in that sense, control points to the increasing abandonment of socialization and education of the individual subject through interpellation to, and through, national and familial ideological apparatuses. Rather, "control aims at a never-ending modulation of moods, capacities, affects, potentialities, assembled in genetic codes, identification numbers, ratings profiles and preference listings; that is to say, bodies of data and information (including the human body as information and data)." Control works at the molecular level of organic and nonorganic bodies, self-organizing but open and unstable distributed networks whose informational substrate potentializes "life itself," thus producing quantum effects that are multiplied across the intercalated strata of self-differing, multiplicious assemblages.[6]

Throughout this study of the new media assemblage of contemporary Hindi-Urdu cinema I have shown how such assemblages in their various integration with forms and institutions of biopower (economic, transnational, bodily, communal, cultural, sexed and gendered, etc.) have become one of the central modalities of control and becoming under globalization in north India. In various ways, this exploration has been a meditation on the ittafaq image: loitering, time pass, bits of sensation, intervals, ontologies of duration. I have argued that media assemblages are continuous multiplicities open to their own specific potential contagions, bodying forth new temporalities, rhythms, tempos, and intensive pulsations. Indeed, one of the fundamental movements of a media assemblage could be mapped as analog infection refunctioning and repotentializing the binary code of the digital.[7] Further, I noted that media assemblages are folded into security functions across the abstract machines of societies turning more and more toward control and management, aiming at the production of populations with specifically modulated affective dispositions. This argument has also been about the production of preindividual sexuality in affective contagions across the topography of contemporary media. In this chapter I aim to flesh out these particular arguments.

I have marked the effective connectivity between the digital and various forms of continuous security, as well as the stochastic resonances of the body as zone of indetermination in the creative event of media assemblages. Securing newly privatized property—from digital cinematic content to the privatized spaces of malltiplexed viewing and consuming—has been an important part of the story of new media in India, and it suggests the lines of struggle for technological access and capital accumulation that the regime of hyperdistribution augurs. Everywhere we turn, it seems, we witness the authorization of secured regimes of passage combining feedback controls on subjective, topographic, and sexual becomings. We have already seen how censorship practice today aims to secure national morality (from pornographic bits), or how current exhibition technology secures the image in the hyperreal seamlessness of the digital, in Dolby's felt sensation in the body, or in DLP's ever "faithful" representation of the film community's intentions. Thus, the question of security has never been far from my concerns in these pages. The new regime of control being instituted everywhere and in everything is part and parcel of the thoroughgoing "liberalization" of India's economy—the privatization of public sector undertakings across the economy is predicated on a logic of securing property and legitimating control: Bollywood turning honorable. One of the first stages of this process is the radical expansion of personal and commercial insurance. In diagramming insurance in its articulation as forms of biopower, I address insurancial technologies as temporal pedagogies that are intertwined with national and diasporic nostalgia, looking specifically at the image-sound regimes that are cobbled together from the half-forgotten detritus of Hindi-Urdu cinema's yesteryears, astrological practices, low-budget digital videography, and the liability laws governing fair disclosure on satellite TV. The question of risk for today's media assemblage opens thought to the changes in the habituations of this media's sensory-motor schema—ittafaq becoming statistical stochasticity. For film culture, narratives, characterization, and star discourses in popular media cannot be dissociated from the transformations in risk technologies in postliberalization India. Today, the media assemblage of liberalization works through the affective disposition of risk, and that is its sexuality where sensation is potential and emergent and value added. More, as I will show, diagramming the confluence of these factors in India yields the specificity of a certain postcolonial branding.

Here the rising production values, the professionalization of acting, new multinational financial structures, and non-resident Indian- or diasporic-oriented themes and lifestyles within contemporary Bollywood narratives are correlates of an overall reorganization of audience segmentation and profit maximization that has emerged through specific techniques of risk minimization. For instance, as I suggested in chapter 3, one of the fundamental blurrings (between classical melodrama and art cinema) going on in the new malltiplex genre of urban/transnational romance-thrillers has brought the agency of the hero into a contingent rather than instrumental relationship to his or her environment by introducing an essential element of nonintegrable chance—hence risk—into social relations.[8] In that sense a crucial aspect of the dramatic tension of these narratives comes not from anything that happens in the narrative, but rather from the contingency endemic to nonequilibrated life itself. There are some signal cinematic markers of this shift; for instance, the introduction of the jump cut—dramatic denouement deferred or never staged, a narrative jumping to a moment of an active negotiation (Veer-Zara [dir. Yash Chopra, 2004], Humko Dewaana Kar Gaye [dir. Raj Kanwar, 2006], and Kwahish [dir. Govind Menon, 2003])—or the acceleration of dramatic diegesis through splicing, digital compositing, and jumpy camerawork. This has given rise to what I would argue is a fundamentally new hero. The agency of chance-harmony, of ittafaq, achieves a new significance by becoming the ambivalent double of the usual hero, a sometimes foe and sometimes savior: chance-fate becoming endemic risk. Today's subject must reorient her or his romantic interests and pleasures in relation to a radically contingent present and an uncertain future. My argument is that the new media assemblage has established a feedback loop relationship between this decisive formal shift in the codes of Bollywood narrative and the heterogeneous implantation of insurancial technologies in India. This feedback loop is a communication channel where information passes through the random noise of the everyday, and where modulations, intervals, phase transitions, becomings, and surplus value find a certain volatile (in)coherence. This becoming-movement of the assemblage is what I will diagram as the new dispensation of the ittafaq image.

Risk here is emerging as the dominant formation, but within it and functioning parallel to it are other subjugated or disqualified (without necessarily being resistant) knowledges, with their own moral, affective, and material economies. Clearly, in contemporary South Asia and its diasporas insurance and astrology are two linked technologies of managing the risky future, not as a tradition-modernity dyad in a discourse on postmodernity but as singularities in an enfolded basin of attraction that structures without stabilizing specific kinds of relays. As we shall see, the conceptions of risk, of the future, of human intervention, and hence relations of power are both divergent and intertwined in these two technologies. Indeed, there are many forms of insurance—South Asian astrology, with its own vocabularies and practices, its own affects (sensory-motor schemata) and singularities, is being reintegrated into globalized forms of risk management through the very connectivities of the media assemblage.

Yeh risky hai (It's risky): On the spirit of Lily

How is India's globalizing media assemblage connected to new technologies that aim to manage the risky future?[9] For quite some time, what has been notorious in Hindi-Urdu film culture is the risk associated with film production, distribution, and exhibition—80 percent of the films fail at the box office, and so, taking a page from Hollywood's reintegration in the 1980s, policymakers, producers, and Indian entertainment moguls have sought to operationalize this cinema's expanded media assemblage. Weekly, it seems, industry observers present facts and figures on the precarious state of the film industry in India, even as the financial base of the industry elites is inoculated from the dangers of black-market (and specifically Pakistani) money through Central Bureau of Investigation anticorruption probes and criminal sweeps and legitimized by such things as industry status, Hollywood-Bollywood (and now, again, Lollywood)[10] collaborative production, and transnational finance and insurance. An unpredictable public, ever fickle in its fast-changing tastes, ever savvy in its acquisition of pirated media streams, and hence ever differentiated in its address, is the core of this multicentered risk. These risks are managed in various ways within the media assemblage—which suggests that the new disciplines of India's globalizing economy are at once fiscal and spiritual (and hence no opposition can be stabilized between the two). So that while the idea of insuring Hindi-Urdu films has taken off in the past five years,[11] older practices rooted in an alternative cosmology, temporality, ritual-habituations, and subjectivity help to insure, as it were, the auspicious commencement of a film's shooting (the ritual legitimacy of the highly publicized mohourut for most films is confirmed by an astrologer, supervised by a pundit, and organized through standardized Brahmanical rituals) or a small-town theater owner's periodic crises centered on court cases, labor struggles, the first day, first shows of the superhits, communal riots, sabotage or "theft" by staff members, and sharp cost increases for basic utilities. Prayer and consulting astrologers or spiritual guides are forms of risk management for many, if not all, of the owners that I spoke with in Bhopal.

But risk also inheres in the act of diagramming a media assemblage. Consider this fragment from my field notes. *May, 2004. The first, and only, story I heard about the pir's mazaar was from Varun.* At every moment of what was to come, I felt lost, I couldn't find my bearings. The story starts in the toilet. I found myself standing next to Varun in the gent's toilet in Goonj Bahadur (Lily Talkies's younger brother, so to speak; a single screen theater with around eight hundred seats). Varun had guided me into the loo, pointing to the stains above the urinals. "They rub stones on the walls and use them to clean their dicks, to dry every last drop of piss," he said. He was talking about the working-class Muslim male patrons of this theater. It seemed important to Varun to mark his difference from "them," even as the reason we were standing in the men's toilet at Goonj was so that he could tell me about the Muslim spirit that watches over Lily-Goonj. Varun had dated a Muslim girl once, but they parted—for many reasons, but certainly critical to this turning away was Varun's own turning more and more to the Hindu chauvinist factions in the region (the Bajrang Dal, RSS, and BJP are very active in Bhopal, which at one point the Hindu fascists called the future capital of the coming Hindu *rashtra*). Why this happened is a complex story, having to do as much with business ties (the upper echelon of entrepreneurs in the city are largely Hindu and overwhelmingly pro-BJP), ethnic solidarity (as a descendant of Sindhi refugees, Varun and his family have always been anti-Pakistan, but this too seems open to change), and psycho-biographies (pressures from his family to marry a Sindhi girl, growing health problems, and the ups and downs of the family business). But at the moment, Varun was enjoying himself, showing me the shrine he had had built to the Pir. It was in the cleaning closet of the gents toilet of Goonj, a six-by-twelve-foot room that the staff had once used to store cleaning equipment.

It was freshly whitewashed and painted green, the color sacred in popular Islam. On a ledge to the right sat an iconically framed picture of Shirdi Sai Baba (an early twentieth-century saint from Maharastra, claimed by both Hindus and Muslims). Someone had just lit sandalwood incense sticks. Taking off our shoes before we entered, we prayed silently together. Later, Varun told me the story of how, at the suggestion of his Sikh manager, S. P. Singh, he consulted a well-known Hindu astrologer. He had warned Varun that he must appease the Pir, and that somewhere close to Lily-Goonj a *mazaar* (sacred burial site) existed that must be watched over and tended to by the owners. He took me to the burial site that he found two streets over from the theater, and over which he had assumed all maintenance responsibilities. We covered our heads with cloth, lit incense, and Varun said a (Hindu) prayer.

The appeasement, however, involved a midnight adventure of digging a hole four feet deep just beyond the grounds of Lily, and finding there a cup of water miraculously buried (he said that he and Singh did find it); Varun was instructed to submerge the cup with the water still in it before dawn in the Narmada River, which was some hours away. He and Singh sped to the river in the early hours of the morning. Completely naked in bone-chilling river water at four in the morning, Varun fulfilled the astrologer's instructions. He also tells me that Singh was sitting in the car laughing at him.

Varun has "regular" insurance too (both personal and for Lily-Goonj); indeed, it's probable that his best friend's wife sold it to him (she's a very successful insurance agent in the city). But he insists that such devotion to the well-being of the Pir's spirit has helped him escape not only death threats, court cases, and movie flops but an actual attempt on his life. Late one night during the middle of a particularly rowdy jubilee run of a blockbuster movie, as Varun was leaving the office, local toughs wanting to pressure him for special treatment and exclusive tickets surrounded him, but inexplicably he was able to slip past them into his car, just as one of them glanced a knife off his car mirror. He sped away, never to be troubled by the (same) lads again.

The disposition toward risk in this set of practices articulates technologies of time (managing the shrine and burial site, appeasements, astrologers, haunting) with the communalized histories of exhibition practices. For Varun the haunting of the Pir was of a piece with owning and running a theater in a largely Muslim neighborhood. Praying at the shrines and the appeasement was also not incongruent with his own Hinduism, and it was given final legitimation by the Hindu astrologer. I can't say with any confidence how seriously Varun took it all; he certainly paid meticulous attention to the specifics of it, and even performed the rituals with some verve, but there also seemed to be a current of levity running through it all. But maybe I'm projecting? Regardless, the "loo shrine" has become legendary for Muslims in the area, and both men and women worship there regularly.

Risk and Sexuality

In the History of Sexuality, Volume 1 and in the lectures collected in "Society Must Be Defended" Foucault argues that from the middle of the nineteenth century onward sexuality in the West exists "at the point where body and population meet";[12] in the lectures he goes on to name one of the nodal points of this fateful meeting "insurance." At this intersection of forces, Foucault suggests, discourses, institutions, affects, and temporalities form a functional assemblage in the body of racialized (degenerate), sexualized (debauched), and classed (disciplined) subjects: "Debauched, perverted sexuality has effects at the level of population, as anyone who has been sexually debauched is assumed to have a heredity. Their descendant also will be affected for generations, unto the seventh generation and unto the seventh of the seventh and so on. This is the theory of degeneracy: given that it is the source of individual diseases and that it is the nucleus of degeneracy, sexuality represents the precise point where the disciplinary and regulatory, the body and the population, are articulated."[13] I wish to draw this thought out in a consideration of "insurancial" technologies in India and its diasporas as a specific transformation of the ecologies of ittafaq. First, as temporal disposition, the ittafaq assemblage implicates the subject in a paradoxical sexualization of chance. This sexualization occurs in the shifting durations of correlated and probabilistic media intervals that are assembled today across platforms and interconnected digital streams. Second, on another scale of media intervals, what we note is that transnational insurance companies are beginning to underwrite popular Bombay film productions, and are further one of the main sponsors of sitcoms, news shows, and movies on satellite TV channels. This implies that to think about sexuality in relationship to what I am calling the media assemblage of Bollywood necessitates that we understand the specific disciplines tied to the production of consuming bodies, and the management and calculation of specific kinds of returns from the increasingly segmented audience-populations of the popular media assemblage. If part of the disciplinary practices put into place through this assemblage includes the management and surveillance of individual and collectivized bodies (in class-segregated screening rooms in multiplexes, or balcony and stall seating in single-screen talkies, through the discourse of the fan, through a stylized mode of address in new genres, through advertising, through fashion, through norms and branding of the star's body), it is by regulating audience populations that the thought of cinema aggregates audiences, calculating risks, nurturing probabilities, and maximizing returns. If, as Foucault suggests, sexuality is the point of articulation of population and body, diagramming the ittafaq ecology in cinematic narratives, media practices, and everyday life helps us to push our analysis of this assemblage's motor-sensory schema in the direction of the specific temporal pedagogies, or ethical scripts orienting subjects toward the future.

Risk: A Brief History

Ulrich Beck, in an article reflecting on his diverse research into the sociology of risk, asks the following question: "What do events as different as Chernobyl, global warming, mad cow disease, the debate about the human genome, the Asian financial crisis and the September 11th terrorist attacks have in common? They signify different dimensions and dynamics of world risk society."[14] For Beck the speeding up of modernization has produced a gulf between the world of quantifiable risk in which we think and act "and the world of non-quantifiable insecurities that we are creating."[15] The interval between calculations of risk and the production of insecurities is especially lucrative for the insurance market, no doubt, but as Beck goes on to show, risk and control have always been of a piece and the specific form the risk assemblage has taken under contemporary globalization scenarios is a kind of "de-bounding" along three continua: space, time, and the social. Thus, risk becomes a technology of controlling what is more and more uncontrollable or even calculable. That does not stop its proliferation in India and in other emerging economies of the global South. Indeed, its effectivity is something of a precondition for a more intensive integration into the global economy. As P. C. James, the executive director of the Insurance Regulatory and Development Authority of India, puts it, insurance is to be thought of as an "instrument of mitigation" by empowering poor and disadvantaged populations and by shifting the burden of social regulation from the state to insurancial technologies and bureaucracies. The point is that unlike Beck's naive reduction of global risk technologies to a Western phenomenon (that is, to a force "exogenous" to developing societies), what we find is that risk finds moments of folding inside and outside together every moment in time. By seeming to extend the postcolonial vocation of development, insurance technologies saturate not only discursive strategies of nation-building (what Ranajit Guha once called the *maa-baap* [mother-father] function of Indian governmentality)[16] but proliferate particular affective dispositions toward the future through segmenting populations as a function of their propensity to risk.

So what is the history of risk management in India? Geeta Patel's pioneering work on insurance, pensions, and modes of governmentality in colonial India has enabled a new thinking about questions of sexuality, the body, and the capillary functioning of colonial power.[17] Her work situates the physics of colonial rule within specific technologies of nurturing the sympathies of a subject population through the calculations necessary for insuring one's own livelihood and security. What we can see in the subsequent history of colonial and postcolonial trajectories of insurance is that, from a mode of governmentality operating at the capillary point of power's exercise in colonial India, insurance has become a form of regulating populations, norming lifestyles, and implanting calculation technologies in the very body of the potentially global Indian: a biopower of risk nurtures probabilities of the aleatory.

Colonial life insurance in India started in the year 1818 when the Oriental Life Insurance Company set up offices in Calcutta. Although that company failed in 1834, the practice of insurance had taken hold among both colonizer and colonized, and thus by the second decade of the nineteenth century Madras Equitable began transacting life insurance business in the Madras Presidency in 1829 (numerous, mostly British companies were founded throughout the nineteeth century).[18] The colonial archives of insurance business in India, however, really began in 1914 when the Government of India started publishing returns of insurance companies in India.[19]

In postcolonial India, the Insurance Amendment Act of 1950 reorganized certain aspects of the colonial legislation concerning insurance. Just after independence, numerous insurance companies had been either taken over by Indians or were run jointly with foreign companies, and according to industry watchers the level of competition was high; there were also allegations of unfair trade practices. Nehru's administration nationalized the insurance industry in 1956 by creating the public sector undertaking Life Insurance Corporation of India (LIC), which absorbed 154 Indian insurers as well as 16 non-Indian insurers and also 75 provident societies.[20] From 1956 until the late 1990s the insurance industry remained a public sector undertaking; in keeping with the liberalization of the economy, toward the end of the last decade insurance was reopened for private sector investment, and foreign companies entered the market in significant numbers.[21]

Thus the explosion of transnational insurance offerings in India is a relatively new phenomenon given that the industry's gradual deregulation began around the mid-1990s and culminated in the Insurance Regulatory and Development Authority Act of 1999 (which went into effect on April 19, 2000). Around this time the public sector undertaking General Insurance Coorporation (GIC) began offering a new set of insurance products that would insure an expanded range of risks while excluding others. For instance, the new policy offers to insure customers against material damages arising out of natural calamities and also the loss of "fidelity of employees"; the policy will not, however, provide insurance for losses arising from defective design and materials, corrosion and rust, or, crucially, destruction of property in riots. So in what is being pragmatically excluded and included as insurable risks we also have an image of a regularized social life in India: a crumbling infrastructure is a manageable risk, but a volatile social structure (i.e., communal riots) is not—as least not yet.[22]

From 2000 to 2005, the market share of private insurance companies in India has gone from close to zero to 26 percent; the penetration of life insurance has increased from 1.7 percent (premium income as a proportion of GDP) in 2000 to 2.6 percent in 2005 (the global average is 4.7 percent), although most of this growth has been in the urban areas only.[23] Since the advent of private insurance firms in 2000, India's insurance market has grown by 20 percent per year; the first-year premium of the life insurance segment has grown 260 percent between 2000 and 2005. What this reflects is the differentiated production of consumer desire for risk technologies. Yet, in a familiar slight of hand, the neoliberal press is pitching the insurance market itself as a "buyer's market": a microtemporality of control as the advent of "choice." As *Business Today* put it, "The real achievement of the private insurance firms . . . is the fact that insurance is no longer a sellers' market. On the back of innovative product offerings, and new distribution channels (think Bancassurance, corporate agencies, even direct selling through the internet) it has become a buyers' market."[24]

Risk and Liberalizing India

Let me further situate the notion of "risk" in India. Niranjan Pant has put the concept in the framework of the creation of an insurance regulatory agency in liberalizing India: risk indicates, simply, a situation where an exposure to loss exists. The existence of risk may have a deterrent effect on capital accumulation, and consequently on capitalist growth; the problem from the point of a liberalizing economy is how to make risk productive. Insurance devices deal with risk through sharing, and in its simplest aspect it is imbued with two fundamental characteristics: first, it transfers risk from one person to a group; second, it facilitates the sharing of losses, on some supposedly "equitable" basis, by all members of the group. For Pant, insurance must be seen from both an individual as well as a social point of view; for the individual, insurance presents an economic device whereby the individual substitutes a small certain cost (the premium) for a large uncertain financial loss (the contingency insured against) that would exist if it were not for the insurance. Socially, insurance functions to "reduce and eliminate" risk through the process of combining a sufficient number of homogeneous exposures into a group, and making the losses predictable for a group as a whole: "Insurance creates a counterpart of risk, which is security."[25] From the point of view of national development, insurance, by removing the fear of risk from economic calculation, is said to "stabilize" the economy, trade, and commerce; it also contributes to the national economy by creating new "value added," optimizing the use of venture capital, and generating investment funds through premiums; thus, there is a positive correlation between the economic development of a country and the amount that people spend on insurance.

Insurance, risk, loss, development, and security are the terms (some new and some quite old) that are transforming an economic agenda of liberalization and market relations in India into concrete social relations with their own collective and subjective practices. As Fredric Jameson rightly argues, perhaps the most significant aspect in all of this "is the impact of the new value abstractions on everyday life and lived experience, and this is a modification best articulated in terms of temporality." Although he contrasts temporality with "image theory," I will show that the two articulate each other and are dimensions of each other in the contemporary biomediasphere. Jameson's argument helps to disentangle the dynamics of the stock market from the older cyclical rhythms of capitalism generally. Those patterns of "boom and bust, accumulation of inventory, [and] liquidation" imprint a "generational rhythm on individual life." Such rhythms also function to create a vague impression of a political alternation between Left and Right, between dynamism and conservatism or reaction. Such temporal cycles are distinct from the newer process of the consumption of investment as such, "the anxious daily consultation of the listings, deliberations with or without your broker, selling off, taking a gamble on something as yet untested (one imagines a Whitmanesque list opening up, expansive, celebratory, reveling in the ideology of democratic 'participation')." For Jameson, writing in the context of Western economic temporalities, there seems to be a narrowing of the quotidian time frame, which gives a sense of urgency to daily activity. Thus, a novel and "more universal microtemporality accompanies and as it were condenses the rhythms of quarterly 'profit taking' (and is itself intensified in periods of crisis and uncertainty)."[26] How universal is this microtemporality? Jameson falls prey to the problem of causal redundancy when he situates the explanatory frame of temporal shifts only at the level of global economic changes; indeed, as the experience of India shows, there is both a narrowing and expansion of time in the new dispensation of ittafaq, and its (multiple) causality would have to be found in the nonlinear dynamics of the media assemblage.

However, we can suggest that generally the crucial mechanism of this microtemporality is the capacity to calculate the future. As one advertisement for Max New York Life (New York Life's Indian avatar) puts it:

Ultimately, it just boils down to one thing: your outlook towards life. Life is not a fixed formula. It's really to each his own. Which is why, there are some of us who take things on the run, rush headlong into the future and cross bridges once we get there. That's one kind of life. Then, there's the other. Where things are planned. Where the future's forecasted. Where you don't just know the next step. You know the next fifty. That's where life insurance comes in. Life insurance is all about living. Living in peace. Comfortable in the knowledge that you and yours are protected. Now, which kind of life do you lead? Better still, which kind of life would you like to lead?[27]

The temporality of risk here is articulated through a complex assemblage: a pedagogy of the future (which life should you lead?), an implicitly gendered, classed mode of address (you and yours), lifestyle heterogeneity (to each "his" own), secure knowledge and knowledge securing comfort, and finally a definitive yet limited (the next fifty steps) calculation of risk. I will address each of these elements in turn, but let me take up the last point first.

Gerda Reith points out that "risk" is not real but rather a measure of calculation or "a means of quantifying that reality."[28] It is moreover a temporal relationship to an essentially uncertain future: the subject of risk is a future-oriented subject. As François Ewald notes, "Risk is a neologism of insurance, said to derive from the Italian word risco which meant 'that which cuts,' hence 'reef' and consequently 'risk to cargo on the high seas.' "[29] The term was first used in the mid-seventeenth century, and it brought time and uncertainty into a quantifiable relation: "Quite simply, the risk of an event occurring was the probability of it happening over a stated period of time. The practice of insurance as a means of guarding against uncertainty developed almost simultaneously, and was an attempt to protect the individual from the threat of these newly predictable events."[30] Daniel Defert marks the advent of insurance in industrial society "with the invention of a technique for managing a population and creating funds for compensating damages, an emerging technology of risk which was originally devised by financiers, before later becoming a paradigm of social solutions to all cases of non-labour: first that of industrial accidents, then sickness and old age, and finally unemployment."[31]

In the twentieth century new forms of scientific inquiry radically questioned the predictability of insurance technologies, and a new model was developed "that moved away from the ideal of perfect knowledge in certain conditions, and replaced it with one based on partial knowledge and risk minimization," at that moment "the ideal of certainty is replaced with an ongoing exercise in probability calculation."[32] In this temporality, since the identification of something as "a risk" refers to some necessarily partial knowledge of future danger, its threat seems to be located within the boundaries of human intervention. One of the central operations of this technology is that providing a temporal orientation for the calculation of risk territorializes the uncertain future as a domain accessible to individual agency in the present, thus creating an effect of navigable space, self-realization, and control. Reith suggests that "such a projection acts as a stimulus to the individual, whose forward movement is animated by the awareness and negotiation of risks."[33]

But what kind of individual is this? Ewald in fact argues that insurance functions through a quite specific mode of individualization. In his analysis, a risk is first of all a characteristic of the population it concerns. No one can claim to evade it, to differ from the others like someone who escapes an accident. Insurance individualizes, it defines each person as a risk, but the individuality it confers no longer "correlates with an abstract, invariant norm such as that of the responsible juridical subject." Rather, it is an individuality relative to that of other members of the insured population—in other words "an average sociological individuality."[34] (This is the birth, in other words, of what Deleuze called the "dividual" in societies of control.)[35] The overall effect of this, notes Defert, is to open up a population to "indefinite analysis" into more and more finely detailed subclasses of risk. Insuring a population means classifying it and subdividing it in line with different scales and degrees of risk and with "an analysis of behaviours, thresholds, marginal categories which are first excluded, then treated as special subclasses while excluding still more marginal groups, and so on."[36] This indefinite, indeed infinite, concatenation of risk analysis bodies forth a new subjective form in insurance technologies. Thus, to be embedded in a temporality that would provide for the future does not just mean not living from day to day and arming oneself against ill fortune, but also mathematizing one's commitments. Fundamentally, it means no longer resigning oneself to the decrees of providence and the blows of fate but instead transforming one's relationship with nature, the world, and God so that "even in misfortune, one retains responsibility for one's affairs by possessing the means to repair its effects."[37]

Returning to my earlier analysis of the embodied malltiplex and the contagions of cinema's media assemblage, this new future-oriented subjective form is embodied in an entire sensory-motor assemblage (clichés, habits) of digital algorithms, audiovisual technologies, autonomic processes, and the (indeterminate) flesh of the body: the biomediated body. Although my use of the term biomedia is not rooted in the biological humanness of the body, the notion of biomediation is central to diagramming a media contagion. As Eugene Thacker usefully notes, the reconditioning of the body in biomedia "is complex enough that it invites a perspective that sees not the machine opposed to the human, and not the artificial opposed to the natural, but a particular instance in which the 'bio' is transformatively mediated by the 'tech,' so that the 'bio' reemerges more fully biological." Recalling my elaboration of interpenetrating multiplicities, and unlike other biomedical instances of body-technology meetings (robot-assisted surgery, prosthetic limbs, artificial organs), the meeting of the body and technology in biomedia is not based on a juxtaposition of components (human or machine, natural or artificial—a quantitative multiplicity). Rather, biomedia facilitates and establishes conditionalities, enables operativities, and encourages the biological as biological in terms of dynamic feedback loops and emergent properties. As Thacker states: "A key component to the questioning of biotechnology is the attention paid to the ways in which biomedia consistently recombine the medium of biomolecular systems with the materiality of digital technology. The biological and the digital domains are no longer rendered ontologically distinct, but instead are seen to inhere in each other; the biological 'informs' the digital, just as the digital 'corporealizes' the biological."[38] Part of what I have sought to show throughout this study is that the transformative mediation of the body by the media assemblage—the body is one of its connectivities—produces a "bio" that is no longer "fully biological" but rather is a continuous and partially virtual multiplicity, returning the body to an unmediated (potentializing) incipience. This incorporeal materiality is the shifting substrate of what Clough has called nonhuman "affect economies."

In the new affect economies of control societies, not only is there necropolitics, which Achille Mbembe argues returns to colonization as well as moves forward to the present conditions of terrorism and counterterrorism, but there also is the meshing of politics, of biopolitics, with an economy of affect.[39] Directed at the potentializing of "affect itself," bodily capacities and the value that they generate have become unhinged from the human body–species. Here in the exceptional zones of biomediation bodily capacities arise out of nonorganic life. The tendency is to deliver life from the body as organism and its particular dependencies on spaces or forms, where being is reduced to corporeal manifestation in space or position in the chronological continuum of time (an implicit revision, thus, of Thacker's residual "humanism"). Rather, there is in biomediation a "more direct reach to non-organic life. So, the managing and the controlling of statistical risks across populations in relationship to organic life, the valuing of life differently in relationship to different populations, at different scales of living, now extends to capital accumulation in the domain of affect in the attempt to capture the productivity of the complexity of non-organic life, its capacity for self-organization."[40]

Consider in this regard the explosion of "cat bonds." Melinda Cooper in her essay "Pre-Empting Emergence: The Biological Turn in the War on Terrorism" argues that there has been a decisive shift in the conceptualization, management, and deployment of risk in relation to the biopolitcs of our present state of emergency. In this scenario war is no longer waged in the defense of the state (the Schmittian philosophy of sovereign war) or even human life (humanitarian warfare; the human as bare life, according to Agamben; sovereign is he who decides on the state of exception for a given human population) but in *the name of life in its biospheric dimension, incorporating meteorology, epidemiology and the evolution of all forms of life, from the microbe upwards.*" The extension of preemptive warfare to include the sphere of environmental and biopolitics "conflates the eternalization of war with the evolution of life on earth—as if permanent war were simply *a fact of life,* with no other end than its own crisis-driven perpetuation."[41]

Cooper extends this analysis into the economic domain, where one application of catastrophe risk has been the invention of new speculative instruments such as "cat bonds," which since the mid 1990s have allowed reinsurers to hedge for natural and technological disasters on the capital markets. A catastrophe bond is somewhat like a municipal bond, except if the catastrophe occurs the "principal goes away to deal with the catastrophe."[42] Cat bonds typically pay a higher percentage than other bonds; reinsurers, insurers, commercial banks, hedge funds, and investment advisors usually are the buyers; and financial houses, insurance companies, and hedge funds issue them to increase the pool of available capital to cover the large risks of, for instance, packages of credit card debts, mortgages, or automobile loans, and *force majeure* events such as earthquakes, floods, and hurricanes. As the risk analyst John Quartermain notes, the application of cat bonds to Internet *force majeure* events seems straightforward, except, of course, "that probability matrices are needed to write them."

But, as Cooper astutely shows, cat bonds can cover not only natural and aerospace catastrophes, which are now regularly traded, but more recently "proposals have been made to issue titles for everything from acts of terrorism to climate change and genetic accidents." The usefulness of the catastrophe bond, in place of the more cautious asset investments of the past, is again commonly attributed to the very nature of the catastrophe event, which reinsurance companies declare to be uninsurable, "at the limits even of the calculable." The problem of mathematizing catastrophe by trading on the potential for accidents associated with the new biotechnologies demands algorithms that "think the unthinkable and quantify the unquantifiable." The cat bond resolves the apparent dilemma by transforming uncertainty itself into "a tradable event, protected by a legally binding contract. In the process, it invents a form of property right that seeks to capture the speculative biological future at its most unpredictable—literally, before it has even emerged."[43]

This preemption of emergence in the floatation of cat bonds is of a piece with a transformation in the affective valence of risk subjects' relation to the future—"from euphoria to panic to fear, or rather alertness (a state of fear without foreseeable end)."[44] In India cat bonds seem to be on the verge of taking off, and they may in fact turn out to be a way for foreign banks to sidestep the insurance machine altogether. Already in 2003, as the *Economic Times* of India reported, foreign banks were exploring ways of issuing quasi-insurance products to domestic corporations, bringing them into direct competition with insurance companies in India; these banks were planning to block off insurance companies and directly approach domestic firms, helping them reduce insurance costs.[45]

My argument in this chapter attempts to think about these disparate analyses together in a critical recasting of the media assemblage internal to the transformation of risk technologies in India. Simply, these postcolonial insurancial technologies today are perhaps the single most powerful modality of biomediation across material substrates (bodies, populations, biotechnologies, life itself), technologies of communication (Internet, TV, cinema), and affect economies (the microtemporalities of globalization). In what follows, I explore more closely one such biomedia assemblage.

Assemblage, Media, and Risk Revisited

In the case of postliberalization India, we must note that the ittafaq assemblage mediates insurance technologies and spiritual practices by articulating the two, often through the mode of address common to Hindi-Urdu narratives. In that sense India and its diasporas are witness to the emergence of a new perceptual mode of power (TV plus insurance) modulating moods, affective dispositions, and temporal orientations in the bodies of a heterogeneous population through the habituated sensory-motor schema of popular cinema.[46] Indeed, we should tie this emergence to a specifically globalized technology, one that assembles national identity, familial traditionalism, and a Hindu-ized transnationalism to the reimagining of the nation-family in the diaspora. I am of course referring to the ensemble of financial, productive, tele-informational, cultural, and now insurance (or prudential) discourses, products, subjective forms, institutions, desires, and populations associated with the non-resident Indian and the cultures of neoliberal economics.[47] As I have suggested throughout this study, there has been a crucial refunctioning and repotentializing of these technologies in Hindi-Urdu popular media. New potential, new functions: refunctioning unfolds through a kind of contagious proliferation in the affective lives of consumers of different media such as satellite TV and the Internet, and retooled or refunctioned spaces like the malltiplex, YouTube, and MySpace, or cultural events like DJ parties, both giving form to and in turn formed by emergent, untimely subjectivities: the media assemblage as morphogenetic feedback loop. The affective disposition of these untimely subjects draw on proleptic temporalities of risk and security, new sensory-motor schemata rooted first and foremost in a nostalgic re-presentation of lost cinematic tableaux and "golden era" hits, and through specific prudential practices of sexuality, savings, acquisition, and projection into a supposedly already calculated future.

Here I wish to look specifically at the relationships embedded in the image-sound regimes of insurance technologies advertising and in "spiritual healer" ads. I am interested in these two forms of biomediation because I believe they reference a way of thinking about time, the subject and globalization that complicates notions of national development, the binary between tradition and modernity, emerging market economies, and remediated religious practices, as well as the idea of a subject's self-actualization.

Consider a TV ad for New York Life that was often seen on various satellite channels from 2003–2005: shot in black and white with digital video technology, an extremely rare version of the 1968 Chevy Impala convertible pulls up to the "Village Bird Shop," and a young Indian boy directs his grandfather in buying a cage full of birds. As they pull away, "Aa Chal Ke Tujhe"—a popular song from the 1964 Kishore Kumar vehicle *Door Gagan Ki Chhaon Mein*—lilts

Aa chal ke tujhe
Main leke chaloon
Ek aise gagan ke thale
Jahan gham bhi na ho
Asoon bhi na ho
Bus pyaar hi pyaar pale
Ek aise gagan ke thale
Jahan door nazar dour aaye
Azad gagan lehair aaye . . .

(Come, I will take you to a kind of place where there is no sadness, no tears, only love, only love, toward a kind of sky where your eyes can wander far, where a free sky will wash over you . . .) As the boy and his grandfather pull over by the side of the road and release the birds into the welcoming and apparently free skies an intertitle reads, " . . . a timeless moment." Cut to a digital image of the New York Life building: as the shot pans upward toward its pinnacle, passing American flags waving on the balustrade, another intertitle reads, "with you every moment in time."

Or consider another ad on the satellite channels. An irate father walks into the family room of a palatial home where his daughter (doodling with pen and paper) and wife (with rollers in her hair, filing her nails) recline leisurely on separate loveseats. He then bellows in a parody of filmi-family dialogue: "Anita what is this? Art school? You want to go to art school? Did you hear Mother-of-Anita? Your daughter wants to go to art school! Your daughter will become a cartoonist!"[48] Mother: "What are you telling me for? You have spoiled her!" [Daughter giggles.] Father: "Become a doctor, an engineer, a lawyer, but a cartoonist?" Turning to a three-sided mirror, in a symphonic crescendo of melodramatic angst, he continues his rant: "A daughter of our family can never become a cartoonist as long as I am alive!" Turning back, he finds his daughter still doodling. Grabbing the drawing out of her hands, he asks "What are you drawing?!" It is a caricature of the father, and he guffaws despite himself. Then, a deep voiceover in Indian-British English states: "Whatever career your child chooses, we can help." The father, turning back to his daughter, slightly assuaged, states in Hindi: "It's good, but I'm not that fat either, yaar [friend]." They embrace, and the three take a stroll out by the picture-perfect pool. The voiceover in English comments: "At MetLife we do many things to help you secure the future. Education planning is one of them."

26. " . . . a timeless moment": advertisement on satellite TV for New York Life, 2005.

27. "With you every moment in time": advertisement on satellite TV for New York Life, 2005.

The final example is another MetLife ad targeting the diaspora. Working in an American firm, a retiring Indian professional is presented with a retirement package consisting of a trip to Europe. On the way into their hotel, he and his wife notice a group of white "hippies," seemingly Hare Krishna devotees, holding banners welcoming "Guruji." The next morning, the husband wraps his wife's saffron shawl around his shoulders and takes in the fresh air on the balcony of their fourth-story room. The devotees mistake the retiree for Guruji, and start bowing to him. With a sly roll of his eyes, calculating and taking utter joy in throwing the dice, he strikes the correct Guruji pose. And suddenly he has thousands of devotees. The last shots are of his wife reaching out and angrily grabbing her shawl off his shoulders. Voiceover: "Some people leave their retirement to chances. How are you planning yours?"

These ads focus the viewers' attention by associating levels of experience through indices of security-fear. For their addressees, who are usually male and upper-class, risks do not arise essentially from domestic conflict, and in fact any specifiable risk is strategically elided from the carefully massaged frame of the ad, just as is a general sense of precarious well being. Risks are hinted at as naturally occurring, unpredictable forces (the simple advent of old age, or the perverse proclivities of an artsy daughter) that act on families and that must be contended with if the future is to be not merely livable (by which is meant middle-class comfort and security) but a domain for the actualization of freedom—the birds in flight, the drawing of the self-actualized daughter, and the sly roll of the eyes playing at holiness are all indices that focus attention toward this possible freedom. It is useful to recall here what Charles Sanders Peirce once wrote of indices: "A rap on the door is an indication. Anything that focuses the attention is an indication. Anything which startles us is an indication, in so far as it marks the junction between two portions of experience. Thus a tremendous thunderbolt indicates that something considerable happened though we may not know precisely what the event was. But it may be expected to connect itself with some other experience."[49] When insurancial media unfold through techniques of attention that generalize a particular mood across a human multiplicity—the mood of a liberalizing ittafaq ecology—there is a certain autonomization of fear-security as both thought process and embodied sensation. As Brian Massumi suggests in his analysis of North American counterterrorism, fear can now operate as the nonphenomenal background of existence, or outside "in-which of experience" (the virtualization of fear), in its role as the affective tone or generic context for a way of life. Certainly it can also still be contained, featuring as a particular life's phenomenal content. In addition, it can function "purely self-demonstratively, as a self-sufficient thought process unencumbered by the bodily activation still necessarily accompanying it." Crucially, Massumi adds, which of these modes, or which combination of them, will be in operation at any given point depends on the "regime of external signs in play, the nature of the contexts through which they multiply, the acquired skills of suppression impressed on the bodies populating those contexts, and the techniques of attention in operation (for example, as associated with the media, in particular as they disseminate themselves more widely and finely through the social field, assisted by miniaturization and digitization)."[50]

Keeping this in mind, we return to an Indian insurancial assemblage that splits in its enunciation, forking along different lines of flight: the digitally produced narrative and soundtrack, usually in Hindi, couched in specifically filmic idioms, either unfolds as a melodramatic narrative launched by the backward glance of an aged retiree ruminating fondly over well-spent years, and culminating in the placidity of secure domesticity, or of the dramatization of chance encounters across various mobilities (transnational travel, tourism, imagined diasporas) and life's phase transitions (retirement, graduation, familial growth, etc.). The soundtracks to these ads are taken from the song archives of classical Bollywood—that is, fifties- and sixties-era Lata, Asha, Kishore, Mukesh, and Rafi (in other words targeting a population that is just now turning sixty-five, which could be taken as perhaps the initial act of population segmentation in this assemblage). From another space and time, the voiceover, usually in English, offers the bemused viewer the century-old expertise and accumulated knowledge embodied in the insurance firm itself. MetLife itself becomes a faithful repository of expert knowledge waiting to secure your too-risky future. That this is done through specific techniques of population segmentation, statistics, probability, and information gathering is, however, largely absent or only implicit; rather, "since they are supposed to be providing security," the insurance institutions need to be associated with a "quasi-infinite longevity": "With insurance one comes to experience a sort of dilation of timescales, stretched out to span not just one generation of lifetime but several, and thus positing the survival of society for an indefinite future."[51] Every one of life's events, its infinitesimal phase transitions, some planned, others sheer ittafaq, becomes an occasion to attend to the quality of one's security by quantifying risk.

Notice, then, how the ittafaq assemblage shifts the parameters of this longevity. First, as I noted above the ittafaq image has often been associated with the transition from dialogue to song, when the perplexity of chance is harmonized in the affective uptake of (nostalgic) music. At moments in these ads, this harmonizing of chance is also the mooring of newness in memory, as well as in the sensory-motor circuit tying chance to sound, that is, by increasing the probability that an assemblage of information will pass through the channel with the least amount of noise. More, by linking the probability of an event to its distributed but unequal effects across a population these commercials open the body to more and more finely modulated renderings of, precisely, harmonizing with the future.

Put another way, a sentimentalized rendering of a moment of painful but also well-planned-for change comes to figure the addressee of insurance and the specific relationship to the risks of the future. The temporality of the prudential subject of insurance is stretched over a sentimentalized lifetime, while the lost past of India as aural memory, as homeland, returns as one of the idyllic fruits of security. Simultaneously, time is projected beyond the subject's death into the future through the biological inevitability and persistent responsibilities of heterosexual reproduction. Insurance thus is a global technology that by being "with you every moment in time" offers up a monument to life, saturating time with the paradoxical values and sensations of security, death, loss, freedom, noncalculability, and maximalization. That paradoxical security covers the lives of loved ones after one's own death draws the addressee of insurance into a temporality that escapes and moors itself in mortality (one ad focuses on the undying love of a young boy whose father, although dead, both returns as a comforting ghost and guarantees a certain return through his life insurance policy—New York Life: a promise kept by those who have gone). This temporality has, therefore, both a gender (in its addressee) and a moral (in its temporal orientation).

Indeed, this enunciation is split along a number of different dimensions of change in this ecology of sensation: norms of heterosexual reproduction already embedded within melodramatic Hindi-Urdu filmic narratives and songs are transposed onto a temporality of securing the future; cultural belonging signified through linguistic and national authenticity within the framework of the family is both deterritorialized and sutured by a metadiscourse in English of self-actualization and security; finally, norms of the family, of security, and of cultural literacy are reorganized explicitly in its segmented mode of address, which targets certain audience populations and excludes others, thereby turning bodily norms into technologies of segmenting a target population in terms of lesser and greater risk.

My claim here is that the insurancial imaginary diagrammed (as opposed to only represented) in these TV ads institutes what Ewald has called a new type of objectivity that gives to the familiar event a reality that changes its nature: "By objectivizing certain events as risks, insurance can invert their meanings: it can make what was previously an obstacle into a possibility. Insurance assigns a new mode of existence to previously dreaded events; it creates value."[52] If in the nineteenth century the West saw the transformation of class struggle between worker and owner through the calculation of risk and a solidarizing of an average sociological population through statistical probabilities, this mutation attests to the emergence of new affective dispositions toward not only justice and responsibility but also time, causality, destiny, desert, and providence. For Ewald, with insurance and its philosophy, "one enters a universe where the ills that befall us lose their old providential meaning: a world without God, a laicized world where 'society' becomes the general arbiter answerable for the causes of our destiny."[53] What I find compelling about this argument is that it situates risk in the transformation of the affect of microtemporality, but the implicit narrative of secularization is simply not convincing. What we find in the context of India (and in many other globalizing spaces around the world) is that new media technologies have assembled practices of time from very different cosmologies (secular, agnostic, and sacred) on the same technological platform, and their viral proliferation through interpenetrating media streams cannot be understood with anything other than a nonlinear history of affective dispositions coevolving on the plane of the machinic phylum.

The Ittafaq of Spiritual Healer Ads

Time is all about the dangers of the present in the ads for Peer (Pir) Syed Sahib, Pundit Maharaj, and Ajmeri Baba, and no amount of quantification will be able to master these dangers.[54] These ads, typically shot in a kind of low-budget digital video style, begin by montaging images of suffering South Asians (usually dressed in modern, or Western clothing) creeping over backgrounds of barren trees and grey, snowy skies; as the spiritual healer is announced (often with his benevolent and glowing "time-worn" face-logo filling the screen), the scenes and background change to celebrating subjects dressed in kurtas and saris, embracing in a perpetual spring.

Although these spiritual healers rarely have websites of their own (they have a pervasive presence in diasporic print media), one can get a description of their powers on matrimonial websites (which gives one a sense of the

28. Advertisement on satellite TV for Peer (Pir) Syed Saab, "spiritual healer," 2005.

29. Black magic: advertisement on satellite TV for Pir Syed Saab, "spiritual healer," 2000.

domain of effectivity that has been for centuries mapped by such astrologers and healers). Thus on the Perfect-Partner.com website we read that Ajmeri Baba is an "internationally famous astrologer [with] over 100 years family experience who solves all your problems including love, matrimony, business, depression, black magic etc., and removes all your problems once and forever"; while Syed Sahib has been "established in the UK for the past 66 years, and with spiritual prayers and miraculous tabeezes, Sahib Jee can solve all worries and problems only in a few days."[55] In an advertisement that was censured by the Advertising Standards Authority in the United Kingdom for its false and misleading claims, Pundit Maharaj announces his powers to solve "business & financial problems, career, depression, separated from the person you love, domestic problems regarding husband, wife or children, health, exams, studies or any other problem at all . . . Pundit Jee will solve your problems 100% guaranteed to your satisfaction . . . guarantee to break black magic & evil spirits in 72 hours."[56]

In the spiritual healer ads on satellite TV we can note that the insistence of generations of experience forms a correlate to the age-old stability of the transnational insurance firm: the branding strategies of insurance and astrology here dovetail. However, there are signal differences of the domain of validity claimed by the astrology as opposed to the insurance agent. For the astrologer and his pastoral subjects, problems to be solved (rather than risks to be avoided) arise from the lures and deadends of a globalized modernity (privileging diasporic settings, their target audience) that pit family member against family member, or from black magic inflicted on the family from outside forces. The family and the pastoral form of power of *maa-baap* are the two instruments of this technology.[57] The familial subject to which these ads are addressed is, in other words, a kind of spiritual warden of the home (and the home here is extended to include the business world of the immigrant husband and wife), who receives guidance, chants, and other spiritual aids from a guru-father (i.e., a baba/pir) for a "nominal fee" (around $500). Thus while insurance practices work to instill a sense of managing the future by indexically associating security with the inevitability of life's externalized flows and events, spiritual healer ads present dramatically traumatic tableaux (with little or no dialogue-sound transitions) awakening or returning an individual to the totality of problems that are presently misshaping modern domestic and business life and then guiding that individual beyond them. In this sense, unlike the serial calculations of the future embedded in the insurancial imaginary, the future of the spiritual healers comes to us bifurcated as either a continuing downward spiral into abject misery or the possibility of a final dissolution of uncertainty and worry in faith. In one is an economic calculation minimizing the risks of an essentially random future in exchange for a monthly premium, and in the other is the desire to eliminate that randomness and achieve complete security through a faithful economic exchange. The two are folded together in the same media interval, producing a kind of morose alertness through indices associating two different forms of experience (security and freedom) through tableaux of fear and release.

Note, however, that within these spiritual healer ads and between these ads and the insurance ads enunciation is split again through the criteria of truth telling, and that is accomplished by appending a simple disclaimer after a momentary fade to black at the end of the healer ads. "Zee TV USA, Inc. expressly disclaims and is not responsible for the accuracy or validity of any representations, commitments or other statements made by the party presenting this program. Any questions or complaints concerning this program must be directed to the appropriate party and not to Zee TV USA, Inc." By disqualifying these ads in terms of accuracy and validity, in other words, of truth, what the TV channel is able to do is both protect itself from any legal risks arising from the claims made by these ads, and situate the risk technologies of MetLife within a legitimate terrain of an unproblematic effectivity.[58] On the one hand, this disqualification is further intensified by the contrast in production values that the two sets of ads presents to the viewer—a meticulously produced, digitally rendered cinematic mode of address in the service of an insurancial imaginary telling little epics of how best to secure the future versus a low-budget digital video technology flashing anxious and dramatic scenes of lower-middle class domestic conflict, digital animation symbolizing supernaturally induced bad luck, and spiritual depression directed at resolving the perennial crises of life through a complete dissolution in a healing faith. On the other hand, these multiple disqualifications of spiritual healing enable both spiritual healer and insurance company to transmit information over the same communication channel because they each have demarcated separate domains of intervention—separated in relationship to class, temporality, domesticity, truth, and spirituality.

To conclude, we can see that on one level there is a kind of war for truth and subjective form being waged on the shared terrain of these two technologies, and the stakes would seem to be nothing less than securing the future itself. I have argued that the ittafaq assemblage has entered a new dispensation, and that its effects must be diagrammed in terms of what strategies produce specific affective dispositions regarding chance, harmony, risk, and security: how to master the turbulence of the future. Across its many levels—discursive, biomediated, intensive, subindividual, and populational—a new multiplicity is forming between national-diasporic spirituality and insurance technology, with a globalizing popular digital media assemblage acting as a kind of catalytic connector, and the media interjects its own turbulence into the connectivity. Through this assemblage different risks, temporalities, life problems, and moral and economic values are produced and become effective. Who will lay claim to best controlling the future? Which temporality can best manage the traumas of globalization for a diasporic-oriented nation? What predictive technologies can guarantee a secure future and a trouble-free present? Or rather must the modern global Indian develop multiple temporalities, some calculable, some curable, and others not? What subjective form can meet the challenges of the future and establish a sense of cultural belonging simultaneously, or are risk management and spiritual healing precisely the kinds of technologies that body forth globalization's heterogeneous and articulated becomings? Ittafaq becoming pure nonharmonized chance, ittafaq is time at the edge of chaos. Clearly, between risk management and spiritual healing two separate but interconnected domains of intervention have been demarcated for two irreducibly different technologies, whose very conception of the future, of risk, and control diverge and double back on each other. Between these two technologies of the future a sexuality is being born that attempts to correlate norms of both family and body with temporalities of risk, providence, and the life of the spirit, a sexuality rooted in the contagious flows of life itself, but whose preindividual sensations are potentialized in the very resonances of correlated populations and events. It is not a sexuality of risk, then, but a sexuality of emergent turbulence: today, Luciana Parisi and Tziana Terranova tell us, money has the most intimate relationship with turbulence: "On the one hand [flows of capital] are notoriously subjected to the unpredictability of turbulence; on the other hand they increasingly work through turbulence even by investing in it. Through venture capital, money looks for profitable innovations within fluidity, moving away from the solid state of planning and calculated risks to the hazardous, short-term world of upstart companies and emerging trends. It is not by chance that in this historical moment the decoded flows of capitalism show a marked preference for biotechnology labs and high tech firms, that is, for example, for a type of technoscience which makes fluidity, molecules and turbulence its central concern."[59] A new regulatory mechanism of population is thus constituted as a paradoxical control without control. Through market-driven cultures of media entertainment, authentic spirituality, bodily pleasure, and secure investment, risk and spirituality catalyze together: insurance-effects of the media assemblage. This ecology of sensation constellates through pure resonance the representations, affects, financial structures, and emergent social practices of dominant Hindi-Urdu media.

CONCLUSION

Clinamedia

I concluded chapter 4 with these observations: A new regulatory mechanism of population is constituted as a paradoxical control without control.
Through market-driven cultures of media entertainment, authentic spirituality, bodily pleasure, and secure investment, risk and spirituality catalyze
together: insurance-effects of the media assemblage. This ecology of sensation constellates through pure resonance the representations, affects, financial structures and emergent social practices of dominant Hindi-Urdu
media. What finally are the implications of this argument? In this volume
I have sought to grapple with, and perhaps to speculate on, the becomings
implicated in certain order words of a new media assemblage in India: first
day, first show, malltiplex, astrology, talkie, honorable, time pass, branding, agency, security, freedom, risk. I have attempted to situate each as
strata with their own nested timescales, topologies, affordances, and tendencies, together forming the multiplicity of an assemblage undergoing a
phase transition.

It should be clear by now that the tendencies I have tried to situate within
specific processes of individuation are what makes this a study of specifically
Hindi-Urdu media. In these pages, I have diagrammed an emergent sensorimotor schema that stretches back to the habituated loitering of colonial
bazaar culture, to the nonlocalized performances of vernacular oral litera-
tures, and to the rituals of first day, first show, and one that tends toward a
future shadowed by the value-added strategies of the malltiplex, insurance,
and cell phone. Yet I should specify further what the question of language
has to do with media assemblages, since these tendencies also resonate

across transnational timespaces quite apart from any language medium. I believe that by drawing out a globalizing field of synaesthetic media becomings, a language-centered analysis becomes inadequate. Clearly language itself must be understood as a topological field, where in the basin of attraction organized by the specificity of Hindustani vernacular connectivities form through habits and echoes of speech in the improvisation of language use; in vernacular performance we find emergent properties of collective enunciation (or language-gestures, aural space, and sonic styles—think of the assemblage between actor, singer, and poet in the performance of Naseeruddin Shah gesturing the songs of Jagjit Singh, singing the poetry of Mirza Ghalib).[1] Thus, the analysis of language in media becomes a matter of the creation of sense, sensation, sensorimotor circuits.

Even so, we tend to forget the other intensive processes tied to other topological fields that are not language oriented or consciousness based. Opening thought in their direction would be a kind of desubjugation of knowledge, as both historical content and form of thought.[2] For these intensive fields establish their own connectivities with language, but whose effects also bare the traces of a different untimely, something that we have diagrammed as variable configurations of media durations. The interminable and unmediated ittafaq is such a configuration, in which the chance and harmony of a prior dispensation of temporality is again individuated, invested by infolding technologies of risk and fate. And then, diverging from itself, the suspense between chance and harmony becomes without resembling the interval that is both anticipated in habit and potentialized in the movement of viewers about to step out for a first day, first show, or fast-forward during the well-known song. These media intervals have become a style of inattention in the audiovisual aesthetic of contemporary Indian music videos, and they diverge yet again into the different forms of filmic duration (jump cuts, faster narratives, extracted song sequences never simply resembling but diverging from each other). This suspense must be understood bodily, as proprioceptive habits, as the capacities of life itself (from the microbe and beyond)[3] assembling with the nonhuman, and utterly confounding the boundaries between human and nonhuman, silicon- and carbon-based "life." This is to analyze media by assembling disparate effects of sensation modulating bodily capacities: sexuality as a continuous ecology of sensation. When sexuality becomes the mattering of sensation—the co-implication, co-evolution of sensation in self-organizing matter—thought is directed to those forms of pleasure, autonomic processes, and the overflow of value in the production of population-specific effects that constitute the conditions of becoming of historically actualized sexualities—sexualities that will always be exceeded and thus potentialized by the intensive processes that traverse their phase space. In this sense, understanding sexuality as an ecology of sensation incorporating both carbon- and silicon-based life means situating the preindividual life of a population (racial, ethnic, national) not in terms of its already actualized history but in terms of its potential futures. Bernard Steigler, in drawing on Andre Leroi-Gourhan's thesis that the ethnic group "is less a past than a becoming," suggests a definition of collective identity that charts a population in its functional interface between social reproduction, geographical specificity, and technical practices: "The unity of the ethnic group is governed by the relation to time, more precisely, the relation to a collective future sketching in its effects the reality of a common becoming . . . Ethnic unity is essentially momentary and in perpetual becoming: it is never acquired since it does not proceed from an origin that would be shared by the people composing the ethnic group: ethnic unity is conventional, without any other origin than a mythical one."[4] Instead, what is specific to a given population is its interface with its geography and the technology it makes functional on the machinic phylum: its mutating associated milieu (Simondon), its potential assemblages (Deleuze).

What would it mean for sensation to write its own history as preindividual, resonant singularities assembling on the plane of the machinic phylum? I have attempted to coordinate the order words in the diagram of a topological multiplicity—the media assemblage is embodied in stochastic events that swerve from their trajectories. The shifts in these trajectories suggest a decisive phase transition in the creative experience of media consumption today. I have focused on the potential invested in exhibition value, in which vectors of different modes of power active in this assemblage form regimes of passage, discursive practices, perceptual dispositions, and temporal relations. Taken together this is the emergent order of a new sensorium. The diagram produced in these pages constellated certain basins of attractions in unstable relations of motion, volatile feedback loops, and intensified channels of communication, where the malltiplex, the digital, the brand logo, and the pirated captured and potentialized the practices of, for instance, first day, first show, time pass, and the ittafaq image.

In these pages I have been speculating on the virtual affects of this assemblage. By virtual affects I mean capacities to affect and be affected by forces of pure resonance, immanent to a given arrangement of actual media technologies and the practices of consumption that are their actualizing events; open sets of virtual affect would constitute the vector field (or phase space) of an assemblage—the affordances and tendencies of becoming. Considering India's globalizing media assemblage, we have come across numerous forces of resonance cross-hatching the series of events that I have argued are particularly relevant in considering this phase transition. What are the different relations of motion that such affects enable and habituate? How can we jam dominant habituations, attend to sensorimotor schema, and create something new, perhaps an untimely experience through this media dominant? In this study I have sought to approach the different events of media, partially actualized and also virtual, as a way to remain open to potential lines of flight that register a certain disgust with dominant media and affirm a multiplicious delirium. That's right, a disgusted delirium: something monstrous, overdetermined, and contained, like a statistical multitude poised and brooding on its own becoming. But the transitions are folded into each other, and each fold is a labyrinth, as Borges reminds us.

For some years after the advent of liberalization in India, one dominant trend of potentializing and capturing screen space in cinema was product placement, and although this is still very much a part of Bollywood's hyperconsumerism, there has been a gradual decrease of product placement in Hindi-Urdu cinema. Instead, now whole segments are shot as if they were in fact commercials for a product—just think of the tea and bank segments of *Baghban* (dir. R. Chopra, 2003), where a scene showcasing product and logo at once unfolds through enframing the living and working space of the elderly couple grappling with social obsolescence, as veritable vehicles for Amitabh Bachchan's career as product endorser (the ups and downs of Brand Bachchan). It is as if commercial film were approaching its most ancient vocation, that of a mode of pure commerce without static image, through the rituals of life, or as if neoliberal consumerism were Spinoza's unformed substance with an infinity of attributes. Certainly, if affect is the chief modality of the media assemblage, where accumulation and the virtual happen simultaneously, then not only bare life but life itself are the targets and instruments of a new form of power.

Can we say, then, that the media assemblage today is in the process of establishing new rituals of life, in the real subsumption of life itself? More specifically, the process of divergence, and differentiating, within a media assemblage means that the relation between the medium (internet loitering, the cell phone, bar, dance club, talkie-malltiplex, digital video and audio, Shahrukh Khan, DJ barat) and its informational substrate—that is, the relation between an actualized form of media and its potential contagion as navigable data—is a matter of sensation.

I have attempted to show a media assemblage in the throes of becoming, where an indeterminate synaesthesia displaces vision (iconic frontality) as the sensory dominant of contemporary media, and the swerves of this displacement are at once forms of capture and modes of potentialization, the particular order of its mutation. Both "THX's science of sensation" and the malltiplex's contagious social swerves, both quantity and quality in the event of media: this is the production of value, value extraction, and accumulation in the realm of affect, across platforms. But the platforms are never neutral, constituted by their own potentializing and capturing processes. (There are direct and indirect implications for political resistance in this fact.) We should note, however, that potential and capture are not a dialectic, if we take this word to mean a relation to the analogies, contradictions, identities, and resemblances of representation, the sutured structures of language-culture. The formless and substanceless realm of value-potential will always be in excess of any regime of capture, but there is no hope in that given the sterile neutrality of the virtual.[5] (And perhaps the necessity to write with hope today says more about the inability of contemporary radical thought to deal pragmatically with the particular problems of our present than anything specifically hopeful in itself.) So we can now return to the questions that I posed at the start of this study: What is the function of this excess? What specific political charge should we "assign" to this excess within the informational matrix of contemporary media assemblages? I have sought to define this excess as the morphogenetic process of assembling capacities to affect and be affected in conditions that are far from equilibrium, where resonating populations swerve and form thresholds in the evolution of media (critical events), self-organizing a general phase transition in the entire assemblage. It is precisely this affective process that has been invested through and through by the adventures of capital. Thus there are both indices and actualizations of new control mechanisms in the media assemblage. But they are mechanisms, with quite specific but reverberating movements of individuation, by which I mean neither a subject nor an essence but events that exceed their actualization, patterned but mutating. This suggests ways of finding an untimely media in the fluxes of its intervals, in the thought of its (non)actualized capacities and incipiencies. Here in the affective flux and habituation of attention the potential for new assemblages seethes not as resistant excess, but as processes that can be tinkered with, hacked, pirated, and refunctioned—and controlled through the very evolution of a new functional order.

This is what the media assemblage does, not what it means, not what it resembles but how it assembles. The media assemblage is not then primarily a regime of signs, although it has its order-words and its discursive practices, its imagistic regimes, with their own functions and quanta, and its language-gestures. Primarily, though, the media assemblage in the context of globalization is a sensation machine, which taps directly and without mediation into the body's affects serially across specific media, entering into the synaptic arrangements of our proprioception, becoming self-causing, and in ways independent of the medium itself. But when this happens this experience-before-experience is no longer a part of the media assemblage as such, but enters a realm of pure tendencies to affect and be affected, where past (tendencies plus capacities) and future (probabilities plus chance swerve) mix freely in pure resonance without presence, without ever being actualized. This is as much a nonhuman process as it is embodied in the open-ended communication channels of the human nervous system, and it involves the body, as Deleuze reminds us, in a whole atmosphere of world.[6]

This may seem contradictory, and I wish to address directly the following question: in what way are the untimely becomings immanent to the media assemblage transversal to any given medium, in other words unmediated, and how does the medium enter back into the media assemblage? The actualized media assemblage of globalization in India bears traces, as I have suggested, of something that exceeds it in every one of its singular events, and that is a multiplicity of specific tendencies of media contagions, the capacities of a given population for limitless redistribution-resegmenation, techno-genetic connections of the dynamic openness of bodies to data-memory machines, of topological urban spaces, and the capacious body. The media assemblage organizes this multiplicity by prodding, automating, diverting, and preempting the emergence of capacities and tendencies (the processes of individuation), and in the process it is in turn reorganized through these changing capacities and revalued tendencies that combine at critical points/events (singularities). I have argued that as partly actualized events media assemblages articulate bodily dispositions and sensoria, thus linking populations across fluxes of races, classes, genders, and sexualities (each with their own nested but different time scales). These regimes of sensation have self-organizing dynamisms in the proliferation of variously connected technologies, the contagions of felt-thought, and the syne-kine-anesthesia of the body. The example I have returned to repeatedly is the DJ barat. In these religious media events, digital aural technology taps bodily synaesthesia unfolding the form of a quasi-sacred (barat), quasi-profane (clubland) ritual, thereby potentializing both the body and the rituals themselves with unexpected results. It is the media assemblage as biogram, as ontogenetic and topological, returning sound-image-movement to its own incipiencies and self-causing dynamics, but also within the basin of attraction demarcated by the barat. There are many media here, the assembling media of digital audio, dance club imagistics, filmi narrative segments, trucks with speakers, lighting, and fog machines, power-generator push carts, Hindi-Punjabi songs, kinesthetic-synaesthetic bodies, and so on, and each has its specific affordances or functions, dimensions of change, resonance, and dynamisms, intensive properties of sonic pulsion and haptic visuality, frames of attention or affective dispositions, and topological connectivities that give form to individuated elements. Emergent properties become effective as the resultant distribution of the interactions of each of these elements. Thus, the individuation of a media assemblage is that which takes shape from an unformed field of forces and matter, and actualizes the substance or the matter shaped by the form in this particular way. The media assemblage has both form and substance through this medium, but it is not exhausted by that actuality since the force of such expressions of form and substance arises from an open and multiplicious field of potentiality whose connectivities are approximate (asymptotic) and resonant, open to sudden shocks, slight divergences, and subtle contagions. It is the media as pure it-tafaq: chance and harmony. This is why the DJ barat is both delirious youth subculture and post-Hindutva urban capture, but neither can totalize what the event is in the process of its becoming.

And what is that becoming? To respond I return to the notion of clina-media (and I will only speculate on its future lines of research here), which draws on Ilya Prigogine's and Isabelle Stengers's hypothesis on the origins of the universe. They refunction the Epicurian intuition about the emergence of the material world through the *clinamen* (or "swerve"): "A declining arrow of time." Prigogine and Stengers cite Lucretius's well-known passage from *On the Nature of the Universe*: "Sometimes at uncertain times and places, the eternal, universal fall of the atoms is disturbed by a very slight deviation—the clinamen. The resulting vortex gives rise to the world, to all natural things."[7] In developing this notion for their argument for self-organizing, dissipative structures, Prigogine and Stengers note that the clinamen, "this spontaneous, unpredictable deviation," "attempts to explain events such as laminar flow ceasing to be stable and spontaneously turning into turbulent flow. Today hydrodynamic experts test the stability of fluid flow by introducing a perturbation that expresses the effect of molecular disorder added to the average flow. We are not so far from the clinamen of Lucretius!"[8] As Luciana Parisi and Tziana Terranova gloss it, the clinamen is "the smallest angle by which an atom deviates from a straight line . . . This deviation (clinamen) is the generator of differential energy and matter, an anti-Platonic ontology of becoming." Throughout this volume I have followed the processes and events of media swerving, resonating, reaching critical thresholds, and generating a new order: a new media assemblage, clinamedia. Clinamedia is the very condition of creativity—the intensive processes of becoming—immanent to the assemblage of bodies, populations, and media flows today.[9] To define media in terms of its swerves, intervals, and durations is to produce functional diagrams of becomings through the events of media rather than their representations. Clinamedia presents us with a method of following the trajectory of correlations in a given basin of media attractions. Given that these trajectories swerve and form resonant populations of events, clinamedia can potentially form a new order between image-sound streams, practices of consumption, and protocols of control. This marks, I believe, a research agenda to come.

My argument in this study has been that when media criticism returns to a thought of the proprioceptive body assembling with new media, when thought approaches a multiplicious field of continuous intensive self-variations, singularities, affects, and tendencies, then criticism becomes a diagram in which past and future are joined together in (non)experiences of the untimely. Such media criticism produces functional diagrams of proprioceptive technologies that, by directly tapping into a body's capacities, proliferate through events that happen before conscious experience, but whose effects are nonetheless real in that potential tendencies can be actualized and can refunction the materialities and vectors of the field. Hindi-Urdu clinamedia today is involved in the topological connectivities of digital media, and these connectivities are forming new basins of attraction: security-risk-data-interval: that is, time pass. Without doubt, the proprioceptive technologies of the clinamedia assemblage in India are investing in this bodily creation of the audiovisual, mixing improvisationally the digital and the analog, the media of unmediated affectivity, and thus constantly producing an overflow of value, memory, intensity. Broadly, we could say that the basin of attraction defining the cinematic assemblage of media (which assembles differently with radio, oral media, Internet, and

TV) has entered another potentializing phase of nonequilibrium, as the resonant affects and tendencies of the cinematic assemblage become volatile and are refunctioned through dynamic connectivities with new media and their global financial structures, with hyperdistributed consumption practices and their singular spacetimes, and with microsegmented populations and their processes of individuation. To open thought, then, both to and in this topological field of clinamedia assembling bodies and the contagious circulation of untimely becomings has been to think politically about those strategies where individually and collectively we give into a kind of quantum tweaking, whose proliferating effects are noncalculable, never fully actualized, and potentially resonant.

Introduction

1 The term "Bollywood" is thoroughly problematic, as Madhav Prasad has pointed out in "This Thing Called Bollywood." His suggestion that its rise to dominance is indissociable from the global emergence of the non-resident Indian (NRI) as delocalized center of the nation is crucial for my qualified use of the term throughout this study.

2 Manohla Dargis, "Hollywood's Crowd Control Problem," *New York Times*, March 5, 2006, www.nytimes.com (accessed March 5, 2006).

3 On "domain of validity," see Prigogine, *The End of Certainty*, 29. Prigogine is quoting Leon Rosenfeld who states that "no physical concept is sufficiently defined without the knowledge of its domain of validity."

4 On "unpredictable, but patterned, trajectories," see Weber and Depew, "Natural Selection and Self-Organization," 41. See also Varela, Thompson, and Rosch, *The Embodied Mind*, 110; and Prigogine, *The End of Certainty*, 78–88, 122.

5 Foucault, "*Society Must Be Defended*," 251–52. See also Foucault, *The History of Sexuality*.

6 See Sobchack, *Carnal Thoughts*, 54.

7 On Indian cinema's active audience, see Srinivas, "The Active Audience"; see also Desai, Dudrah, and Rai, "Bollywood Audiences."

8 For instance, Susan Buck-Morss writes, "The nervous system is not contained within the body's limits. The circuit from sense-perception to motor response begins and ends in the world. The brain is thus not an isolable anatomical body, but part of a system that passes through the person and her or his (culturally specific, historically transient) environment . . . we will call this aesthetic system of sense-consciousness, decentered from the classical subject, wherein external sense-perceptions come together with the internal images of memory and anticipation, the 'synaesthetic system' " ("Aesthetics and Anaesthetics," 12–13).

9 On duration as ontology, see Deleuze, "Bergson, 1859–1941" and *Bergsonism*. Another lineage of this thought is from Martin Heidegger's definition of *Wesen* as

"enduring as presence" (das *Währen als Gegenwart*) (*An introduction to Metaphysics*, 59; see also "The Question Concerning Technology"). This presence, as Deleuze shows, need not be figured as a metaphysics of being (Derrida's critique of presence in ontotheology is inescapable here), but rather can be thought as an empiricism of becoming.

10 I elaborate the concept of resonance later in this introduction, but I take my inspiration from Deleuze's "On Gilbert Simondon"—his inspired reading of Simondon's work on intensive individuation. Simondon's influence is legible throughout Deleuze's work during this period, especially *Difference and Repetition* and *Logic of Sense*. See also Aracagök, "Decalcomania, Mapping and Mimesis"; and, of course, Simondon, *On the Mode of Existence of Technical Objects* and "The Genesis of the Individual."

11 On the postcolonial genealogy of contagion, see Foucault, "The History of Sexuality" and *The History of Sexuality*; Porter and Hall, *The Facts of Life*; Mason, *The Making of Victorian Sexuality*; and Laqueur, *Making Sex*. For the articulation of concerns around domesticity and working-class sanitation, see Poovey, *Making a Social Body*. Ann Stoler's work has long argued for a Foucauldian critique of a politics of sentiment, and her research into the specificities of the "alienation of affections" and "disaffections" form the anxieties of colonial governance and shape its interventions in the home; see her "A Sentimental Education"; "Sexual Affronts and Racial Frontiers"; "Casting for the Colonial," (with Karen Strassler); "Making Empire Respectable"; *Race and the Education of Desire*; and (edited with Frederick Cooper) *Tensions of Empire*. See also Adams, "The Familial State"; Hunt, *The Family Romance of the French Revolution*; and Vergès, *Monsters and Revolutionaries*. See also Nelson, *National Manhood*; and Sanchez-Eppler, *Touching Liberty*.

12 On contagion and the aleatory in game theory, see Morris, "Contagion"; Ehrhardt, Marsili, and Vega-Redondo, "Diffusion and Growth in an Evolving Network"; and López-Pintado, "Contagion and Coordination in Random Networks."

13 On dissipative structures, Manuel Delanda notes: "The structures generated by turbulent flows are called 'dissipative structures' because they use a pattern of eddies inside eddies [and flows within flows] to transport energy from higher scales to lower scales, where it can be dissipated as heat. Heat transport, normally considered a source of waste, is made into a source of order: channeling and dissipating energy across a hierarchy of nested eddies can generate complex patterns by amplifying and stabilizing small random fluctuations" (*War in the Age of Intelligent Machines*, 60).

14 Regarding the biopolitical settlement of the Bush administration, see Pease, "The Global Homeland State."

15 By post-Hindutva I don't mean to imply that India has left behind its Hindu chauvinist "phase." Rather, after the fall of the Babri Masjid in 1992, India entered a period of political and economic crisis that has in every way been marked by the piecemeal creation of upper-caste Hindu hegemony, what in an article for

Z *Magazine* in 1990 I called India's "new Brahmanism." It is in the wake of this rise and consolidation of Hindu nationalism as an all-India politics that I am calling post-Hindutva.

16 Gopalan, *Cinema of Interruptions*, 129. Gopalan's recent work, "The Short Student Film," on the short film made by student filmmakers in India is I think a brilliant shift toward considering the different modernities lived in the durations of this form.

17 See Arnold, "Aspects of Production and Consumption in the Popular Hindi Film Song Industry."

18 These provocative suggestions concerning media synaesthesia open new lines of thought for Indian media studies by returning to one of the oldest forms of understanding the pleasures of the body: rasa theory. As many critics have noted, Bharat-muni's sixth-century *Natya-shastra* provides South Asians with a ready matrix with which to experience not only Bollywood but a good samosa as well (see Rao, *Acoustical Perspective on Raga-Rasa Theory*; Waterhouse, ed., *Dance of India*; Patnaik, *Rasa in Aesthetics*; Mukherjee et al., eds., *Rasa*; and Mishra, *Bollywood Cinema*). As Richard Schechner argues in a provocative and programmatic article, rasa also means "'juice,' the stuff that conveys the flavour, the medium of tasting. The juices of eating originate both in the food and from the body. Saliva not only moistens food, it distributes flavours. Rasa is sensuous, proximate, experiential. Rasa is aromatic. Rasa fills space, joining the outside to the inside. Food is actively taken into the body, becomes part of the body, works from the inside. What was outside is transformed into what is inside. Moreover, an aesthetic founded on rasa is fundamentally different than one founded on the 'theatron,' the rationally ordered, analytically distanced panoptic" (Schechner, "Rasaesthetics" 29). Historically, then, this reading of rasa discourse as elite Brahmanic pedagogy is complicated by the fact that the *Natyasastra* was the only one of the Vedas that was to be enjoyed by all castes; moreover, when the text says that the sons of Bharata (the purported author of the *Natyasastra*) ridiculed the sages and were therefore cursed to be born Sudras, one meaning of this historically is that drama was the profession of the "lower" castes, or Dalits. Note also that the first play performed by Bharata—composed by Brahma (one of the most revered of the gods) and performed at his request—is a "Samavakara" called "Amrta-Manthana," which is supposed to enlighten the audience "about duty (dharma), prosperity (artha = earning wealth), and desire (kama = the inner urge in man)" (22). Graham Ley argues in a similar vein concerning the "discipline of the allocation of Sanskrit and Prakrit speech to characters (in chapter 18)"; he suggests that this discipline acknowledges the distinctions of caste and the demeaning circumstances that may qualify caste status, while the modes of address to be followed in drama . . . secure conformity with the established order" ("Aristotle's *Poetics*, Bharatmuni's *Natyasastra*, and Zeami's Treatises," 195). If the *Natyasastra*, then, could be thought of in our contemporary terms as the most "democratic" of Vedas, one whose history bears the marks of caste struggles and

the memory of Dalit resistance to Brahman hegemony, we would like to think of rasa not as an abstract theory of sensual pleasure but as a coded discipline symptomatic of what Laura Marks terms a kind of contagion of the skin of media. The task of a critical rasa theory of media would be to extract lines of flight and create enabling deformations in the media assemblage and its habituated and potential body. On the one hand we see these deterritorializations fetishistically "minoritized" in the disciplines and norms of rasa. On the other hand, we write to engage with and solicit that "something other" in the clichés of Hindi-Urdu media's rasa: contagion.

19 See Varela, Thompson, and Rosch, The Embodied Mind; and Pessoa, Thompson, and Noe, "Finding Out about Filling-In."

20 "MPEG," Webopedia, www.webopedia.com (accessed February 21, 2006). Discrete Cosine Transform is a technique for representing waveform data as a weighted sum of cosines and results in what is called lossy compression, which approximates some of the coefficients to reduce the amount of data. See also Mitchell, "The Work of Art in the Age of Biocybernetic Reproduction," 484.

21 Benjamin locates a special place for affect in the production of habituations, a notion that is useful here to keep in mind: "Buildings are received in a twofold manner: by use and by perception. Or, better: tactilely and optically. Such reception cannot be understood in terms of the concentrated attention of a traveler before a famous building. On the tactile side, there is no counterpart to what contemplation is on the optical side. Tactile reception comes about not so much by way of attention as by way of habit. The latter largely determines even the optical reception of architecture, which spontaneously takes the form of casual noticing, rather than attentive observation. Under certain circumstances, this form of reception shaped by architecture acquires canonical value. For the tasks which face the human apparatus of perception at historical turning points cannot be performed solely by optical means, that is, by way of contemplation. They are mastered gradually—taking their cue from tactile reception—through habit" (Benjamin, "The Work of Art in the Age of Its Technological Reproducibility," 120).

22 See Chow, "A Souvenir of Love"; and Jameson, The Cultural Turn.

23 For an explication of this notion of a mode being in another mode, see Spinoza, Ethics, 32–33. Seymour Feldman in his introduction to the volume notes that Spinoza uses the word "in" with the sense of "logically dependent on, logically contained in" (22). In other words, to grasp the dynamism of the media assemblage we must understand each of its elements as dependent on each other and contained in each other: that is, the implicate order of media (recalling David Bohm in Wholeness and the Implicate Order), or a thought of media that approaches a plane of immanence where the DJ party and technologies of insurance are contained within or folded into each other.

24 On the ontogenesis of a singularity or a haecceity, see Simondon, "The Genesis of the Individual."

25 For more on the topological image center, see Massumi, "Fear (the Spectrum Said)."

26 See Martin, *The Financialization of Everyday Life*.

27 As Miriam Hansen notes in her justly famous essay on the mass production of the senses, "The first major transvaluation of the concept of classical cinema came with post-1968 film theory, in the all-round critique of ideology directed against the very system celebrated by Bazin. In this critique, formulated along Althusserian and Lacanian lines and from Marxist and later feminist positions, classical Hollywood cinema was analyzed as a mode of representation that masks the process and fact of production, turns discourse in diegesis, history into story and myth; as an apparatus that sutures the subject in an illusory coherence and identity; and as a system of stylistic strategies that weld pleasure and meaning to reproduce dominant social and sexual hierarchies" (Hansen, "The Mass Production of the Senses," 63). On functionality, see Hayles, *How We Became Posthuman*, 47.

28 I am working with a notion of nonlinear causality developed by Deleuze in *The Logic of Sense*, 33 (see also 148–68), and elaborated by Delanda, *War in the Age of Intelligent Machines* and *A New Philosophy of Society*, 30–31; and Shaviro, "Deleuze's Encounter with Whitehead." See also Massumi, "Realer than the Real."

29 See Keyman and Koyuncu, "Globalization, Alternative Modernities and the Political Economy of Turkey," 106. The authors' reliance on preformed concepts such as modernity and traditionalism undercuts the newness of the particular form of economic sociality emerging in Turkey today; I argue for another model of criticism in my analysis of spiritual healing and insurance. See also Kalb, "From Flows to Violence."

30 See Jameson, *The Seeds of Time*.

31 See Massumi, "Fear (the Spectrum Said)": "In other words, affective modulation operates co-optively at what Gilbert Simondon calls the 'pre-individual' level. By pre-individual he does not mean 'within the individual' but rather 'at the limit between the subject and the world, at the limit between the individual and collective.' That limit is the body activatable—the bodily irritability that is the generic 'material quality' of human life" (46).

32 Hansen, "Digitizing the Racialized Body, or The Politics of Universal Address," 125.

33 Petersen, "Mundane Cyborg Practice," 80. See Bakardjieva, *Internet Society*; Balsamo, *Technologies of the Gendered Body*; Barad, *Meeting the Universe Halfway*; Hansen, *Bodies in Code*; and Wegenstein, *Getting under the Skin*.

34 Foucault, *Security, Territory, Population*, 1.

35 O'Regan, "A National Cinema," 139.

36 Cory Doctorow's work on digital rights management is particularly useful in sorting out the legal and social issues involved in the frantic development of these technologies of security. See Doctorow, www.craphound.com (accessed August 2007).

37 See Hardt and Negri, *Empire*, 45.

38 In suggesting that "the sexual act is in time what the tiger is in space," Georges Bataille argued that to analyze sexuality requires "thinking on a level with a play of forces that runs counter to ordinary calculations, a play of forces governed not by necessity but precisely by its contrary, 'luxury' " (*The Accursed Share*, 12). Bataille famously contrasted productive and nonproductive expenditure as the essential problem of human existence, and I wish to draw on this troubling notion of excess and sumptuary relations in the context of an analysis of what is becoming of Bollywood's media assemblage in the age of globalization. Moreover, this analysis of becoming and of the body in and of media assemblages articulates a line of flight from feminist film and media criticism that has shifted attention to the specificities of the consuming body in the context of an overall analysis of gendered power and the gendered image. See Bean, "Technologies of Early Stardom and the Extraordinary Body"; Studlar, *This Mad Masquerade*; Bruno, *Streetwalking on a Ruined Map*; Gunning, "The Cinema of Attractions"; Hansen, "Of Mice and Ducks" and "Benjamin and Cinema"; Doane, "Technology's Body"; and Buck-Morss, "Aesthetics and Anaesthetics."

39 Historically, the term "metro" has referred to Mumbai (Bombay), Kolkata (Calcutta), Delhi, and Chennai (Madras); more recently, Bangalore, Hyderabad, and two or three more cities (Indore, Pune) have also come to be thought of as metros. Generally, the term designates a kind of cosmopolitan space within the nation —one that, since liberalization, has been integrated more and more tightly with transnational economic and cultural circuits. Bhopal, the capital of Madhya Pradesh, although populated by well over two million people, has always been thought of in the popular imaginary (even after the Union Carbide disaster in 1984) as the hinterland of northern India—in one recent commercial on the satellite channel B4U, a Mumbai taxi driver explains that people come from all over to pursue their dreams in the film industry, even "from as far away as Bhopal."

40 As Manuel Delanda reminds us, the structures generated by turbulent flows are called dissipative structures because they use a pattern of eddies inside eddies and flows within flows to irreversibly transport energy from higher scales to lower scales, where it can be dissipated as heat. "Heat transport, normally considered a source of waste, is made into a source of order: channeling and dissipating energy across a hierarchy of nested eddies can generate complex patterns by amplifying and stabilizing small random fluctuations" (*War in the Age of Intelligent Machines*, 60). See also Dyke, "Cities as Dissipative Structures." For a general theory of nonlinear dissipative media (where media is defined as any such medium), see Barenblatt, Ivanov, and Shapiro, "On the Structure of Wave Fronts in Nonlinear Dissipative Media." On resonance and chaos theory, see Prigogine, *The End of Certainty*; and for the evolutionary implications of dissipative structures, see Varela, Thompson, and Rosch, *The Embodied Mind*. Note that I am not arguing that media assemblages are *like* dissipative structures but rather that they are dissipative in their very processes.

41 I owe this insight to a conversation with Patricia Clough, on the eve of her lecture on the self-measuring capacities of in-formation.

42 Vacarme, "'I Am Sure That You Are More Pessimistic Than I Am . . . ,'" 116.

43 Deleuze, "Control and Becoming," 170–71.

ONE *"First Day, First Show"*

1 "Dalit" is a Sanskrit word meaning burst, split, broken, crushed, or destroyed, and since the nineteenth century it has come to mean downtrodden. It is used in reference to untouchables (Harijans), outcastes, scheduled castes, and others living in an exploited social state (see "Countries of the World," www.photius. com, accessed February 16, 2006). Human Rights Watch notes that "Dalit is a term first coined by Dr. B. R. Ambedkar, one of the architects of the Indian constitution of 1950 and revered leader of the Dalit movement. It was taken up in the 1970s by the Dalit Panther Movement, which organized to claim rights for 'untouchables,' and is now commonly used by rights activists. 'Untouchables' are those at the bottom of, or falling outside of, India's caste system. Administrative parlance now employs the term 'scheduled castes,' while rights activists and the population more generally employ the term 'Dalits'" (see Human Rights Watch, http://hrw.org, accessed February 16, 2006).

2 A proprioceptor is defined in the *Oxford English Dictionary* as "any sensory structure which receives stimuli arising within the tissues (other, usually, than the viscera); esp. one concerned with the sense of position and movement of a part of the body." Hence, proprioception is the reception of information by proprioceptors and its interpretation. The contexts for proprioception are in fact neural pathways as well as the memory of the flesh—in muscles and fibers. It is the stuff of both neuroscience and science fiction. To directly control and modulate proprioception seems like the very dream of not only Western (military) science but advertising as well (Hollywood and the military coincide in the affective economies of societies of control, as Patricia Clough has pointed out). For interesting recent science fiction stories dealing with proprioception, see Dann, ed., *The Nebula Awards Showcase 2005*; Cory Doctorow's brilliant "0wnz0red"; and Jeffrey Ford's lovely "The Empire of Ice Cream."

3 For "biogram," see Massumi, *Parables of the Virtual*: "It has been suggested that extending the concept of the diagram into the biogram might be a vector worth pursuing. Formal topologies are not enough. The biogram is a lived topological event. It is onto-topological. It is the event of experience folding back on itself for its own furtherance, its continuing becoming. Onto-topological means ontogenetic. The biogram is experience reaccessing its powers of emergence, for more effect" (207). See also Simondon, "The Genesis of the Individual." Conceptually, there are direct precursors within Indian film and media criticism that have enabled this thought of biogramming media assemblages. There is the line of analysis that has shown how Bombay cinema's fragmented mode of

production can be diagrammed (exemplary here is the careful work of both Ravi Vasudevan and Madhav Prasad); there is also the work on the hybrid media genealogies of the popular film form; as Esha Niyogi remarks in "Modern Shakespeares in Popular Bombay Cinema": "Spearheaded by the cosmopolitan Parsis who had acquired wealth and prominence through modern business enterprises and western education, this theatre was an important channel through which translocal influences (Victorian melodrama, Shakespearean and seventeenth-century British drama, non-western oral traditions such as Persian folktales) flowed into Indian performance traditions in the late nineteenth and early twentieth centuries. Although the dramatic tradition had originated in the colonial academy, its producers and performers soon undertook commercial ventures, becoming attentive to popular tastes. . . . These alterations involved changing the very ways in which the 'constants' of human existence were being conceptualized in performance" (27). My argument is that this reconceptualization of human existence happened through a particular shift in the nature and connectivity within and among these media: a new sensorium came into being with the birth of popular mass culture in twentieth-century India. This is one instantiation of what I am calling the media assemblage.

4 For an ongoing engagement with the problem of communal violence, trauma, the body, and language in the South Asian context, see Das, "Trauma and Testimony," "Our Work to Cry, Your Work to Listen," "The Spatialization of Violence," and "Violence and the Work of Time"; and Das and Kleinman, introduction to *Remaking a World*.

5 In north India, paan is a very popular mixture of beetle nut, tobacco, anise seed, spices, and juices wrapped in an edible leaf.

6 These ruminations owe a great deal to Mary N. Woods's lecture on art deco in Miami Beach, Havana, and Mumbai, which was delivered on December 13, 2002, at the Alliance Française in Mumbai.

7 The term itself was not coined until the 1960s as an abbreviation of the hallmark International Exposition of Decorative and Industrial Modern Arts staged in Paris between April and October 1925. During the 1920s and 1930s, the movement was known as modernism or the "style moderne." See Fischer, "Greta Garbo and Silent Cinema," 86.

8 Ibid. See also Todd, "Decadent Heroes."

9 Fischer, "Greta Garbo and Silent Cinema," 87.

10 Fischer argues that art deco had a particularly strong gender inflexion: "Deco can be divided into two broad schools that might be imagined along traditional lines of gender. On the one hand, there was the 'feminine' curvilinear mode that favored such saccharine imagery as 'rose[s], . . . garlands . . . baskets of flowers, fountains, . . . doves, female deer . . . and nudes.' On the other hand, there was the 'masculine' geometric pole in which 'curves gave way to angularity and motifs of design tended to be . . . dynamic'"; and "While her representation has its roots in the romanticized, ubiquitous woman of Art Nouveau (depicted with wild,

flowing hair), in Deco this archetype becomes more austere and modern. As Winokur remarks, the 'Deco shape—a compression and elongation of the Victorian woman's body—would remain a representational norm for at least the next three decades'" ("Greta Garbo and Silent Cinema," 88–89).

11 Quoted in Fischer, "Greta Garbo and Silent Cinema," 88.

12 Also known as the Earle, the Eagle Theater was a porn house for much of the 1980s. It was designed by John Eberson, the architect extraordinaire of art deco cinema. On *Maximum City*, see Mehta, *Maximum City*.

13 Vasudevan, "Addressing the Spectator of the 'Third World' National Cinema," 312.

14 For architecture as framing, see Cache, *Earth Moves*; and Hansen, "Wearable Space."

15 As Jawaharlal Nehru wrote, India's "urge towards synthesis, derived essentially from the Indian philosophic outlook, was the dominant feature of Indian cultural, and even racial, development. Each incursion of foreign elements was a challenge to this culture, but it was met successfully by a new synthesis" (*The Discovery of India*, 76).

16 To get a sense of the cosmopolitan aspirations of such schools, and thus of the kind of environment that *Mohabbatein* is referencing, it is useful to note that in 2004, for example, the first twenty graduates of the school all attended prestigious schools and universities across the globe (see Doon School, www .doonschool.com, accessed December 2006).

17 This aspect of contemporary globalizing Indian cinema is taken up in the Tamil context by Anand Pandian, who explores the picturization of landscape from an affective perspective in "Cinematic Landscapes of Affect: Framing Feelings in Tamil Commercial Film."

18 This seems to me the radical implications of Shilpa Phadke's work, in "Dangerous Liaisons," on gender, caste, and loitering in Mumbai's public sphere. See also her essay coauthored with Shilpa Ranade and Sameera Khan, "Why Loiter? Radical Possibilities for Gendered Dissent," forthcoming.

19 See Jain, "Gods in the Bazaar," "Muscularity and Its Ramifications," "More than Meets the Eye," and *Gods in the Bazaar*; Ray, "The Bazaar" and *The Felt Community*; Freitag, "South Asian Ways of Seeing, Muslim Ways of Knowing" and "The Realm of the Visual"; Taylor, "Penetrating Gazes"; Pinney, "'A Secret of Their Own Country'"; and Hughes, "House Full." See also Derne and Jadwin, "Male Hindi Filmgoers' Gaze"; Haynes, "Market Formation in Khandesh"; and Ghosh, "The Postcolonial Bazaar."

20 Jain, "More than Meets the Eye," 67.

21 Quoted in Haynes, "Market Formation in Khandesh," 292, 299.

22 As is well known, Bharatmuni defined Rasa as the cumulative result of *vibhava* (stimulus), *anubhava* (involuntary reaction), and *vyabhicari bhava* (voluntary reaction). "For example, just as when various condiments and sauces and herbs and other materials are mixed, a taste is experienced, or when the mixing of

materials like molasses with other materials produces six kinds of taste, so also along with the different *bhavas* [emotions] the *sthayi bhava* [permanent emotions experienced 'inside'] becomes a rasa" (*Natyasastra*, 55).

23 See Deleuze, "Postscript on Societies of Control."

24 Spivak has warned about "information retrieval," and today we must be equally suspicious of "resistance retrieval." See Spivak, "Can the Subaltern Speak?" and "Subaltern Studies."

25 See Phadke, "Dangerous Liaisons."

26 It might seem to the uninitiated that this is a gross rendition of Bhopali Hindi—that is, more like something Soorma Bhopali from *Sholay* might whine. However, I have attempted to render the particular rolling "r" and syllable additions that I find so distinctive of Bhopali Hindi as best I could.

27 For this analysis of the part-object I draw on Massumi's generative reading of capital in "The Political Economy of Belonging" in *Parables for the Virtual*, 73.

28 See Hughes, "Is There Anyone Out There?" and "Pride of Place."

29 There is no opposition implied in the phrase "material and expressive." See Delanda, *A New Philosophy of Society*.

30 Massumi, *Parables for the Virtual*, 85.

31 Ibid., 27.

32 See ibid., 88.

33 For a detailed accounting of such dynamics in the fields of evolution, philosophy, biology, physics, history, and mathematics, see Deleuze, *Difference and Repetition*. See also Prigogine, *The End of Certainty*; Bohm, *Wholeness and the Implicate Order*; Kaufmann, *At Home in the Universe*; Weber and Depew, "Natural Selection and Self-Organization," and Varela, Thompson, and Rosch, *The Embodied Mind*.

34 Dave Kehr, "Shot in Los Angeles, but Bombay All the Way," *New York Times*, December 20, 2002, www.nytimes.com (accessed January 2003).

35 Massumi, *Parables for the Virtual*, 83–84.

36 Ibid.; 84.

37 The word "catalysis" has a certain connotational heterogeneity that Massumi exploits brilliantly. Part of the definition of the word in the *Oxford English Dictionary* is as follows: "1. Dissolution, destruction, ruin. Obs. rare. 2. Chem. The name given by Berzelius to the effect produced in facilitating a chemical reaction, by the presence of a substance, which itself undergoes no permanent change. Also called contact action."

38 As Massumi notes, proliferating communication technologies "*give body to relationality as such* and as set in motion—as the passing on of the event. . . . Every 'enclosure' is encompassed by a pure immanence of transition. The medium of 'communication' is not the technology. It is the interval itself: the moveability of the event, the displacement of change, relationality outside its terms, 'communication' without content, communicability" (Massumi, *Parables for the Virtual*, 86).

39 See Johnston, "Machinic Vision."

40 But why pose the question of time first? Simply because in duration is becoming. Temporality is the fundamental mode of indetermination that many thinkers have tied to affect (Bergson, Deleuze, Massumi, Clough, Parisi, Grosz, and, despite his overemphasis on space, Hansen), but I will also continue to think of this affective, intensive, presensate modality of change as an articulation of specific regulatory regimes (or molar, massified habituations).

41 Massumi, *Parables for the Virtual*, 90.

42 Ibid., 76.

43 See Dickey, *Cinema and the Urban Poor in South India*; Sivathamby, *Tamil Film as a Medium of Political Communication*; and Srinivas, "Film Culture, Politics, and Industry."

TWO *Contagious Multiplicities*

1 *Mother India*, starring Nargis and Sunil Dutt, was one of the most important articulations of the national in the idioms of the cinematic epic. It won national awards and acclaim from public figures like Nehru. Raj Kapoor and Nargis in their roles as national representatives in the mid-1950s toured the Soviet Union and were received like royalty by adoring Russian fans. See Bakshi, "Raj Kapoor."

2 See Chakravarty, *National Identity in Indian Popular Cinema, 1947–1987*.

3 See the "Objectives of Film Certification" on the website of the Central Board of Film Certification (www.cbfcindia.tn, accessed July 20, 2005), which states that (a) the medium of film remains responsible and sensitive to the values and standards of society; (b) artistic expression and creative freedom are not unduly curbed; (c) certification is responsible to social changes; (d) the medium of film provides clean and healthy entertainment; and (e) as far as possible, the film is of aesthetic value and cinematically of a good standard. See also Frederick Noronha, "Censors Continue to Stifle Indian Filmmaking," *Indo-Asian News Service*, December 4, 2004 (http://in.movies.yahoo.com, accessed July 20, 2005).

4 Delanda, *War in the Age of Intelligent Machines*, 3.

5 Ilya Prigogine, in *The End of Certainty*, 39, suggests that Poincaré resonances are derived from the frequencies of moving particles; I am extending this thought as a general frame through which trajectories and populations within a media assemblage can be diagrammed.

6 This is pointed out, in another context, by Hardt and Negri in *Empire*, 24–25.

7 Prasad, *Ideology of the Hindi*, 43.

8 Massumi, *Parables of the Virtual*, 116.

9 Jha, "Lyrical Nationalism," 49.

10 Ibid., 51.

11 On singularity or haecceity, see Simondon, "The Genesis of the Individual."

12 As Alfred North Whitehead writes: "Time is known to us as the succession of our acts of experience . . . But this succession is not pure succession: it is the

derivation of state from state, with the later state exhibiting conformity to the antecedent. Time in the concrete is the conformation of state to state, the later to the earlier, and the pure succession is an abstraction from the irreversible relationship of settled past to derivative present" (Whitehead, *Symbolism: Its Meaning and Effect* [1959], 35, quoted in Griffin, *Physics and the Ultimate Significance of Time*, 14.

13 More specifically, one could cite the very telling passages in the 1927–1928 *Report of the Indian Cinematograph Committee*: "Primarily the cinema is an instrument of recreation. It affords the cheapest and most popular form of entertainment to the mass of the people. It is a well-recognized maxim that there should be as little interference as possible with the recreations of the people. But in this respect some differentiation has been made in the majority of countries between the cinema and other forms of entertainment, such as the state. There are two reasons for this differential treatment of the cinema. One reason is that the cinema appeals to a much wider audience. The number of persons who witness a successful play is infinitesimal compared with the vast numbers who witness a successful film. The second reason is that the film has a special and peculiar appeal. It has to achieve its effect visually, without the aid of the spoken word. The result is an exaggeration of physical expression and suggestive action. Every device is employed in order to intensify the visual impression, such as the well-known device of the 'close-up,' and thus a peculiarly direct and vivid impression is produced upon the mind of the spectator" (1). The mass nature of the media is at issue, as well as the bodily effects of the aesthetic form, and hence the necessity of censorship.

14 Dave Kehr, "Shot in Hollywood, but Bombay all the Way," *New York Times*, December 20, 2002.

15 From the perspective of a media assemblage we must note that *Kaante* was one of the first films released with explicit tie-ins with the multiplex boom that was just getting underway in India. Its theatrical release—and it was simultaneously released in Los Angeles, New York, Bombay, Delhi, London, and Calcutta—in India was tied in with specific marketing schemes at various multiplexes. For instance, INOX set up a huge vault that patrons were invited to crack. See Bhavanashi Ramakrishna, "Smarter than the Smart: Cinema Marketing," *Theatre World*, April-June 2003, 19.

16 Chute, "Bollywood Rising," 35–36.

17 South Asian critics have provided different frameworks through which to view Hindi-Urdu films. For instance, Bollywood as cheap imitation: Ayesha Jalal, in her brilliant mimicry of Sadat Hasan Manto, pens a satirical letter to Uncle Atal Bihari Vajpayee (then prime minister of India), admonishing him that his policies are only strengthening the position of the jihadis in Pakistan: "Worse still, you played straight into the hands of the jihadis by suspending all forms of communication, air, rail or otherwise with Pakistan. Even more than the government, the jihadis want the people of Pakistan to have no contact whatsoever with

Indian infidels. Your misguided decision so rattled Musharraf that he in turn banned all Indian television channels in Pakistan, heightening the misery of an already depressed nation for whom the ridiculous fantasies that are the trademark of your Hindi film industry is the only form of cheap entertainment available. (When I wrote good film scripts, there was only Hollywood and no imitation called Bollywood.) There has been a dramatic increase in the suicide rate in several Pakistani cities, and you are contributing to this by keeping tensions with Pakistan at fever pitch" (Jalal, "A Letter to India"). For his part, Vijay Mishra argues for "the interweaving of relatively autonomous fragments within the main narrative structure" (Bollywood Cinema, 30). The conception of Indian popular cinema's nonnarrative structure is developed by Gopalan in Cinema of Interruptions.

18 See "Dilip Kumar: Bollywood Allstar," Pyara.com, www.pyara.com (accessed May 5, 2003).

19 "Star Profile: Suchitra Sen," Filmfare, August 5, 1955, 12–13.

20 Vasudevan, "Addressing the Spectator of the 'Third World' National Cinema," 312.

21 Ibid.

22 Ibid., 314, 312, 313.

23 Guzzetti, "Narrative and the Film Image," 379. Guzetti remarks that Andre Bazin in What Is Cinema? makes the crucial distinction between decoupage, which is the division of the action into shots, and montage, which is a more narrow term tied to the editing of those shots.

24 Vasudevan, "Addressing the Spectator," 315.

25 Ibid., 315–16.

26 We should note here that this criticism is enabled but not enclosed by a certain advance in technology. The DVD-video capture technology through which I have captured the images shown in the accompanying illustrations enabled me to go backward and forward frame by frame to analyze the exact configuration of decoupage and montage. However, these signs of another agency had already been signaled by Vasudevan in his recognition of the suspenseful empty doorway.

27 In Earth Moves Bernard Cache writes that "no value has been attributed to the interval that separates the cause from the realization of its effect. For a cause to produce an effect, this interval must be filled. For in and of themselves, the set of causes that produce an effect are only frames of probability. One never knows how the interval will be filled; otherwise, everything that is known about the interval would cross over to the side of the cause, and all one would have done is to define a more restricted frame of probability. And if, by any chance, no indeterminacy remained in the interval, the cause would become identical to the effect and nothing new could happen at all. . . . Intervals always remain and intercalated phenomena always slip into them, even if they finally break the frames of probability apart" (23). The question of nonlinear causality or quasi causality is central to what Gilles Deleuze maps in relationship to timespaces of virtuality—see in particular Boundas, ed., The Logic of Sense. Manuel Delanda, Brian Massumi,

and Steven Shaviro have all written about the importance of this concept in contemporary thought. See Shaviro, "Deleuze's Encounter with Whitehead," 17; Massumi, "Realer than the Real"; Varela et al., *The Embodied Mind*, 196; and Delanda, *Intensive Science and Virtual Philosophy*. I return to the nonlinear causality of the interval in my conclusion.

28 Rushton, "What Can a Face Do?" 225.

29 Ibid., 226.

30 Morson, "Narrativeness," 61.

31 Ibid., 61–62, 68.

32 What are some of the "other potentialities"? For instance, we can consider that Paro's subsequent proud rejection of Devdas is made possible by the complexly delineated agency given by this segment; or that at a particular moment, Devdas could very well have run off with Paro, if only, if only. . . .

33 See Thompson, "The Concept of Cinematic Excess."

34 Bhansali further pursues the possibilities of these algorithms in *Black* (2005); see "Something 'Special' in Bollywood," *Sunday Herald Entertainment*, June 19, 2005, www.deccanherald.com (accessed August 1, 2005); and Lakshmi B. Ghosh, "Bollywood Goes All Out for Special Effects," *Hindu*, September 6, 2005, www .hindu.com (accessed October 1, 2006).

35 For this critique of representation, see Deleuze, *Difference and Repetition*.

36 "An assemblage is precisely this increase in the dimensions of a multiplicity that necessarily changes in nature as it expands its connections. There are no points or positions in a rhizome, such as those found in a structure, tree, or root. There are only lines" (Deleuze and Guattari, *A Thousand Plateaus*, 8). To diagram an assemblage is also to mark the changing nature of the diagram itself: how does the nature of film criticism change as the diagram itself shifts? In other words, what multiplicities become indispensable for the new connectivities of the assemablage? Cinema bodies "forth machinic assemblages of desire and collective assemblages of enunciation. No significance, no subjectification: writing to the nth power. . . . An assemblage, in its multiplicity, necessarily acts on semiotic flows, material flows, and social flows simultaneously" (21–22). See also Johnston, "Machinic Vision," 28. Delanda further clarifies the nature of multiplicious assemblages by suggesting that recent scientific studies of affect (capacities) have shifted to consider the capacity to form novel assemblages when objects are put into functional relations with one another; "An individual organism will typically exhibit a variety of capabilities to form assemblages with other individuals, organic or inorganic" (*Intensive Science and Virtual Philosophy*, 72).

37 Bolter and Grusin, *Remediation*, 55.

38 I am aware that there is a blurring of physical, biological, and social dissipative systems here. At moments of great theoretical ferment a certain blurring can be productive and lead to new clarity. It seems fairly uncontroversial today to suggest that popular media and its consumption is a dissipative system; what does become fraught is specifying the precise way in which media is dissipative.

For instance, if the information in a media assemblage produces entropy (as all dissipative systems do), what is the exact nature of the difference of this informational entropy from chemical or biological processes? This must be further specified and elaborated.

39 See Spinoza, *Ethics*.

40 The sociological debate about the independence/interdependence of cognition and affect is vast. Generally the literature has sought to isolate affect and assimilate it to the "meaning making" process of cognition, and to do so by assuming a body in equilibrium rather than in duration. See Patwardhan, "Exposure, Involvement and Satisfaction with Online Activities."

41 See "Rural Labour Enquiry Report on General Characteristics of Rural Labour Households (55th Round of N.S.S.) 1999–2000," Indian Labour Bureau, http://labourbureau.nic.in (accessed April 20, 2004); and Behar, "Madhya Pradesh." Madhya Pradesh is also one of the only states in India to publish not one but two human development reports (although because of category confusion the two are not largely comparable; see Viswanathan, "Human Development Report for Madhya Pradesh."

42 The debates about the effects of globalization in India have focused on the increasing impoverishment of the working peoples in the subcontinent, the possible new modes of unequal capital accumulation for transnational corporations, and the cultural implications of deregulated image flows for "national traditions" (see Shroff, "Globalisation"; Bharucha, "Politics of Culturalisms in an Age of Globalisation"; Chatterjee, "Empire after Globalisation"; and Thomas, "Trading the Nation"). These arguments share a common ground on the questions of ideology, representation, labor, and inequalities in globalization. My argument is focused more on the diagrams of power immanent to certain transnationalized flows (even when, or better especially when, their contexts of operation are seemingly entirely circumscribed by the nation-state). For the (ab)use of the term in postcolonial theory see Chowdhury, "Interrogating 'Newness.'"

43 Hoogvelt, *Globalization and the Postcolonial World*, 131.

44 See Harvey, *The New Imperialism*; Kaplan and Grewal, *Scattered Hegemonies*; Mbembe, "Necropolitics"; Wallerstein, *The Decline of American Power*; Stiglitz, *Globalization and Its Discontents*; and Sassen, *Globalization and Its Discontents* and *De-nationalization*.

45 Don Kalb, "From Flows to Violence." See also Kalb, *Expanding Class* and "Localizing Flows."

46 For instance, Ankie Hoogvelt states that "between 1975 and 1985 an estimated $165–200 billion were placed by individual investors from the Third World in the international financial markets. This is surely the critical difference between the earlier, expansive phase of capitalism and today's 'imploding' phase. In the earlier prewar period, when nearly 44 percent of all international long-term lending (including foreign direct investment) went to the regions of Africa, Asia and Latin America, it found its way into the development of railways, port

installations, mines and factories. . . . Today, however, the regime of privatisa-
tion and deregulation imposed by the World Bank and IMF structural adjustment programmes, have created a climate of what is euphemistically called
'financial openness' in which the Third World bourgeoisie are less restricted and
more enabled than ever before to channel their nation's wealth to the financial
markets and institutions of the core countries. In so doing, they can participate
in the economies of the core of the world system, while their countries cannot"
(*Globalization and the Postcolonial World*, 84).

47 Ibid., 88.

48 Ibid., 111.

49 The literature on this new regime of capitalist security is complex and growing,
as only one study of a very important Indian city indicates: see Heitzman, "Geographic Information Systems in India's 'Silicon Valley.' "

50 Adkins, "The New Economy, Property and Personhood," 115, 118.

51 Ibid., 119.

52 Ibid., 113.

53 Ibid., 114.

54 Brishti Guha, "Economic Consequences of Microelectronic and Telecom Revolution."

55 See Clough et al., "Notes Toward a Theory of Affect Itself"; see also Clough and
Halley, eds., *The Affective Turn*.

56 Thacker, *Biomedia*.

57 On affect accumulation, see Clough's introduction to *The Affective Turn*.

58 See Deleuze and Guattari, *A Thousand Plateaus*, 409–10.

59 Simondon, *On the Mode of Existence of Technical Objects*, 13. Simondon argues for a
technical culture in which humans would arrive at an understanding of the technical object in terms of both its elements and "its integration into the functional
ensemble" (96). It is clear that a conceptual genealogy of both an assemblage as
continuous multiplicity and the virtuality constitutive of machinic evolution must
pass through the brilliant work of Simondon. This passage is also of course cited
in Stiegler, *Technics and Time*, 71. Stiegler goes on to note that "what is proper to
the industrial technical object is a tendency toward the unification of parts in a
whole, which tendency is not due to the person making the object and thinking
by functions, but to the synergetic necessity that most often is unplanned, and
that is affirmed within the object in the course of its functioning" (75).

60 Delanda, *War in the Age of Intelligent Machines*, 6–7.

61 Ibid., 20.

62 See the website of the Extropy group at www.extropy.org (accessed September
10, 2007). For an incisive critique of Extropian free-market utopianism see
Foster, *The Souls of Cyberfolk*, 17.

63 See Dyke, "Cities as Dissipative Systems." As Dyke's analysis suggests, diagramming this assemblage shows us that there are interrelations between the social

structures of globalization and the rate of material flow required to sustain them. Or, in other words, it tells us that the "entropy debt" incurred by dissipative media assemblages can be paid in several ways: that the information content of the assemblage is necessarily connected to the rate of material flow needed to sustain it. "For example, just to fix ideas, the standard line (since Hume) has it that economic systems have moderate scarcity as their condition. But scarcity is not the primary condition for an economy. What economies rest on are gradients. They depend on finding ways of keeping material flow at a suitable rate" (359).

64 See Harvey, *The Condition of Postmodernity*; and Virilio, *Speed and Politics*.

65 Kalb, "From Flows to Violence," 178. See also Wood, *Empire of Capital*, xi.

66 Kalb, "From Flows to Violence," 183–84.

67 Thomas, "Trading the Nation," 276–77.

68 See Hirst, "The Global Economy"; Hirst and Thompson, *Globalisation in Question*; Dore, *Stockmarket Capitalism*; Amsden, *The Rise of "The Rest"*; Wade, *Governing the Market*; Weiss, *The Myth of the Powerless State*; and Weiss, ed., *States in the Global Economy*.

69 Kalb, "From Flows to Violence," 184.

70 Ibid. Kalb goes on to argue that the global-commodity-chain school of political economy "countered the trickle-down assumption of global marketization by pointing out that markets were not anonymous hidden hands but rather structured relations of power between nodes in a network in which the weak found it practically impossible to improve their relative positions vis-a-vis the strong. While design, research and development, and marketing functions remained controlled by the North, southern producers found it very hard to move upwards in the chain of added value and seemed to be condemned to low barrier/low skill/low value added activities. This was not only the case in simple commodity productions but also in manufacturing and large foreign direct investment (FDI) layouts. The accelerating integration of China and South Asia in Northern networks since the mid-1980s had enormously expanded the supply of unskilled and medium skilled workers. This was resulting in an intensifying downward pressure on income among workers and firms in global commodity chains in sub-Saharan Africa and parts of Latin America, as well as in increased feminization of labor forces. Rather than marketization per se, it turned out to be positionality within the chain, as well as the class relations and path-dependence of regional systems within the world economy, that explained the outcomes. Marketization now appeared in a different light: instead of leading to trickle down, it served to bloc upward trajectories by continuously enlarging the reserve army of labor. It turned out to be a force for monopolistic control rather than democratic participation. It allowed capitalists to structurally depress incomes in manufacturing. Maquiadoras of Tijuana were out-competed by Chinese producers" ("From Flows to Violence," 185). See also Fernandes, "Nationalizing 'the Global.'"

71 For a critique of competing interpretations of India's postliberalization political economy, see Reed and Kundu, "Corporate Capitalism in Contemporary South Asia."

72 McGuire, "Economic Liberalisation and India," 83.

73 Ibid., 86.

74 The projected date to wipe out the revenue deficit is 2008. See Roy, "World Bank and Government of India on Same Wavelength," Rediff.com, August 13, 2003, http://us.rediff.com (accessed September 20, 2003). For a historical overview of the process of globalization from 1947 to 2004, see the revisionist article by Nayak, Chakravarti, and Rajib, "Globalization Process in India."

75 The devaluation of the rupee is shown in the following data: June 9, 2000: $1 = Rs. 42.91; January 29, 2002: $1 = Rs. 48.31; June 26, 2005: $1 = Rs. 43.50.

76 As John McGuire put it at the end of a decade of liberalizing reforms: "Certainly, the majority of Indians seem to have suffered a severe setback since the advent of the reforms. Over six million went below the poverty line in the year following the reform, as opposed to the annual 10–15 million who had moved above it for the previous decade. Similarly, the rate of registered unemployment has risen rather than fallen, as 'Sick Industries' have been closed. During the same period, education and health expenditure have been cut back in real terms as have food subsidies. . . . At the very least, one-third of India's population have had their capacity to purchase food severely constrained, with millions eating less, as the per capita daily net availability of grain and pulse per person has fallen from 510 gm in 1991 to 461 gm in 1995–96. Yet, while people literally starve, there remains 37 million tons of surplus food grain. . . . While economic liberalisation has produced growth it has been of a certain type and it had benefited the chosen few. For the large number of Indians it has increased exploitation" ("Economic Liberalisation and India," 88).

77 See the "Current Statistics: Macroeconomic Indicators" section of *Economic and Political Weekly*, May 21, 2005, www.epw.org.in (accessed March 4, 2006). See also Nagaraj, "Industrial Growth in China and India." Nagaraj, who is fairly sanguine regarding India's macroeconomic potential, notes that "realising India's growth potential would call for overcoming some of the widely accepted problems currently faced by the industrial sector. As is known, industrial output growth has decelerated since around the mid-1990s for about seven years now. There is little evidence to suggest acceleration of output and export growth on a trend basis after the initiation of the economic reforms in the early 1990s. Constraints on growth seem to be mainly from the demand side as agriculture growth slowed down in the 1990s, and infrastructure investment has steadily declined since the late 1980s. Further, small enterprises and unregistered manufacturing have been adversely affected by lack of credit and its high cost" (2170). India's real GDP grew 8.4 percent in 2006; from 2005 to 2008, it has averaged more than 8 percent, more than double the 3.5 percent during the three decades prior to 1980; as this book went to press, total trade in goods and services was

around 45 percent of GDP, from 17 percent in 1990. This situation is largely the source of the optimism currently fueling much direct foreign investment in India. See "India on Fire," *Economist*, February 3–9, 2007, 69–71.

78 "Out of a total labour force of 406 million, around 397 million are in the workforce, the remaining 9 million (2.2 percent of total workforce) are what is known as 'openly unemployed' i.e. they did not have any work during last 365 days. Out of this 397 million workforce in the country, 28 million are employed in the organised sector. 369 million workers are in the unorganised sector which includes about 236 million workers employed in the agricultural and related activities. The remaining 133 million are in the non-agricultural activities which include about 19 million workers employed in the small scale industries, 30 million home based workers (6.5 million handloom weavers, 4.5 million artisans and craft persons, 4.4 million beedi workers, etc.)" (Press Information Bureau, Government of India, http://pib.nic.in, accessed June 1, 2006). For recent reviews of labor, see Sundar, "Labour Flexibility Debate in India"; and Subramanian, "Deregulation and Labour Policies in a Public Sector Firm."

79 De Haan and Dubey, "Poverty, Disparities, or the Development of Underdevelopment in Orissa"; and Kabra, "Displacement and Rehabilitation of an Adivasi Settlement."

80 For zones of exception, see Agamben, *Homo Sacer* and *States of Exception*; and Mbembe, "Necropolitics."

81 As Thomas writes in "Trading the Nation": "The only luxury that some nations from the South enjoy is an approved timetable towards the eventual deregulation of some sectors" (278). In fact, what the global south is confronted with is liberalization on every economic front—the end of tariffs, subsidies, the opening up to foreign investments in national markets, financial sectors and so on, based on the principle of nondiscrimination and reciprocity, referred to in WTO-speak as "most favoured nation" status (MFN). In other words, when AT&T invests in a particular telecommunications sector in India, it will be on the basis of their MFN status and the same guarantees for incentives, tax breaks, and so on as given by a domestic competitor, even if such terms were to go against the interests of domestic industry and national priorities. This reaching into the heart of domestic policy resulting in the imposition of globally conformist regulatory disciplines is a primary objective of the WTO.

82 See Rajan, *Biocapital*.

83 Appadurai, "Spectral Housing and Urban Cleansing," 627–28.

84 See Keyman and Koyuncu, "Globalization, Alternative Modernities and the Political Economy of Turkey."

85 Kvetko, "Can the Indian Tune Go Global?" 184.

86 While the broadcasters maintained the official line and abstained from any criticism of the government, the privately owned and politically plural press offered a critical framework within which Indian journalism evolved. The relative autonomy of the print media was a significant factor in strengthening democracy

in India, although the press remained elitist in its approach and perspectives. More importantly, the investigative, often adversarial, role of print journalists contributed to the creation of an early-warning system for serious food shortages and thus a preventive mechanism against famine. See Thussu, "Privatizing the Airwaves," 126.

87 "India Pay TV Market to Be $7 billion+ by 2010: MPA," *Indiantelevision.com*, March 2, 2006, www.indiantelevision.com (accessed October 10, 2007).

88 Murdoch's STAR channel, for example, felt that its mainly U.S.-originated programming was only reaching a tiny, though influential and wealthy, urban audience. It therefore started adding Hindi subtitles to Hollywood films broadcast on its twenty-four-hour channel STAR Movies and dubbing popular U.S. soaps into Hindi. In 1996, STAR Plus began telecasting locally made programs in English and Hindi, in addition to Western programs. Other global players have followed the market leader in Asia by localizing their products to reach a wider market and increase advertising revenues: the Discovery Channel, which started broadcasting to India in 1995, dubs its documentaries in Hindi; and BBC World regularly broadcasts "India-specific" programs, including news in Hindi. See Thussu, "Privatizing the Airwaves," 127.

89 See Virdi, "Indian Film and TV," 75.

90 Juluri, "Music Television and the Invention of Youth Culture in India," 368.

91 Ibid., 372.

92 According to Wikipedia, the term BitTorrent "is a peer-to-peer file sharing (P2P) communications protocol. BitTorrent is a method of distributing large amounts of data widely without the original distributor incurring the entire costs of hardware, hosting and bandwidth resources. Instead, when data is distributed using the BitTorrent protocol, each recipient supplies pieces of the data to newer recipients, reducing the cost and burden on any given individual source, providing redundancy against system problems, and reducing dependence on the original distributor" (www.en.wikipedia.org, accessed September 1, 2007).

93 Of course, it seems that BitTorrent as a global technology, which assembles packets of data across the globe without regard for distribution territory, will make this rather difficult. But Pesce is right to suggest that a new business model will be first on the agenda of the corporate media conglomerates in the coming years; what that will be is as yet still unclear.

94 Hull, *Entropy, Information, and Evolution*, 5–6.

95 "No Sale," March 2, 2007, Internet Archive, www.archive.org (accessed September 14, 2007).

96 "The Kamla Bhatt Show: BitTorrent's Ashwin Navin on Bollywood and India," May 21, 2007, YouTube, www.youtube.com (accessed October 10, 2007).

97 3G is the third-generation International Telecommunications Union specification for mobile communications (replacing digital personal communication services). On 3G, see "3G," Webopedia, http://Wi-fiplanet.Webopedia.com (accessed September 27, 2007). On 3G in India, see Shailaja Neelakantan, "Forget

2G, India has 3G Plans," Gigaom, http://gigaom.com (accessed February 27, 2007).

98 "India Adds 6.79 Million Mobile Phone Users in November," *Financial Express*, December 14, 2006, www.financialexpress.com (accessed September 14, 2007).

99 I should also note that the actual production of these increasingly more compact phones is an extremely exploitative process in various East Asian locations: "In a factory in Thailand making motors for Nokia phones, employees work with lead solder and have to buy their own protective masks and gloves because the company wants to save on 'overhead.' Lead solder contains 40% lead and is so dangerous that it has been banned from electronics by several European regulations. Instead of protective equipment, the workers are given milk to filter the toxins from their blood. Several sick workers were hospitalised and diagnosed with dangerous levels of lead poisoning" ("Workers Poisoned in Nokia and Motorola Factories," SOMO—Centre for Research on Multinational Corporations, December 1, 2006, www.somo.nl, accessed September 1, 2007). See also Wilde and de Haan, "The High Cost of Calling: Critical Issues in the Mobile Phone Industry," SOMO—Centre for Research on Multinational Corporations, September 1, 2007, www.somo.nl (accessed September 27, 2007).

100 "Mobile Value Added Services in India: A Report by IAMAI & eTechnology Group@IMRB," December 2006, 15.

101 "Mobile Value Added Services in India," 11–12. I owe a debt of gratitude to Smita Rajan, whose generosity and guidance has been invaluable in this research on new media.

102 Given what I had argued about the ticket as virtual object in the media event of first day, first show, the growing trend in multiplexes across India to enter into a symbiosis with a VAS service provider for automated ticket booking systems shows that it is in the virtual realm (affect) of the functional object that value streams mutate and generate new sources of capital accumulation, folding m-commerce into the affective capacities of dominant media itself. See Anuradha Ramamirtham, "IVR System Eases Ticket Bookings at Adlabs Cinemas," cxotoday.com, October 8, 2007, http://www.cxotoday.com (accessed October 10, 2007).

103 "Movies & Music are the passion of India. Most of the rich content available to the end users revolves around these two, with Ringtones of popular Bollywood songs, Wallpapers of movie leads and games developed around movie themes" ("Mobile Value Added Services in India," 13).

104 "Mobile Value Added Services in India," 13. "Currently entertainment-based VAS applications are driving the market both in value and volume terms. These have a very high perceived value as apart from basic entertainment, these can also be a means of self expression by the end user. This explains the success of Entertainment VAS despite the fact that its practical value is minimal. . . . However, perceived value will increase in the future as new utility applications are developed catering to different niche segments; like location based services." (18)

105 "Mobile Value Added Services in India," 14.

106 More specifically, the "end user" sends the service request in an SMS form. The request goes to a server managed by the Platform enabler on behalf of the operator. The content is arranged by the Operator from the Content Aggregator who procures it from the Content developer. This content is forwarded to the Platform enabler who stores it in the server. The server automatically and instantaneously entertains the request from the customer as all these VAS are preloaded into the server ("Mobile Value Added Services in India" 25).

107 "The electronic image, that is, the tele and video image, the numerical image, coming into being, either had to transform cinema or to replace it, to mark its death. . . . The new images no longer have any outside (out-of-field), any more than they are internalized in a whole; rather, they have a right side and a reverse, reversible and non-superimposable, like a power to turn back on themselves. They are the objects of a perpetual reorganization, in which a new image can arise from any point whatever of the preceding image. The organization of space here loses its privileged directions, and first of all the privilege of the vertical which the position of the screen still displays, in favour of an omni-directional space which constantly varies its angles and co-ordinates, to exchange the vertical and the horizontal. And the screen itself, even if it keeps a vertical posture by convention, no longer seems to refer to the human posture, like a window or a painting, but rather constitutes a table of information, an opaque surface on which are inscribed 'data,' information replacing nature, and the brain-city, the third eye, replacing the eyes of nature. Finally, sound achieving an autonomy which increasingly lends it the status of image, the two images, sound and visual, enter into complex relations with neither subordination nor commensurability" (Deleuze, *Cinema 2*, 265). And this for essential reasons has always been the condition of popular Indian cinema—its becoming TV before TV. The voice does not belong to either the actor or the singer but to the relation that is established between them. One is reminded here of a story that the famous actor Shammi Kapoor tells of his first hearing of the death of Mohammad Rafi, the playback singer who sang to life some of Kapoor's most memorable characters. Sitting in the prayer hall of a temple, a man leans over to Shammi and whispers, "Your voice has gone today." Almost immediately he realizes that Rafi saab had passed. In Hindi cinema, the lip-sync has always meant that the relationship of the visual to sound, or subject to voice would be tenuous, itself predicated on variations not determined by the codes of the real, or even of narrative.

108 Dolby Professional Motion Picture Technologies, www.dolby.com.

109 See Rombes, "Avant-Garde Realism." See also Lev, *The Language of New Media*.

110 See Chion, *The Voice in Cinema*.

111 "Low Frequency Effect," Phillips Microtechnology, www.tvtower.com (accessed July 24, 2006).

112 See Sandeep Mittal, "The Next Frontier?" *Theatre World*, April-June 2003, 31. Mittal notes that aside from the design issues—stadium seating's steep angle can be a problem, with front rows generally twenty-five feet from the ceiling, and rear rows ten feet from the ceiling; hanging the speaker array from the roof can also be an issue, since most cinemas in India have ceiling fans for the rear rows given the high costs and power requirements of air conditioning—the human ear can detect horizontal separation of sound, but vertical separation may in fact distract rather than add to the reality effect of digital sound.

113 Hansen, *New Philosophy*, 103.

114 Ibid., 115, 120.

115 For the body as center of indetermination, see Bergson, *Creative Evolution*; and Deleuze, *Bergsonism*.

116 For the singular importance of the Lucas-Spielberg brand of franchise-oriented blockbuster moviemaking—perhaps the original media assemblage models developed in the 1970s and perfected in the 1980s, see Schatz, "The New Hollywood," 195–96.

117 "THX—The Science of Sensation," www.thx.com (accessed April 7, 2007).

118 "The result is that cinema audiences experience movies that look and sound great. They enjoy: Precise audio localization that tracks the action across the screen; a wide frequency range that delivers higher highs and lower lows; a naturally balanced sound and planned sight lines so that every seat is the 'best in the house'; accurate, true-to-life images; highly intelligible dialog and decreased distortion; a clearer, more realistic movie-going experience. If you're a cinema owner, THX certification puts you in an elite class of cinemas that enjoy tangible benefits of certification. In addition to offering your audience an optimal cinematic experience, you gain a competitive advantage with clear bottom-line rewards. Independent consumer research shows that movie-goers recognize and prefer the THX brand when selecting a cinema" ("THX—The Science of Sensation," www.thx.com, accessed September 30, 2006).

119 "Interview with Tim Schafbuch: THX—An Overall Cinema Experience," *Theatre World*, January-March 2003, 40.

120 Although according to Real Image Media Technologies, the Indian marketer of DTS technologies, there are currently around nine hundred DTS cinemas in India, mostly in the south; see "The Road to 892 Cinemas: How DTS Came to India—and Stayed!" Real Image, www.real-image.com (accessed May 1, 2003).

121 "INOX All Set to Enter Multiplex Business," *The Financial Express*, May 1, 2002, www.financialexpress.com (accessed May 1, 2008).

122 The tie-up will ensure INOX preferential access to all real estate development by Pantaloon; see "State of the Multiplex Industry in India," *Cinema Systems*, October 2006, www.cinema-systemsindia.com (accessed January 26, 2008).

123 Pantaloon Group, "Company Vision," www.pantaloon.com (accessed February 3, 2003).

124 Muskan Talkies (owned by former Congress chief minister Digvijay Singh) and Raj Cinemas are currently the only two DTS theatres in Bhopal. It is not uncommon for such DTS theaters to suspend its operation (but not the advertisement) of the technology for everyday use to avoid burdensome maintenance repairs.

125 Quoted in Sergi, *The Dolby Era*, 38.

126 Headed by Diwan Rahul Nanda, and based in Bombay, the TopsGroup Security company (founded in 1970) boasts of a workforce of thirty thousand highly trained, experienced, vetted, and nonunionized laborers. It went from a turnover of 4 million rupees per year to over 1.44 billion rupees in 2005. The company's ascendance is an indication of India's entrance into the global stage of societies of control.

127 Thomas, "Trading the Nation," 283.

128 Tara Sinha, personal communication, March 10, 2000, Bhopal, India.

129 Kvetko, "Can the Indian Tune Go Global?" 185. Kvetko ties the emergence of Indipop perhaps a little too instrumentally to the privatization of sound in the media assemblage of globalization; nonetheless, I find his argument to be an interesting one: "The influence of this music on Indipop artists can be clearly heard in the increasing use of 'riff-based' compositions, as opposed to the typically 'ragabased' music of films. For example, Lezz Lewis and Hariharan of the successful Indipop duo known as The Colonial Cousins sit together with an acoustic guitar when writing songs. The chords and riffs they choose dictate the form of the song. Film song composers, on the other hand, pick out single notes on a harmonium (a small organ with hand-pumped bellows) in order to find a memorable melody. Later, a music arranger will fill in the background with accompanying chords, but the organization of the film song is determined by the melody and lyrics. Furthermore, the overall structures of many Indipop songs are formed around moments of harmonic tension and release. Similar to many Western pop songs, 'the hook' is deferred by a sequence of chords to create the effect of a buildup. Only then, after we have been kept in anticipation, do we reach a moment (often intentionally brief) of musical release. In many ways, I find this to be a fetishization of the act of listening itself, and it stands in direct opposition to what several film music directors told me: 'If the audience can't sing along within the first few seconds, the song will never be a success' " (184–85).

130 Sundholm, "Listening to Film," 91.

131 This is shorthand for a vast corpus of scholarly work on affect, media, algorithms, and the analog—and I explain at length throughout this and subsequent chapters exactly what I mean by this formula. Much of the literature is cited in various notes below. But for contagious affectivity, see specifically Guattari, *Chaosmosis*, 2.

132 Fernandes, "Nationalizing 'the Global,' " 613.

133 On synaesthesia, see Massumi, *Parables for the Virtual*, 191; see also Cytowic, *The Man Who Tasted Shapes*; Harrison and Baron-Cohen, eds., *Synaesthesia*; Dann,

Bright Colors Falsely Seen; and Sobchack, *Carnal Thoughts*, 67. On the sympathies of assemblages, see Deleuze and Parnet, *Dialogues*. On the sympathy involved in intuition and instinct, see Bergson, *Creative Evolution*, 176.

134 The digital is not the final exit of "the Real" in cinema—it may indeed be its apotheosis: the digital technologies of deep memory (one take can be up to an hour long, as opposed to the nine-minute capacity of the analogue camera's magazine) produces, or gives off the effect of, a total reality "editing itself." See Rombes, "Avant-Garde Realism."

135 As a crucial affective register for the diaspora, nostalgia is also an important pedagogy of the future: one day we will return to the land of such wonders that are no more. The number and quality of exhibitions, shows, and installations that commemorate Bollywood for the Indian diaspora has greatly expanded in the past three years. See, for instance, "Cinema India: A part of Image and Identity," March 19, 2004 to June 20, 2004, the Gas Hall, BM&AG Chamberlain Square, Birmingham, United Kingdom, www.bmag.org.uk. Moreover, these satellite channels are crucial for nonmetro diasporic formations. As one of my field research interviewees put it, "Most of [my interest in Bollywood] came from all these channels that became available to us . . . B4U and Zee TV and TV Asia. I mean, those channels weren't available in Minnesota for the longest time and they just, kind of came about a few years ago. And the more I watch that stuff the more I got into all of it and all the different movies and all the different countdown [shows], like song shows and all sorts of those type of things" (Interview with "Anjali," October, 2003, New York City). These field research interviews (which I conducted by myself, except for two done jointly with Dr. Rajinder Dudrah) consist of fifteen taped conversations with locally based Bollywood fans in the New York City area conducted over the course of three months from August to October 2003. The work was funded by a British Academy International Scholars grant, and conceived in collaboration with Dr. Rajinder Kumar Dudrah of the University of Manchester.

136 For diagram, see Deleuze, *Foucault*; for biogram, see Massumi, *Parables for the Virtual*, 186–87. See also Delanda, "Deleuze, Diagrams, and the Open-Ended Becoming of the World"; and Rajchman, "Diagram and Diagnosis."

137 Currier, "Feminist Technological Futures," 325.

138 The *Oxford English Dictionary* defines anastomosis as "Intercommunication between two vessels, channels, or distinct branches of any kind, by a connecting cross branch. Applied originally to the cross communications between the arteries and veins, or other canals in the animal body; whence to similar cross connexions in the sap-vessels of plants, and between rivers or their branches; and now to cross connexions between the separate lines of any branching system, as the branches of trees, the veins of leaves, or the wings of insects."

139 Guattari, *Chaosmosis*, 35. On dynamical processes in Deleuze, see Delanda, *Intensive Science and Virtual Philosophy*.

140 Deleuze, *Bergsonism*, 38.

141 I believe that this is a reductive reading of Haraway's cyborg imagery (as long as one refuses the relegation of the cyborg to merely the imagistic register). Indeed, insofar as the critique of affective labor within capital necessitates blurring the boundaries of organism and technology, which is what Haraway argues in her "Cyborg Manifesto," a continuous assembling of capacities through feedback looped relations is implied.

142 Currier, "Feminist Technological Futures," 329. For a decisive critique of the prosthetic notion of the body's potential, see Massumi, *Parables for the Virtual*, 116.

143 Guattari, *Chaosmosis*, 39. For the critique of autopoesis as self-enclosed system, see Pearson, *Germinal Life*; Maturana and Varela, *Autopoiesis and Cognition*; and Clough, "The Affective Turn." This would also be rather different from the self-enclosure characteristic of Maturana and Varela's autopeosis—see Hayles, *How We Became Post-Human*.

144 Bolter and Grusin, *Remediation*, 44.

145 Ibid., 238.

146 Deleuze and Guattari, *A Thousand Plateaus*, 8.

147 Currier, "Feminist Technological Futures," 323. In his essay on Foucault, Deleuze makes clear the genealogy of this thought in his own work: "So this is our definition of a group of statements, or even a single statement: they are multiplicities. It was Reimann in the field of physics and mathematics who dreamed up the notion of 'multiplicity' and different kinds of multiplicities" (13). He goes on to note that Husserl (in *Formal and Transcendental Logic*) and Bergson (in *Time and Free Will*) both drew on the concept of multiplicity for their own philosophical concepts, but Foucault's *Archeology of Knowledge* represents "the most decisive step yet taken in the theory-practice of multiplicities" (14). See also the discussion of continuous multiplicities in Deleuze and Guattari, *A Thousand Plateaus*, 482–88.

148 Parisi, "Information Trading and Symbiotic Micropolitics"; see also Parisi, *Abstract Sex*.

149 Parisi, "Information Trading and Symbiotic Micropolitics," 42–43.

150 See Brian Massumi, *Parables for the Virtual* and *A User's Guide to Capitalism and Schizophrenia*; Manovich, *The Language of New Media*; Crary, *Techniques of the Observer* and *Suspensions of Perception*; Levy, *Cyberculture*; Shaw and Weibel, eds., *Future Cinema*; Deleuze, *Cinema 1*, *Cinema 2*, and *Bergsonism*; Guattari, *Chaosmosis*; Shaviro, *The Cinematic Body*; and Sobchack, *Carnal Thoughts*.

151 Tim Lenoir, foreword to Hansen, *New Philosophy for New Media*, xiv.

152 See Bergson, *Creative Evolution*.

153 Hansen, *New Philosophy* 4.

154 See also Patricia Clough's *Autoaffection*—her important critique of the body and technology as "autoaffection." Much of my consideration of Hansen's provocative and inspiring thought was made possible through delightful and energizing conversations with Clough.

155 Massumi, *Parables for the Virtual*, 29.

156 Hansen, *New Philosophy*, 7, 8.

157 Ibid., 176.

158 Ibid., 133.

159 Ibid.

160 This is a question that traces its line of force back to Martin Heidegger's concept of *Enframing*; see "The Question Concerning Technology." For an important
problematization, see also Athanasiou, "Technologies of Humanness, Aporias
of Biopolitics, and the Cut Body of Humanity": "'The essence of modern technology,' he [Heidegger] argues, 'shows itself in what we call Enframing,' *Ge-stell*:
the setting up and hunting down of nature as standing-reserve, the ordering
and challenging of nature to unconceal itself. . . . The translation by the word
'skeleton' would not be inappropriate for another reason as well: it echoes the
corporeal implications of Enframing; more specifically, it signals a claim upon a
crumbling and perished corporeality, evidenced by—or, rather, *revealed as*—the
very remains of those reduced to a standing-reserve, deemed unfit to live. Despite
Heidegger's somewhat neutral employment of Enframing, his notion is itself
charged with strong implications of the biopolitical propriety underwriting the
skeletal power to body forth beings and things, to challenge them forth within
the configuration, the 'Frame-work,' of modern technology" (134–35). It could
be argued that Hansen's conception of framing is more rigorously addressed in
his article on architecture and the new media—see his "Wearable Space."

161 Hansen, *New Philosophy*, 74, 82.

162 See Hansen, "The Mass Production of the Senses," 67.

163 Massumi suggests another aspect of framing that Hansen seems to disregard
entirely: namely, framing as a capturing and containing of variation. "But in the
history of sport, as with virtually every collective formation, the codification of
rules follows the emergence of an unformalized proto-sport exhibiting a wide
range of variation. The formal rules of the game capture and contain the variation. They frame the game, retrospectively, describing its form as a set of constant relations between standardized terms. A codification is a framing derivative
that arrogates to itself the role of foundation. It might be argued that all founda-
tions are of this nature: ex post facto regulatory framings rather than effective
foundings" (*Parables for the Virtual*, 71).

164 Massumi, *Parables for the Virtual*, 62.

165 Chun, *Control and Freedom*; this phrase appeared in her presentation as keynote
speaker for the 2007 Film and Literature Conference at Florida State University.

166 Russell, "Deleuze's Dick," 51.

167 Thomas, "Trading the Nation," 285.

168 Indeed, as Sonwalkar notes in "India: Makings of Little Cultural/Media Imperialism?" in South Asia today people in Pakistan, Sri Lanka, and Nepal are as worried about Indianizatio, as they are of Westernization. See also Pashupati, Sun,
and Mcdowell, "Guardians of Culture, Development Communicators, or State

Capitalists?" 253–54; and Rajagopal, "The Rise of National Programming" and *Politics after Television.*

169 "Hollywood meets Bollywood," *Hindu*, June 19, 2003, www.hindu.com (accessed February 15, 2007); "The Trailblazer: Producer/Director Ram Gopal Varma," *Time Asia*, October 20, 2003, www.time.com (accessed March 2, 2004).

170 For an analysis of a local negotiation of media in a tribal community in south India, see Jayaprakash, "Remote Audiences Beyond 2000."

171 As a comparison, Bordwell notes that "in 1999 and 2000 the average shot length of a typical Hollywood film in any genre was likely to run 3 to 6 seconds. . . . Editors tend to cut at every line and insert more reaction shots than we would find in the period 1930–1960. Admittedly, by building dialogue scenes out of brief shots, the new style has become slightly more elliptical, utilizing fewer establishing shots and long-held two-shots. . . . Classical continuity contains built-in redundancies: shot/reverse shots reiterate the information about character position given in the establishing shot, and so do eyelines and body orientation. For the sake of intensifying the dialogue exchange, filmmakers have omitted some of the redundancies provided by establishing shots. At the same time, though, fast-cut dialogue has reinforced premises of the 180-degree staging system. When shots are so short, when establishing shots are brief or postponed or nonexistent, the eyelines and angles in a dialogue must be even more unambiguous, and the axis of action must be strictly respected" ("Intensified Continuity," 17).

172 Benjamin, *The Arcades Project*, 116–17.

173 Interview with "Anjali," October 2003, New York City.

174 See Derrida, *Positions*, 40–41.

175 For the notion of a system of transformations, see Foucault, "History of Systems of Thought," 199–202.

176 *Hat ke* means something that is a little outside of the norm—a kind of masala film whose effects are not tracked by the functional segmentations of a population. It is something tangential, but always also at only one remove. "Fold" refers to when the fetish of white virginal skin (Bollywood's heroines, from Saira Banu to Kareena Kapoor) folds into the fetish of the good South Asian (the Hindu NRI computer techie), and thus a new multiplicity—where sexuality and race form as a connectivity to and with the exteriority of the nation—is in the becoming.

177 Traversing these sites like a dream or nightmare, the touch of cinema is a mode of contagion. And sometimes vision itself becomes tactile: Hindi-Urdu cinema is in other words a haptic medium. In thinking about commercial Hindi cinema as a haptic media event I am following the work of both Deleuze and, especially, Laura Marks. See Deleuze, *Francis Bacon*; and Marks, *The Skin of the Film*. As Daniel Smith explains, in his elaboration of *Logic of Sensation*, "what Deleuze . . . terms haptic space (from the Greek verb apto, to touch) is a space in which there is no longer a hand-eye subordination in either direction. It implies a type of seeing distinct from the optical, a close-up viewing in which 'the sense of sight behaves just like the sense of touch'" ("Deleuze on Bacon," xxxii). Indeed, Deleuze, in a

way that suggests something of the "to come" of the future anterior, warns that "one can remain entangled in the figurative givens and the optical organization of representation; but one can also spoil the diagram, botch it, so overload it that it is rendered inoperative. . . . The diagram is thus the operative set of asignifying and nonrepresentative lines and zones, line-strokes and color patches. And the operation of the diagram, its function, says Bacon, is to be 'suggestive.' . . . Because they are destined to give us the Figure, it is all the more important for the traits and color-patches to break with figuration. . . . In order to be converted into a fact, in order to evolve into a Figure, they must be reinjected into the visual whole; but it is precisely through the action of these marks that the visual whole will cease to be an optical organization; it will give the eye another power, as well as an object that will no longer be figurative" (82–83). Precisely, this is the affect of touch. In extending and transforming this experience of vision through our memory of other senses (touch only being one of them), Laura Marks argues that the skin of a film "offers a metaphor to emphasize the way film signifies through its materiality, through a contact between perceiver and object represented . . . to think of film as a skin acknowledges the effect of a work's circulation among different audiences, all of which mark it with their presence. . . . Film (and video) may be thought of as impressionable and conductive, like skin. . . . I want to emphasize the tactile and contagious quality of cinema as something we viewers brush up against like another body" (The Skin of the Film, xii). Rather than reducing the haptic quality of media assemblages to the function of metaphor, what we see is that the haptic opens the habitual pedagogies of cinema to its potential contagions, constantly transforming its own conditions and contexts of operation through interpenetrating multiplicities: satellite TV, fashionable desires, the latest saris, instantaneous Internet, Stardust, fan identity, affect, Shahrukh's aura, the slow duration of a movie set. Methodologically, the diagram of the media assemblage would begin from the point of exhibition as event; from the concept of audience as social flows desiring; from the positionality of a criticism that is intent upon its own functionalities (or nature).

178 I have always wanted to write a new history or science fiction of Bhopal. There is an originary Hindu narrative of the founding of Bhopal: Bhojpal, meaning dam built by Bhoj Parmar (AD 1010–1055), was the original name of the area of settlement (whose dams are still extant and considered engineering marvels). Although archaeological sources suggest that Bhopal was already a principality in the time of Sher Shah (1539–1545) (Verma, The Freedom Struggle in the Bhopal State, 1–2), it is generally believed that Dost Mohammed Khan founded the Bhopal dynasty. Dost Mohammed was born in Afghanistan, then settled in Lohari, Jalalabad. After having killed a Pathan, and fearing reprisals, Dost Mohammed fled to Delhi during the first years of Bahadur Shah's reign. He then joined the Moghul army in its march to Malwa against the Marathas. According to the nationalist historian Rajendra Verma, anarchy and disorder ruled the day in northern and central India (The Freedom Struggle in the Bhopal State, 2–3). This account is in keeping

with the colonial historiography of the area as well: "No better illustration," writes C. E. Luard (ably assisted in his information gathering by the gazetteer officer Munshi Kudrat Ali), "of the lawlessness . . . and the decay of the central power could be given than the story of the rise of this Afghan adventurer, who in the space of a few years was able to purchase the lease of an imperial district and rise by the power of his sword alone to be the founder of a line of independent princes" (Luard, *Bhopal State Gazetteer*, 10.) In keeping with the "great deeds of great men" approach of this kind of history, it was Dost Mohammed who, after a series of military adventures and political intrigues, first assumed the title of Nawab in 1722. Four years later, in 1726, he died at the age of sixty-six.

179 Later she explained the term "coir" (pronounced "coy-ar"): "It is a by-product of coconut, actually the scraping of the hair kind of things on the surface of a dried coconut shell (its husk). It is widely used in India to stuff chairs and mattresses. It is quite cheap. Coir mattresses are supposed to be very good for the back. When a chair's upholstery wears off, you can see coir peeping out at corners. Sometimes in real old and poverty-stricken movie halls in small towns of India, one can even feel the coir poking! And then of course, it is a heaven for bugs! Ouch, now I am going very gross."

180 This analysis has benefited from reading Priya Jaikumar's nicely written *Cinema at the End of Empire: A Politics of Transition in Britain and India.*

181 See the National Film Development Corporation (NFDC) website, www .nfdcindia.com (accessed October 1, 2006).

182 See Stoler, *Race and the Education of Desire* and *Carnal Knowledge and Imperial Power.*

183 *Report of the Indian Cinematograph Committee (1927–28)*, 34.

184 See Bataille, "The Notion of Expenditure," in which he writes of the bourgeoisie's "humiliating conceptions of restrained expenditure" (124). See also Bataille, *The Accursed Share*, vol. 1, 45–61, vols. 2 and 3, 197–257, and *Erotism* 164–96.

185 See Central Board of Film Certification, "Certification," www.cbfcindia.tn.nic.in (accessed October 1, 2006).

186 See Central Board of Film Certification, "Objectives of Film Certification," www .cbfcindia.tn.nic.in (accessed October 1, 2006).

187 Central Board of Film Certification, "Detailed Guidelines for Certification," www.cbfcindia.tn.nic.in (accessed October 1, 2006).

188 Central Board of Film Certification, "Cut List Details for Pagal Jiwani," www .cbfcindia.tn.nic.in (accessed October 1, 2006).

189 Central Board of Film Certification, "Film Cut Details. Film: Hello Girls," www .cbfcindia.tn.nic.in (accessed October 1, 2006).

190 The classic study of continuing relevance here is Stokes, *The English Utilitarians and India.*

191 See Foucault, *"Society Must Be Defended."*

192 Volga, "To Censor or Not to Censor."

193 See Thomas, "Indian Cinema."

194 As Volga writes: "In the days before independence, zamindars tended to invest their profits from agriculture into hotels, clubs and films that were springing up in the fast growing towns. This was partly because the British directly or indirectly controlled most industry and the local zamindars lacked the money or the guts to enter that area as competitors. The rajas of Challapalli, Mirzapur and Pithapuram were among the early producers of films in Andhra Pradesh. A few businessmen from Rayalseema soon joined them. Almost till 1970 film producers were mainly from the agricultural landowning class. In 1966 when the government lifted prohibition the arrack business blossomed forth. Huge profits both black and white were then ploughed into the film industry and laundered clean in the process. So the seventies saw many arrack contractors turn film producers. The eighties saw a spurt in the growth of urbanisation and real estate became the easy way to make money. Real estate business too became the breeding ground for crime and violence" ("To Censor or not to censor," 17). What seems to me a new governing logic (recapitulating base-superstructure) in such arguments is the quarantining of the sensation machine (commercial/bodily assemblage of cinema becoming media) as a direct reflection of its finance. None of this history can be excluded in a consideration of Indian commercial cinema's media assemblage; indeed part of the story of this cinema's globalization is the corporatization of its financial base.

195 Volga, "To Censor or Not to Censor."

196 Geeta Seshu, "Pornography—Certification Vs Censorship," IndiaNest.com, August 11, 2002, www.boloji.com (accessed October 1, 2006).

197 Jaikumar, "More Than Morality," 86.

198 Ibid., 87.

199 Ibid., 94, 95.

200 Vijay Anand, who passed away in 2004, is the director of such films as *Guide* (1965) and *Tesri Manzil* (1966), and brother to legendary actor Dev Anand.

201 Seshu, "Pornography—Certification vs Censorship."

202 Ibid.

203 Two excerpts from my field notes are relevant here. November 26, 2000 (from my notes in Mumbai): What an experience. I wanted to go see *Astitva*, ended up at Jamuna Palace Talkies. At first I thought that that was the Hindi pronunciation of Gemini. Turned out to be a "C" movie venue. Dikait Queen, and the intermission trailer! "Final Judgement" with that Brubaker guy! The narrative—well basically it's about this group of journalists that goes somewhere to the north of MP— they were sure to show a map of MP (pre-Chatishghar). There is a photographer and two couples. They're in north MP. A community of tribals which is matrilineal, women-empowering. The soundtrack was key: There was this one song, and the rest of the soundtrack came from the Last Temptation of Christ! The tribals are being harassed by a corrupt police chief. There are extended scenes of police officers (a man & woman) torturing the tribals. Tie up the women and beat them mercilessly. There is talk that the tribals are sexually licentious, cannibalistic.

The journalist meets the anthropologist who has gone native. The anthro has married into the tribe, and their daughter is one of the leaders. The whole film is atrociously dubbed. A love affair develops between the queen and one of the journalists. The long, slow pan up the woman's body, too excess. Again and again. A sadistic movie. It was like these set pieces. Right—that's why the form of the sex-spliced flick is the exact same form as a Hindi flick. Notice the resolution of the police question? One bad seed. Notice another narrative: Modernity, reason, the West, and male completes the eastern, oriental, wild, virgin, woman. And then again the valorization of tribal cultures—the legitimation of them as cultures—a whole way of life that can be learned and changed.

December 15, 2000: "Kali ki Saughund." It was a "C" dacait film, with Dharmendra (playing Sultan Daccu) and Shakti Kapoor (playing the evil Thakur), and that very popular woman star who is always in these women daccu films—Satnam Kaur (Sundeep Unnithan, "Bandolier Babes," *India Today*, November 20, 2000). The first paragraph of the article begins: "The writhing heroine is in the process of 'losing her honour' to the troika of the lala, thakur and thanedar. Macho hero Dharmendra wades in throwing punches and snorting his trademark 'kutey kameenay.' But he's too late to prevent the humiliated woman from becoming a vengeance-seeking dacoit" (70). This is literally the whole of the story. What I immediately noted down was the extremely bad dubbing and editing. Not to mention that some of the film that was used was obviously either very old or used already. The movie begins with Reshma running away from policemen, she finds her way into the forest and goes to sleep, waking up the next morning she is apprehended by some of Sultan Daccu's men, who take her to their leader. Reshma then recounts her story to Sultan. Which begins a flashback: Sis a teacher in the "city." She gets a posting in the "village." Her brother, Amar, is a police officer (who interestingly wears an ear ring, hmmm). She has another younger brother and a mother. The younger brother is obsessed with Rakhee, and the bond between brother and sister. She joins her post in the village, and learns that the Tahkur, the Lala, and the Police Inspector are in cahoots with local alcohol lords to keep the village under their domination. The first point of contention between Reshma and this nexus is on the very issue of education: the nexus realizes that education will awaken the villagers and their domination will be threatened; they then take steps to keep the villagers from going to her school. Reshma, trying to find justice for a villager beaten up by the Thakur, goes to the District Magistrate, but apparently to no avail (this scene of her confronting the DM is not shown). She goes back to the city, and meets Amar and mother on Rakhee, but her younger brother has gone to the village to seek her out, and do the raksha bandan ceremony.

It is at this moment that a scene occurs which is narratively completely unmotivated—three men are sitting on a cot, drinking whiskey. They call for more water from "Bhabhi," and the next thing you know one of the men goes into the house and assaults this woman. He takes her saree off and her blouse and the camera lingers over her naked breasts. The assailant then starts to fondle her breasts, but it looks more like a massage, and he then starts pinching her breasts. The most crucial thing about this whole scene, other than the near complete nonresistance of the woman, is the soundover: the heavy breathing of a man and woman is ensconced between flutelike music. This scene lasts for about five minutes, and then the assailant suddenly hears something, and runs off. He is fully clothed the whole time. The camera is at once frantic and meticulous—the breasts of the woman is what arrests the camera's gaze, and all the action is performed by the man, while the woman simply lies there. (This sense of sex as basically an extension of male activity was repeated in the jokes that were going round among the talkie attendants when I sat with them later.) Next scene is of Reshma's younger brother in the village. There he has a run-in with the local goondas, and they kill him off. Reshma coming back to the village finds the body of her dead brother, and applying his blood as a teeka (reminiscent of khoon bhari maang), she takes an oath to Kali—hence the title, Kali ki Saughand. In a fit of rage, she then kills one of the Takur's men, for which she is arrested. But immediately after her arrest, the Thakur, the Lala, and one or two others, gang rape her. First, Thakur slaps her, and then they throw her down and repeatedly rape her. This scene is crucial, because the breasts of the woman who is being raped are not Reshma's. Obviously, the body is different. There is a cut shot, where you see hands running over this headless torso of a woman, and then shots of a writhing Reshma, who is seemingly yelling and screaming, but again this is belied by the voiceover—the same heavy breathing of a man and woman, accompanied by a vigorous flute music. Interspersed between shots of a writhing Reshma, are shots of the Thakur and his colleagues thrusting into the camera (apparently Reshma), and shots of a dancing shiva murthi, or is it a dancing kali? Reshma is sentenced to hang to death, and she runs away from the police. This ends the flashback.

Hearing her tale, Sultan has pity on her plight and takes her into her gang, and trains her himself in shooting and riding. From here, the combo of Sultan and Reshma quickly dispatches the corrupt power nexus. The complication comes when Reshma's brother is posted in the village, and is committed to apprehending his sister. Her mother also moved to the village and adds poignancy to the scenes, supposedly. Once there, Amar falls for a new village girl, who is also on the lookout for Sultan and his gang. They perform two or three regular Hindi film type songs. Between all this violence and love scenes, there is another random scene of sex on a cot. Intriguingly, all the rape/sex scenes happen on cots inside houses, except Reshma's rape which happens on the floor of Thakur's house. In the next couple of scenes, we see Sultan is being ambushed on his weekly Kali Darshan pooja, and Amar in an attempt to apprehend him is fought off by Reshma, but succeeds in shooting Sultan who dies. There is a Jonny Lever type character who provides the information that leads to Sultan's death, and he also provides comic relief I guess, and who is in love with one of the village girls. He is killed by two of Reshma's gang, and they attempt to rape her, but are killed by Amar's girlfriend, but not before they off the girl first. Reshma until this point is referred to as a messiah and kali ki avatar; after this the sympathy is supposed to shift seemingly. In the next scene, we see Thakur's daughter getting married, and then a song and dance (quite lewd), and Reshma riding, riding with her gang. Finally, the song over, she arrives and quickly dispatches the Inspector and the Thakur. Her brother also arrives just in time to tell her to halt, but she shoots the gun out of his hand, her mother picks up the gun, and shoots her daughter dead, a la *Mother India*. Cannot forget that I saw a police officer in full uniform in the balcony seats, leaving the show with everyone else. Women's body types.

204 Sobchak, "The Scene of the Screen," 153.

205 Taran Adarsh, "Wake Up Call for Producers!" *Trade Guide*, February 24, 2001, 5.

206 Anupama Chopra, "Size Doesn't Matter," *India Today*, March 12, 2001, 78.

207 Ibid., 79.

208 That is, 94 percent of the tickets were sold on the first day or first weekend, depending on which source is referenced.

209 Quoted in Chopra, "Size Doesn't Matter," 79.

210 See Bataille, *The Accursed Share*, vol. 1, 45–61, vols. 2 and 3, 197–257, and *Erotism*, 164–96.

211 See Laxmi Srinivas's "The Active Audience": "In India, the social dimension of the movie event appears exaggerated when compared to the West. Public places such as cinema theatres are centres of group experience in contrast to many Western societies, where it is now an acceptable practice to see a movie, or even eat at a restaurant by oneself. Movie experiences in India involve families, friends and coworkers. Groups maybe composed of 4 to 8, even 10 individuals or more. Families include all ages—even infants are brought to the theatre and toddlers and the elderly are part of the group. The camaraderie in moviegoing is evident in the crowds emptying out of the theatres. People emerge as a group, and there is a lot of talk and laughter. Men are to be seen smoking, their arms slung around one another's shoulders, laughing, or holding hands with either a female or male friend and viewing companion. Women are seen laughing and chatting or holding the hand of a male companion or children. Families emerge, with a child carried by a male or female parent or the elderly carefully guided down the steps by a family member" (160).

THREE *"The Best Quality Cinema Viewing"*

1 "The military and the alphabet soup of Fed cops gave birth to the Valley. After WWII, all those shipbuilder engineers and all those radar engineers and the tame academics at Cal Tech and Cal and Stanford sorta congealed, did a bunch of startups and built a bunch of crap their buds in the Forces would buy. . . . Two generations later, the Valley was filled with techno-determinists, swagger-

ing nerd squillionaires who were steadfastly convinced that the money would flow forever and ever amen. Then came Hollywood, the puny $35 billion David that slew the $600 billion Goliath of tech. They bought Congresscritters, had their business model declared fundamental to the American way of life, extended copyright ad [infinitum/nauseam] and generally kicked the shit out of tech in DC" (Doctorow, "0wnz0red," 113–14). Later, I will return to this story's treatment of Hollywood, technology, and copyright.

2 Ibid., 118.

3 Ibid., 123.

4 Ravi Deshpande, "A Taste of Technology," *Expressions*, August-November 1999, www.abhivyakti.org.in (accessed October 1, 2006).

5 There are moments in this chapter when I refer to the multiplex as a specific exhibition space and so I use the narrow term, and other moments when I use the term malltiplex to emphasize the space as an assemblage of media and retailing. Pragmatically speaking, the terms are today interchangeable in India.

6 Dodona Research, www.dodona.co.uk (accessed October 1, 2006).

7 Aparna Krishnakumar, "Multiplex Owners on Expansion Spree," Rediff.com, March 2, 2005, www.rediff.com (accessed January 26, 2008).

8 See "Exhibition Infrastructure," Meeting of State Information and Broadcasting Ministers, November, 2001, www.ficci.com (accessed January 29, 2008).

9 See "PVR Limited," http://ipan.com (accessed October 1, 2006).

10 "Bollywood Tonight," Asia Network, March 7, 2005.

11 See "Mumbai Multiplexes" on the SmasHits webpage, August 27, 2003, www.smashits.com (accessed October 1, 2006).

12 For phase transitions, see Delanda, *Intensive Science and Virtual Philosophy*, 121–25.

13 Massumi, *Parables for the Virtual*, 30.

14 Says Henri Bergson of movement: "Mechanism . . . would consist in seeing only the positions [point A and point B]. Finalism would take [the order of point A and point B] into account. But both mechanism and finalism would leave on one side the movement, which is reality itself. In one sense, the movement is more than the positions and less than their order: for it is sufficient to make it in its indivisible simplicity to secure that the infinity of successive positions as also their order be given at once—with something else which is neither order nor position which is essential, the mobility. But in another sense, the movement is less than the series of positions and their connecting order; for, to arrange points in a certain order, it is necessary first to conceive the order and then to realize it with points, there must be the work of assemblage and there must be intelligence, whereas the simple movement of the hand contains neither . . . it is not made up of elements" (*Creative Evolution*, 91; see also page 128: "Life in general is mobility itself "). As Deleuze, Guattari, and Massumi have been saying ever since: follow the movements.

15 On relative accumulation, see Bichler and Nitzan, "Dominant Capital and the New Wars," 255–327.

16 Massumi, *Parables for the Virtual*, 134–35.

17 As Félix Guattari puts it: "The semiologies of signification play in keys with distinctive oppositions of a phonematic or scriptural order which transcribe enunciations into materials of signifying expression. Structuralists have been content to erect the Signifier as a category unifying all expressive economies: language, the icon, gesture, urbanism or the cinema, etc. They have postulated a general signifying translatability for all forms of discursivity. But in so doing, have they not misunderstood the essential dimension of machinic autopoiesis? This continual emergence of sense and effects does not concern the redundancy of mimesis but rather the production of an effect of singular sense, even though indefinitely reproducible" (*Chaosmosis*, 37; see also the critique of Lacan on page 48).

18 Massumi, *Parables for the Virtual*, 155–57.

19 Quoted in Deleuze, *Cinema 2*, 63.

20 See Simondon, *On the Mode of Existence of Technical Objects*, 64–68.

21 For an elaboration of the viewer as user in the human-computer interface of new media, see Manovich, *The Language of New Media*, 205.

22 See "Interview—Jeffrey L. Waaland: A 'Golden Link' to a Combined Cause," *Theatre World*, March 2005, 24–26, 25.

23 See Bazin, "The Myth of Total Cinema," 20; and Manovich's treatment of Bazin in the light of recent digital compositing in cinema (*Language of New Media*, 185).

24 Following Lev Manovich's analysis of the logic of new media as "individualized customization," I situate the media assemblage of Bollywood film in terms of the mathematization of the image and its modularity (see *The Language of New Media*, 27, 30).

25 Massumi, *Parables for the Virtual*, 35. Massumi elaborates on affect thus: "Proprioception [is] defined as the sensibility proper to the muscles and ligaments as opposed to tactile sensibility (which is "exteroceptive") and visceral sensibility (which is "interoceptive"). Tactility is the sensibility of the skin as surface of contact between the perceiving subject and the perceived object. Proprioception folds tactility into the body, enveloping the skin's contact with the external world in a dimension of medium depth: between epidermis and viscera. The muscles and ligaments register as conditions of movement what the skin internalizes as qualities: the hardness of the floor underfoot as one looks into a mirror becomes a resistance enabling station and movement; the softness of a cat's fur becomes a lubricant for the motion of the hand. Proprioception translates the exertions and ease of the body's encounters with objects into a muscular memory of relationality. This is the cumulative memory of skill, habit, posture. At the same time as proprioception folds tactility in, it draws out the subject's reactions to the qualities of the objects it perceives through all five senses, bringing them into the motor realm of externalizable response" (59). "Visceral sensibility immediately registers excitations gathered by the five "exteroceptive" senses even before

they are fully processed by the brain. . . . The immediacy of visceral perception is so radical that it can be said without exaggeration to precede the exteroceptive sense perception. It anticipates the translation of the sight or sound or touch perception into something recognizable associated with an identifiable object. . . . The dimension of viscerality is adjacent to that of proprioception, but they do not overlap. The dimension of proprioception lies midway between stimulus and response, in a region where infolded tactile encounter meets externalizing response to the qualities gathered by all five senses. It performs a synthesis of those intersecting pathways in the medium of the flesh, thus open to its own quasi corporality. Viscerality, though no less of the flesh, is a rupture in the stimulus-response paths, a leap in place into a space outside action-reaction circuits. Viscerality is the perception of suspense. The space into which it jolts the flesh is one of an inability to act or reflect, a spasmodic passivity, so taut a receptivity that the body is paralyzed until it is jolted back into action-reaction by recognition. Call it the space of passion" (60–61). "Call proprioception and viscerality taken together—as two complementary dimensions of the "medium"-depth perception most directly implicated in the body's registration of the in-betweenness of the incorporeal event—mesoperception. Mesoperception is the synesthetic sensibility: it is the medium where inputs from all five senses meet, across subsensate excitation, and become flesh together, tense and quivering. Mesoperceptive flesh functions as a corporeal transformer where one sense shades into another over the failure of each, their input translated into movement and affect. Mesoperception can be called sensation for short" (62).

26 Teo, "Postmodernism and the End of Hong Kong Cinema," 176.

27 "IMAX opens venue in China," Film Journal International, May 2004, 49. On the specifications for IMAX, see "70 mm film," Wikipedia, http://en.wikipedia.org (accessed May 20, 2008).

28 "World News," Variety, October 23, 2003, 13. For a recent example of the U.S. development strategy for "stadium seating" multiplexes, see "Consolidated Growth: Theatres and Technology in Expansion Mode," Film Journal International, November 2004, 50–52.

29 See "Christie Digital Cinema," www.christiedigital.com (accessed October 1, 2006); and "Korea's Successful Movie Industry," Christie Kino Notes 1(1) (2003): 4.

30 Ashoke Nag, "Plexes Pump B.O. Volume," Variety, March 8–14, 2004, 18.

31 See Manuel, Cassette Culture.

32 See ibid., 28–30.

33 One can see in this integration of expenditure in the multiplex (think of Fame Ad Labs in Wadala, Mumbai) a corrective to Bataille's own nostalgic romanticism of the transgressive excess: "In former times value was to unproductive glory, whereas in our day it is measured in terms of production: Precedence is given to energy acquisition over energy expenditure. Glory itself is justified by the consequences of a glorious deed in the sphere of utility. But, dominated though it is

by practical judgment and Christian morality, the archaic sensibility is still alive: In particular it reappears in the romantic protests against the bourgeois world; only in the classical conceptions of the economy does it lose its rights entirely" (*The Accursed Share*, 29). This romantic conception of excess has a genealogy in Romantic-era physiognomy—see Gigante, "The Monster in the Rainbow."

34 Sharma, "India's Experience with the Multiplex."

35 A film titled *Time Pass* was playing for a couple of weeks in summer 2000 (I was not able to see it, however). The film title was a kind of running joke between patrons and theater staff, a code word for sheer useless expenditure. Moreover, the phrase kept returning in my interviews with cinemagoers: going to see a movie was nothing other than time pass, it was just the quality of that passage that differed from one movie to the next, from one movie hall to the next. More recently, a very odd (grotesque even) film by the same title was released (dir. Chander Mishra, 2004); it narrates the story of a Hindu college boy trying to seduce a Christian girl amid Hindu-Muslim riots in Bombay.

36 Fuzzy sets are defined as sets whose elements have degrees or gradients of membership.

37 For the notion of open time in narratology, see Morson, "Narrativeness." He writes: "And what gives a moment presentness? In a phrase, open time. For a present moment to matter, to have real weight, more than one thing must be possible at the next moment. We may define open time as the excess of possibilities over actualities. For a determinist, one and only one thing can happen at any given moment; what did not happen could not have happened. In open time, at least one thing that did not happen could have. Think of the moment in War and Peace when Rostov, with 'his keen sportsman's eye,' realizes that if he and his men charge the French at this moment, they will rout them, but if he waits, the configuration of the French troops climbing the hill will change and the opportunity will be lost. Rostov may charge or not, and his choice matters. Or consider Dmitri Karamazov holding a pestle over his father's head and trying to decide whether to kill him. He could do either, that is the whole point. The examples are endless" (62).

38 Almost every movie theater owner I spoke with in Bhopal had some story to tell about students commandeering the projection room, and demanding the re-screening of key songs.

39 In considering this experience of open time in Bollywood cinemagoing it would be useful first to provincialize the Hollywood dominant, and second, to question if Hollywood's temporal pedagogies were ever that total in the first place even in the West. Consider in this regard some "temporal strategies" of every day life used by the Surrealists and the Situationists to interrupt the dead time of capitalist alienation. As Conrad Russell states: "An example of this kind of temporal interruption can be found in Breton's Second Manifesto of Surrealism, 'the simplest Surrealist act consists of dashing down into the street, pistol in hand, and firing blindly, as fast as you can pull the trigger, into the crowd.' Paul D. Miller

identifies this as a 'psycho-social critique' of the regimentation of time and culture in industrial society. The Surrealists parodied the monotony imposed by the industrialization of time through the activity of crétinisation, where 'hours and hours going round in loops on city trams' aimed at disalienation from the very empty repetition it mimicked. This activity of dérive, or drift, 'has an immediate shattering effect on calculated time.' Through the shards of clock-time, another temporality appears, marked by 'oneiric continuity,' as opposed to the fragmented state of Debord's 'commodity time'" ("Against Dead Time," 200). See also Doane, *The Emergence of Cinematic Time*.

40 Chatterjee has put this regime and its insecurities most succinctly, as follows: "The era of globalisation has seen the undermining of national sovereignty in crucial areas of foreign trade, property and contract laws and technologies of governance. There is overwhelming pressure towards uniformity of regulations and procedures in these areas, overseen, needless to say, by the major economic powers through new international economic institutions. Can one presume a convergence of interests and a consensus of views among those powers? Or could there be competition and conflict in a situation where international interventions of various kinds on the lesser powers are both common and legitimate? One significant line of potential conflict has already emerged: that between the dollar and the euro economic regions. A second zone of potential conflict is over the control of strategic resources such as oil. A third may be emerging over the spectacular surge of the Chinese economy that could soon make it a potential global rival of the western powers. These were the kinds of competitive metropolitan interests that had led to imperialist annexations and conflicts in the 19th century" ("Empire after Globalisation," 4156).

41 Sharma, "India's Experience with the Multiplex."

42 Sinclair and Harrison, "Globalization, Nation, and Television in Asia," 46.

43 There is, Hebdige continues, no doubt a tangled, contradictory dynamic that gives force to music visualization, "but the more immediate economic pressures seem clear enough: the decline in record sales worldwide, the fragmentation of markets, the collapse of any kind of unitary youth market" ("Digging for Britain," 149).

44 Gopalan, *Cinema of Interruptions*, 129.

45 See Brooks, "Pedagogy of the Dispossessed."

46 Calvin Sims, "'Synergy': The Unspoken Word," *New York Times*, October 5, 1993, C1, 18; quoted in Balio, "A Major Presence in the World's Markets," 208.

47 Balio, "A Major Presence in the World's Markets," 210.

48 See Schatz, "The New Hollywood," 192.

49 Corbett, "The Big Picture," 26.

50 Jameson, *The Seeds of Time*, 134–35.

51 Ibid., 144.

52 See Massumi, *Parables for the Virtual*, 27, for a critique of the "waning of affect" in postmodernity arguments. For the influential inaugural argument, see Jameson,

"Postmodernism," 64. For a rather uncritical adoption of that viewpoint (in an otherwise quite suggestive essay), see Sobchak, "The Scene of the Screen."

53 Chalmers, "Lighting the Way," 34.

54 Simondon, *On the Nature of Technical Objects*, 36.

55 "Who Says You Can't Be Cutting Edge and Tried and True?—DLP Technology Overview," Digital Light Processing, Texas Instruments, http://dlp.com (accessed November 30, 2006).

56 On the conceptual dominance of cinematic realism in new media, see Manovich, *Language of New Media*, 184–211; and for a trenchant critique, see Hansen, *New Philosophy for New Media*.

57 "Who Says You Can't Be Cutting Edge and Tried and True?"

58 Varela et al., *The Embodied Mind*, 162, 167.

59 Chalmers, "Lighting the Way," 34.

60 Manovich, *Language of New Media*, 139.

61 GDC Technology Private Limited is a Singapore incorporated company. It is a subsidiary of the Hong Kong Public Listed Company named Global Digital Creations Holdings Limited. "GDC Technology pioneers digital post-production, delivery and presentation technologies"; see "Mega Media Announces 1st Digital Cinema Encoder in Southeast Asia," Digital Cinema Today, June 17, 2005, www.dcinematoday.com (accessed November 30, 2006).

62 "Sathyam Cinemas Brings 'RDX' to India," Kannada Galatta, October 2006, http://kannada.galatta.com (accessed November 30, 2006).

63 Rohini Mohan, "DLP Technology Enters India," Hindu, May 22, 2005, http://www.hindu.com (accessed November 30, 2006).

64 Ganesh S. "DLP: A Cinematic Revolution," *Theatre World*, March 2005, 38–39, 39.

65 Doctorow, "0wnz0red," 110–11.

66 See "Chilkat AES & RSA Encryption Component 2.2.0," Infotech Location, www.itlocation.com (accessed November 30, 2006). "Chilkat Crypt.NET is an advanced encryption component that offers both RSA public-key encryption with digital signatures as well as symmetric encryption algorithms including AES (Rijndael), Blowfish, and Twofish. It provides the ability to easily create digital signatures for files or memory data, or verify digital signatures against incoming data or files. It allows for the use of any Cryptographic Service Provider, including Smart Card implementations from 3rd-party vendors. It also provides easy access to information about digital certificates and the ability to add and delete certificates from certificate stores found in the registry, filesystem, or even directly in memory."

67 Doctorow, "0wnz0red," 110.

68 "Digital Cinema," *Theatre World*, March 2005, 34. See also Jason Power's recent article in *Theatre World* where he elaborates on an open-file format for use in digital cinema: "The Digital Cinema Package format contains all the digital information needed to play the movie, including the images, sound, and subtitles. The

Digital Cinema Package can be thought of as a big box containing all the parts of the movie. If you open the box, you will find smaller boxes called Reels—these are similar in concept to film reels as they each represent a section of the movie, although the length is not limited as it is with film. Each Reel box will contain the elements for that section of the movie—for example, images, sound, and subtitles. The package film is based on a format called MXF (Material eXchange Format), which makes it very flexible—essentially the boxes can be as big or small as you like, and there is no limit to the number or type of pieces of content you can put inside them. . . . In the future, this could simplify distribution and enable exhibitors in multilingual areas to choose which language to play. When the package is created by the film distributor, they will also create Playlists which tell the system which boxes in the package to play when. . . . These Playlists would also make it possible for the distributor to include cuts of the movie—a PG version might have certain sections omitted, or even replaced with alternative images and audio. These features are very similar to the structures already found on many DVD disks in a home" ("MXF: Global Standard File," *Theatre World*, March 2005, 37).

69 Bolter and Grusin, *Remediation*, 67.

70 See Muffoletto, "Top Ten Trends in Multiplex Design," 26–27.

71 Ibid., 26.

72 The copy from the website continues: "Golden Link delivers the leading brands for our full range of foodservice equipment, supplies, and packaging to deliver the highest quality and value in concessions items. Having great suppliers is only half the solution, our 'Gold Net' of worldwide distributors and manufacturers serves the top box office countries in the world bringing concessionaires a 1-stop shop solution" (Golden Link, Inc., www.goldenlinkinc.com, accessed October 10, 2007). See also "Interview—Jeffrey L. Waaland: A 'Golden Link' to a Combined Cause," *Theatre World*, March 2005, 24–26.

73 Muffoletto, "Top Ten Trends in Multiplex Design," 27.

74 Deleuze and Guattari, *What Is Philosophy?* 167.

75 For strategies and tactics, see Certeau, *The Practice of Everyday Life*; for an analysis that extends Certeau into new media studies, see Manovich, *The Language of New Media*, 268, 280. One element of the media assemblage of the Indian malltiplex, which will come to have a decisive impact on not only the future of exhibition in India but on globalization in the region itself, is the impending crisis in energy production and distribution. Where will the energy come from, and how best can it be delivered to consumers? Privatization analysts insist that India needs up to $75 billion of investment in the power sector alone if it is to maintain its current rate of growth, and with a fiscal deficit of 9 percent of gross domestic product, private and foreign money will be crucial. In 2005, India produced 112,500 megawatts of power but had a deficit of 7–11 percent. Consumption grows 10 percent a year, but annual per capita consumption is only 500 kilowatts hours, compared with China's 939 and 8,747 in the United States. "Power-Hungry India

Faces a Stifling Energy Crisis," *Daily Times*, September 8, 2005, www.dailytimes .com (accessed November 30, 2006). See also the lecture from the former CIA head of South Asian Affairs, Sumit Ganguly, "India Needs Energy and the US," Rediff.com, September 2, 2005, http://in.rediff.com (accessed November 30, 2006). In the older media assemblage, a functional combination of state-generated power and devoted, privately owned generators was able to meet most of the needs of the major theaters in any given city in north India, but not without extended power outages, cutbacks in usage, and numerous other problems arising out of the negotiation of theater owners with often corrupt and bureaucratic state electricity boards responsible for power generation. With the gradual privatization of state-owned power companies [begun in 1991], this system of energy distribution is becoming nonfunctional.

76 Interview with Varun Moolchandani, Bhopal, June 20, 2004.

77 Metalight Productions Pvt. Ltd., India, www.metalightindia.com (accessed November 30, 2006).

78 Zubair Ahmed, "India Readies for Shopping Mall Boom," BBC News, October 4, 2005, http://news.bbc.co.uk (accessed October 10, 2007).

79 See "Getting Cheaper and Better," *Economist*, February 3–9, 2007, 64–65.

80 Sanjay Sharma, "How Profitable Is the Mall Business in Reality?" Gurgoan Scoop, www.gurgoanscoop.com (accessed June 1, 2008).

81 For a contextualization of the BJP's "India shining" campaign, on which around 2 billion rupees were spent running up to the 2004 elections, see: "India Shining . . . Feel Good vs Fail Good," *India Infoline*, February 10, 2004, www .indiainfoline.com (accessed November 30, 2006).

82 K. Sunil Thomas, "Boom or Bust," *The Week*, December 5, 2004, www.the-week .com, (accessed November 30, 2006).

83 Quoted in Thomas, "Boom or Bust." It is also no coincidence that the mall-multiplex has come to be seen as an articulation of consumerism and delocalization in Bangalore. In the recent violence that marked the death of the Kannada film star Rajkumar, the linkages between antiglobalization movements and cultural identity focused popular rage on the legacies and phase transitions of Rajkumar's media assemblage. See Sudha Ramachandran, "Bengaluru: 'We Want Our City Back!'" *Asian Times Online*, April 22, 2006, www.atimes.com (accessed November 30, 2006).

84 As one proprietor-consultant stated on a Mumbai-based real estate website: "A mall proprietor has to very carefully place his tenants/anchor tenants. Attracting consumers of high socio-economic profiles should not be the only ones on the agenda. People in India are family oriented. Thus families form [the] biggest shopping segments [and] varied entertainment avenues are to be insured to attract this segment" ("Mall: A Multiplex Boom," Accommodation Times, www.accommodationtimes.com, accessed November 3, 2006).

85 K. Sunil Thomas, "Boom or Bust," *Week*, December 5, 2004, www.the-week.com (accessed November 30, 2006). One might say, then, that the multiplex is a re-

turn globally to the cinema of attractions of early-twentieth-century film culture. As Vasudevan notes, "In contrast to the Hollywood mode of continuity cinema or narrative integration, [Tom] Gunning argues that early cinema was exhibitionist. The character's look into the camera indicated an indifference to the realist illusion that the story tells itself without mediation. The films displayed a greater interest in relaying a series of views and sensations to their audience rather than following a linear narrative logic. These elements were to be increasingly transcended in the Hollywood cinema's abstraction of the spectator as individuated consumer of its self-enclosed fictional world. In the process, the audience, earlier understood to be composed of workers and immigrants, was "civilized" into appreciating the bourgeois virtues of a concentrated, logical, character-based narrative development" ("Addressing the Spectator of the 'Third World' National Cinema," 319). See also Gopalan, *Cinema of Interruptions*, 25.

86 Buck-Morss, "Aesthetics and Anaesthetics," 22.

87 Sharma, "India's Experience with the Multiplex."

88 It would be useful in this regard to track what happens to the traditional balcony seating in the new multiplexes; many of the multiplexes I have visited in Delhi (PVR), Mumbai (Wadala IMAX), and Bangalore (Forum Mall) had no balconies. Instead, they had introduced "gold class" screenings, with complimentary drinks and dinner in plush reclinable seating. However, given the multiple directions that multiplexing can go in India, it comes as no surprise that other multiplexes have retained balcony seating (for instance, the Innovative multiplex in Maruthahalli, Bangalore).

89 Ishvinder Kaur, "PVR Cinemas, Bangalore: The Paradigm Resurrection!" *Theatre Magic*, March 2005, 8.

90 Ibid., 14.

91 "Interview: Matthew Heyman," *Theatre World*, June 2005, 14.

92 Benjamin, "The Origins of German Tragic Drama," 230; quoted in Patke, "Benjamin's Arcades Project and the Postcolonial City," 8.

93 Deleuze and Guattari, *What Is Philosophy?* 173.

94 See Jameson, *The Seeds of Time* and "Notes on Globalization as a Philosophical Issue." See Manovich, *The Language of New Media*.

95 Manovich, *The Language of New Media*, 205.

96 Benjamin, *The Arcades Project*, 406.

97 Ibid., 107.

98 Deleuze, *Bergsonism*, 32.

99 Massumi, *Parables for the Virtual*, 113.

100 This collection of data as customer profiling has become central to value added e-commerce, and it is part of the set of relations that Bruce Sterling has called "spime": "You use your credit card to make an online purchase of one bottle, an act that integrates it into your own spime management inventory system while at the same time linking you to its customer management software. This link already holds the bottle's unique ID code, history of ownership, geographical

tracking hardware and software to establish its place in space and time, and numerous other data. Now your personal data is added to that to assist with further development of the object—direct customer profiling" (Thomas, "The End of Cyberspace and Other Surprises," 386–87; see also Bruce Sterling, "When Blobjects Rule the Earth," SIGGRAPH, Los Angeles, 2004, www.boingboing.net, accessed October 30, 2007).

101 Regarding the samosa, see Kalra, "The Political Economy of the Samosa."

102 This is copy for Ricos concession products from an advertisement that ran in *Theatre World*, March 2005, 21.

103 For a useful contextualization of the discourses and practices that surround the NRI, see Desai, *Beyond Bollywood*, chapter 7: "Sex in the Global City: The Sexual and Gender Politics of the New Urban, Transnational and Cosmopolitan Indian Cinema in English."

104 Some examples include: Hrithik Roshan, Ashwariya Rai, and Aamir Khan ("A-grade" film stars) and Coke and Pepsi stands outside and inside the movie hall; the image and effects of new technologies (doubling the bodily effects of digital sound, Dolby logos and CDs become objects of a modernizing desire, for instance); the connectivities of new media (Internet, cable, and satellite amplify and thereby change the nature of star discourses and fan practices); and pedagogical temporalities centered on facilitating different forms of consumption (shorter films, detachable, highly stylized song-dance sequences, the gradual elimination of the intermission, the partitioning of screening times through an analytic of audience segmentation, and the proliferation of liabilities and the consequent pedagogies of chances and risks of the present, nationalist-diasporic-primordial belongings).

105 Massumi, *Parables for the Virtual*, 58.

106 Hansen, *New Philosophy for New Media*, 265–66.

107 As one website puts it, "*Kabhi Khushi Kabhi Gham* is a Bollywood film released in India and countries with large NRI populations on December 14, 2001. Its popularity was predetermined by virtue of possessing many of the biggest names in the Bollywood film industry: Amitabh Bachchan, his wife Jaya Bhaduri, Shah Rukh Khan, and his frequent costar Kajol (who had announced she would retire after the movie), along with rising stars Hrithik Roshan and Kareena Kapoor. This was also director Karan Johar's follow up to the immensely popular *Kuch Kuch Hota Hai*. The film was the first Bollywood feature to see a theatrical release in Germany with German subtitles. The story starts with a flashback to earlier, happier times that went astray, and then shows the characters working to right things. This basic plotline, and many of the jokes and characters within, are directly lifted from *Kuch Kuch Hota Hai*—for instance, Shah Rukh Khan and Kajol were not only the romantic leads in both movies, but they play characters with the same names. However, masala romances don't exist for the fresh, original plotlines, and in other regards *Kabhi Khushi Kabhi Gham* excels. The actors are charismatic, the soundtrack by Sandesh Shandilya and brothers Jatin Pandit &

Lalit Pandit (with Adesh Shrivastava composing the single "Shava Shava") is excellent, and the art direction is colorful, glossy, and dream-like, with elaborate sets and massive dance sequences, often done in beautiful hues of red and gold. One noticeable aspect of the movie is that the latter half takes place principally in London, where several of the characters are supposedly studying to earn their MBA at Oxford. While the use of foreign locations has been relatively common since being popularized in *Dilwale Dulhania Le Jayenge*, this movie, along with *Kal Ho Naa Ho*, ranks as one of the most amusing blendings of Bollywood sensibilities and a foreign setting" (NebulaSearch, www.nebulasearch.com, accessed November 30, 2006).

108 Bordwell, "Intensified Continuity," 24.

109 Manovich, *The Language of New Media*, 134–35.

110 Lata's disavowal of the raunchy remix video says a lot about the discourse around sexuality, family, and work in the film music industry. "I must say it's really strange that though I was known to sing sober songs, most of the remixed numbers are mine. 'Kaanta lagaa,' for instance, had another context when I sang it. I feel sorry for the girl who was seen in the music video of 'Kaanta lagaa.' I've heard she's from a decent family. Why wasn't she stopped by her family? Ambition? If she did it with their consent, then god help them. I struggled hard to get where I am. That's why I am still here" ("I Have Never Harmed Other Singers: Lata," *Indiaglitz*, September 29, 2004, www.indiaglitz.com, accessed November 30, 2006).

111 Bolter and Grusin, *Remediation*, 19.

112 Ibid., 70.

113 Ghosh, "An Uncertain 'Coming of the Book,'" 25. See also Joshi, "In Another Country"; Orsini, *Hindi Public Sphere, 1920–1940*; Naregal, *Language, Politics and Elites in the Public Sphere*; Darnton, "Literary Surveillance in the British Raj" and "Book Production in British India, 1850–1900"; Eisenstein, *The Printing Press as an Agent of Change*; Martin and Febvre, *The Coming of the Book*; and Anderson, *Imagined Communities*.

114 Ghosh, "An Uncertain 'Coming of the Book,'" 48, 44.

115 Ibid., 27–28.

116 Ibid., 28.

117 Ibid., 33. See as well Rosie Thomas's argument that "there is of course good evidence that Hindi films have evolved from village traditions of epic narration, and the dramas and the characters, as well as the structure, of the mythological epics are regularly and openly drawn upon" ("Indian Cinema: Pleasures and Popularity," 123).

118 "The oral traversed the domain of the written through other significant routes as well. Performances based on the mangal kavya and panchali texts offered multifarious points of intervention and negotiation between the written text and its audience. These religious ballads celebrating the various forms of the goddess Shakti—Manasa the snake goddess, Sitala the goddess of fever and smallpox,

Chandi, and others—seem to have sprung from the oral traditions of nomadic lower castes, which then became gradually sanskritized over time. As Edward Dimock points out, the mangal kavya poems were simultaneously part of the written and oral traditions and thus continued to be recited during worship and festive gatherings. While some of them were sanitized and drawn into Brahmanical circles, the popular performance tradition continued to thrive and almost invariably escaped fixation by writing" (Ghosh, "An Uncertain 'Coming of the Book,'" 34–35).

FOUR *"With You Every Moment in Time"*

1 See Brooks, *The Melodramatic Imagination.*

2 See Niyogi, "Modern Shakespeare in Popular Bombay Cinema"; and Vasudevan, "Addressing the Spectator of the 'Third World' National Cinema."

3 One Internet source describes the jump cut in this way: "In film, [a jump cut is the] radical transition between two camera shots. Jump cuts will cause viewer disorientation and are sometimes used deliberately to create that effect. However, they are usually accidents that happen as a result of such factors as an extreme change in subject, size, camera angle, screen direction or position, or a camera shift from moving action to a stationary shot. If a jump cut happens too often, the viewer may become irritated and lose interest in the action on the screen" (Answers.com, www.answers.com, accessed February 8, 2008).

4 It is in fact the more subtle cuts in space that give duration to the ittafaq image; that is, the sense of an event still expanding and not exhausted is communicated in a certain continuity of spatial markers from one shot to the next, a compressed interval. This is best brought out in the scene of confrontation in *Veer Zara*: Mariam Hayaat Khan (Kirron Kher) confronts Veer Pratap Singh (Khan) and we shift to the balcony after the play of fearful gazes.

5 Deleuze, "Control and Becoming," 174. One sees, however, that Foucault also conceptualized time much as he did the body—as palimpsest. Thus power is articulated on time, etc. But, exactly like the body in that it is a continuous multiplicity, time is merely another name for a phase transition—i.e., movement, framing, territory. See Cache, *Earth Moves.*

6 Clough, "Affect and Control," 360. See also Clough et al., "Notes Towards a Theory of Affect Itself."

7 This is a point that is best brought out by Eugene Thacker in *Biomedia*, chapters 2 and 3, in which he elaborates a form of criticism that pushes bioinformatics to consider its ethical relation as a movement of virtualization.

8 Examples of the new genre include, among others, *Dil Chahta Hai* (dir. Farhan Akhtar, 2001), *Chalte Chalte* (dir. Aziz Mirza, 2003), *Hum Dil De Chuke Sanam* (dir. S. L. Bhansali, 1999), *Saathiya* (dir. Shaad Ali, 2002), *Lakshya* (dir. Farhan Akhtar, 2004), *Kal Ho Na Ho* (dir. Nikhil Advani, 2003), *Hum Tum* (dir. Kunal Kohli, 2004), *Murder* (dir. Anurag Basu, 2004), *Jism* (dir. Amit Saxena, 2003),

Aetbaar (dir. Vikram Bhatt, 2004), Road (dir. Rajat Mukherjee, 2002), Naach (dir. Ram Gopal Varma, 2004), Black (dir. S. L. Bhansali, 2005), Veer-Zara (dir. Yash Chopra, 2004), Chameli (dir. Sudhir Mishra, 2004), Humko Dewaana Kar Gaye (dir. Raj Kanwar, 2006), and Home Delivery (dir. Sujoy Ghosh, 2005). This last film crosses genres as much through its stars as through its mise-en-scène: Rahul Bose and Kareena Kapoor have each branded a certain kind of cinema anew: Kapoor has taken the aura-seduction of the Bollywood bombshell and actually exploded it, and Bose has taken the incredible virtuality—or openness to new connectivities—of the present moment as an occasion to rearticulate in "a new grammar" (his own words) the art of popular cinema. For a brilliant discussion of the group of filmmakers associated with Bose, see Desai, Beyond Bollywood, chapter 7.

9   See Reith, "Uncertain Times."

10 Lollywood is the stereotypical name for Pakistani cinema.

11 According to a recent article in the Hindu, filmmakers and television produc-
    ers all over India are "warming up to the need for insuring their production
    risks. This year, most of the prominent Hindi movies opted for film insurance,
    including Lakshya, Main Hoon Na, Hum Tum, Deewar, Dhoom and Masti. Among
    the yet to be released, big-budget Bollywood films that have sought cover are
    Swades, an Ashutosh Gowarikar/UTV project, Ketan Mehta's The Rising, Mukta
    Arts' Kisna, Yash Chopra's Bunty Aur Babli and Karan Johar's Kaal, according to
    industry sources. . . . Unlike other general insurance products, film insurance is
    usually a customised offering. The premium could vary from film to film and the
    extent of risk cover of the production. The product usually covers fire, serious ill-
    ness or death of lead actors, failure of equipment, etc." (Latha Venkatraman and
    Rukmani Vishwanath, "Bollywood Warming Up to Risk Cover—United India
    Designing Product for TV Serials," Hindu, September 14, 2004, www.thehindu-
    businessline.com, accessed November 30, 2006). The leading firm offering in-
    surance policies to filmmakers in India is United India Insurance Co. Ltd., www
    .uiic.co.in (accessed November 30, 2006). Radhika Mehta states that "today the
    Indian general insurance market is valued at Rs 14,000 crore. It is growing at a
    rate of 20 per cent and is expected to reach Rs 45,000 crore in about 10 years.
    Private players have already gained a 10 per cent share in three years. No mean
    achievement when compared to the growth rates of countries like South Korea
    and Thailand, where the private sector took 15 years to gain a 15 per cent share
    of the market. India has 14 private players in life insurance and 12 players in the
    general insurance sector. . . . The per capita spending on insurance in India is
    $9, compared with $2,500 in the US and $50–100 in Southeast Asia. The rise in
    the number of nuclear families will provide an impetus for growth. However,
    this needs to be supported with parallel developments in the industry. . . . The
    greatest barrier to insurance is penetration. [Quoting Dalip Verma, managing
    director, Tata-AIG:] 'The strength lies in building the back end. Products need to
    be supported efficiently through identification of affinity and social groups and

market segmentation'" ("Future Perfect," Tata-AIG General Insurance, www
.tata.com, accessed November 30, 2006).

12 Foucault, "*Society Must Be Defended*, 251–52. See also Foucault, *The History of Sexuality, Vol. 1*.

13 Foucault, *Society Must Be Defended*, 252.

14 Beck, "The Terrorist Threat: World Risk Society Revisited," 39.

15 Ibid., 40.

16 See Guha, *Dominance without Hegemony*.

17 See Patel, "Hindsight."

18 In the last three decades of the nineteenth century the following companies were started in the Bombay Presidency alone: Bombay Mutual (1871), Oriental (1874), and Empire of India (1897) (all of these firms were joint Indian-British collaborations). Overall, British firms such as Amberly Life Assurance, Royal Insurance, and Liverpool and London Globe Insurance dominated the field. See Bhattacharya and Rane, "History of Insurance in India," Center for Civil Society Publication, www.ccsindia.org, 379 (accessed March 3, 2005).

19 The Indian Life Assurance Companies Act of 1912 was the first statutory measure to regulate the life insurance business. Later in 1928 the Indian Insurance Companies Act was legislated to enable the British government to collect statistical information about both life and non-life insurance business transacted in India by Indian and foreign insurers, including provident insurance societies. In 1938, with a view "to protecting the interest of insuring public, the earlier legislation was consolidated and amended by the Insurance Act 1938 with comprehensive provisions [for] detailed and effective control over the activities of insurers" (Bhattacharya and Rane, "History of Insurance in India," 379).

20 The General Insurance Business (Nationalisation) Act of 1972 nationalized the general insurance business in India effective from January 1, 1973 (Bhattacharya and Rane, "History of Insurance in India," 381).

21 Ibid., 380.

22 See "July 1997 Insurance Review," Ipan, www.ipan.com (accessed November 30, 2006); and the General Insurance Corporation of India website at www .gicofindia.com (accessed November 30, 2006). See also Pant, "Insurance Regulation and Development Bill: An Appraisal." A few years later, in the late 1990s, GIC offered another insurance scheme that was met with outright rejection from many quarters. As stated in a commentary in *Economic and Political Weekly*: "The Rajeshwari Mahila Kalyan Bima policy, the GIC scheme as it stood when it was announced, was a ridiculous and callous attempt to 'compensate' women in distress. Launched by the prime minister on March 19 [1999] the scheme covered women in the age group 10 to 75 and offered insurance against disability caused by rape at an annual premium of Rs 15 for a period of one to five years. The extent of insurance coverage depended on the degree of disability: the compensation for permanent disability would be 25,000 and Rs 12,500 for loss of a limb or eye. The scheme also offered insurance against disability caused from surgical

operations, from snake-bites, drowning, murder and terrorist activity. Interestingly, the assessment of the degree of disability would depend on a doctor's report, a doctor of the insurer's choice. The scheme drafted by Oriental Insurance, originally meant to cover risks that women faced, included rape reportedly at the instance of the government" ("Women: Unviable Scheme," March 20–26, 1999, www.epw.org.in, accessed November 30, 2006). As women's groups immediately pointed out (causing the withdrawal of the scheme), it seemed to acknowledge the government's inability to protect women from rape and to compensate them after the event.

23 "Five Years After," *Business Today*, December 18, 2005, 112. In comparison, China's life insurance penetration is 2.3 percent and non-life insurance is 1.03 percent; while in the United States it is 4.38 and 5.23 respectively.

24 Ibid., 112. "Among the new products launched by private sector life insurers is the unit-linked insurance plan (ULIP). Today, seven out of 10 policies sold by private insurers are ULIPs. The popularity of equity-linked ULIPs may have to do with the stock market's performance over the past 12 months" (112). Bancassurance is the selling of insurance and banking products through the same channel, most commonly through bank branches selling insurance. The sales synergies available have been sufficient to be used to justify mergers and acquisitions. See Money Terms, http://moneyterms.co.uk (accessed October 10, 2007).

25 Pant, "Development Agenda for Insurance Regulation."

26 Jameson, "The End of Temporality," 703–4.

27 "Ultimately, It Just Boils Down to One Thing—Your Outlook Towards Life," advertisement in *The Layman's Guide to Insurance* (one of the "Outlook Money Books," supported by Max New York Life).

28 Reith, "Uncertain Times," 385. See also Heise, "Toxins, Drugs, and Global Systems."

29 Ewald, "Insurance and Risk," 199. See also Ewald, "Two Infinities of Risk."

30 Reith, "Uncertain Times," 389.

31 Defert, "'Popular Life' and Insurance Technology," 211.

32 Reith "Uncertain Times," 394. Reith further notes that "since absolute certainty of future events was impossible, the best course of action was simply risk minimization, and this could be achieved by the rational calculation of relevant factors. In such models, the notion of risk represents an order of knowledge that has given up all hope of certainty, instead concerning itself with calculating degrees of probability and belief. . . . Contrary to the optimistic Enlightenment belief that greater knowledge brings greater certainty, this application of risk makes clear that the more knowledge we have, the less certain we become, and the ideal of certainty is replaced with an ongoing exercise in probability calculation" (394). I am drawing here as well on the force of Ian Hacking's *The Taming of Chance*. Hacking describes how in the 1930s the "laws of physics, which had long been the model of impersonal and irrevocable necessity, were shorn of their magisterial power. . . . By 1936 they described only the probabilities of the future

course on any individual particle. . . . The 1930s pulled physics, and hence all law, away from determinism" (116).

33 Reith, "Uncertain Times," 396.

34 Ewald, "Insurance and Risk," 203.

35 See Deleuze, *Foucault* and *Negotiations*. See also Clough, "Affect and Control."

36 Defert, "'Popular Life' and Insurance Technology," 219.

37 Ibid., 207.

38 Thacker, *Biomedia*, 6–7.

39 See Mbembe, "Necropolitics."

40 Clough, "The Affective Turn," 8–9.

41 Cooper, "Pre-empting Emergence," 129.

42 John Quarterman, "Perilocity," http://riskman.typepad.com (accessed March 2, 2007).

43 Cooper, "Pre-empting Emergence," 121.

44 Cooper, 128.

45 "Foreign Banks Bond in Times of Catastrophe," *Economic Times*, Friday, July 11, 2003, http://economictimes.indiatimes.com (accessed February 3, 2007). In another report, the *Economic Times* noted that "a group of bankers led by Credit Suisse First Boston, a Swiss investment bank . . . helped FIFA, the world football federation, insure the world's most popular sporting event against terrorism and other risks. Such coverage has been hard and expensive to come by since September 11th 2001. AXA, a French insurer, backed out of insuring the 2002 tournament in Asia after that day's attacks. So this time FIFA turned to the capital markets: in September it issued $260m of 'cancellation bonds,' the first transfer of terrorist risk to public investors. These will receive a handsome yield in return for underwriting the risk of cancellation. If the tournament is called off, they will lose three-quarters of their principal. The offering is the latest twist on catastrophe bonds ('cat bonds'), through which investors have in the past assumed the financial risk of big natural disasters. Since cat bonds were first issued in 1997, after Hurricane Andrew in Florida and a huge earthquake in San Francisco caused reinsurance premiums to rocket, over $6.3 billion has been issued, according to Swiss Re, a reinsurer. So far this year, $900m of catastrophe risk has been transferred in this way" ("Latest Twist in Catastrophe Bonds," *Economic Times*, January 5, 2004, http://economictimes.indiatimes.com, accessed March 2, 2007).

46 On the perceptual mode of power, see Massumi, *Parables for the Virtual*, 31–48.

47 As Niranjan Pant has noted: "Whether proactive or reactive, regulation of economic affairs such as insurance has essentially a prudential air about it. This is where it is different from 'government,' which is mainly an administrative device. Although, therefore, in the tripartite division of state polity into legislature, judiciary and executive, the economic regulatory institutions are clubbed with the executive; the need to insulate 'regulation' from the core executive is being progressively recognised everywhere. Regulation is not as much about enforcing pre-set laws, as it is about promotion, development and facilitation of the spread

of prudential practices of business and financial reporting. This requires the regulators to develop acutely sensitive eyes and ears for market developments. Regulation must provide legal, non-arbitrary, policy responses to the roadblocks of the business, especially where business itself fails to respond by its self-fixing mechanism" ("Insurance Regulation and Development Bill: An Appraisal," *Economic and Political Weekly*, Nov. 6, 1999, http://www.epw.org.in, accessed November 30, 2006).

48 The scene is reminiscent of the stormy early relationship between strict, paranoid patriarch and besotted daughter in love with working-class loafer, which turns into the greatest horror film in modern Bollywood history: Shyam and Tulsi Ramsay's *Purana Mandir* (1984).

49 Peirce, "What Is a Sign?" 8.

50 Massumi, "Fear (the Spectrum Said)," 44.

51 Ewald, "Insurance and Risk," 209. We should note that part of the struggle around knowledge and practice that is being waged in and through these ads with the creation of insurance expertise is a subjugation of a much older practice of security among working class and lower-middle-class South Asians. For instance, the collective saving schemes called "Committees" in North Indian Muslim communities have long preexisted insurance technologies and were aimed at pooling resources and providing for community members in moments of distress (interview with Zaida Begum, October 2004).

52 Ewald, "Insurance and Risk," 200.

53 Ibid., 208.

54 For the importance of non-Western healing practices among the diaspora, see, for example, Dein and Sembhi, "The Use of Traditional Healing in South Asian Psychiatric Patients in the U.K."; and Haller, "Let It Flow."

55 See Perfect-Partner.com at www.perfect-partner.com (accessed March 7, 2007). For opposing views, see "Ajmeri Baba Ripped Me Off Big Time," Hindustan.net, http://hindustan.net (accessed March 7, 2007).

56 See the ruling by the Advertising Standards Authority, www.asa.org.uk (accessed November 30, 2006).

57 See Guha, *Dominance without Hegemony*.

58 There have been complaints lodged by consumers of spiritual healer products in the United Kingdom with the Advertising Standards Authority (an independent, self-regulatory body for nonbroadcast advertisements, sales promotions, and direct marketing in the United Kingdom). On March 13, 2002, a public complaint was lodged against Pundit Maharaj, from Hampshire, West Yorkshire, that questioned the advertiser's claims and ability to fulfill the guarantees, and objected that the advertisement could mislead and exploit vulnerable people. The complaint was upheld, and the ASA noted that the "advertiser sent no evidence to show that he guaranteed his services or that he refunded dissatisfied clients. The Authority considered that he had not substantiated the claim that he guaranteed unconditionally to resolve all a client's difficulties and problems.

It also considered that the implication that he did so could mislead and exploit vulnerable people. The Authority asked the advertiser to remove that misleading implication and all references to guarantees from his future advertisements. It advised him to consult the Committee of Advertising Practice Copy Advice team before advertising again" (Advertising Standards Authority, http://www.asa.org .uk, accessed November 30, 2006).

59 Luciana Parisi and Tiziana Terranova, "Heat-Death: Emergence and Control in Genetic Engineering and Artificial Life," ctheory.net, May 10, 2000, www .ctheory.net (accessed October 1, 2007).

Conclusion

1 See the TV serial *Mirza Ghalib* (dir. Gulzar, 1988).

2 On subjugated knowledge, see Foucault, *"Society Must be Defended,"* 7–8.

3 As the U.S. Department of Energy website for the Microbial Genome Project states: "Microbes, which make up most of the earth's biomass, have evolved for some 3.8 billion years. They have been found in virtually every environment, surviving and thriving in extremes of heat, cold, radiation, pressure, salt, acidity, and darkness. Often in these environments, no other forms of life are found and the only nutrients come from inorganic matter. The diversity and range of their environmental adaptations indicate that microbes long ago 'solved' many problems for which scientists are still actively seeking solutions" ("Microbial Genomics at the U.S. Department of Energy," http://microbialgenomics.energy .gov, accessed March 7, 2007).

4 Steigler, *Time and Technics*, 55–56. See also Audouze, "Leroi-Gourhan, a Philosopher of Technique and Evolution."

5 Gilles Deleuze insists on the sterility of the virtual quasi-cause in the *Logic of Sense*, and Manuel Delanda explores this theme in *Intensive Science and Virtual Philosophy*; as does Stephen Shaviro in "Deleuze's Encounter with Whitehead," 17, www .shaviro.com (accessed January 7, 2007).

6 Deleuze, *Cinema 2*, 63.

7 Quoted in Prigogine and Stengers, *Order Out of Chaos*, 141.

8 Ibid. For his part, Gilbert Simondon tied the clinamen to the very individuation of singularities thus: "Anything that contributes to establishing relations already belongs to the same mode of existence as the individual, whether it be an atom, which is an indivisible and eternal particle, or prime matter, or a form. The atom interacts with other atoms through the clinamen, and in this way it can constitute an individual (though not always a viable one) across the entire expanse of the void and the whole of endless becoming" ("The Genesis of the Individual," 298). Of course, atoms are not indivisible or eternal, but Simondon's theory of individuation decisively breaks with the substantialist and hylomorphic viewpoints on becoming through the concept of the clinamen.

9 Luciana Parisi and Tiziana Terranova, "Heat-Death: Emergence and Control in Genetic Engineering and Artificial Life," ctheory.net, 5/10/2000, www.ctheory .net (accessed October 1, 2007). See Prigogine and Stengers, *Order Out of Chaos*; and Prigogine, *The End of Certainty*. See also David Borgo, whose analysis, in *Sync or Swarm*, of complexity theory and its relation to popular, improvisational musical forms seems particularly open to what I am calling clinamedia.

BIBLIOGRAPHY

Adams, Julia. "The Familial State: Elite Family Practices and State-Making in the Early Modern Netherlands." *Theory and Society* 23 (1994): 505–39.

Adkins, Lisa. "The New Economy, Property and Personhood." *Theory, Culture and Society* 22(1) (2005): 111–30.

Agamben, Giorgio. *Homo Sacer*. Trans. Daniel Heller-Roazen. Stanford, Calif.: Stanford University Press, 1995.

———. *States of Exception*. Trans. Kevin Attell. Chicago: University of Chicago Press, 2005.

Amsden, Alice. *The Rise of "The Rest": Challenges to the West from Late-Industrializing Economies*. New York: Oxford University Press, 2003.

Appadurai, Arjun. "Spectral Housing and Urban Cleansing." *Public Culture* 12(3) (2000): 627–51.

Aracagök, Zafer. "Decalcomania, Mapping and Mimesis." *Symploke* 13(1–2) (2005): 283–302.

Arnold, Alison. "Aspects of Production and Consumption in the Popular Hindi Film Song Industry." *Asian Music* 24(1) (1992–1993): 122–36.

Athanasiou, Athena. "Technologies of Humanness, Aporias of Biopolitics, and the Cut Body of Humanity." *Differences* 14(1) (2003): 125–62.

Audouze, Françoise. "Leroi-Gourhan: A Philosopher of Technique and Evolution." *Journal of Archaeological Research* 10(4) (2002): 277–306.

Bakardjieva, Maria. *Internet Society: The Internet in Everyday Life*. London: Sage Publications, 2005.

Bakshi, Rajni. "Raj Kapoor." In *The Secret Politics of our Desires: Innocence, Culpability and Indian Popular Cinema*, ed. Ashis Nandy. New Delhi: Zed Books, 1998. 92–133.

Balio, Tino. "A Major Presence in the World's Markets." In *The Film Cultures Reader*, ed. Graeme Turner. New York: Routledge, 2002. 206–18.

Balsamo, Anne. *Technologies of the Gendered Body: Reading Cyborg Women*. Durham, N.C.: Duke University Press, 1997.

Barad, Karen. *Meeting the Universe Halfway: Quantum Physics and the Entanglement of Matter and Meaning.* Durham, N.C.: Duke University Press, 2007.

Barenblatt, G. I., M. Ya. Ivanov, and G. I. Shapiro. "On the Structure of Wave Fronts in Nonlinear Dissipative Media." *Archive for Rational Mechanics and Analysis* 87(4) (1985): 293–303.

Bataille, George. *The Accursed Share*, vol. 1. Trans. Robert Hurley. New York: Zone Books, 1998.

———. *The Accursed Share*, vols. 2 and 3. Trans. Robert Hurley. New York: Zone Books, 1991.

———. *Erotism: Death and Sensuality.* San Francisco: City Lights, 1988.

———. *Visions of Excess.* Trans. Allan Stoekl. Minneapolis: University of Minnesota Press, 1985.

Bazin, Andre. *What Is Cinema?* Ed. and trans. Hugh Gray. Berkeley: University of California Press, 1967–1971.

Bean, Jennifer M. "Technologies of Early Stardom and the Extraordinary Body." *Camera Obscura* 48(16) (2001): 1–57.

Beck, Ulrich. "The Terrorist Threat: World Risk Society Revisited." *Theory, Culture and Society* 19(4) (2002): 39–55.

Behar, Amitabh. "Madhya Pradesh: Experiment with Direct Democracy." *Economic and Political Weekly* 38(20) (2003): 1925–27.

Benjamin, Walter. *The Arcades Project.* Trans. Howard Eiland and Kevin McLaughlin. Cambridge, Mass.: Belknap Press, 1999.

———. "Paris: The Capital of the Nineteenth Century." Trans. Howard Eiland. In *Selected Writings*, vol. 3., ed. H. Eiland and M. Jennings. Cambridge, Mass.: Belknap Press, 2003. 32–49.

———. "The Work of Art in the Age of Its Technological Reproducibility" (1939). In *Selected Writings*, vol. 4., ed. H. Eiland and M. Jennings. Cambridge, Mass.: Belknap Press, 2006. 101–33.

Bergson, Henri. *Creative Evolution.* Trans. Arthur Mitchell. New York: Dover Publications, 1998.

Bharatmuni. *Natyasastra.* Ed. and trans. Anand Rangacharya. New Delhi: Munshiram Manoharlal Publishers, 1996.

Bhattacharya, Arjun, and O'Neil Rane. "History of Insurance in India." Center for Civil Society. www.ccsindia.org (accessed March 3, 2005).

Bichler, Shimshon, and Jonathan Nitzan. "Dominant Capital and the New Wars." *Journal of World Systems Research* 10(2) (2004): 255–327.

Bohm, David. *Wholeness and the Implicate Order.* New York: Routledge, 2002.

Bolter, Jay David, and Richard Grusin. *Remediation.* Cambridge, Mass.: MIT Press, 1999.

Bordwell, David. "Intensified Continuity: Visual Style in Contemporary American Film." *Film Quarterly* 55(3) (2002): 16–28.

Borgo, David. *Sync or Swarm: Improvising Music in a Complex Age.* New York: Continuum, 2006.

Brooks, Dwight E. "Pedagogy of the Dispossessed: Race, Gender and Critical Media Literacy in the 'Malltiplex.'" *Symploke* 10(1–2) (2002): 71–88.

Brooks, Peter. *The Melodramatic Imagination: Balzac, Henry James, Melodrama, and the Mode of Excess*. New Haven, Conn.: Yale University Press, 1995.

Bruno, Giuliana. *Streetwalking on a Ruined Map: Cultural Theory and the City Films of Elvira Notari*. Princeton, N.J.: Princeton University Press, 1993.

Buck-Morss, Susan. "Aesthetics and Anaesthetics: Walter Benjamin's Artwork Essay Reconsidered." *October* 62 (1992): 3–41.

Cache, Bernard. *Earth Moves*. Trans. Anne Boyman. Cambridge, Mass.: MIT Press 1995.

Certeau, Michel de. *The Practice of Everyday Life*. Trans. Steven Randall. Berkeley: University of California Press, 1984.

Chakravarty, Sumita S. *National Identity in Indian Popular Cinema, 1947–1987*. Austin: University of Texas Press, 1993.

Chalmers, Hilary. "Lighting the Way: Osram's Paul Caramagna Discusses the Changing Role of Cinema Projection." *Film Journal International* 108(4) (2005): 34.

Chatterjee, Partha. "Empire after Globalisation." *Economic and Political Weekly* 39(37) (2004): 4155–64.

Chion, Michel. *The Voice in Cinema*. Ed. and trans. Claudia Gorbman. New York: Columbia University Press, 1999.

Chow, Rey. "A Souvenir of Love." In *At Full Speed: Hong Kong Cinema in a Borderless World*, ed. Esther Yau. Minneapolis: University of Minnesota Press. 209–20.

Chowdhury, Kanishka. "Interrogating 'Newness': Globalization and Postcolonial Theory in the Age of Endless War." *Cultural Critique* 62 (2006): 126–61.

Chun, Wendy. *Control and Freedom*. Boston: MIT Press, 2005.

Chute, David. "Bollywood Rising: A Beginner's Guide to Hindi Cinema." *Film Comment* 38(3) (May/June 2002): 35–40.

Clough, Patricia. "Affect and Control: Rethinking the Body 'Beyond Sex and Gender.'" *Feminist Theory* 4(3) (2003): 359–64.

———. *Autoaffection*. Minneapolis: University of Minnesota Press, 2000.

———. "The Affective Turn: Political Economy, Biomedia, and Bodies." *Theory, Culture and Society* 25(1) (2008): 1–22.

Clough, Patricia, and Jean Halley, eds. *The Affective Turn: Theorizing the Social*. Durham, N.C.: Duke University Press, 2007.

Clough, Patricia Ticineto, Greg Goldberg, Rachel Schiff, Aaron Weeks, and Craig Willse. "Notes Toward a Theory of Affect Itself." *Ephemera* 7(1) (2007): 60–77.

Cooper, Melinda. "Pre-empting Emergence: The Biological Turn in the War on Terror." *Theory, Culture and Society* 23(4) (2006): 113–35.

Corbett, Kevin J. "The Big Picture: Theatrical Moviegoing, Digital Television, and Beyond the Substitution Effect." *Cinema Journal* 40(2) (2001): 17–35.

Crary, Jonathan. *Suspensions of Perception*. Boston: MIT Press, 1999.

———. *Techniques of the Observer: On Vision and Modernity in the Nineteenth Century*. Boston: MIT Press, 1990.

Currier, Diane. "Feminist Technological Futures: Deleuze and Body/Technology Assemblages." *Feminist Theory* 4(3) (2003): 321–38.

Cytowic, Richard E. *The Man Who Tasted Shapes: A Bizarre Medical Mystery Offers Revolutionary Insights into Emotions, Reasoning, and Consciousness*. New York: Warner, 1993.

Dann, Jack, ed. *The Nebula Awards Showcase 2005*. New York: Penguin, 2005.

Dann, Kevin T. *Bright Colors Falsely Seen: Synaesthesia and the Search for Transcendental Knowledge*. New Haven, Conn.: Yale University Press, 1998.

Darnton, Robert. "Literary Surveillance in the British Raj: The Contradictions of Liberal Imperialism." *Book History* 4 (2001): 133–76.

Das, Veena. "Trauma and Testimony: Implications for Political Community." *Anthropological Theory* 3(3) (2003): 293–307.

———. "Our Work to Cry, Your Work to Listen." In *Mirrors of Violence: Communities, Riots and Survivors in South Asia*, ed. Veena Das. Delhi: Oxford University Press, 1990. 345–99.

———. "The Spatialization of Violence: A "Communal" Riot in Delhi." In *Unraveling the Nation*, ed. Kaushik Basu and Sanjay Subrahmanyam. Delhi: Penguin Press, 1995. 198–225.

———. "Violence and the Work of Time." In *Signifying Identities: Anthropological Perspectives on Boundaries and Contested Values*, ed. Anthony P. Cohen. London: Routledge, 2000. 59–75.

Das, Veena, and Arthur Kleinman. Introduction. In *Remaking a World: Violence, Social Suffering, and Recovery*, ed. Veena Das, Arthur Kleinman, Margaret Lock, Mamphela Ramphele, and Pamela Reynolds. Berkeley: University of California Press, 2001. 1–31.

Defert, Daniel. " 'Popular Life' and Insurance Technology." In *The Foucault Effect*, ed. Graham Burchell et al. Chicago: University of Chicago Press, 1991. 211–34.

De Haan, Arjan, and Amaresh Dubey. "Poverty, Disparities, or the Development of Underdevelopment in Orissa." *Economic and Political Weekly* 40(22–23) (2005): 2321–30.

Dein, Simon, and Sati Sembhi. "The Use of Traditional Healing in South Asian Psychiatric Patients in the U.K.: Interactions between Professional and Folk Psychiatries." *Transcultural Psychiatry* 38(2) (2001): 243–57.

Delanda, Manuel. "Deleuze, Diagrams, and the Open-Ended Becoming of the World." In *Becomings: Explorations in Time, Memory, and Futures*, ed. Elizabeth Grosz. Ithaca, N.Y.: Cornell University Press, 1999.

———. *A New Philosophy of Society*. New York: Continuum, 2006.

———. *War in the Age of Intelligent Machines*. New York: Zone Books, 1991.

Deleuze, Gilles. "Bergson, 1859–1941." In *Desert Islands and Other Texts*, ed. David Lapoujade. New York: Semiotexte, 2004. 22–31.

———. *Bergsonism*. Trans. Hugh Tomlinson and Barbara Habberjam. New York: Zone Books, 1990.

———. *Cinema II: The Time-Image*. Trans. Hugh Tomlinson and Robert Galeta. Minneapolis: University of Minnesota Press, 1986.

———. "Control and Becoming." *Negotiations*. Trans. Martin Joughin. New York: Columbia University Press, 1997. 169–76.

———. *Difference and Repetition*. Trans. Paul Patton. New York: Columbia University Press, 1994.

———. *Foucault*. Trans. Sean Hand. Minneapolis: University of Minnesota Press, 1988.

———. *Francis Bacon: The Logic of Sensation*. Trans. Daniel Smith. Minneapolis: University of Minnesota Press, 2005.

———. *The Logic of Sense*. Trans. Mark Lester. New York: Columbia University Press, 1990.

———. "On Gilbert Simondon." In *Desert Islands and Other Texts, 1953–1974*, ed. David Lapoujade, trans. Michael Taormina. New York: Semiotexte, 2004. 86–89.

———. "Postscript on Societies of Control." *October* 59 (1992): 3–7.

Deleuze, Gilles, and Félix Guattari. *A Thousand Plateaus*. Trans. Brian Massumi. Minneapolis: University of Minnesota Press, 1987.

———. *What Is Philosophy?* Trans. Hugh Tomlinson and Graham Burchell. New York: Columbia University Press, 1994.

Deleuze, Gilles, and Claire Parnet. *Dialogues*. Trans. Hugh Tomlinson and Barbara Habberjam. New York: Columbia University Press, 1977.

Derne, Steve, and Lisa Jadwin. "Male Hindi Filmgoers' Gaze: An Ethnographic Interpretation." *Contributions to Indian Sociology* 34 (2000): 243–69.

Derrida, Jacques. *Positions*. Trans. Alan Bass and Henri Rense. Chicago: University of Chicago Press, 1981.

Desai, Jigna, Rajinder Dudrah, and Amit S. Rai. "Bollywood Audiences" (editorial). *South Asian Popular Culture* 3(2) (2005): 79–82.

Deshpande, Ravi. "A Taste of Technology." *Expressions* 3 (August-November 1999). www.abhivyakti.org.in (accessed October 1, 2006).

Dickey, Sara. *Cinema and the Urban Poor in South India*. New York: Cambridge University Press, 1993.

Doctorow, Corey. "0wnz0red." In *Nebula Awards Showcase 2005*. Ed. Jack Dann. New York: ROC, 2005. 103–30.

Doane, Mary Ann. *The Emergence of Cinematic Time*. Cambridge, Mass.: Harvard University Press, 2002.

———. "Technology's Body: Cinematic Vision in Modernity." *Differences* 5(2) (1993): 1–23.

Dore, Ronald. *Stockmarket Capitalism: Welfare Capitalism, Japan and Germany versus the Anglosaxons*. New York: Oxford University Press, 2000.

Dyke, C. "Cities as Dissipative Structures." In *Entropy, Information, and Evolution*. Ed. B. Weber, D. Depew, and J. Smith. Cambridge, Mass.: MIT Press, 1990. 355–67.

Ehrhardt, George, Matteo Marsili, Fernando Vega-Redondo. "Diffusion and Growth in an Evolving Network." *International Journal of Game Theory* 34 (2006): 383–97.

Eisenstein, Elizabeth L. *The Printing Press as an Agent of Change*. 2 vols. Cambridge: Cambridge University Press, 1979.

Ewald, François. "Insurance and Risk." In *The Foucault Effect*, ed. Graham Burchell et al. Chicago: University of Chicago Press, 1991. 197–210.

———. "Two Infinities of Risk." In *The Politics of Everyday Fear*, ed. and trans. Brian Massumi. Minneapolis: University of Minnesota Press, 1993. 221–28.

Fernandes, Leela. "Nationalizing 'The Global': Media Images, Cultural Politics and the Middle Class in India." *Media, Culture and Society* 22 (2000): 611–28.

Fischer, Lucy. "Greta Garbo and Silent Cinema: The Actress as Art Deco Icon." *Camera Obscura* 16(3) (2001): 83–112.

Ford, Jeffrey. "The Empire of Ice Cream." In *The Nebula Awards Showcase 2005*, ed. Jack Dann. New York: Penguin, 2005. 292–23.

Ford, Russell. "Deleuze's Dick." *Philosophy and Rhetoric* 38(1) (2005): 41–71.

Foster, Thomas. *The Souls of Cyberfolk*. Minneapolis: University of Minnesota Press, 2005.

Foucault, Michel. *The History Of Sexuality. Vol. 1.: An Introduction*. Trans. Robert Hurley. New York: Vintage, 1990.

———. "The History of Sexuality." In *Power/Knowledge*, ed. Colin Gordon. New York: Pantheon, 1980. 183–93.

———. "History of Systems of Thought." In *Language, Counter-Memory, Practice*. Trans. Donald Bouchard. Ithaca, N.Y.: Cornell University Press, 1977. 199–202.

———. *Security, Territory, Population*. Ed. Michel Senellart, trans. Graham Burchell. New York: Palgrave, 2007.

———. "Society Must Be Defended." Trans. David Macey. New York: Picador, 2003.

Freitag, Sandria B. "The Realm of the Visual: Agency and Modern Civil Society." *Contributions to Indian Sociology* 36 (2002): 365–97.

———. "South Asian Ways of Seeing, Muslim Ways of Knowing: The Indian Muslim Niche Market in Posters." *Indian Economic and Social History Review* 44 (2007): 297–331.

Ghosh, Anindita. "An Uncertain 'Coming of the Book': Early Print Cultures in Colonial India." *Book History* 6 (2003): 23–55.

Ghosh, Bhishnupriya. "The Postcolonial Bazaar: Thoughts on Teaching the Market in Postcolonial Objects." *Postmodern Culture* 9(1) (1998). http://muse.jhu.edu (accessed January 29, 2008).

Gigante, Denise. "The Monster in the Rainbow: Keats and the Science of Life." *PMLA* 117(3) (May 2002): 433–48.

Gopalan, Lalitha. *Cinema of Interruptions*. London: BFI, 2002.

———. "The Short Student Film." Paper presented at the conference Cinema South Asia, University of Pennsylvania, February 2008.

Griffin, David Ray. Introduction. In *Physics and the Ultimate Significance of Time*, ed. David Ray Griffin. Albany: State University of New York Press, 1986. 1–48.

Guattari, Félix. *Chaosmosis*. Trans. Paul Bains and Julian Pefanis. Bloomington: Indiana University Press, 1995.

Guha, Brishti. "Economic Consequences of Microelectronic and Telecom Revolution." *Economic and Political Weekly* 35(31) (2000): 2725–29.

Guha, Ranajit. *Dominance without Hegemony: History and Power in Colonial India.* Cambridge, Mass.: Harvard University Press, 1998.

Gunning, Tom. "The Cinema of Attractions: Early Film, Its Spectator and the Avant-Garde." In *Early Cinema: Space, Frame, Narrative,* ed. Thomas Elsaesser. London: British Film Institute, 1990. 56–67.

Guzzetti, Alfred. "Narrative and the Film Image." *New Literary History* 6(2) (winter 1975): 379–92.

Haller, Dieter. "Let It Flow: Economy, Spirituality and Gender in the Sindhi Network." *Anthropological Theory* 5(2) (2005): 154–75.

Hansen, Mark B. N. *Bodies in Code: Interfaces with Digital Media.* New York: Routledge, 2007.

———. "Digitizing the Racialized Body, or The Politics of Universal Address." *SubStance* 33(2) (2004): 107–33.

———. *New Philosophy for New Media.* Cambridge, Mass.: MIT Press, 2004.

———. "Wearable Space." *Configurations* 10 (2002): 321–70.

Hansen, Miriam. "The Mass Production of the Senses: Classical Cinema as Vernacular Modernism." *Modernism/Modernity* 6(2) (1999): 59–77.

———. "Benjamin and Cinema: Not a One-Way Street." *Critical Inquiry* 25 (1999): 306–43.

———. "Of Mice and Ducks: Benjamin and Adorno on Disney." *South Atlantic Quarterly* 92(1) (1993): 27–61.

Haraway, Donna. "A Cyborg Manifesto: Science, Technology, and Socialist-Feminism in the Late Twentieth Century." In *Simians, Cyborgs and Women: The Reinvention of Nature.* New York: Routledge, 1991. 149–81.

Hardt, Michael, and Antonio Negri. *Empire.* Cambridge, Mass.: Harvard University Press, 2001.

Harrison, John E., and Simon Baron-Cohen, eds. *Synaesthesia: Classic and Contemporary Readings.* Cambridge: Blackwell, 1996.

Harvey, David. *The Condition of Postmodernity.* Cambridge, Mass.: Blackwell Publishers, 1989.

———. *The New Imperialism.* New York: Oxford University Press, 2003.

Hayles, Katherine. *How We Became Posthuman.* Chicago: University of Chicago Press, 1999.

Haynes, Douglas E. "Market Formation in Khandesh, c. 1820–1930." *Indian Economic and Social History Review* 36 (1999): 275–302.

Hebdige, Dick. "Digging for Britain." In *Black British Cultural Studies,* ed. Houston Baker, Manthia Diawara, and Ruth Lindeborg. Chicago: University of Chicago Press, 1996. 120–62.

Heidegger, Martin. *An Introduction to Metaphysics.* Trans. Ralph Manheim. New York: Doubleday, 1961.

———. "The Question Concerning Technology." In *The Question Concerning Technology and Other Essays,* ed. William Lovitt. New York: Harper Torchbooks, 1977. 3–35.

Heitzman, James. "Geographic Information Systems in India's 'Silicon Valley': The Impact of Technology on Planning Bangalore." *Contemporary South Asia* 12(1) (2003): 57–83.

Hirst, Paul. "The Global Economy: Myths or Reality?" In *The Ends of Globalization: Bringing Society Back In*, ed. Don Kalb, Marco Van Der Land, Richard Staring, Bart Van Steenbergen, and Nico Wilterdink. Lanham, Md.: Rowman and Littlefield, 2000. 107–25.

Hirst, Paul, and Grahame Thompson. *Globalisation in Question.* Cambridge: Polity Press, 1996.

Hoogvelt, Ankie. *Globalization and the Postcolonial World: The New Political Economy of Development.* Baltimore: Johns Hopkins University Press, 2001.

Hughes, Stephen. "House Full: Silent Film Genre, Exhibition and Audiences in South India." *Indian Economic and Social History Review* 43 (2006): 31–62.

———. "Is There Anyone Out There? Exhibition and the Formation of Silent Film Audiences in South India." Ph.D. dissertation, University of Chicago, 1996.

———. "Pride of Place." *Seminar* 525 (May 2003). www.india-seminar.com (accessed February 10, 2008).

Hull, David L. "Introduction." In *Entropy, Information, and Evolution*, ed. B. H. Weber, D. J. Depew, and J. D. Smith. Cambridge: Bradford Books, 1988. 1–8.

Hunt, Lynn. *The Family Romance of the French Revolution.* Berkeley: University of California Press, 1992.

Jaikumar, Priya. *Cinema at the End of Empire: A Politics of Transition in Britain and India.* Durham, N.C.: Duke University Press, 2006.

———. "More than Morality: The Indian Cinematograph Committee Interviews (1927)." *Moving Image* 3(1) (2003): 82–109.

Jain, Kajri. *Gods in the Bazaar.* Durham, N.C.: Duke University Press, 2007.

———. "Gods in the Bazaar: The Subjects of Calendar Art," *South Asia: Journal of South Asian Studies* 21(1) (1998): 91–108.

———. "More than Meets the Eye: The Circulation of Images and the Embodiment of Value." *Contributions to Indian Sociology* 36 (2002): 33–70.

———. "Muscularity and Its Ramifications: Mimetic Male Bodies in Indian Mass Culture." *South Asia: Journal of South Asian Studies* 24(1) (2001): 197–224.

Jalal, Ayesha. "A Letter to India: In Manto's Spirit." *Economic and Political Weekly* 37 (44–45) (2002): 4526–29.

Jameson, Fredric. *The Cultural Turn: Selected Writings on the Postmodern, 1983–1998.* New York: Verso, 1998.

———. "Notes on Globalization as a Philosophical Issue." In *Cultures of Globalization*, ed. Fredric Jameson and Masao Miyoshi. Durham, N.C.: Duke University Press, 1998. 54–77.

———. *The Seeds of Time.* New York: Columbia University Press, 1996.

Jha, Priya. "Lyrical Nationalism: Gender, Friendship, and Excess in 1970s Hindi Cinema." *Velvet Light Trap* 51 (2003): 43–53.

Jayaprakash, Yesudhasan Thomas. "Remote Audiences beyond 2000: Radio, Everyday Life and Development in South India." *International Journal of Cultural Studies* 3(2) (2000): 227–39.

Johnston, John. "Machinic Vision." *Critical Inquiry* 26 (1999): 27–48.

Joshi, Priya. *In Another Country: Colonialism, Culture, and the Development of the English Novel in India*. New York: Columbia University Press, 2002.

Juluri, Vamsee. "Music Television and the Invention of Youth Culture In India." *Television and New Media* 3(4) (November 2002): 367–86.

Kabra, Asmita. "Displacement and Rehabilitation of an Adivasi Settlement: Case of Kuno Wildlife Sanctuary, Madhya Pradesh." *Economic and Political Weekly* 38(29) (2003): 3073–78.

Kalb, Don. *Expanding Class: Power and Everyday Politics in Industrial Communities, The Netherlands 1850–1950*. Durham, N.C.: Duke University Press, 1997.

———. "From Flows to Violence: Politics and Knowledge in the Debates on Globalization and Empire." *Anthropological Theory* 5(2) (2005): 176–204.

———. "Localizing Flows: Power, Paths, Institutions, and Networks." In *The Ends of Globalization: Bringing Society Back In*, ed. Don Kalb, Marco Van Der Land, Richard Staring, Bart Van Steenbergen, and Nico Wilterdink. Lanham, Md.: Rowman and Littlefield, 2003. 1–32.

Kalra, Virinder S. "The Political Economy of the Samosa." *South Asia Research* 24(1) (2004): 21–36.

Kaplan, Caren, and Inderpal Grewal. *Scattered Hegemonies*. Minneapolis: University of Minnesota Press, 1994.

Kaufmann, Stuart. *At Home in the Universe: The Search for the Laws of Self-Organization and Complexity*. New York: Oxford University Press, 1996.

Kaur, Ishvinder. "PVR Cinemas, Bangalore: The Paradigm Resurrection!" *Theatre Magic* (March 2005): 8–16.

Keyman, E. Fuat, and Berrin Koyuncu. "Globalization, Alternative Modernities and the Political Economy of Turkey." *Review of International Political Economy* 12(1) (2005): 105–28.

Krishnakumar, Aparna. "Multiplex Owners on Expansion Spree." Rediff India Abroad, March 2, 2005. www.rediff.com (accessed January 26, 2008).

Kvetko, Peter. "Can the Indian Tune Go Global?" *Drama Review* 48(4) (winter 2004): 183–92.

Laqueur, Thomas. *Making Sex: Body and Gender from the Greeks to Freud*. Cambridge, Mass.: Harvard University Press, 1990.

Levy, Pierre. *Cyberculture*. Trans. Robert Bononno. Minneapolis: University of Minnesota Press, 2001.

Ley, Graham. "Aristotle's *Poetics*, Bharatmuni's *Natyasastra*, and Zeami's Treatises: Theory as Discourse." *Asian Theatre Journal* 17(2) (2000): 192–214.

López-Pintado, Dunia. "Contagion and Coordination in Random Networks." *International Journal of Game Theory* 34 (2006): 371–81.

Luard, C. E. *Bhopal State Gazetteer*, vol. 3. Calcutta: Government Printing, 1908.

Manovich, Lev. *The Language of New Media*. Cambridge, Mass.: MIT Press, 2000.

Manuel, Peter. *Cassette Culture: Popular Music and Technology in North India*. Chicago: University of Chicago Press, 1993.

Marks, Laura. *The Skin of the Film*. Durham, N.C.: Duke University Press, 1999.

——. *Touch*. Minneapolis: University of Minnesota Press, 2002.

Martin, Henri-Jean, and Lucien Febvre. *The Coming of the Book: The Impact of Printing, 1450–1900*. Trans. G. Gerard. London: Verso, 1997.

Martin, Randy. *The Financialization of Everyday Life*. Philadephia: Temple University Press, 2002.

Mason, Michael. *The Making of Victorian Sexuality*. 2 vols. New York: Oxford University Press, 1994.

Massumi, Brian. "Fear (the Spectrum Said)." *positions* 13(1) (2005): 31–48.

——. *Parables for the Virtual: Movement, Affect, Sensation*. Durham, N.C.: Duke University Press, 2001.

——. "Realer than the Real: The Simulacrum According to Deleuze and Guattari." Australian National University. www.anu.edu (accessed July 1, 2007).

——. *A User's Guide to Capitalism and Schizophrenia: Deviations from Deleuze and Guattari*. Boston: MIT Press, 1992.

Maturana, Humberto, and Francisco Varela. *Autopoiesis and Cognition*. Boston: Reidel, 1980.

Mbembe, Achille. "Necropolitics." *Public Culture* 15(1) (2003): 11–40.

McGuire, John. "Economic Liberalisation and India: New Rhetoric, Old Theme." *South Asia* 21(1) (1998): 77–89.

Mehta, Suketu. *Maximum City: Bombay Lost and Found*. New York: Vintage, 2005.

Mishra, Vijay. *Bollywood Cinema*. New York: Routledge, 2001.

Mitchell, W. J. T. "The Work of Art in the Age of Biocybernetic Reproduction." *Modernism/Modernity* 10(3) (2003): 481–500.

Morris, Stephen. "Contagion." *Review of Economic Studies* 67 (2000): 57–78.

Morson, Gary Saul. "Narrativeness." *New Literary History* 34 (2003): 59–73.

Muffoletto, Jack. "Top Ten Trends in Multiplex Design." *Film Journal International* 108(6) (2005): 26–27.

Mukherjee, Bimal et al., eds. *Rasa: The Indian Performing Arts in the Last Twenty-Five Years*. Calcutta: Anamika Kala Sangam Research and Publications, 1995.

Mukherjee Reed, Ananya Kundu, and Apurba Kundu. "Corporate Capitalism in Contemporrary South Asia." *Contemporary South Asia* 9(2) (2000): 127–39.

Nagaraj, R. "Industrial Growth in China and India." *Economic and Political Weekly* 40(21) (2005): 2163–71.

Naregal, Veena. *Language, Politics and Elites in the Public Sphere*. New Delhi: Permanent Black, 2001.

Nayak, Amar K. J. R., Kalyan Chakravarti, and Prabina Rajib. "Globalization Process in India: A Historical Perspective since Independence." *South Asian Journal of Management* (January-March 2005): 7–22.

Nehru, Jawaharlal. *The Discovery of India*. New York: Oxford University Press, 1990.

Nelson, Dana. *National Manhood: Capitalist Citizenship and the Imagined Fraternity of White Men*. Durham, N.C.: Duke University Press, 1998.

Niyogi, Esha De. "Modern Shakespeares in Popular Bombay Cinema." *Screen* 43(1) (2002): 19–40.

O'Regan, Tom. "A National Cinema." In *A Film Culture Reader*, ed. Graeme Turner. New York: Routledge, 2002.

Orsini, Francesca. *Hindi Public Sphere, 1920–1940: Language and Literature in the Age of Nationalism*. New Delhi: Oxford University Press, 2002.

Pant, Niranjan, "Insurance Regulation and Development Bill: An Appraisal." *Economic and Political Weekly* 34(45) (1999): 3166–68.

Parisi, Luciana. *Abstract Sex: Philosophy, Bio-Technology, and the Mutations of Desire*. New York: Continuum, 2004.

———. "Information Trading and Symbiotic Micropolitics." *Social Text* 22(3) (2004): 25–49.

Parisi, Luciana, and Tiziana Terranova. "Heat-Death: Emergence and Control in Genetic Engineering and Artificial Life." *CTheory*, May 10, 2000. www.ctheory.net (accessed October 1, 2007).

Pashupati, Kartik, Hua Lin Sun, and Stephen D. Mcdowell. "Guardians of Culture, Development Communicators, or State Capitalists? A Comparative Analysis of Indian and Chinese Policy Responses to Broadcast, Cable and Satellite Television." *Gazette: The International Journal for Communication Studies* 65(3) (2003): 251–71.

Patel, Geeta. "Hindsight: Embodying Finance before and after 1857." Paper presented at the Thirty-third Annual Conference on South Asia, October 15–17, 2004, Madison, Wisconsin.

Patke, Rajeev. "Benjamin's Arcades Project and the Postcolonial City." *Diacritics* 30(4) (2000): 3–14.

Patnaik, Priyadarshi. *Rasa in Aesthetics: An Application of Rasa Theory to Modern Western Literature*. New Delhi: D. K. Printworld, 1997.

Patwardhan, Padmini. "Exposure, Involvement and Satisfaction with Online Activities: A Cross-National Comparison of American and Indian Internet Users." *Gazette: The International Journal for Communication Studies* 66(5) (2004): 411–36.

Pearson, K. A. *Germinal Life: The Difference and Repetition of Deleuze*. New York: Routledge, 1999.

Pease, Donald. "The Global Homeland State: Bush's Biopolitical Settlement." *boundary 2* 30(3) (2003): 1–18.

Sanders, Charles Peirce. *Essential Peirce*, vol. 2. Ed. N. Houser et al. Bloomington: Indiana University Press, 1998.

Pesce, Mark. "Piracy Is Good? New Models for the Distribution of Television Programming." Mindjack. www.mindjack.com (accessed June 15, 2008).

Pessoa, Luiz, Evan Thompson, and Alva Noe. "Finding Out about Filling-In: A Guide to Perceptual Completion for Visual Science and the Philosophy of Perception." *Behavioral and Brain Sciences* 216 (1998): 723–48.

Petersen, Søren Mørk. "Mundane Cyborg Practice: Material Aspects of Broadband Internet Use." *Convergence: The International Journal of Research into New Media Technologies* 13(1) (2007): 79–91.

Phadke, Shilpa. "Dangerous Liaisons: Women and Men: Risk and Reputation in Mumbai." *Economic and Political Weekly* 42(17) (2007): 1510–18.

Phadke, Shilpa, Shilpa Rawade, and Sameera Khan. "Why Loiter? Radical Possibilities for Gendered Dissent." In Melissa Butcher and Selvaraj Velayutham, eds., *Dissent and Cultural Resistance in Asia's Cities*, forthcoming.

Pinney, Christopher. " 'A Secret of Their Own Country'; Or, How Indian Nationalism Made Itself Irrefutable." *Contributions to Indian Sociology* 36 (2002): 113–50.

Poovey, Mary. *Making a Social Body: British Cultural Formation, 1830–1864.* Chicago: University of Chicago Press, 1995.

Porter, Roy, and Lesley Hall. *The Facts of Life: The Creation of Sexual Knowledge in Britain.* New Haven, Conn.: Yale University Press, 1995.

Prasad, M. Madhava. *The Ideology of Hindi Film: A Historical Construction.* New York: Oxford University Press, 2000.

———. "This Thing Called Bollywood." *Seminar* 525. www.india-seminar.com (accessed February 24, 2006).

Prigogine, Ilya. *The End of Certainty: Time, Chaos, and the New Laws of Nature.* New York: Free Press, 1996.

Prigogine, Ilya, and Isabelle Stengers. *Order Out of Chaos, Man's New Dialogue with Nature.* New York: Bantam Books, 1984.

Rai, Amit S. "India's New Brahmanism." *Z Magazine* (July-August, 1991): 31–38.

———. *Rule of Sympathy: Sentiment, Race, and Power, 1760–1860.* New York: Palgrave, 2002.

Rajagopal, Arvind. *Politics after Television: Hindu Nationalism and the Reshaping of the Public in India.* Cambridge: Cambridge University Press, 2001.

———. "The Rise of National Programming: The Case of Indian Television." *Media, Culture and Society* 15(1) (1993): 91–111.

Rajchman, John. "Diagram and Diagnosis." In *Becomings,* ed. Elizabeth Grosz. Ithaca, N.Y.: Cornell University Press, 1999.

Rao, Suvarnalata. *Acoustical Perspective on Raga-Rasa Theory.* New Delhi: Munshiram Manoharlal Publishers, 2000.

Ray, Rajat Kanta. "The Bazaar: Changing Structural Characteristics of the Indigenous Section of the Indian Economy before and after the Great Depression." *Indian Economic and Social History Review* 25 (1988): 263–318.

———. *The Felt Community: Commonality and Mentality before the Emergence of Indian Nationalism.* New York: Oxford University Press, 2002.

Reith, Gerda. "Uncertain Times: The Notion of 'Risk' and the Development of Modernity." *Time and Society* 13(2/3) (2004): 383–402.

Report of the Indian Cinematograph Committee (1927–28). Paris: Crastre, 2007.

Rombes, Nicholas. "Avant-Garde Realism." *C-Theory: Event-Scenes,* E135, January 19, 2005. www.ctheory.net (accessed December 1, 2006).

Roy, Subir. "World Bank and Government of India on Same Wavelength." Rediff. com, August 13, 2003. http://us.rediff.com (accessed September 20, 2003).

Rushton, Richard. "What Can a Face Do? On Deleuze and Faces." *Cultural Critique* 51 (2002): 219–37.

Russell, Conrad. "Against Dead Time." *Time and Society* 11(2/3) (2002): 193–208.

Sanchez-Eppler, Karen. *Touching Liberty: Abolition, Feminism, and the Politics of the Body*. Berkeley: University of California Press, 1993.

Sassen, Saskia. *Globalization and Its Discontents*. New York: New Press, 1998.

———. *De-nationalization*. Princeton, N.J.: Princeton University Press, 2003.

Schatz, Thomas. "The New Hollywood." In *The Film Cultures Reader*, ed. Graeme Turner. New York: Routledge, 2002. 184–205.

Schechner, Richard. "Rasaesthetics." *TDR: The Drama Review* 45(3) (2001): 27–50.

Sergi, Gianluca. *The Dolby Era: Film Sound in Contemporary Hollywood*. New York: Manchester University Press, 2004.

Seshu, Geeta. "Pornography—Certification vs Censorship." Boloji.com. August 11, 2002. http://www.boloji.com (accessed October 1, 2006).

Sharma, Aparna. "India's Experience with the Multiplex." *Seminar* 525. www.india-seminar.com (accessed November 20, 2006).

Shaviro, Stephen. *The Cinematic Body*. Minneapolis: University of Minnesota Press, 1993.

———. "Deleuze's Encounter with Whitehead." The Pinocchio Theory blog, May 16, 2007. www.shaviro.com/Blog (accessed July 1, 2007).

Simondon, Gilbert. "The Genesis of the Individual." In *Incorporations*, ed. Jonathan Crary and Sanford Kwinter. New York: Zone Books, 1992. 297–319.

———. *On the Mode of Existence of Technical Objects*. Trans. Ninian Mellamphy. London: University of Western Ontario, 1980 [1958].

Sinclair, John, and Mark Harrison. "Globalization, Nation, and Television in Asia." *Television and New Media* 5(1) (2004): 41–54.

Sivathamby, Karthigesu. *Tamil Film as a Medium of Political Communication*. Madras: New Century Book House, 1981.

Sobchack, Vivian. *Carnal Thoughts: Embodiment and Moving Image Culture*. Berkeley: University of California Press, 2004.

Spinoza, Baruch. *Ethics*. Trans. Samuel Shirley. Indianapolis: Hackett Publishing, 1992.

Spivak, Gayatri Chakravorty. "Can the Subaltern Speak? Speculations on Widow-Sacrifice." In *Marxism and the Interpretation of Culture*, ed. Cary Nelson and Lawrence Grossberg. Urbana: University of Illinois Press, 1988. 271–313.

———. "Subaltern Studies: Deconstructing Historiography." In *Subaltern Studies IV*, ed. Ranajit Guha. New Delhi: Oxford University Press, 1985. 330–63.

Srinivas, Lakshmi. "The Active Audience: Spectatorship, Social Relations and the Experience of Cinema in India." *Media, Culture and Society* 24(2) (2002): 155–73.

Srinivas, S. V. "Film Culture, Politics, and Industry." *Seminar* 525. www.india-seminar.com (accessed July 1, 2006).

Sterling, Bruce. "When Blobjects Rule the Earth." SIGGRAPH, Los Angeles, 2004. www.boingboing.net (accessed October 30, 2007).

Stiegler, Bernard. Technics and Time. Vol. 1: The Fault of Epimetheus. Trans. Richard Beardsworth and George Collins. Stanford, Calif.: Stanford University Press, 1998.

Stiglitz, Joseph. Globalization and Its Discontents. London: Allen Lane, 2002.

Stokes, Eric. The English Utilitarians and India. New York: Oxford University Press, 1990.

Stoler, Ann. Carnal Knowledge and Imperial Power. Berkeley: University of California Press, 2002.

———. "Making Empire Respectable: The Politics of Race and Sexual Morality in 20th Century Colonial Cultures." In American Ethnologist 16(4) (1989): 634–60.

———. Race and the Education of Desire: Foucault's History of Sexuality and the Colonial Order of Things. Durham, N.C.: Duke University Press, 1995.

———. "A Sentimental Education: European Children and Native Servants." In Fantasizing the Feminine: Sex and Death in Indonesia, ed. Laurie Sears. Durham, N.C.: Duke University Press, 1995.

———. "Sexual Affronts and Racial Frontiers." In Comparative Studies in Society and History 34(2) (1992): 514–51.

Stoler, Ann, and Frederick Cooper, eds. Tensions of Empire: Colonial Cultures in a Bourgeois World. Berkeley: University of California Press, 1997.

Stoler, Ann, and Karen Strassler. "Casting for the Colonial." In Comparative Studies in Society and History 42(1) (2000): 4–49.

Studlar, Gaylyn. This Mad Masquerade: Stardom and Masculinity in the Jazz Age. New York: Columbia University Press, 1996.

Subramanian, Dilip. "Deregulation and Labour Policies in a Public Sector Firm: Mixed Results at ITI." Economic and Political Weekly 40(22–23) (2005): 2265–74.

Sundar, K. R. Shyam. "Labour Flexibility Debate in India: A Comprehensive Review and Some Suggestions." Economic and Political Weekly 40(22–23) (2005): 2274–86.

Sunder Rajan, Kaushik. Biocapital. Durham, N.C.: Duke University Press, 2006.

Sundholm, John. "Listening to Film." Review of Communication 3(1) (2003): 90–93.

Sonwalkar, Prasun. "India: Makings of Little Cultural/Media Imperialism?" Gazette 63(6) (2001): 505–19.

Taylor, Woodman. "Penetrating Gazes: The Poetics of Sight and Visual Display in Popular Indian Cinema." Contributions to Indian Sociology 36 (2002): 297–322.

Teo, Stephen. "Postmodernism and the End of Hong Kong Cinema." In The Film Cultures Reader, ed. Graeme Turner. New York: Routledge, 2002. 174–83.

Thacker, Eugene. Biomedia. Minneapolis: University of Minnesota Press, 2004.

Thomas, Pradip N. "Trading the Nation: Multilateral Negotiations and the Fate of Communications In India." Gazette 61(3–4) (1999): 275–92.

Thomas, Rosie. "Indian Cinema: Pleasures and Popularity." Screen 26(3–4) (May-August 1985): 116–31.

Thomas, Sue. "The End of Cyberspace and Other Surprises." *Convergence* 12 (2006): 383–91.

Thompson, Kristin. "The Concept of Cinematic Excess." In *Narrative, Apparatus, Ideology*, ed. Philip Rosen. New York: Columbia University Press, 1986. 130–42.

Thussu, Daya Kishan. "Privatizing the Airwaves: The Impact of Globalization on Broadcasting in India." *Media, Culture and Society* 21 (1999): 125–31.

Todd, Drew. "Decadent Heroes: Dandyism and Masculinity in Art Deco Hollywood." *Journal of Popular Film and Television* 32(4) (2005): 168–81.

Vacarme. " 'I Am Sure That You Are More Pessimistic Than I Am . . . ': An Interview with Giorgio Agamben." Trans. Jason Smith. *Rethinking Marxism* 16(2) (2004): 115–24.

Varela, Francisco, Evan Thompson, and Eleanor Rosch. *The Embodied Mind*. Cambridge, Mass.: MIT Press, 1991.

Vasudevan, Ravi S. "Addressing the Spectator of the 'Third World' National Cinema: The Bombay 'Social' Film of the 1940s and 1950s." *Screen* 36(4) (1995): 305–24.

Vergès, Françoise. *Monsters and Revolutionaries: Colonial Family Romance and Métissage*. Durham, N.C.: Duke University Press, 1999.

Verma, Rajendra. *The Freedom Struggle in the Bhopal State: A Gambit in the Transfer of Power*. New Delhi: Intellectual Publishing House, 1984.

Virdi, Jyotika. "Indian Film and TV: An Introduction." *Jump Cut* 43 (July 2000): 75.

Virilio, Paul. *Speed and Politics*. New York: Semiotexte, 1986.

Viswanathan, Renuka. "Human Development Report for Madhya Pradesh." *Economic and Political Weekly* 34(22) (1999): 1314–15.

Volga. "To Censor or Not to Censor: Film and Public Policy." *Economic and Political Weekly* 35(18) (2000): WS17–20.

Wade, Robert. *Governing the Market: Economic Theory and the Role of Government in East Asian Industrialization*. Princeton, N.J.: Princeton University Press, 2004.

Wallerstein, Immanuel. *The Decline of American Power: The US in a Chaotic World*. New York: New Press, 2003.

Waterhouse, David, ed. *Dance of India*. Mumbai: Popular Prakashan, 1998.

Weber, Bruce H., and David J. Depew. "Natural Selection and Self-Organization: Dynamical Models as Clues to a New Evolutionary Synthesis." *Biology and Philosophy* 11 (1996): 33–65.

Wegenstein, Bernadette. *Getting under the Skin: Body and Media Theory*. Cambridge, Mass.: MIT Press, 2006.

Weiss, Linda. *The Myth of the Powerless State*. Ithaca, N.Y.: Cornell University Press 1998.

———, ed. *States in the Global Economy: Bringing Domestic Institutions Back In*. Cambridge: Cambridge University Press, 2003.

INDEX

affect: bazaar and, 41; becoming and, 216; body and, 12–15, 32, 50, 124, 139, 166, 197; branding and, 15; capitalist accumulation and, 61, 77, 90–91, 196, 216; circulation and, 100; connectivity and, 12; consumerism and, 6, 216; contagion and, 123; control and, 196; disposition and, 199; ethics and, 58; excess and, 168; film exhibition and, 32; governmentality and, 190; habit and, 16, 54, 107; Hansen on, 92; interval and, 20; ittafaq and, 180; labor and, 78; machinic as, 53; malltiplex and, 50, 136–39, 146, 162; media assemblage and, 5–6, 9, 78, 106, 162, 185; modes of perception and, 24; multiplex and, 148, 156; nation and, 79; pre-individual and, 5, 16, 23, 56; resonance and, 216; risk and, 198; security and, 153, 185; sensation and, 70; sexuality and, 14; sound and, 99; synaesthesia and, 107–8; THX technology and, 128; time and, 205; time pass and, 167; transitivity and, 52; virtual and, 139, 179; waning of, 148
Agamben, Giorgio, 20
art deco, 44, 50; affect and, 32; film exhibition and, 26, 36; film posters and, 30; history of, 27; Hollywood and, 29; postcolonial deployment of, 29
assemblage: art deco and, 27; as body, 105; defintion of, 100, 234n36; duration and, 5, 12; energy and, 157; Hindi-Urdu cinema and, 57; insurance and, 188–89, 194, 203; ittafaq and, 203, 208; language and, 212; loitering and, 38; machinic phylum and, 79; mutation and, 3; sensory-motor schema as, 195; vision as, 150
astrology: Hindi-Urdu cinema and, 184; India and, 185; insurance and, 18; media assemblage and, 211; spiritual healer ads and, 207; TV and, 14
audience, 62; antagonisms and, 49; Bhopal and, 33; body and, 189; censorship and, 124; collective viewing practices and, 116; consumption and, 90–91, 117; crowd control and, 46; discipline and, 189; globalization and, 76, 84; gradient and, 87; Hindi-Urdu cinema and, 63, 129–30; Hollywood and, 109; hyperdistribution and, 86–87; kathakata and, 177; marketing and, 87; multiplex and, 147–49, 161; new filmic genres and, 129–30; niche and, 128; passive

audience (*cont.*)

viewers and, 123; population and, 137, 204; pornography and, 127; re-organization of, 184; re-segmentation and, 6; security and, 136, 151–52; segmentation and, 145; sound and, 91–92; spiritual healer ads and, 207; THX technology and, 128

Bachchan, Amitabh, 33
barat: DJ culture and, 171–72
basin of attraction, 212
bazaar: loitering and, 38, 40; media assemblage and, 40, 160, 176; sensation and, 40; sound and, 98
Beck, Ulrich, 189
becoming: being and, 52; body and, 15, 216; branding and, 76; cinema and, 8, 27, 143–44; clinamedia and, 52, 217; death and, 114; *Devdas* (2002) and, 67; DJ culture and, 217; ecology of sensation and, 212; emergence and, 16; energy and, 157; event and, 52; field of potential and, 54, 58; framing and, 107–8; globalization and, 70, 183; habit and, 17, 24; Hindi-Urdu cinema and, 12, 129–30; information and, 84; *ittafaq* and, 41, 209; loitering and, 38; malltiplex and, 134–37, 162; matter and, 138; media and, 111; media assemblage and, 5, 9, 13, 50, 216; multiplicity and, 130; narrative and, 65; non-human and, 93; politics of, 115; risk and, 186; sexuality and, 18, 168; subjectivity and, 65; time and, 53, 167; untimely and, 12, 16, 20, 199, 216
Benjamin, Walter, 160, 164
Bergson, Henri, 103, 105; on duration, 53; on movement, 255n14
Bharatiya Janata Party (BJP), 10, 82; censorship and, 126

bhava: affect and, 41; cell phone and, 90; loitering and, 51; rasa theory and, 223n18, 229n22
Bhopal, 7, 186; audience and, 128, 142; communalism and, 98; DJ culture and, 135, 170–71; ethnography of, 72; film exhibition and, 9–10, 24–25, 33, 50, 97, 100, 157; globalization and, 73–74; history of, 249n178; Lily Talkies in, 116; media assemblage and, 23; media diagram of, 18; *Mohabbatein* and, 25; piracy and, 84, 96, 175; pornography and, 127
biogram, 217, 227n3
biomedia, 56; affect and, 91; body and, 195; definition of, 78; Doctorow on, 133; globalization and, 76; Hindi-Urdu cinema and, 115; risk and, 198
biopolitics: affect and, 196; attention and, 87; body and, 7, 166; censorship and, 120; cinema and, 10; connectivity and, 71; control and, 182; emergence and, 197; exhibition and, 19; India and, 83, 184; interval and, 20; malltiplex and, 36; media assemblage and, 5, 176, 183; phase transition and, 168–69; probability and, 190; racism and, 122; risk and, 108; sensation and, 17
biopower, 4
bits, 184; cinema and, 128; as filmic segment, 123; pleasure and, 165; pornography and, 127, 251n203; as song-dance sequence, 129; time and, 183
BitTorrent, 86–87
body, 17; affect and, 12–15, 32, 50, 124, 139, 166, 197; analog and, 11; art deco and, 27, 32; audience and, 24, 189; autonomic process and, 36, 42; biomedia and, 91, 198; biopolitics and, 7, 166; censorship and, 121, 124; as center of indetermination, 4, 53, 105,

184; cinema and, 126; clinamedia and, 217, 219; connectivity and, 12, 57, 135, 170; consumption and, 117; contagion and, 54, 123, 248n177; control and, 182; cyborg and, 12; discipline and, 189; DJ culture and, 12, 170–72, 179; ecologies of sensation and, 59; embodied mind and, 150; emergence and, 14; ethics as capacities and, 58; event dimension and, 53; excess and, 130; film exhibition and, 7, 24, 30, 43, 45; Foucault on, 188; framing and, 106–8, 247n163; globalization and, 3, 70; habit and, 12, 166; Hansen on, 92; indetermination of, 196; information trading and, 105; insurance and, 203; *ittafaq* and, 180; *kathakata* and, 177; kinesthesia and, 115; loitering and, 38, 42; machinic phylum and, 25; malltiplex and, 36, 136–39, 163–64, 167; Massumi on, 202; media and, 27; media assemblage and, 4, 9, 25, 41, 169; media contagion and, 50; memory and, 216–17; modulation of, 78; multiplex and, 110, 134; multiplicity and, 99–100, 108; mutation and, 3, 108; new media and, 16; non-linear dynamics and, 5; openness and, 140; perception and, 199; politics of, 24; population and, 3, 15, 136; potential of, 56, 105–6; pre-individual and, 9; proprioception and, 111, 151, 168, 217; representation and, 104; security and, 153; sensation and, 3, 53, 71, 216; sensorium and, 43, 157; sensory-motor schema and, 68, 107; sexuality and, 168, 188, 190; Shahrukh Khan and, 113; sound and, 99; synaesthesia and, 138; technology and, 14; time and, 143–44; topology and, 12; transitivity and, 52; untimely and, 16; value and,

36, 162; virtual and, 72; vision and, 150; volatility of, 15

Bollywood, definition of, 221n1

branding: affect and, 15, 18; astrology and, 207; cell phones and, 89; Dolby and, 91–92; globalization and, 76; malltiplex and, 143; media assemblage and, 123; multiplex design and, 155; as order word, 211; qualitative difference and, 143

Buck-Morss, Susan, 160

capital: affect and, 77, 197, 214; assemblage and, 123; BitTorrent and, 86; feedback loop and, 71; film finance and, 38, 191; flight of, 75; globalization and, 74; India and, 82–84; machinic phylum and, 78, 80; markets and, 76; media assemblage and, 44, 184; mobility and, 75; non-resident Indian and, 167; postcolonial criticism and, 17; security and, 94; turbulence and, 209; virtualization and, 49

cat bonds: biopolitics and, 197; emergence and, 197; preemption and, 198

cell phones: India and, 88–89; media assemblage and, 212

censorship, 122; Hindi-Urdu cinema and, 119–21; nationalism and, 123

Central Board of Film Certification (CBFC), 119

Chopra, Yash, 34

C.I.D. (film), 179

cinema, 15, 59, 118; affect and, 162, 167; art deco and, 30; audience and, 130; becoming and, 111; biopolitics and, 10, 166; body and, 4; chance and, 180; connectivity and, 145; consumption and, 155; contagion and, 196; contagious multiplicity and, 12; Deleuze on, 27; digital and, 149; DJ cinema (*cont.*)

culture and, 170–71; duration and, 144–45; emergence and, 14; excess and, 130; film exhibition, 2, 9–10, 26, 134, 157, 186; globalization and, 70; Hong Kong and, 141; *ittafaq* and, 180; loitering and, 35; malltiplex and, 141, 146; media assemblage and, 2–5, 9, 13, 98, 164; multiplex and, 161; nationalism and, 35, 55; new genres and, 184; perception and, 199; phase transition and, 135; pornographic bits and, 127–28; productive expenditure and, 118; proprioception and, 157; risk and, 198; security and, 153; sensation and, 24, 126; temporality and, 163; time and, 143–44; time pass and, 166; TV and, 145; xenon lamps and, 149. *See also* Hindi-Urdu cinema

Cinema of Interruptions (Gopalan), 8, 144

clinamedia, 19; art deco and, 33; becoming and, 52, 217; contagion and, 87; creativity and, 182; habit and, 59; Hindi-Urdu cinema and, 217; loitering and, 54; media assemblage as, 217, 273n9

clinamen, definition of, 217, 272n8

Clough, Patricia, 77, 182, 196

connectivity: affect and, 12; affective labor and, 78; art deco and, 26, 32; basin of attraction and, 212; becoming and, 53; biomedia and, 196; biopolitics and, 71; body and, 135, 163, 170; cinema and, 146; clinamedia and, 217; diagram and, 19, 145; digital and, 71; duration and, 52, 59; excess and, 140; feedback loops and, 16, 71; film exhibition and, 24; first day, first show and, 50; globalization and, 76; habit and, 17; intensity and, 212; interval and, 19; *ittafaq* and, 182; loitering and, 35, 38, 41; malltiplex

and, 134–35, 146; media assemblage and, 8, 27, 70, 117; multiplex and, 147; multiplicity and, 44, 56, 103; nationalism and, 35; resonance and, 217; security and, 183; sexuality and, 14; speed and, 108; spiritual healer ads and, 208; temporality and, 42; value and, 158; viral marketing and, 71

contagion: affect and, 167; body and, 54, 123, 248n177; ecology of sensation and, 53; exhibition and, 118; malltiplex and, 154; media assemblage and, 6, 50, 55, 71; media studies and, 19; modality of, 57, 105; multiplicity and, 100; sensation and, 126

continuous multiplicities, 11. *See also* multiplicity

Cooper, Melinda, 197

creative indetermination, 5

Currier, Diane, 100

Dalit, definition of, 227n1

Defert, Daniel, 194

Delanda, Manuel, 78; biopolitics and, 7

Deleuze, Gilles, 100, 195, 222n10; cinema and, 27; on control, 182; on machinic phylum, 78; on the virtual, 65

Devdas (film, 1955), 27, 62–65

Devdas (film, 2002), 27, 67–68

diagram: affect and, 18, 106; becoming and, 130; biogram as, 5, 84, 100, 147; biomedia and, 196; body and, 12; branding and, 185; connectivity and, 71; contagion and, 50; criticism and, 217; duration and, 168–69; dynamic threshold and, 138; emergence and, 36; film exhibition and, 24, 44; information and, 84; *ittafaq* and, 182, 185, 189; malltiplex and, 134–37, 145; media assemblage and, 3, 11–12,

14, 25, 213; representation and, 12, 14, 138; risk and, 20, 186; sensory-motor schema and, 114; transitive mode of power and, 52; untimely and, 16, 29

diaspora: art deco and, 27; Bhopal and, 33; Bollywood and, 110; capital and, 15; Hindutva and, 199; insurance and, 19, 202; time and, 14

digital, 9, 20; affect and, 16; audio-visual technologies and, 99; BitTorrent and, 87; body and, 107; branding and, 138; cliché and, 195; clinamedia and, 218; connectivity and, 71; contagion and, 50; control and, 5, 7; *Devdas* (2002) and, 68; digital light processing (DLP), 149; Disney and, 165; DJ culture and, 171, 179; duration and, 188; ecology of sensation and, 136; emergence and, 135; encryption and, 10; film exhibition and, 24; Hansen on, 92; Hindi-Urdu cinema and, 73, 113; insurance and, 199; *ittafaq* and, 182; media assemblage and, 70, 100, 175–76, 216; multiplex and, 155–56, 162; narrative and, 185; navigable data as, 11; perception and, 170; security and, 151–53, 183; sensation and, 178; sound and, 91–92; spiritual healer ads and, 205, 208; virtual and, 105

Digital Light Processing (DLP), 149, 175

discourse: identity and, 3

discursive strategies, 6

DJ culture, 10; audiovisual database and, 182; *barat* and, 171; Bhopal and, 170; class composition and, 171–72; Hindi-Urdu cinema and, 170, 179; India and, 170–71; Manovich on, 169–70; media assemblage and, 11, 217; synaesthesia and, 217

DJ Rekha, 171

Doctorow, Cory, 133, 152–53

Dolby, 61; branding of, 92; consumption of, 8; film exhibition and, 24, 33; logo and, 175; malltiplex and, 134; pirating and, 91; security and, 151–52; sensation and, 184; THX technology and, 92–93

duration: affect and, 16, 53; average shot duration, 169; becoming and, 115; Bergson on, 53; body and, 107, 144; Bollywood and, 143; cinema and, 144–46; clinamedia, 218; commodification and, 163; connectivity and, 19; contagion and, 6; diagram and, 12, 169; ecology of sensation and, 59; Hindi-Urdu cinema and, 41; interval as, 45; *ittafaq* and, 189; malltiplex and, 136; media event and, 117; multiplicity and, 164; ontology and, 5, 17, 301; synaesthesia and, 139; untimely and, 212; virtual and, 50. *See also* time

dynamic threshold: becoming and, 9; media assemblage and, 6. *See also* nonlinear dynamics

Eagle Theatre (New York City), 30

ecology: affect and, 5; media assemblage and, 17

ecology of sensation, 8, 13, 140; affect and, 18; body and, 59; connectivity and, 136; event and, 52; first day, first show and, 49; insurance and, 204; interval and, 45; *ittafaq* and, 182; loitering and, 35; media assemblage and, 211; pre-individual as, 9; as sexuality, 3–4, 9, 50, 59, 168, 212; turbulence and, 209–10

embodiment, 3

emergence: audience and, 85; becoming and, 12; cell phones and, 88–90; cinema and, 135; clinamedia and, 217; co-dependence and, 20; *Devdas* (1955) and, 65; diagram and, 14, 36;

emergence (*cont.*)

culture and, 179; event and, 49, 51; excess and, 12; film exhibition and, 24; habit and, 25; Hindi-Urdu cinema and, 41; insurance and, 205; *ittafaq* and, 180, 182; machinic phylum and, 79; media assemblage and, 117, 140, 217; perception and, 199; phase space and, 55; phase transition and, 59; preemption and, 197–98; pre-individual and, 5, 18; self-organizing dynamics and, 149; sensation and, 70–71; technology and, 50; virtual and, 58. *See also* nonlinear dynamics

entropy: feedback loops and, 71

Eros Entertainment, 1

event: first day, first show and, 49; folding and, 50

Ewald, François, 194

excess: Hindi-Urdu film and, 118; media assemblage, 13, 215; multiplicity and, 140; potential and, 15; time and, 13; virtual and, 12, 215

exhibition: art deco and, 27, 32, 42; audience and, 9, 49, 136, 144–45; beyond the "metros," 96; Bhopal and, 9; bits and, 184; body and, 157; class antagonism and, 144; design and, 56; DJ culture and, 171, 179; energy and, 157; event and, 10, 43, 51; excess and, 118; film exhibition, 2, 9–10, 26, 134, 157, 186; first day, first show and, 42; globalization and, 135, 167; Hollywood and, 147; India and, 151, 157; intervals and, 19; Lily Talkies and, 10; loitering and, 35, 38; machinic phylum and, 25; media assemblage and, 99; multiplex and, 110, 147, 161; populations and, 45; pornography and, 127; risk and, 186, 188; security and, 153; sensation and, 24; sexuality and, 168; sound and, 92–93; temporality and, 163; TV

and, 90; value and, 76, 213; xenon lamps and, 149

feedback loop, 71; affect and, 16, 56, 166; biomedia and, 196; media assemblage and, 4, 6, 27, 185; sensorium and, 213

feminism, 4, 17, 100; becoming and, 115; contagion and, 6; multiplicity and, 103

first day, first show, 33, 38; Bhopal and, 42; definition of, 23; movie tickets and, 45

Foucault, Michel, 3, 188

genre segmentations, 12

Ghosh, Anindita, 176

globalization: cultural production and, 76; economic networking and, 75; India and, 81; local microstates and, 81; markets and, 76; media assemblage and, 74; neo-liberalism and, 74; telecommunication and, 75

Gopalan, Lalitha, 8, 144

governmentality: insurance and, 190; liberalization and, 73; *maa-baap* and, 190

Grosz, Elizabeth, 100

Guattari, Félix, 100; on machinic phylum, 78, on representation, 256n17

habit: affect and, 16, 54, 107; attention and, 58; audience and, 125; becoming and, 17; body and, 12, 166; cliché and, 195; co-evolution and, 71; connectivity and, 212; contagion and, 50; creative indetermination and, 17; emergence and, 25; *ittafaq* and, 180, 212; jamming of, 214; loitering and, 36; malls and, 158; malltiplex and, 136, 144–45, 163–64; media assemblage and, 3, 7, 11, 25, 36, 41, 99, 168–69, 186; multiplex and, 148; ontology of durations and, 13; pre-individual and, 84, 117; print technology and, 176; sensation and, 61, 71, 105; time and, 186

Hansen, Mark B. N., 16, 92, 105–6

Hindi-Urdu cinema, 6, 17, 30, 54; assemblage and, 57; audience and, 63, 129–30; becoming and, 12; Bhopal and, 72; biopolitics and, 183; bits and, 128; connectivity and, 57; consumerism and, 217; *Devdas* (1955) and, 63; DJ culture and, 175, 179; duration and, 41; exhibition and, 49, 51; first day, first show and, 46; genres and, 60; as global commodity, 115; golden age, 63; information and, 111; insurance and, 184; loitering and, 38; media assemblage and, 8, 25, 71, 146, 183, 242n107; narrative and, 62, 66; new genres and, 129, 266n8; non-resident Indian and, 33, 167; organization of, 34; piracy and, 97; risk and, 72, 186, 267n11; sensation and, 25; song-dance sequence and, 146; speed and, 108; virtual and, 144

Hindutva, 7; Bhopal and, 10; DJ culture and, 217; exhibition and, 25; nation and, 127; nationalism and, 34

Hollywood: China and, 141; India and, 109; malltiplex and, 147

Hong Kong cinema, 62

Hoogvelt, Ankie, 75, 80

Hughes, Stephen, 43

identity: becoming and, 212; body and, 5; contagion and, 71; *Devdas* (1955) and, 63; diagram and, 115; diaspora and, 114; ecology of sensation and, 4; excess and, 12; hybridity and, 6; Indian television and, 85; loitering and, 41; media assemblage and, 14; multiplicity and, 100, 104; perception

and, 199; representation and, 68, 168; resistance and, 140; sexuality and, 3, 14, 59, 139

individualization: Ewald on, 195

information: globalization and, 75, 80; intervals and, 19

insurance, 212; astrology and, 18; Beck on, 189–90; biomedia and, 199; biopolitics and, 108; cat bonds and, 197–98; cinema and, 38; control and, 184; definition of, 188–89; diaspora and, 14; exhibition and, 186–87; globalization and, 189, 191; history in India, 190–92; India and, 185; insecurities and, 190; media assemblage and, 169, 185, 198, 211; MetLife and, 202; new type of objectivity as, 205; New York Life and, 199–200; pre-individual and, 115; risk and, 191, 199; security and, 200–203; spiritual healer ads and, 207–8; temporality and, 203

intensity: duration and, 5; first day, first show and, 49; movie tickets and, 44

interval, media, 19

ittafaq: definition of, 179; *Devdas* (1955) and, 67; Hindi-Urdu cinema and, 179; as image center, 19, 41, 180, 183, 185, 203, 213

Jain, Kajri, 36

Jameson, Fredric, 15, 148, 163, 193

Jha, Priya, 57

Juluri, Vamsee, 85

jump cut, 182, 185

Kaante (film), 61

Kapur, Geeta, 63

kathakata, 177

Khan, Shahrukh, 1, 34, 111

Kumar, Dilip, 62

Kvetko, Peter, 98

Lily Talkies, 6; construction of, 116; DJ
culture and, 170–71; exhibition and,
10; Goonj Bahadur Talkies and, 187;
sound and, 97

loitering, 13; affect and, 41; cell phone
and, 123; clinamedia and, 54; film
exhibition and, 26, 35–36; first day,
first show and, 50; Hindi-Urdu cinema and, 38; ittafaq and, 183; media
and, 182; media assemblage and, 41,
51, 160, 166, 211, 216; non-linear dynamics and, 38; patterned trajectory
as, 55; piracy and, 41; print technology and, 176–77; time pass and, 144

machinic phylum: affect and, 205;
becoming and, 213; capital and,
78, 81; emergence and, 149; India
and, 82; malltiplex and, 161; media
assemblage and, 25, 123; multiplicity and, 163; pre-individual and, 84;
sensation and, 213; sound and, 98;
TV and, 86

Main Hoon Na (film), 1, 180

malltiplex: becoming and, 166; biopolitics and, 36; body and, 41, 50,
165; branding and, 213; China and,
141; connectivity and, 146; consumerism and, 147; definition of, 36;
design and, 156; diagram and, 135;
embodiment and, 195–96; excess
and, 168; exhibition and, 51, 135–36;
genre and, 130; globalization and,
84, 139; habit and, 36, 159, 163;
history of, 136; India and, 141–42,
156–57; marketing and, 141; media
assemblage and, 141, 211–12; multiplex and, 155; mutagen and, 168;
new filmic genres and, 129, 184–85;
non-resident Indian and, 130;
pleasure and, 144–45; pre-individual
and, 117; refunctioning and, 199;
restructuring of value and, 158; risk

and, 161; security and, 151; sensation
and, 154, 163, 217; sensorium and,
142; space and, 163; temporality and,
163; time and, 38, 167; time pass
and, 38, 167; TV and, 146; value and,
161–62; virtual and, 139, 167

Manovich, Lev, 163

Massumi, Brian, 5, 46, 53, 103, 106, 137,
165; on affect, 139, 256n25; biopolitics and, 7; on catalysis, 230n38; on
cultural coding, 50; on sensation,
202; on structure, 49

Mbembe, Achille, 196

media assemblage, 123, 214; affect
and, 5–6, 9, 78, 106, 162, 185; art
deco and, 26, 30; attention and, 87;
audience and, 130; bazaar and, 40;
becoming and, 5, 10, 27; Bhopal and,
23; biomedia and, 196; BitTorrent
and, 86; body and, 4, 9, 25, 41, 169;
Bollywood and, 108; cell phones and,
88–90; cinema and, 2–5, 9, 13, 98,
164; clinamedia as, 217; co-emergence
and, 140; connectivity and, 11,
56, 184; consumption and, 117;
contagion and, 55–56, 71, 125, 196;
definition of, 6, 56, 70; diagram and,
14; digital and, 100; discipline and,
189; as ecology, 18, 56, 87–88, 124;
emergent properties and, 88–89;
energy and, 157; ethics and, 58,
59; evolution of sensation and, 56;
excess and, 13, 215; exhibition and,
32, 99; far-from-equilibrium condition of, 11; feedback loop and, 186;
film music and, 98; first day, first
show and, 49–50; globalization and,
14–15, 70, 74, 90; habit and, 3, 7, 11,
25, 36, 41, 99, 168–69, 186; Hindi-
Urdu cinema and, 8, 25, 71, 146, 183,
242n107; history and, 176; Hollywood and, 109; India and, 212; interval and, 20; ittafaq and, 182; kathakata

and, 177; life itself and, 214; loitering and, 36, 41; machinic phylum and, 79; malltiplex and, 135, 141, 144, 155; modality and, 52; multiplicity and, 103, 111, 183; mutagen and, 134; mutation and, 108; nationalism and, 35; new dominant, 54; order words of, 211; politics of, 71, 115; pragmatics and, 216; pre-individual and, 18; print technology and, 176; qualitative change of, 146; resistance and, 41; risk and, 20, 186, 198; security and, 84, 108, 154; sensation and, 40, 93, 176–78, 216; sexuality and, 54; sound and, 98; spiritual healer ads and, 208; synaesthesia and, 68; time and, 19; transitive mode of power of, 52; untimely and, 7, 199, 216; value and, 161; vector field and, 170; virtual and, 8, 17, 58, 72, 139–40

media contagions, 59

media event, 3, 6

media studies: argument regarding, 19; assemblage theory and, 3; body and, 16; Hansen on, 105; media assemblage and, 5; South Asia and, 38

memory, 301; body and, 42, 216; cinema and, 144; clinamedia and, 219; DJ culture and, 171; exhibition and, 98; insurance and, 203; loitering and, 41; media assemblage and, 175; media studies and, 17; nationalism and, 34; sensory-motor circuit and, 203

Mohabbatein (film), 10, 25, 33–35, 48, 52; corporate media strategies and, 49; exhibition practices and, 45; first day, first show and, 42

Morson, Gary Saul, 66, 182

multiplex, 10; affect and, 156, 162; art deco and, 27; design innovations in, 154–55; diagram and, 145, 147; emergence of, 135; exhibition and, 110, 151; genre and, 41; Hindi-Urdu cinema and, 18; history of, 142, 147; India and, 36, 73, 161; malls and, 161; Massumi on, 165; perception and, 107; screening times and, 145; security and, 168; sensation and, 61; synaesthesia and, 135; THX technology and, 94; time and, 140

multiplicity, 45; audience and, 59; biomedia and, 196–97; body and, 99–100, 108; contagion and, 76; continuous, 11; duration and, 143–44, 164; film exhibition and, 32, 44; identity and, 104; *ittafaq* and, 180; malltiplex and, 134, 136, 155; media assemblage and, 4–6, 19, 99, 146, 156, 211; mood and, 202; politics and, 115; population and, 122; qualitative, 6; quantitative, 57; racism and, 122; sensation and, 163; sensorium and, 163; spiritual healer ads and, 208; time and, 103; topology and, 214; transitive mode of power and, 53; two types of, 103, 246n147; virtual and, 62, 65, 91, 103, 138, 140

mutagen: becoming and, 134; sensation and, 56

mutation, 3

narrative: female agency and, 64; narrativeness, 66

National Film Development Corporation (NFDC), 118

nation-state, 80

new media, 2

niche markets, 77

nonlinear dynamics: causality and, 225n28; dissipative structures and, 222n13, 226n40, 234n38; film exhibition and, 24; *ittafaq* and, 193; machinic phylum and, 78; media assemblage and, 15, 38, 56; sensation and, 70 non-resident Indian (NRI), 13, 129, 184, 198; BitTorrent and, 88; Hindi-Urdu cinema and, 33, 42, 167; security and, 144

ontology: duration and, 5, 221n9; excess and, 13

Parisi, Luciana, 105, 209, 218
patriarchal power in Hindi cinema, 63
Peirce, Charles Sanders, 202
perception: Bergson on, 105; center of indetermination and, 15
Pesce, Mark, 86–87
Petersen, Søren Mørk, 16
phase transition: biopolitics and, 169; BitTorrent and, 86–88; duration and, 129; ecology of sensation and, 136; emergence and, 59; excess and, 13, 215; feedback loop and, 185; globalization and, 79; Hindi-Urdu cinema and, 38, 129–30; information and, 84; machinic phylum and, 78; malltiplex and, 147; media assemblage and, 19, 113, 211, 214; multiplicity and, 103; ontology and, 17. See also nonlinear dynamics
piracy, 55; affect and, 18; BitTorrent and, 56; black market and, 115; branding and, 213; copyright and, 97; digital and, 151; Dolby and, 96; excess and, 216; exhibition and, 154; habit and, 11; India and, 96; logo and, 175; loitering and, 41; malltiplex and, 135; media flows and, 100; media streams and, 186; movie tickets and, 44; music cassettes and, 142
population: audience and, 25, 204; insurance and, 195
postcolonial criticism, 4, 17, 26, 36, 126; contagion and, 6; media studies and, 3; nationalism and, 32; subjectivity and, 6; untimely and, 29

poverty in India, 82–83
Prasad, Madhava, 8, 57
pre-individual: affect and, 5, 16, 23, 56; biopolitics and, 17; body and, 9; capital and, 77; contagion and, 71; ecology of sensation and, 212; emergence and, 5, 18; excess and, 13; habit and, 71; machinic phylum and, 79, 84, 214; sensation and, 140, 209; sexuality and, 3, 53, 183; time and, 168; virtual and, 91
Prigogine, Illya, 217
print technology, 176
proprioception: definition of, 227n2; diagram and, 19; malltiplex and, 154; media assemblage and, 5

queer studies, 4

Rai, Aishwarya, 1, 34, 46, 49, 67
rasa theory, 40
real subsumption, 78
Reith, Gerda, 194
Report of the Indian Cinematograph Committee (1927–28), 118, 125
representation, 3; affect and, 215; body and, 5; censorship and, 122, 130; clinamedia, 218; diagram and, 13, 18, 138; digital and, 185; ecology of sensation and, 210; exhibition and, 168; functionality and, 14; Hindi-Urdu film and, 6, 62; iconic and, 30; media assemblage and, 14, 211; multiplicity and, 104; mutation and, 66; sensorium and, 99; spiritual healer ads and, 207
resonance, 17, 55; becoming and, 216; clinamedia and, 219; connectivity and, 19; contagion and, 6; Devdas (1955) and, 67; ecology of sensation and, 210; Hindi and, 42; interval and, 19, 45; loitering and, 42; machinic phylum and, 78; media assemblage

and, 2, 5, 211; sensation and, 3; virtual and, 216

risk: astrology and, 185; audience and, 185, 204; Beck on, 189; biopolitics and, 108; cat bonds and, 197–98; clinamedia and, 219; diagramming and, 186; disposition toward, 188, 199; Hindi-Urdu cinema and, 35, 186; history in India and, 191; India and, 186, 190, 192; insurance and, 194, 202; *ittafaq* and, 19, 54, 203; malltiplex and, 137, 161, 182; media assemblage and, 7, 20, 198, 211; multiplex and, 186; multiplicity and, 44; as order word, 193; population and, 71; probability and, 195; spiritual healer ads and, 207; subjectivity and, 198; time and, 212

security, 159; becoming and, 199; biopolitics and, 166; capital and, 94; censorship and, 121; clinamedia and, 219; colonial power and, 191; connectivity and, 183; control and, 50, 184; digital and, 51, 151–52; ecology of sensation and, 136; globalization and, 84; India and, 97, 193; insurance and, 200–203; *ittafaq* and, 182; malltiplex and, 136, 145, 153, 166; media assemblage and, 108, 183; multiplicity and, 44; as order word, 193, 211; piracy and, 142, 154; print technology and, 176; profit and, 168; risk and, 20, 72, 161; spiritual healer ads and, 207; time and, 204

Sen, Suchitra, 62–65

sensation: affect and, 70; anticipation and, 67; art deco and, 27; bazaar and, 40; becoming and, 294; biopolitics and, 17; bits and, 128; body and, 3, 53, 71, 216; branding and, 92; censorship and, 124–25; cinema and, 24, 126; codification

and, 56, 71; co-emergence and, 140; contagion and, 168; Deleuze on, 156; deterritorialization and, 56; Dolby and, 184; duration and, 45; ecology and, 8, 11, 13, 140; embodiment and, 202; film exhibition and, 7, 24, 97; globalization and, 70, 84; habit and, 61, 71, 105; Hindi-Urdu cinema and, 25; iconicity and, 32; intervals and, 19; *ittafaq* and, 183, 212; language and, 212; loitering and, 35; machinic phylum and, 79, 214; malltiplex and, 135–37, 143, 154–55, 294; media assemblage and, 40, 93, 176–78, 216; modulation and, 123; multiplicity and, 104, 163–64; piracy and, 96; population and, 3; as regularity, 139; security and, 204; sensory-motor schema and, 138; sexuality and, 53, 67, 117; Sobchak on, 4; sound and, 91; spiritual healer ads and, 209; synaesthesia and, 68, 94, 107; technology and, 72; THX technology and, 128; time and, 144, 217; time pass and, 143–44, 164; value and, 41; viral marketing and, 59; virtual and, 138; vision and, 150

sensorium: body and, 163; co-evolution and, 53; ecology of sensation and, 135, 221n8; emergence and, 214; exhibition and, 43, 54; feedback loop and, 166; malltiplex and, 135, 142; media assemblage and, 15; multiplex and, 61; sound and, 99; time pass and, 167

sensory-motor schema, 13–14; becoming and, 67; Bollywood and, 115; Deleuze on, 27; diagram and, 114; DJ culture and, 11; film exhibition and, 24; habit and, 138; indetermination and, 106; *ittafaq* and, 189; perception and, 198; time and, 12 sexuality: affect and, 185; art deco and, 32; autonomic processes and, 54; body and, 168, 188, 190; censorship and, 126; cinema and, 119; discipline and, 189; ecology of sensation as, 3–4, 9, 50, 59, 168, 212; exhibition and, 168; film exhibition and, 24; filmic representation and, 125; Foucault on, 3, 188; globalization and, 70; identity as, 14; insurance and, 189, 191; *ittafaq* and, 182; mallti- plex and, 136; media assemblage and, 7, 164; pre-individual and, 53, 183; risk and, 199; sensation and, 53, 67, 117; spiritual healer ads and, 209; subjectivity and, 3

Simondon, Gilbert, 16, 78, 139, 149

Sobchack, Vivian, 4, 128

sound, Dolby, 91

spiritual healer ads, 205, 207–9, 271n58

spiritual healing, 14

Spivak, Gayatri Chakravorty, 6

Stengers, Isabelle, 217

Stiegler, Bernard, 25, 213

subjectivity: female agency and, 65; financialization and, 115; Hindi-Urdu film and, 9; interval and, 20

Sunder Rajan, Kaushik, 83

synesthesia, logo as, 15

technology: capital and, 76

television: BitTorrent and, 86–87; cell phones and, 89; India and, 84; Indian cable channels and, 84

temporality: cinema and, 163; insur- ance and, 194; media and, 163; narrative and, 66; present and, 166; security and, 145

Terranova, Tziana, 209

Thacker, Eugene, 78, 196

time: affect and, 53, 197; art deco and, 26; becoming and, 53, 167; bits and, 128; capital and, 14; causality and, 205; clinamen and, 217; econ- omy and, 193; embodiment and, 38; emergence and, 14; film showings and, 145; globalization and, 77; habit and, 11; Hindi-Urdu popular culture and, 15; identity and, 213; insurance and, 194–96, 203–4, 208; *ittafaq* and, 209, 212; malltiplex and, 36, 41, 167; multiplicity and, 103; nar- rative and, 30; ontology and, 13; per- ception and, 167; practices of, 186; resonance and, 42; risk and, 188; screening and, 117; sensation and, 3, 144, 217; sound and, 99; spatial- ization and, 80; spiritual healer ads and, 205; time pass and, 38, 143–44, 164–66; utopia and nostalgia as, 12; value and, 193. *See also* untimely

time pass: affect and, 166; cinema-going and, 164; clinamedia and, 219; definition of, 143, 163; Hindi-Urdu cinema and, 163; *ittafaq* and, 183, 215; loitering and, 41; media assem- blage and, 211; movie-going as, 119; pleasure and, 144; print technology and, 177; as sensorium, 167

tinkering: affect and, 215; media assem- blage and, 4

topology, 19; becoming and, 12; bits and, 165; cinema and, 2; digital and, 138; media assemblage and, 38; value added and, 49

transitive mode of power, 52–53

turbulence: media assemblage and, 6; sexuality and, 209

tweaking: clinamedia and, 219

unpredictable but patterned trajectories, 8, 15, 53, 70, 182, 221n4. *See also* nonlinear dynamics

untimely: becoming and, 12, 16, 20, 199, 216; Bollywood and, 143–44; clina- media and, 217, 219; embodiment and, 16; excess and, 215; intensity and, 212; media assemblage and, 2, 7, 199, 216

value: abstraction and, 193; affect and, 123; sensation and, 294
"value added" applications and services, 88
Varela, Francisco, 150
Varma, Ram Gopal, 110
Vasudevan, Ravi, 8, 30, 63; on *Devdas* (1955), 62
viral marketing: branding and, 51; contagion and, 87; emergence and, 59; malltiplex and, 168; song-dance sequence and, 146; TV and, 85
virtual: actual and, 103; actualization and, 107, 137; affect and, 139–40, 179, 216; body and, 105–7, 137; capital and, 83; cyborg and, 103; Deleuze on, 65; diagram and, 147; duration and, 50; globalization and, 70, 77; history and, 103; malltiplex and, 136–37, 139, 167; marketing and, 134; media assemblage and, 8, 17, 58, 72, 139–40; multiplex and, 165; multiplicity and, 62, 65, 91, 103, 138, 140; mutational and, 143–44; narrative and, 66; non-human and, 107; partialities and, 196; potential and, 104–5; pre-individual and, 91, 139; representation and, 215; resonance and, 216; sensation and, 138; topology and, 138

"0wnz0red" (Doctorow), 133, 152–53

Amit S. Rai is an associate professor of English at
Florida State University. He is the author of *Rule of
Sympathy: Sentiment, Race, and Power, 1750–1850*.

Library of Congress Cataloging-in-Publication Data
Rai, Amit, 1968–
Untimely Bollywood : globalization and India's new
media assemblage / Amit S. Rai.
   p. cm.
Includes bibliographical references and index.
ISBN 978-0-8223-4394-3 (cloth : alk. paper)
ISBN 978-0-8223-4412-4 (pbk. : alk. paper)
1. Motion picture industry—India—Bombay.
2. Mass media—India. 3. Motion pictures—India.
4. Globalization—India. I. Title.
PN1993.5.I8R275 2009
302.23'430954—dc22   2008052620